THE ENGLISH POETS

T. H. WARD.

VOL. II.

THE SEVENTEENTH CENTURY:

BEN JONSON TO DRYDEN.

THE

ENGLISH POETS

SELECTIONS

WITH CRITICAL INTRODUCTIONS

BY VARIOUS WRITERS

AND A GENERAL INTRODUCTION BY

MATTHEW ARNOLD

EDITED BY

THOMAS HUMPHRY WARD

VOL. II

BEN JONSON to DRYDEN

Granger Index Reprint Series

BOOKS FOR LIBRARIES PRESS
FREEPORT, NEW YORK

First Published 1885
Reprinted 1971

INTERNATIONAL STANDARD BOOK NUMBER:
0-8369-6245-1

LIBRARY OF CONGRESS CATALOG CARD NUMBER:
77-149119

PRINTED IN THE UNITED STATES OF AMERICA

CONTENTS.

BEN JONSON.

[Born 1573; educated at Westminster School and (according to Fuller) at St. John's College, Cambridge. After a brief connexion with the trade of his step father, a master-bricklayer, he served as a volunteer in the Low Countries, and settled in London as a playwright not later than 1597. His first important comedy, *Every Man in his Humour*, was acted 1598; his first tragedy, *Sejanus*, 1603. His masques chiefly belong to the reign of James I, more especially to its earlier part. He wrote nothing for the stage from 1616 to 1625. After this he produced a few more plays, without permanently securing the favour of the public. Of these plays the last but two was *The New Inn*, the complete failure of which on the stage provoked Jonson's longer *Ode to Himself*. He enjoyed however in his later years, besides a fluctuating court patronage, the general homage of the English world of letters as its veteran chief. He died in London, August 6, 1637. The First Folio edition of his Works, published in 1616, included the Book of *Epigrams*, and the lyrics and epistles gathered under the heading *The Forest* in the same Folio: the Second Folio, published posthumously in 1641, contained the larger and (as its name implies) supplementary collection, called *Underwoods* by its author.]

Though the readers of Ben Jonson are relatively few, there is no securer fame in our literature than his. He lived long, and ended his days in a very different world of letters as well as of politics from that upon which, after his return from military service in the Netherlands, he had launched the earliest of his great comedies. In his old age, when he had survived both the heat of the quarrels in which he had exulted and the fulness of the popularity which he had contemned,—when his powers were declining and his troubles increasing,—he was generally acknowledged as the chief of his art. His society was courted by grave seniors and by youthful aspirants to literary honours, while by an inner circle of devotees he was venerated as their 'metropolitan in poetry,' and honoured after death with a collection of tributes such as even in that age of panegyrics would have overweighted the remembrance of any other man. During the

Restoration period his reputation as an English dramatist was still second to none, so far as critical opinion was concerned. But a poet's name is not kept green by critical opinion, and the name of a dramatic poet perhaps least of all. In his old age, as Jonson informed King Charles I, the 'less poetic boys' had judged 'parts of him decayed'; to posterity he gradually came to seem over-full and over-difficult. And thus in the end his inability or unwillingness (often expressed with unnecessary frankness) to come to terms with the larger public has revenged itself by his writings having been long and unworthily neglected. To sink irresistibly into the souls of men, or lightly to move the mirth of the multitude, was and is beyond the power of his poetic genius. To dissolve its inspirations in wantonness, or to satisfy coarse appetites with the husks of its fruits, was incompatible with the character of his mind. No writer was ever at once so varied and so serious, so voluminous and so conscientious. Few have been so careful about what they wrote before publication, and so careless about it afterwards. He thought that he could trust his reputation to the judgment of those who can 'understand and define what merit is'; and upon the whole it may be said that both the audience to which he appealed, and that whose opinion he professed neither to love nor to fear, have taken him at his word. His fame as a dramatist—on which his general fame will always essentially depend—must therefore remain within the keeping of those who are 'sealed of the tribe of Ben'; but of these the succession is certain to remain unbroken.

One quite special cause has in the course of time not less unjustly than unfortunately interfered with the posthumous popularity of Ben Jonson. Not only has his poetic fame—as was inevitable—been overshadowed by that of Shakspere; but he was long believed to have entertained, and to have taken frequent opportunities of expressing, a malign jealousy of one both greater and more successful than himself. This rather musty charge was elaborately examined and refuted by Jonson's editor, Gifford, to whose efforts on this head nothing remains to be added, though perhaps here and there something may with advantage be taken away from them. With pen and with tongue Ben Jonson was always, consciously or unconsciously, exerting his critical faculty ; and like his great namesake of the eighteenth century, who in many respects (not including creative gifts) so strangely resembles him, he loved to measure and qualify even the praise which came warmest from his heart. In order to judge of his feelings towards Shakspere, and his opinion of Shakspere's genius, it suffices. to read with candour as well as care the famous lines included in the following selection. If the constitution of the writer's mind, and the circumstances of the writing be taken into account, it may be said with truth that few criticisms at once so generous and so discerning have ever been committed to posterity by one great poet concerning another. At all events it should not be over·looked that the praise which from Jonson weighs heaviest—the praise of Shakspere's *art*—was precisely that of which many generations delighting in the poet's 'native woodnotes wild' failed to understand the meaning.

As a matter of course, Jonson is chiefly remembered as a dramatist, though his labours as such very far from exhausted his extraordinary powers of work, and though for ten years (beginning with that of Shakspere's death) he never wrote for the stage at all. Indeed, though he declared his profits as a playwright to have been extremely small, it seems to have been necessity rather than choice which turned his efforts in this direction. In the spirited *Ode to Himself* (of which the date is uncertain, but which probably belongs to some time near 1616), as well as in the lines to Shakspere, he makes no secret of his longing for what seemed to him nobler because freer forms of poetry. But though he not long afterwards (1619) told Drummond of Hawthornden in one of his famous *Conversations*, 'that he had an intention to perfect an epic poem entitled Heroologia, of the Worthies of this Country roused by Fame, and to dedicate it to his country,' nothing came of the project. Nor would it appear that the burning of his library, for which he execrated 'the lame Lord of Fire' in a vivacious series of his favourite heroic couplets, consumed together with the MS. of his *English Grammar* and of his Aristotelian notes for his Translation of Horace's *Art of Poetry*, any original poem of special length or importance. Exclusively, therefore, of his dramas and masques, and of a few *translations from the Latin Poets* professing to be nothing more than such, Jonson's poetical remains consist only of the three collections mentioned at the head of this notice. How far the last of these, the *Underwoods*, which comprises epistles, epigrams, and lyrics of various kinds, was prepared or even designed for publication by Jonson, is unknown.

The lyrics in Jonson's *dramas* are extremely few, as becomes a dramatist who (as he rather too tersely expresses it) strove not only to set 'words above action,' but 'matter above words.' Indeed, with the exception of two or three pretty songs (of which one, exquisitely rendered from a Latin original, and another, afterwards reprinted in an enlarged form in the *Underwoods*, are cited to exemplify the light touch at the command of Jonson's not always laborious fingers) none of these often charming and always disturbing obstacles to dramatic interest interfere with the steady progress of his plays. The stately choruses in the tragedy of *Catiline* stand on a different footing from that of more or less desultory songs.

Even in Jonson's *masques*,—a form of poetry which owes to him not indeed its origin, but its establishment as a species in our literature—though the lyrical element necessarily forms an integral part of the composition, yet the importance attached to it by the author is unmistakeably secondary. Nor is the reason of this far to seek. From one point of view, indeed, it is right and proper to insist upon the essential differences between a masque and a drama, and upon the consequent absurdity of applying the same standards of criticism to both. From another point of view it is equally true that it is the dramatic element, or the element of action, in the masque as treated by Jonson, which constitutes the differerce between it and a mere 'disguising'—a difference which in th.: case of earlier masques had no existence at all. According to his wont, Jonson was above all anxious to 'furnish the inward parts' of the masques, barriers and other entertainments composed by him, and in an age when, by the caprice of fashion and according to the inevitable law of change, a taste for these 'transitory devices' had largely superseded the love of the drama, to offer nothing that was not both 'nourishing and sound.' Hence whether it was a municipal 'invention in the Strand,' to the body of which he had to 'adapt his soul,' or a hint of the Queen's which he had to develope as ladies' hints sometimes require, his aim was chiefly to give something of dramatic life as well as of deeper meaning to his occasional pieces. Not only was he resolved that so far as in him lay 'painting and carpentry' should *not* be (as he thought Inigo Jones strove to make them) ''he soul of masque'; but even the songs and dances, indispensable though they were in one sense, were in another to be, so to speak, adventitious. Thus while his masques contain more dramatic life than those of any of his contemporaries, and reveal more poetic purpose than those of any other English writer except Milton, the lyrical part of them, though always adequate, rarely challenges special admiration. The extract in heroic couplets from the *Hymenæi* furnishes a typical instance of the thought expended by Jonson upon what in most other hands would have been a mere conventional personification ; the short *adagio* from the *Fortunate Isles* shows how fully competent he was to marry words to the required movement of dance or song. A longer extract from *Pleasure Reconciled to Virtue* would have been necessary to bring into fullest relief what was owed to Jonson by the writer of the greatest—without rival or parallel—of all English masques. Is it inconceivable that our poets should recur, less tentatively than they have hitherto done, to a poetic form so peculiarly suitable for giving expression to the more varied intellectual life of these latter times as was that which Jonson virtually secured to our literature ?

Among his detached pieces the *Epigrams* were the favourites of 'honest' Ben Jonson himself,—'the ripest,' as he called them, 'of his studies.' It is unnecessary to point out (though the poet had to do so in the admirable lines addressed to his 'mere English' critic) that his conception of the forms and functions of an epigram was the wider one entertained by the Ancients ; and that therefore his purpose in the large majority of these poems is *not* to work rapidly up to a point at the close. If this be borne in mind, the felicitous terseness of these *Epigrams*, and of those pieces in the *Underwoods* which belong to the same class, will not be denied the admiration which it deserves. Some are witty, in the narrower sense of the term,—nearly all in the broader. Their sarcasm, where they contain such, directs itself against various types of men and women— among them, much to Jonson's credit, rather against those whom he might have been expected to flatter than those whom he might have been expected to assail. But the Fastidious Brisks were as genuine an abomination to Ben Jonson as the Zeal-of-the-land Busies, and this though he to some extent depended for his bread as well as for his sack upon the good-will of the Court and courtiers. And it may be said in passing that though like all his brother-dramatists he was loyally devoted to the Crown[1], he was free-spoken even to the most august of his patrons, and constantly recurs to the commonplace but wholesome maxim that it is the

[1] He has been credited (but erroneously) with the authorship of the National Anthem.

love, not the fear, of his subjects upon which a monarch ought to rely.   But Jonson's satirical epigrams are both less effective and less elaborate than those of a directly opposite tendency.   Few of our Jacobean or Caroline poets have equalled him in pregnancy of panegyric—whether his theme was the praise of statesmen like the elder or the younger Cecil, or of men of letters varying in kind and degree from Selden, whom he salutes as 'monarch of letters,' to the poet's fellow-dramatists.   Nor was he less happy when the object of his poetic homage was a gentle woman, like the Countess of Bedford celebrated in the lines cited below.   And his Epitaphs, among which room could only be found here for two of the most pathetic, remain unsurpassed, not only for a condensed force which we are accustomed to find in Jonson, but also for a tender grace which he is not so usually supposed to have possessed.

In the collection called the *Forest*, small as it is, Jonson has done the greatest justice to the variety of poetic styles of which (in addition to the dramatic) he was capable.   He here excuses himself for not writing of love, partly on the favourite poets' plea of growing age ; and in truth his muse was comparatively a stranger to Eros.   Yet the little chaplet of tributes to ' Charis ' put together by Jonson in 1624 and inserted in the *Underwoods*, and some charming original and translated pieces to be found elsewhere, show him not only to have written graceful love-poetry himself, but to have furnished examples of it to his younger contemporaries.   Herrick was in his way almost as much indebted to Jonson as Milton was in his.   As a translator or adapter of Classical originals, Jonson was in his element ; his re-settings of favourite gems from Catullus and others were doubtless true labours of love.   For the 'bricklayer' (as his opponents delighted to be historically justified in calling him) had the early nurture of a scholar ; and through life he remained deeply grateful to the famous Camden, his master at Westminster.   That among the Latin poets Horace should have specially attracted him, is easily to be accounted for ; in some of his original Epistles he has all the brightness and all the urbanity of his Roman model—in the fine *Epode* included in the *Forest* he rises to a moral dignity beyond the reach either of Horace or of his later imitators.

For not even a slight summary like the present should exclude from mention among Jonson's characteristics the firm and steady tone of his morality.   In his earlier manhood he twice changed his faith—without the faintest suspicion of interested motives attaching to his conversion—and in his later days he seems to have remained a close student of theology, inclining now to

'those wiser guides
Whom fashion had not drawn to study sides.'

But to a conscientious desire for truth he added a humility of soul towards things divine, which stands in strange and touching contrast to the high mettle and quick temper of his bearing in most other matters. Critics have been known to cry out against having to hear too much about the robustness of Ben Jonson ; but his manliness is inseparable from him, and, as the lines *To Heaven* show, he was not ashamed even of his piety.

A. W. WARD.

ECHO'S LAMENT OF NARCISSUS.

[From *Cynthia's Revels* (acted 1600), Act I, Sc. 1.]

Slow, slow, fresh fount, keep time with my salt tears:
   Yet slower, yet; O faintly, gentle springs:
List to the heavy part the music bears,
   Woe weeps out her division, when she sings.
      Droop herbs and flowers,
      Fall grief in showers,
      Our beauties are not ours;
        O, I could still,
Like melting snow upon some craggy hill,
      Drop, drop, drop, drop,
Since nature's pride is now a withered daffodil.

VENETIAN SONG[1].

[From *Volpone*; or, *The Fox* (acted 1605). Act I. Sc. 6.]

     Come, my Celia, let us prove,
     While we can, the sports of love.
     Time will not be ours for ever;
     He, at length, our good will sever;
     Spend not then his gifts in vain:
     Suns that set may rise again;
     But if once we lose this light,
     'Tis with us perpetual night.
     Why should we defer our joys?
     Fame and rumour are but toys.
     Cannot we delude the eyes
     Of a few poor household spies?
     Or his easier ears beguile,
     Thus removèd by our wile?

[1] Compare Catullus, *Carmen V*. The allusion (not taken from Catullus) in the concluding lines is to a famous Spartan law.

'Tis no sin love's fruits to steal;
But the sweet thefts to reveal,
To be taken, to be seen,—
These have crimes accounted been.

SONG[1].

[From *Epicæne; or, The Silent Woman*, Act I, Sc. 1; 1609.]

Still to be neat, still to be drest,
As you were going to a feast;
Still to be powdered, still perfumed:
Lady, it is to be presumed,
Though art's hid causes are not found,
All is not sweet, all is not sound.

Give me a look, give me a face,
That makes simplicity a grace;
Robes loosely flowing, hair as free:
Such sweet neglect more taketh me
Than all the adulteries of art:
They strike mine eyes, but not my heart.

CHARIS' TRIUMPH.

[One of the ten pieces forming *A Celebration of Charis* in *Underwoods*.
The last two stanzas are sung or said by Wittipol in *The Devil is an
Ass* (acted 1616), Act II, Sc. 2.]

See the chariot at hand here of Love,
    Wherein my Lady rideth!
Each that draws is a swan or a dove,
    And well the car Love guideth.
As she goes, all hearts do duty
        Unto her beauty;
And enamoured do wish, so they might
        But enjoy such a sight,
That they still were to run by her side,
Through swords, through seas, whither she would ride.

[1] A translation from the Latin of Bonnefonius (Jean Bonnefons).

Do but look on her eyes, they do light
    All that Love's world compriseth!
Do but look on her hair, it is bright
    As Love's star when it riseth!
Do but mark, her forehead's smoother
      Than words that soothe her;
And from her arched brows, such a grace
      Sheds itself through the face,
As alone there triúmphs to the life
All the gain, all the good of the elements' strife.

Have you seen but a bright lily grow
Before rude hands have touched it?
Have you marked but the fall o' the snow
    Before the soil hath smutched it?
Have you felt the wool of beaver?
      Or swan's down ever?
Or have smelt o' the bud o' the briar?
      Or the nard in the fire?
Or have tasted the bag of the bee?
O so white,—O so soft,—O so sweet is she!

TRUTH.

[From *Hymenæi*; or, *the Solemnities of Masque and Barriers* at the marriage
of the Earl of Essex, 1606.]

Upon her head she wears a crown of stars,
Through which her orient hair waves to her waist,
By which believing mortals hold her fast,
And in those golden cords are carried even,
Till with her breath she blows them up to heaven.
She wears a robe enchased with eagles' eyes,
To signify her sight in mysteries:
Upon each shoulder sits a milk-white dove,
And at her feet do witty serpents move:
Her spacious arms do reach from east to west,
And you may see her heart shine through her breast.
Her right hand holds a sun with burning rays,
Her left a curious bunch of golden keys,
With which heaven's gates she locketh and displays.

A crystal mirror hangeth at her breast,
By which men's consciences are searched and drest ;
On her coach-wheels Hypocrisy lies racked ;
And squint-eyed Slander with Vainglory backed
Her bright eyes burn to dust, in which shines Fate :
An angel ushers her triumphant gait,
Whilst with her fingers fans of stars she twists,
And with them beats back Error, clad in mists.
Eternal Unity behind her shines,
That fire and water, earth and air combines.
Her voice is like a trumpet loud and shrill,
Which bids all sounds in earth and heaven be still.

THE SHEPHERDS' HOLIDAY.

[From *Pan's Anniversary;* or, *The Shepherds' Holiday:* 1625.]

First Nymph.

       Thus, thus begin, the yearly rites
       Are due to Pan on these bright nights ;
       His morn now riseth and invites
       To sports, to dances, and delights :
         All envious and profane, away !
         This is the shepherds' holiday.

Second Nymph.

       Strew, strew the glad and smiling ground
       With every flower, yet not confound ;
       The primrose drop, the spring's own spouse,
       Bright day's-eyes, and the lips of cows,
         The garden-star, the queen of May,
         The rose, to crown the holiday.

Third Nymph.

       Drop, drop you violets, change your hues
       Now red, now pale, as lovers use,
       And in your death go out as well,
       As when you lived unto the smell :
         That from your odour all may say,
         This is the shepherds' holiday.

Song before the Entry of the Masquers.

[From *The Fortunate Isles and their Union,* 1625.]

Spring all the graces of the age,
    And all the loves of time ;
Bring all the pleasures of the stage,
    And relishes of rhyme ;
Add all the softnesses of courts,
The looks, the laughters and the sports ;
And mingle all their sweets and salts,
That none may say the triumph halts.

Ode to Himself.

[Written after the failure of the comedy *The New Inn,* 'never acted, but most negligently played by some, the king's servants; and more squeamishly beheld and censured by others, the king's subjects,' January 19, 1629.]

Come, leave the loathèd stage,
    And the more loathsome age ;
Where pride and impudence, in faction knit,
    Usurp the chair of wit !
Indicting and arraigning every day
    Something they call a play.
    Let their fastidious, vain
    Commission of the brain
Run on and rage, sweat, censure, and condemn ;
They were not made for thee, less thou for them.

Say that thou pour'st them wheat,
    And they will acorns eat ;
'Twere simple fury still thyself to waste
    On such as have no taste !
To offer them a surfeit of pure bread
    Whose appetites are dead !
    No, give them grains their fill,
    Husks, draff to drink or swill :
If they love lees, and leave the lusty wine,
Envy them not, their palate's with the swine.

No doubt some mouldy tale,
Like Pericles, and stale
As the shrieve's crusts, and nasty as his fish—
 Scraps out of every dish
Thrown forth, and raked into the common tub,
 May keep up the Play-club:
There, sweepings do as well
As the best-ordered meal;
For who the relish of these guests will fit,
Needs set them but the alms-basket of wit.

And much good do't you then:
Brave plush-and-velvet-men
Can feed on orts; and, safe in your stage-clothes,
 Dare quit, upon your oaths,
The stagers and the stage-wrights too, your peers,
 Of larding your large ears
With their foul comic socks,
Wrought upon twenty blocks;
Which if they are torn, and turned, and patched enough,
The gamesters share your gilt, and you their stuff.

Leave things so prostitute,
And take the Alcaic lute;
Or thine own Horace, or Anacreon's lyre;
 Warm thee by Pindar's fire:
And though thy nerves be shrunk, and blood be cold,
 Ere years have made thee old,
Strike that disdainful heat
Throughout, to their defeat,
As curious fools, and envious of thy strain,
May, blushing, swear no palsy's in thy brain.

But when they hear thee sing
The glories of thy king,
His zeal to God, and his just awe o'er men:
 They may, blood-shaken then,
Feel such a flesh-quake to possess their powers,
 As they shall cry: 'Like ours

In sound of peace or wars,
  No harp e'er hit the stars,
In tuning forth the acts of his sweet **reign,**
And raising Charles his chariot 'bove his **Wain.'**

SONG.—TO CELIA[1].

[From *The Forest.*]

Drink to me only with thine eyes,
  And I will pledge with mine ;
Or leave a kiss but in the cup,
  And I 'll not look for wine.
The thirst that from the soul doth **rise,**
  Doth ask a drink divine :
But might I of Jove's nectar sup,
  I would not change for thine.

I sent thee late a rosy wreath,
  Not so much honouring thee,
As giving it a hope, that there
  It could not withered be.
But thou thereon didst only breathe,
  And sent'st it back to me :
Since when it grows, and smells, **I swear,**
  Not of itself, but thee.

EPIGRAMS.

TO MY MERE ENGLISH CENSURER.

To thee, my way in Epigrams seems new,
When both it is the old way, and the true.
Thou sayst that cannot be ; for thou hast seen
Davis [2] and Weever [3], and the best have been,
And mine come nothing like. I hope so ; yet,
As theirs did with thee, mine might credit get,

---

[1] From the (prose) love-letters of Philostratus the younger (about 250 A.D.)
[2] Author of the *Scourge of Folly.*   [3] Compiler of *Funeral Monuments*

If thou 'dst but use thy faith as thou didst then,
When thou wert wont t' admire, not censure [1] men.
Prithee believe still, and not judge so fast :
Thy faith is all the knowledge that thou hast.

ON COURT-WORM.

All men are worms, but this [2] no man.   In silk
'Twas brought to court first wrapt, and white as milk [3];
Where, afterwards, it grew a butterfly,
Which was a caterpillar.   So 'twill die.

TO FOOL, OR KNAVE.

Thy praise or dispraise is to me alike :
One doth not stroke me, nor the other strike.

ON LUCY, COUNTESS OF BEDFORD .

This morning, timely rapt with holy fire,
I thought to form unto my zealous Muse,
What kind of creature I could most desire
To honour, serve, and love, as Poets use.
I meant to make her fair, and free, and wise,
Of greatest blood, and yet more good than great ;
I meant the day-star should not brighter rise,
Nor lend like influence from his lucent seat.
I meant she should be courteous, facile, sweet,
Hating that solemn vice of greatness, pride ;
I meant each softest virtue there should meet,
Fit in that softer bosom to reside.
Only a learned, and a manly soul
I purposed her : that should, with even powers,
The rock, the spindle, and the shears control
Of Destiny, and spin her own free hours.
Such when I meant to feign, and wished to see,
My Muse bade BEDFORD write, and that was she !

---

[1] Censure = criticise.   [2] *This* = this is.   [3] Compare Pope's ' Sporus.'
[4] Wife of Edward, third Earl of Bedford.   She was also sung by Donne
and Daniel.

An Epitaph on Salathiel Pavy, a Child of Queen Elizabeth's Chapel[1].

Weep with me, all you that read
    This little story;
And know, for whom a tear you shed
    Death's self is sorry.
'Twas a child that so did thrive
    In grace and feature,
As Heaven and Nature seemed to strive
    Which owned the creature.
Years he numbered scarce thirteen
    When Fates turned cruel,
Yet three filled zodiacs had he been
    The stage's jewel;
And did act, what now we moan,
    Old men so duly,
As, sooth, the Parcæ thought him one,—
    He played so truly.
So, by error to his fate
    They all consented;
But viewing him since, alas, too late
    They have repented;
And have sought to give new birth
    In baths to steep him;
But being so much too good for earth,
    Heaven vows to keep him.

Epitaph on Elizabeth L. H.

Wouldst thou hear what man can say
In a little? Reader, stay.

Underneath this stone doth lie
As much beauty as could die:
Which in life did harbour give
To more virtue than doth live.

---

[1] These children (called in the next reign Children of Her Majesty's Revels) were trained up to act before the Queen. Salathiel had acted in two of Jonson's plays, in 1600, and in 1601, when he is supposed to have died.

If at all she had a fault,
Leave it buried in this vault.
One name was ELIZABETH;
The other, let it sleep in death,
Fitter, where it died to tell,
Than that it lived at all. Farewell!

AN ODE TO HIMSELF.

[From *Underwoods.*]

Where dost thou careless lie
    Buried in ease and sloth?
Knowledge that sleeps, doth die;
And this security,
    It is the common moth
That eats on wits and arts, and [that][1] destroys them both.

Are all the Aonian springs
    Dried up? lies Thespia waste?
Doth Clarius' harp want strings,
That not a nymph now sings;
    Or droop they as disgraced,
To see their seats and bowers by chattering pies defaced?

If hence thy silence be,
    As 'tis too just a cause,
Let this thought quicken thee:
Minds that are great and free
    Should not on fortune pause;
'Tis crown enough to virtue still, her own applause

What though the greedy fry
    Be taken with false baits
Of worded balladry,
And think it poësy?
    They die with their conceits,
And only piteous scorn upon their folly waits.

[1] 'That' *conj.*

Then take in hand thy lyre ;
    Strike in thy proper strain ;
With Japhet's line [1] aspire
Sol's chariot, for new fire
    To give the world again :
Who aided him, will thee, the issue of Jove's **brain.**

And, since our dainty age
    Cannot endure reproof,
Make not thyself a page
To that strumpet the stage ;
    But sing high and aloof,
Safe from the wolf's black jaw, and the dull **ass's hoof.**

To the Memory of my beloved Master William Shakspeare, and what he hath left us.

[Printed by Gifford in *Underwoods*, but really from the First Folio edition of Shakspeare, 1623.]

To draw no envy, Shakspeare, on thy name,
Am I thus ample to thy book and fame ;
While I confess thy writings to be such,
As neither Man nor Muse can praise too much.
'Tis true, and all men's suffrage. But these ways
Were not the paths I meant unto thy praise;
For seeliest ignorance on these may light,
Which, when it sounds at best, but echoes right ;
Or blind affection, which doth ne'er advance
The truth, but gropes, and urgeth all by chance ;
Or crafty malice might pretend this praise,
And think to ruin where it seemed to raise.
These are, as some infámous bawd or whore
Should praise a matron ; what could hurt her more ?
But thou art proof against them and, indeed,
Above the ill fortune of them, or the need.

[1] Prometheus son of Iapetus.

I therefore will begin : Soul of the age !
The applause, delight, the wonder of our stage !
My SHAKSPEARE, rise ! I will not lodge thee by
Chaucer, or Spenser, or bid Beaumont lie
A little further, to make thee a room[1]:
Thou art a monument without a tomb,
And art alive still while thy book doth live,
And we have wits to read, and praise to give.
That I not mix thee so my brain excuses,—
I mean with great, but disproportioned Muses ;
For if I thought my judgment were of years,
I should commit thee surely with thy peers,
And tell how far thou didst our Lyly outshine,
Or sporting Kyd, or Marlowe's mighty line.
And though thou hadst small Latin and less Greek,
From thence to honour thee, I would not seek
For names, but call forth thund'ring Æschylus,
Euripides, and Sophocles to us,
Pacuvius, Accius, him of Cordova[2] dead,
To life again, to hear thy buskin tread,
And shake a stage ; or when thy socks were on,
Leave thee alone for a comparison
Of all that insolent Greece or haughty Rome
Sent forth, or since did from their ashes come.
Triumph, my Britain, thou hast one to show,
To whom all scenes of Europe homage owe.
He was not of an age, but for all time !
And all the Muses still were in their prime,
When, like Apollo, he came forth to warm
Our ears, or like a Mercury to charm !
Nature herself was proud of his designs,
And joyed to wear the dressing of his lines,

---

[1] In allusion to W. Basse's elegy on Shakspeare, beginning—

> 'Renownèd Spenser, lie a thought more nigh
> To learned Chaucer ; and rare Beaumont, lie
> A little nearer Spenser, to make room
> For Shakespear in your threefold, fourfold tomb.'

[2] Seneca.

Which were so richly spun, and woven so fit,
As, since, she will vouchsafe no other wit.
The merry Greek, tart Aristophanes,
Neat Terence, witty Plautus, now not please;
But antiquated and deserted lie,
As they were not of Nature's family.
Yet must I not give Nature all ; thy Art,
My gentle Shakspeare, must enjoy a part.
For though the poet's matter nature be,
His art doth give the fashion ; and that he[1]
Who casts to write a living line, must sweat
(Such as thine are) and strike the second heat
Upon the Muses' anvil, turn the same,
And himself with it, that he thinks to frame ;
Or for the laurel he may gain to scorn ;
For a good poet 's made, as well as born.
And such wert thou ! Look, how the father's face
Lives in his issue, even so the race
Of Shakspeare's mind and manners brightly shines
In his well turnèd and true filèd lines,
In each of which he seems to shake a lance,
As brandished at the eyes of ignorance.
Sweet Swan of Avon ! what a sight it were
To see thee in our waters yet appear,
And make those flights upon the banks of Thames,
That so did take Eliza and our James !
But stay, I see thee in the hemisphere
Advanced, and made a constellation there !
Shine forth, thou Star of Poets, and with rage
Or influence chide or cheer the drooping stage,
Which, since thy flight from hence, hath mourned like night,
And despairs day but for thy volume's light.

[1] That he = that man.

EPITAPH ON THE COUNTESS OF PEMBROKE

[From *Underwoods.*]

Underneath this sable hearse
Lies the subject of all verse,
SIDNEY'S sister, PEMBROKE'S mother;
Death! ere thou hast slain another,
Learn'd and fair, and good as she,
Time shall throw a dart at thee.

AN EPITAPH ON MASTER PHILIP GRAY.

[From *Underwoods.*]

Reader, stay;
And if I had no more to say
But: 'Here doth lie, till the last day,
All that is left of PHILIP GRAY,
It might thy patience richly pay:
For if such men as he could die,
What surety o' life have thou and I?

EPODE[2].

[From *The Forest.*]

Not to know vice at all, and keep true state,
Is virtue and not Fate;
Next to that virtue, is to know vice well,
And her black spite expel.
Which to effect (since no breast is so sure
Or safe, but she'll procure
Some way of entrance) we must plant a guard
Of thoughts to watch and ward

---

[1] Mary, sister of Sir Philip Sidney (who wrote his *Arcadia* for her), and mother of William Herbert, Earl of Pembroke. She died in 1621, and is buried in Salisbury Cathedral.

[2] The following is only the earlier (general) part of this fine Epode, 'sung to deep ears.'

At the eye and ear, the ports unto the mind,
    That no strange or unkind
Object arrive there, but the heart, our spy
    Give knowledge instantly
To wakeful reason, our affections' king:
    Who, in th' examining,
Will quickly taste the treason, and commit
    Close the close cause of it.
'Tis the securest policy we have
    To make our sense our slave.
But this true course is not embraced by many—
    By many? scarce by any.
For either our affections do rebel,
    Or else the sentinel,
That should ring larum to the heart, doth sleep;
    Or some great thought doth keep
Back the intelligence, and falsely swears
    They are base and idle fears
Whereof the loyal conscience so complains.
    Thus, by these subtle trains
Do several passions invade the mind,
    And strike our reason blind.

To Heaven.

[From *The Forest.*]

Good and great God! can I not think of Thee,
But it must straight my melancholy be?
Is it interpreted in me disease,
That, laden with my sins, I seek for ease?
O be Thou witness, that the reins dost know
And hearts of all, if I be sad for show;
And judge me after, if I dare pretend
To aught but grace, or aim at other end.
As Thou art all, so be Thou all to me,
First, midst, and last, converted One and Three!
My faith, my hope, my love; and, in this state,
My judge, my witness, and my advocate!

Where have I been this while exiled from Thee,
And whither rapt, now Thou but stoop'st to me?
Dwell, dwell here still! O, being everywhere,
How can I doubt to find Thee ever here?
I know my state, both full of shame and scorn,
Conceived in sin, and unto labour born,
Standing with fear, and must with horror fall,
And destined unto judgment, after all.
I feel my griefs too, and there scarce is ground
Upon my flesh t' inflict another wound ;—
Yet dare I not complain or wish for death,
With holy Paul, lest it be thought the breath
Of discontent ; or that these prayers be
For weariness of life, not love of Thee.

WILLIAM DRUMMOND

OF HAWTHORNDEN.

[WILLIAM DRUMMOND was born at the manor-house of Hawthornden near Edinburgh on December 13, 1585, and died there December 4, 1649. His chief poetical works are *Teares on the Death of Mœliades* (Prince Henry), 1613; *Poems*, 1616; *Forth Feasting, a panegyricke to the King's most excellent Majestie*, 1617; *Flowers of Sion*, 1623; *The Entertainment of the high and mighty. monarch Charles*, 1633; *The Exequies of the Honourable Sir Anthony Alexander, Knight*, 1638. Besides these he wrote innumerable political pamphlets, &c., and a considerable historical work. More important are his well-known *Conversations with Ben Jonson*, of which an authentic copy was discovered by Mr. David Laing and printed by him in 1832. A unique copy of the *Poems*, printed on one side of the paper only, and containing Drummond's autograph corrections, is in the Bodleian Library. It varies most curiously from the later editions.]

The interest of Drummond lies chiefly, for a modern reader, in the circumstances of his life. He is one of the earliest instances in our literature of the man of letters pure and simple ; of the man who writes neither for his bread, like the great dramatists his contemporaries, nor to adorn the leisure moments of an active life, like Chaucer and Sir Philip Sidney, but who, when his fortune allows him to choose his career, elects to write for the sake of writing. It is true he travelled, both as a very young man and later ; he corresponded regularly with his Scottish friends at the courts of James and Charles, especially with Sir William Alexander Earl of Stirling, the poet and statesman ; he took part in such royal festivities as a rare chance might bring to Edinburgh ; he keenly felt and sharply criticised the course of public affairs ; but for all this his centre and his home was the beautiful house on the bank of the Esk, into the solitudes of which even the din of Bishops' Wars could scarcely penetrate. Other poets are known by their names alone ; we talk of Jonson and Herrick, of Dryden and Addison ; but Drummond is for all time Drummond of Hawthornden.

His countrymen did not till lately do much honour to Drummond. At the end of the seventeenth century that by which his name was chiefly kept alive was a macaronic poem, *Polemo-Middinia*, which modern criticism hesitates to attribute to his hand. In 1711 Bishop Sage and the Scottish antiquary Thomas Ruddiman published Drummond's works in prose and verse, but this volume, though it still remains the only edition that contains his prose as well as his poetry, is uncritical, and is a tribute to Drummond rather as a politician than as a poet. Fifty years ago, however, Mr. David Laing, to whom Scottish literature and history owe so much, analysed and set in order the mass of manuscript which the last representative of the poet had given to the Society of Antiquaries of Scotland, forty years before. Then followed the Maitland Club edition of his poems (1833); and then, in our own day, came Professor Masson with a characteristic volume, doing for Drummond after his kind what the same biographer had long been doing for Milton after his kind—setting him against a rich background of the circumstances of his time. The dominant impression which we derive from Professor Masson's book is an impression of Drummond in his relation to public events ; of the royalist and episcopalian born to 'unhappy times and dying days'; writing pamphlets, satires, letters at intervals : turning his skill in verse to the service of the Court when occasion served, but brooding in discontent, for the most part silent, over the slow but certain triumph of Argyle and his presbyterians. Yet though this element is essential to our understanding of Drummond, there are other elements in him that have also to be taken into account. He has had a love story, as sweet while it lasted and as pathetic in its end as any that ever inspired a poet ; it is the memory of the fair Mary Cunningham of Barns, who died on the eve of their wedding, that keeps him unmarried till nearly fifty : and, at least till the political clouds close round him, he is, as we said, a man of letters, the friend of Drayton and Sir William Alexander, and the entertainer of Ben Jonson.

Drummond is a literary and even learned poet. With Alexander, he deliberately preferred to write English, as it was spoken in England, rather than his native Scotch. His wealth and his leisure enabled him to surround himself with books ; he was familiar with both ancient and modern literature. An interesting gift of his to the newly founded University of Edinburgh has preserved for us a selection of the very volumes that he read ; English poetry and prose, including works of Bacon and Selden, of Drayton and Donne, of Ben Jonson and Shakespeare ; Latin, French, Italian volumes in great numbers. Moreover, among the *excerpta* from his papers which Mr. Laing printed we find exact lists of the books that he read from period to period, the year's task sometimes extending to forty or fifty separate writers, some of them of the dimensions of Knox's *History of the Reformation*, and Sidney's *Arcadia*, and Lyly's *Euphues*, and Rabelais, and *Amadis de Gaule*. Like every other cultivated man of his day, he had read Marini ; and his copy of Montaigne is extant. His favourite forms of verse are the sonnet, of the Shakespearian rather than the true Italian type, and a short song or madrigal, combining the six-syllabled and the ten-syllabled lines in a very happy way ; but he also uses other metres, such as the heroic couplet, and now and then ventures upon a difficult foreign experiment, as in his two Sextains and his one attempt in *terza rima*. The matter of his verse is described by himself on the title-page of his first miscel-laneous volume of Poems—'Amorous, Funerall, Divine, Pastorall' —the Pastoral being of little account, and the Funeral neither better nor worse than the average of their class. What are really interesting in the poetry that he published during his life are the sonnets and songs directly inspired by Mary Cunningham—sonnets and songs that ring true, and contrast with the cold convention-ality of such poems as the *Aurora* of Drummond's friend Lord Stirling—and the grave *Flowers of Sion*. Among the posthumous poems also are some that are noticeable ; one or two genuine cries of anguish at what the author thought to be the evil of the times, and a few hymns (such as the 'hymns for the week,' following the order of the days of Creation) fit to rank with many of those that have become classical.

Good as are some of the love-sonnets and madrigals, Drummond is best where he is most serious. His deepest interests are meta-physical and religious ; he is for ever taking refuge from the ills of the present in meditations on Death, Eternity, the Christian Doctrine. The Universe, 'this All' as he calls it,—that conception of the earth with its concentric spheres which belonged to the older astronomy,—is an idea on which he dwells in almost mono-tonous fashion. The finest of all his writings, the prose tract called *The Cypresse Grove*, is a discourse upon Death, reminding us, as Mr. Masson well says, of the best work of Sir Thomas Browne ;

the most striking of his poems are certainly those where, as in the sonnet 'For the Baptist,' he presents in his own rich language the severer portions of the Christian history, or the inexhaustible theme of the shortness and the mystery of life. What saves him from becoming wearisome is partly the nobility of his verse at its best, its stateliness and sonorous music; partly his evident sincerity, and his emancipation, speaking generally, from the evil influences that were creeping in to corrupt English poetry at that time. His conceits, where he indulges in them, are bad indeed; the sun to him is

> 'Goldsmith of all the stars, with silver bright
> Who moon enamels, Apelles of the flowers';

the waves that toss the boat that holds his love have their ready explanation :—

> 'And yet huge waves arise; the cause is this,
> That ocean strives with Forth the boat to kiss.'

But these are the accidents of his poetry, and his theory and practice are better learnt from such words as those he sent at an uncertain date to Dr. Arthur Johnston, a writer of Latin verse well known in his day. 'Poesy,' he says, 'subsisteth by herself, and after one demeanour and continuance her beauty appeareth to all ages. In vain have some men of late, transformers of everything, consulted upon her reformation, and endeavoured to abstract her to metaphysical ideas and scholastical quiddities, denuding her of her own habits, and those ornaments with which she hath amused the world some thousand years. Poesy is not a thing that is yet in the finding and search, or which may be otherwise found out.' Such is the mature view of Drummond; the view of a man who has read the best that the poets of all ages have made, has enjoyed it, has assimilated it, and will not allow himself to be drawn away from the main current by the fashion of the day. It is difficult to withhold admiration from a poet who in the first half of the seventeenth century had studied Marini and yet kept himself for the most part free from conceits; and, if we turn from his poetry to his life, it is difficult to withhold sympathy from a man whose private happiness was ruined by a fatal blow, and whose public hopes were wasted in witnessing the steady upward progress of a cause which he regarded with abhorrence.

EDITOR.

SONNETS.

[From the *Poems.*]

In my first years, and prime yet not at height,
When sweet conceits my wits did entertain,
Ere beauty's force I knew, or false delight,
Or to what oar she did her captives chain,
Led by a sacred troop of Phœbus' train,
I first began to read, then lov'd to write,
And so to praise a perfect red and white,
But, God wot, wist not what was in my brain:
Love smil'd to see in what an awful guise
I turn'd those antiques of the age of gold,
And, that I might more mysteries behold,
He set so fair a volume to mine eyes,
   That I (quires clos'd which dead, dead sighs but breathe)
   Joy on this living book to read my death.

Then is she gone? O fool and coward I!
O good occasion lost, ne'er to be found!
What fatal chains have my dull senses bound,
When best they may, that they not fortune try?
Here is the flow'ry bed where she did lie,
With roses here she stellified the ground,
She fix'd her eyes on this yet smiling pond,
Nor time, nor courteous place, seem'd ought deny.
Too long, too long, Respect, I do embrace
Your counsel, full of threats and sharp disdain;
Disdain in her sweet heart can have no place,
And though come there, must straight retire again:
   Henceforth, Respect, farewell, I oft hear told
   Who lives in love can never be too bold

If crost with all mishaps be my poor life,
If one short day I never spent in mirth,
If my spright with itself holds lasting strife,
If sorrow's death is but new sorrow's birth ;
If this vain world be but a sable stage
Where slave-born man plays to the scoffing stars ;
If youth be toss'd with love, with weakness age,
If knowledge serve to hold our thoughts in wars ;
If time can close the hundred mouths of fame,
And make, what long since past, like that to be ;
If virtue only be an idle name,
If I, when I was born, was born to die ;
  Why seek I to prolong these loathsome days?
  The fairest rose in shortest time decays.

Thou window, once which served for a sphere
To that dear planet of my heart, whose light
Made often blush the glorious queen of night,
While she in thee more beauteous did appear,
What mourning weeds, alas ! now dost thou wear?
How loathsome to mine eyes is thy sad sight?
How poorly look'st thou, with what heavy cheer,
Since that sun set, which made thee shine so bright?
Unhappy now thee close, for as of late
To wond'ring eyes thou wast a paradise,
Bereft of her who made thee fortunate,
A gulf thou art, whence clouds of sighs arise ;
  But unto none so noisome as to me,
  Who hourly see my murder'd joys in thee.

Alexis, here she stay'd ; among these pines,
Sweet hermitress, she did alone repair ;
Here did she spread the treasure of her hair,
More rich than that brought from the Colchian mines.
She sate her by these musked eglantines,
The happy place the print seems yet to bear ;
Her voice did sweeten here thy sugar'd lines,
To which winds, trees, beasts, birds, did lend their ear.
Me here she first perceiv'd, and here a morn
Of bright carnations did o'erspread her face ;
Here did she sigh, here first my hopes were born,
And I first got a pledge of promis'd grace :
    But, ah ! what serv'd it to be happy so,
    Sith passed pleasures double but new woe ?

SEXTAIN.

The heaven doth not contain so many stars,
So many leaves not prostrate lie in woods,
When autumn 's old, and Boreas sounds his wars,
So many waves have not the ocean floods,
As my rent mind hath torments all the night,
And heart spends sighs, when Phœbus brings the light.

Why should I been a partner of the light,
Who, crost in birth by bad aspects of stars,
Have never since had happy day nor night ?
Why was not I a liver in the woods,
Or citizen of Thetis' crystal floods,
Than made a man, for love and fortune's wars ?

I look each day when death should end the wars,
Uncivil wars, 'twixt sense and reason's light ;
My pains I count to mountains, meads, and floods,
And of my sorrow partners make the stars ;
All desolate I haunt the fearful woods,
When I should give myself to rest at night.

With watchful eyes I ne'er behold the night,
Mother of peace, but ah! to me of wars,
And Cynthia queen-like shining through the woods,
When straight those lamps come in my thought, whose light
My judgment dazzled, passing brightest stars,
And then mine eyes en-isle themselves with floods.

Turn to their springs again first shall the floods,
Clear shall the sun the sad and gloomy night,
To dance about the pole cease shall the stars,
The elements renew their ancient wars
Shall first, and be depriv'd of place and light,
Ere I find rest in city, fields, or woods.

End these my days, indwellers of the woods,
Take this my life, ye deep and raging floods;
Sun, never rise to clear me with thy light,
Horror and darkness, keep a lasting night;
Consume me, care, with thy intestine wars,
And stay your influence o'er me, bright stars!

In vain the stars, indwellers of the woods,
Care, horror, wars, I call, and raging floods,
For all have sworn no night shall dim my sight.

SONG.

Phœbus, arise,
And paint the sable skies
With azure, white, and red;
Rouse Memnon's mother from her Tithon's bed,
That she thy cáreer[1] may with roses spread;
The nightingales thy coming each where sing;
Make an eternal spring,
Give life to this dark world which lieth dead;
Spread forth thy golden hair
In larger locks than thou wast wont before,

---

[1] Printed *careere* in the Bodleian copy. Elsewhere *cariere* or *carrier*.

And, emperor like, decore
With diadem of pearl thy temples fair:
Chase hence the ugly night,
Which serves but to make dear thy glorious light.
This is that happy morn
That day, long-wished day,
Of all my life so dark
(If cruel stars have not my ruin sworn,
And fates not hope betray),
Which, only white, deserves
A diamond for ever should it mark:
This is the morn should bring unto this grove
My love, to hear and recompense my love.
Fair king, who all preserves,
But show thy blushing beams,
And thou two sweeter eyes
Shalt see, than those which by Peneus' streams
Did once thy heart surprise;
Nay, suns, which shine as clear
As thou when two thou did to Rome appear.
Now, Flora, deck thyself in fairest guise;
If that ye, winds, would hear
A voice surpassing far Amphion's lyre,
Your stormy chiding stay;
Let zephyr only breathe,
And with her tresses play,
Kissing sometimes these purple ports of death.
The winds all silent are,
And Phœbus in his chair,
Ensaffroning sea and air,
Makes vanish every star:
Night like a drunkard reels
Beyond the hills to shun his flaming wheels;
The fields with flow'rs are deck'd in every hue,
The clouds bespangle with bright gold their blue:
Here is the pleasant place,
And every thing, save her, who all should grace.

To Chloris.

[From *Madrigals and Epigrams.*]

See, Chloris, how the clouds
Tilt in the azure lists,
And how with Stygian mists
Each horned hill his giant forehead shrouds;
Jove thund'reth in the air,
The air, grown great with rain,
Now seems to bring Deucalion's days again.
I see thee quake; come, let us home repair,
Come hide thee in mine arms,
If not for love, yet to shun greater harms.

Sonnet to Sir W. Alexander.

The love Alexis did to Damon bear
Shall witness'd be to all the woods and plains
As singular, renown'd by neighbouring swains,
That to our relics time may trophies rear:
Those madrigals we sung amidst our flocks,
With garlands guarded from Apollo's beams,
On Ochills whiles, whiles near Bodotria's streams,
Are registrate by echos in the rocks.
Of foreign shepherds bent to try the states,
Though I, world's guest, a vagabond do stray,
Thou mayst that store which I esteem survey,
As best acquainted with my soul's conceits:
  Whatever fate heavens have for me designed.
  I trust thee with the treasure of my mind.

SONNETS.

[From *Flowers of Sion.*]

Look how the flower which ling'ringly doth fade,
The morning's darling late, the summer's queen,
Spoil'd of that juice which kept it fresh and green,
As high as it did raise, bows low the head :
Right so my life, contentments being dead,
Or in their contraries but only seen,
With swifter speed declines than erst it spread,
And, blasted, scarce now shows what it hath been.
And doth the pilgrim therefore, whom the night
By darkness would imprison on his way,
Think on thy home, my soul, and think aright
Of what yet rests thee of life's wasting day ?
    Thy sun posts westward, passed is thy morn,
    And twice it is not given thee to be born.

For the Baptist.

The last and greatest herald of heaven's King,   .
Girt with rough skins, hies to the deserts wild,
Among that savage brood the woods forth bring,
Which he than man more harmless found and mild :
His food was locusts, and what young doth spring,
With honey that from virgin hives distill'd ;
Parch'd body, hollow eyes, some uncouth thing
Made him appear long since from earth exil'd.
There burst he forth : 'All ye, whose hopes rely
On God, with me amidst these deserts mourn ;
Repent, repent, and from old errors turn.'
Who listen'd to his voice, obey'd his cry ?
    Only the echoes, which he made relent,
    Rung from their marble caves, 'Repent, repent !'

To the Nightingale.

Sweet bird, that sing'st away the early hours,
Of winters past or coming void of care,
Well pleased with delights which present are,
Fair seasons, budding sprays, sweet-smelling flowers ;
To rocks, to springs, to rills, from leafy bowers
Thou thy Creator's goodness dost declare,
And what dear gifts on thee he did not spare,
A stain to human sense in sin that lowers.
What soul can be so sick which by thy songs,
Attir'd in sweetness, sweetly is not driven
Quite to forget earth's turmoils, spites, and wrongs,
And lift a reverent eye and thought to heaven .
  Sweet artless songster, thou my mind dost raise
  To airs of spheres, yes, and to angels' lays.

MADRIGAL.

This world a hunting is,
The prey poor man, the Nimrod fierce is Death ;
His speedy greyhounds are
Lust, sickness, envy, care,
Strife that ne'er falls amiss,
With all those ills which haunt us while we breathe.
Now, if by chance we fly
Of these the eager chase,
Old age with stealing pace
Casts up his nets, and there we panting die.

SONNET TO SIR W. ALEXANDER.

[Appended to *The Cypresse Grove.*]

Though I have twice been at the doors of death,
And twice found shut those gates which ever mourn,
This but a light'ning is, truce ta'en to breath,
For late-born sorrows augur fleet return.
Amidst thy sacred cares and courtly toils,
Alexis, when thou shalt hear wand'ring Fame
Tell Death hath triumph'd o'er my mortal spoils,
And that on earth I am but a sad name ;
If thou e'er held me dear, by all our love,
By all that bliss, those joys Heaven here us gave,
I conjure thee, and by the maids of Jove,
To grave this short remembrance on my grave :
   Here Damon lies, whose songs did sometime grace
   The murmuring Esk ; may roses shade the place !

SIR WILLIAM ALEXANDER,

EARL OF STIRLING (*or* STERLINE).

[Born about 1580, of a family which had for some time owned Menstrie in Clackmannan. In early life he travelled, and on his return, or during his absence, wrote *Aurora, First Fancies of the Author's Youth,* a small volume of sonnets and songs to a real or imaginary lady called Aurora. He became a courtier in 1603, and followed James to London. In 1603 he published at Edinburgh *The Tragedie of Darius*; in 1604 he reprinted it, adding *The Tragedie of Crœsus* and *The Parœnesis to Prince Henry*; in 1607 he reprinted the two tragedies and added *The Alexandrean Tragedy* and *Julius Cæsar,* under the joint title of 'Four Monarchicke Tragedies.' He helped King James in his version of the Psalms. Knighted in 1621, and made Secretary of State for Scotland in 1626, he was raised to the peerage as Viscount Canada in 1630, and created Earl of Stirling 1633. He printed a folio edition of his tragedies and of the religious poem of *Domesday* in 1637, and died 1640.]

Mr. Masson in his life of Drummond pronounces a severe judgment over the grave of Drummond's friend, Sir William Alexander, Earl of Stirling. 'There he lies, I suppose, to this day, vaguely remembered as the second-rate Scottish sycophant of an inglorious despotism, and the author of a large quantity of fluent and stately English verse which no one reads.' He certainly played no very glorious part in the attempts of James and Charles to impose episcopacy on Scotland ; unconscious all the while that he was one of those who were preparing the way for a 'Monarchicke Tragedie' as terrible as ary of the four that he had put into verse. That the bulk of his poetry deserves that neglect which, as Mr. Masson truly says, has befallen it, is not likely to be disputed by those who have tried to read it. The precocious solemnity of his tragedies, all written before his thirtieth year, is too much for the modern reader, however successfully it may have commended the poet to the literary confidences of his pedantic master. With all the sonorousness and wave-like beat of their stanzas, they are meie rhetoric ; they miss the genuine philosophic note of the somewhat similar plays of Alexander's older contemporary, the *Mustapha* and *Alaham* of Lord Brooke.   Still, Lord Stirling was an interesting man both in his life and in his writings, and he deserves to be not quite excluded from a collection of English poems.   His time admired his work ; his books sold ; Habington, Daniel, Drayton, and many other poets praised him ; above all, he was the close friend of Drummond—the Alexis to the Damon of Hawthornden.   His 'century of sonnets' lack indeed the reality and the music of the best of Drummond's, and his Aurora is a vague and shadowy goddess.   But the two sonnets that we quote will show that Drayton had reason for calling him 'that most ingenious knight' ; and the ode that follows, though defaced by one or two blemishes, deals with the commonplaces of the tragic chorus in a way that is not altogether commonplace.

EDITOR.

SONNETS.

[From *Aurora.*]

I envy not Endymion now no more,
Nor all the happiness his sleep did yield,
While as Diana, straying through the field,
Suck'd from his sleep-seal'd lips balm for her sore :
Whilst I embraced the shadow of my death,
I dreaming did far greater pleasure prove,
And quaff'd with Cupid sugar'd draughts of love
Then, Jove-like, feeding on a nectar'd breath.
Now judge which of us two might be most proud ;
He got a kiss yet not enjoy'd it right,
And I got none, yet tasted that delight
Which Venus on Adonis once bestow'd :
    He only got the body of a kiss,
    And I the soul of it, which he did miss.

Love swore by Styx, while all the depths did tremble,
That he would be avenged of my proud heart,
Who to his deity durst base styles impart,
And would in that Latona's imp resemble :
Then straight denounced his rebel, in a rage
He laboured by all means for to betray me,
And gave full leave to any for to slay me,
That he might by my wrack his wrath assuage.
A nymph, that longed to finish Cupid's toils,
Chanced once to spy me come in beauty's bounds,
And straight o'erthrew me with a world of wounds,
Then unto Paphos did transport my spoils.
    Thus, thus I see that all must fall in end,
    That with a greater than themselves contend.

From 'The Tragedy of Darius.'

Chorus 3.

Time, through Jove's judgment just,
Huge alteration brings ;
Those are but fools who trust
In transitory things,
Whose tails bear mortal stings,
Which in the end will wound ;
And let none think it strange,
Though all things earthly change :
In this inferior round
What is from ruin free ?
The elements which be
At variance, as we see,
Each th' other doth confound :
The earth and air make war,
The fire and water are
Still wrestling at debate,
All those through cold and heat
Through drought and moisture jar.
What wonder though men change and fade
Who of those changing elements are made ?

How dare vain worldlings vaunt
Of Fortune's goods not lasting,
Evils which our wits enchant ?
Expos'd to loss and wasting !
Lo, we to death are hasting,
Whilst we those things discuss.
All things from their beginning
Still to an end are running,
Heaven hath ordained it thus ;
We hear how it doth thunder,
We see th' earth burst asunder,
And yet we never ponder
What this imports to us :

These fearful signs do prove
That th' angry powers above
Are mov'd to indignation
Against this wretched nation,
Which they no longer love :
What are we but a puff of breath
Who live assured of nothing but of death?

Who was so happy yet
As never had some cross?
Though on a throne he sit,
And is not vexed with loss,
Yet fortune once will toss
Him, when that least he would;
If one had all at once
Hydaspes' precious stones
And yellow Tagus' gold ;
The oriental treasure
And every earthly pleasure,
Even in the greatest measure
It should not make him bold :
For while he lives secure,
His state is most unsure ;
When it doth least appear
Some heavy plague draws near,
Destruction to procure.
World's glory is but like a flower,
Which both is bloom'd and blasted in an hour.

In what we most repose
We find our comfort light,
The thing we soonest lose
That's precious in our sight;
In honour, riches, might,
Our lives in pawn we lay ;
Yet all like flying shadows,
Or flowers enameling meadows,
Do vanish and decay.

Long time we toil to find
These idols of the mind,
Which had, we cannot bind
To bide with us one day.
Then why should we presume
On treasures that consume,
Difficult to obtain,
Difficult to retain,
A dream, a breath, a fume?
Which vex them most that them possess,
Who starve with store and famish with excess.

BEAUMONT AND FLETCHER.

[JOHN FLETCHER was born in December, 1579, at Rye in Sussex, where his father, who ultimately became Bishop of London, was minister. He was admitted pensioner at Benet College, Cambridge, in 1591 ; and little is known of his life between this date and the period of his connection with Beaumont.

FRANCIS BEAUMONT was the son of Sir F. Beaumont, of Grace-Dieu in Leicestershire, and was born at that place, probably in 1585. He resided for a short time at Broadgates Hall (now Pembroke College), Oxford, and was entered of the Inner Temple in 1600.

Not many years after this we may suppose the friendship between the two poets to have begun. 'They lived together on the Bank side,' in Southwark, 'not far from the Play-house' (the Globe), and wrote for the theatre. The most celebrated of their joint productions were produced probably between 1608 and 1611. But the common life which has been described by Aubrey, and is itself almost a poem (if partly a comic one), must have been disturbed in 1613, when Beaumont married   In the spring of 1616 he died. So far as is known, Fletcher remained single till his death, which took place in August, 1625.]

Coleridge wished that Beaumont and Fletcher had written poems instead of tragedies. It was a bold wish, though not an unfriendly one ; but perhaps we should be readier to echo it if Coleridge had spoken of lyrics rather than of poems generally. The longer poems of Beaumont which remain to us are, on the whole, not remarkable. He composed a free paraphrase of Ovid's *Remedia Amoris*. *Salmacis and Hermaphroditus*, printed as early as 1602, when he was probably seventeen years old, is noteworthy chiefly on that account. In this poem, written in the same metre as Marlowe's *Hero and Leander*, and founded on a passage in Ovid's *Metamorphoses*, there is plenty of luxuriance and facility, but also a superabundance of mere voluptuous description and of frigid conceits. Some of Beaumont's memorial poems are marked by an almost incredible want of taste. But the case is very different with the letter to Ben Jonson, in which 'their merry

meetings at the Mermaid' are described with great animation and
doubtless with truth. By Fletcher there are but three poems
extant; but each has an interest of its own. Two of them are
addressed to 'the true master in his art' and 'his worthy friend,'
Ben Jonson ; and the other, *Upon an Honest Man's Fortune,* is
more than worthy of its place at the end of the comedy which
bears that name. In it we seem to come nearer than usual to the
poet himself, who probably knew too much of 'want, the curse
of man,' but never lost heart or belief in himself, and who has
here described with admirable strength, what Goethe afterwards
felt so keenly, the self-sufficience of the mind and its superiority
to fortune.

> 'Man is his own star, and the soul that can
> Render an honest and a perfect man,
> Commands all light, all influence, all fate ;
> Nothing to him falls early or too late ;
> Our acts our angels are, or good or ill,
> Our fatal shadows that walk by us still.'

These are fine lines, and there are others in the poem as good ;
yet we should hardly be willing to exchange one of the best of
the plays for them. But when we come to the purely lyrical
poems, the songs from the dramas and the speeches from *The
Faithful Shepherdess,* we feel that we are standing on different
ground. Of the passages here selected some belong indubitably
to Fletcher alone, and one, certainly the grandest, to Beaumont
alone. The great lines *On the Tombs in Westminster* are written
in the common rhyming couplets of four accents which have been
so plentifully and so variously used in English poetry. It was a
favourite metre of Fletcher's too, and it is interesting to compare
the difference of its effect in the hands of the two poets. There is
a grave strength in Beaumont's verse, and a concentrated vigour .
of imagination in such lines as

> 'Here are sands, ignoble things,
> Dropt from the ruin'd sides of kings,'

which hardly belongs to Fletcher's lighter nature. On the other
hand, all the qualities of his dramatic verse, its delightful ease and
grace, and its overflowing fancifulness, come out in the lyrical
speeches of the *Faithful Shepherdess.* Milton himself, though he
put a greater volume of imagination and sound into the measure,
never gave it such an airy lightness ; and we must look onwards

to Shelley's 'Ariel to Miranda' for an echo to these lyrics, still sweeter than their melody, and to his 'Music, when soft voices die' for a fellow to 'Weep no more.'

There is the same buoyant grace in Fletcher's songs, and something more. In that age of songs, many a playwright could produce a lyric or two of the stamp which seems to have been wellnigh lost since ; but songs seem to flow by nature from Fletcher's pen in every style and on every occasion, and to be always right and beautiful. If he wants a drinking-song, he can rise to 'God Lyæus, ever young,' or can produce, what on a much lower level is hardly less perfect, the 'Drink to-day and drown all sorrow' of the *Bloody Brother.* The wonderful verses on Melancholy, which suggested *Il Penseroso* and are hardly surpassed by it, come as easily to his call as the mad laughing-song of the same play. 'Sad songs,' like that quoted from *The Queen of Corinth* ; dirges, like the 'Come you, whose loves are dead' of *The Knight of the Burning Pestle,* or the 'Lay a garland on my hearse' ; invocations, prayers to Cupid, hymns to Pan,—each has its own charm, and Fletcher is as ready with his Beggars' or Broom-man's songs, or even with a dramatic battle-lyric like the tumultuous 'Arm, arm, arm, arm !' of *The Mad Lover.* Some of the best of these occur, indeed, in plays of which Beaumont was the joint author ; but a comparison of those lyrics which undeniably belong to each poet alone is perhaps enough to convince us that Fletcher was the author of 'Lay a garland on my hearse,' if not also of 'Come you, whose loves are dead.' Probably however he has touched his highest point in the song from *Valentinian,* 'Hear, ye ladies that despise.' Here the reader will observe (what applies also to another fine song from the same play, 'Now the lusty spring is seen') that the rhythm exactly corresponds in the two stanzas without at all interfering with the spontaneous effect of the whole.

Fletcher was the sole author of *The Faithful Shepherdess,* the forerunner of Milton's *Comus* ; and we may safely assume that no one of the extracts which follow is a joint production of the two poets. But this is not the case with their dramatic works. So complete was their poetical union that it is impossible, in the absence of external evidence, to say with any certainty what part of those plays which belong to both is due to each, or even to describe their separate characteristics. An old tradition contrasted the 'judgment' of the younger poet, who was Jonson's intimate friend, with the fancy and facility of the elder. That

Fletcher possessed the latter qualities is certain ; but we have no reason to attribute to Beaumont any of the deficiencies which the 'faint praise' of 'judgment' might seem to imply.

The opening song of *The Two Noble Kinsmen* has been included in this selection, although it is difficult to attribute it to any one but Shakespeare. On the other hand, 'Take, oh take those lips away,' the first stanza of which occurs in *Measure for Measure*, has been excluded.

A. C. BRADLEY.

LINES ON THE TOMBS IN WESTMINSTER.

[By Beaumont].

Mortality, behold and fear!
What a change of flesh is here!
Think how many royal bones
Sleep within this heap of stones;
Here they lie had realms and lands,
Who now want strength to stir their hands;
Where from their pulpits seal'd with dust
They preach, 'In greatness is no trust.'
Here's an acre sown indeed
With the richest royall'st seed
That the earth did e'er suck in,
Since the first man died for sin:
Here the bones of birth have cried,
'Though gods they were, as men they died':
Here are sands, ignoble things,
Dropt from the ruin'd sides of kings:
Here's a world of pomp and state,
Buried in dust, once dead by fate.

FROM 'THE MAID'S TRAGEDY.'

[By Beaumont and Fletcher.]

Lay a garland on my hearse
  Of the dismal yew;
Maidens, willow branches bear;
  Say, I died true.

My love was false, but I was firm
  From my hour of birth.
Upon my buried body lie
  Lightly, gentle earth!

From 'The Faithful Shepherdess.'

[By Fletcher.]

I.

THE SATYR.

Here be grapes whose lusty blood
Is the learned poet's good ;
Sweeter yet did never crown
The head of Bacchus ; nuts more brown
Than the squirrel's teeth that crack them ;
Deign, O fairest fair, to take them !
For these black-eyed Dryope
Hath oftentimes commanded me
With my clasped knee to climb :
See how well the lusty time
Hath deck'd their rising cheeks in red,
Such as on your lips is spread.
Here be berries for a queen,
Some be red, some be green ;
These are of that luscious meat
The great god Pan himself doth eat :
All these, and what the woods can yield,
The hanging mountain or the field,
I freely offer, and ere long
Will bring you more, more sweet and strong ;
Till when, humbly leave I take,
Lest the great Pan do awake,
That sleeping lies in a deep glade,
Under a broad beech's shade.
I must go, I must run
Swifter than the fiery sun.

II.

THE RIVER GOD TO AMORET.

I am this fountain's god. Below
My waters to a river grow,
And 'twixt two banks with osiers sct,
That only prosper in the wet,
Through the meadows do they glide,
Wheeling still on every side,
Sometime winding round about
To find the evenest channel out.
And if thou wilt go with me,
Leaving mortal company,
In the cool streams shalt thou lie,
Free from harm as well as I ;
I will give thee for thy food
No fish that useth in the mud,
But trout and pike, that love to swim
Where the gravel from the brim
Through the pure streams may be seen ;
Orient pearl fit for a queen
Will I give, thy love to win,
And a shell to keep them in ;
Not a fish in all my brook
That shall disobey thy look,
But, when thou wilt, come gliding by
And from thy white hand take a fly:
And to make thee understand
How I can my waves command,
They shall bubble whilst I sing,
Sweeter than the silver string.

The Song.

Do not fear to put thy feet
Naked in the river swèet ;
Think not leech or newt or toad
Will bite thy foot, when thou hast trod ;
Nor let the water rising high,
As thou wad'st in, make thee cry
And sob ; but ever live with me,
And not a wave shall trouble thee !

III.

THE SATYR.

Thou divinest, fairest, brightest,
Thou most powerful maid and whitest,
Thou most virtuous and most blessed,
Eyes of stars, and golden tressed
Like Apollo ! tell me, sweetest,
What new service now is meetest
For the Satyr ? Shall I stray
In the middle air, and stay
The sailing rack, or nimbly take
Hold by the moon, and gently make
Suit to the pale queen of night
For a beam to give thee light ?
Shall I dive into the sea
And bring thee coral, making way
Through the rising waves that fall
Like snowy fleeces ? Dearest, shall
I catch thee wanton fawns, or flies
Whose woven wings the summer dyes
Of many colours ? get thee fruit,
Or steal from heaven old Orpheus' lute ?
All these I 'll venture for, and more,
To do her service all these woods adore.

FROM 'THE TWO NOBLE KINSMEN.'

[By Shakespeare and Fletcher.]

Roses, their sharp spines being gone,
Not royal in their smells alone,
     But in their hue ;
Maiden-pinks, of odour faint,
Daisies smell-less yet most quaint,
     And sweet thyme true ;

Primrose, first-born child of Ver,
Merry spring-time's harbinger,
     With her bells dim ;
Oxlips in their cradles growing,
Marigolds on death-beds blowing,
     Larks'-heels trim.

All, dear Nature's children sweet,
Lie 'fore bride and bridegroom's feet,
     Blessing their sense !
Not an angel of the air,
Bird melodious or bird fair,
     Be absent hence !

The crow, the slanderous cuckoo, nor
The boding raven, nor chough hoar,
     Nor chattering pie,
May on our bride-house perch or sing,
Or with them any discord bring,
     But from it fly !

From 'Valentinian.'

[By Fletcher.]

I.

Hear, ye ladies that despise,
  What the mighty Love has done;
Fear examples and be wise:
  Fair Calisto was a nun;
Leda, sailing on the stream
  To deceive the hopes of man,
Love accounting but a dream,
  Doated on a silver swan;
Danaë, in a brazen tower,
Where no love was, loved a shower.

Hear, ye ladies that are coy,
  What the mighty Love can do;
Fear the fierceness of the boy:
  The chaste moon he made to woo;
Vesta, kindling holy fires,
  Circled round about with spies,
Never dreaming loose desires,
  Doting at the altar dies;
Ilion, in a short hour, higher
He can build, and once more fire.

II.

SONG TO BACCHUS.

God Lyæus, ever young,
Ever renown'd, ever sung;
Stain'd with blood of lusty grapes,
In a thousand lusty shapes,
Dance upon the mazer's brim,
In the crimson liquor swim;
From thy plenteous hand divine
Let a river run with wine;
God of youth, let this day here
Enter neither care nor fear.

III.

INVOCATION TO SLEEP.

Care-charming Sleep, thou easer of all woes,
Brother to Death, sweetly thyself dispose
On this afflicted prince ; fall like a cloud
In gentle showers ; give nothing that is loud
Or painful to his slumbers ;—easy, sweet,
And as a purling stream, thou son of night,
Pass by his troubled senses ; sing his pain
Like hollow murmuring wind or silver rain ;
Into this prince gently, oh, gently slide,
And kiss him into slumbers like a bride !

From 'The Queen of Corinth.'

[By Fletcher.]

Weep no more, nor sigh, nor groan ;
Sorrow calls no time that 's gone ;
Violets plucked the sweetest rain
Makes not fresh nor grow again ;
Trim thy locks, look cheerfully ;
Fate's hid ends eyes cannot see ;
Joys as winged dreams fly fast,
Why should sadness longer last ?
Grief is but a wound to woe ;
Gentlest fair, mourn, mourn no mo.

From 'The Nice Valour.'

[By Fletcher.]

Hence, all you vain delights,
As short as are the nights
  Wherein you spend your folly !
There 's nought in this life sweet,
If man were wise to see 't,
  But only melancholy ;
  O sweetest melancholy !

Welcome, folded arms and fixed eyes,
A sigh that piercing mortifies,
A look that 's fasten'd to the ground,
A tongue chain'd up without a sound !
Fountain heads and pathless groves,
Places which pale passion loves !
Moonlight walks, when all the fowls
Are warmly hous'd save bats and owls !
A midnight bell, a parting groan,
These are the sounds we feed upon ;
Then stretch our bones in a still gloomy valley ;
Nothing 's so dainty sweet as lovely melancholy.

THOMAS DEKKER.

[In a tract dated 1637, Dekker speaks of himself as a man of threescore years. This is the only clue to his age that has been discovered. He was born in London and apparently lived all his life there, as playwright, pamphleteer, and miscellaneous literary hack. His plays were published separately at various dates from 1600 to 1636. He frequently worked with other dramatists, Webster, Middleton, Massinger, Ford, etc.]

Dekker had several qualities which made him a desirable coadjutor in play-writing. He was a master of the craft of the stage. A man of quick sympathies, unconquerable buoyancy of spirit, infinite readiness and resource, he had lived among the people who filled the theatres, and took a genuine delight in moving them by the exhibition of common joys and sorrows. His whole heart went with his audience, and, though he had not the loftiness of aim of his greatest contemporaries, none of them had a finer dramatic instinct. He knew London as well as Dickens, and had something of the same affection for its oddities and its outcasts. The humour which lights up its miseries, the sunshine which plays over its tears, the simple virtues of the poor and unfortunate, patience, forgiveness, mirthfulness, were the favourite themes of this tender-hearted dramatist. His plays are full of life and movement, of pathos that is never maudlin and humour that is never harsh. Vice always gets the worst of it, hardness of heart above all never goes unpunished, but relenting leniency always comes in to keep retribution within gentle bounds. Virtue is always triumphant, but it is discovered in the most fantastic shapes and the least conventional habiliments. It needs some charity to tolerate such heroes and heroines as Simon Eyre, the mad shoemaker, Candido, the patient citizen, Orlando Friscobaldo, Bellafronta, and other types of strangely disguised goodness, but the dramatist's own love for them, with all their absurd eccentricities, is infectious. He laughs at them heartily, and carries us with him in his humour, but he knows how to change the key and soften laughter into tenderness.

Dekker's verse is naturally graceful and copious, keeping unforced pace with the abundance of matter supplied by his fertile invention. He was not a careful writer. He probably 'never blotted a line,' and one cannot read his plays without wishing that he had 'blotted a thousand.' His intellect had not the intense chemical energy of Shakespeare's, through which no thought could pass unchanged ; and he did not strain after originality as some of his great compeers did, Webster, Jonson, Ford, and Chapman. He poured out in an easy stream whatever came readiest, and his best passages do not run far without being marred by some poor commonplace, tumbled out as it entered the mint, without any new stamp impressed upon it. It is in his songs, interspersed at too rare intervals through his plays, that Dekker appears at his best. He had the most exquisite gift of song. Few of his contemporaries had a harder life, but all the miscellaneous drudgery through which he had to toil for a precarious livelihood failed to destroy his elasticity and spirits, and his songs rise from the earth like bird-songs, clear, fresh, spontaneous. There is genuine lyrical rapture in the notes. Like most town-bred poets, he had a passion for the country, and his fancy is never more happy than when dwelling on rustic delights.

W. MINTO.

CONTENT.

[From *Patient Grissil.*]

Art thou poor, yet hast thou golden slumbers?
        O sweet Content!
Art thou rich, yet is thy mind perplexed?
        O Punishment!
Dost laugh to see how fools are vexed
To add to golden numbers golden numbers?
        O sweet Content, O sweet, O sweet Content!

Work apace, apace, apace, apace,
Honest labour bears a lovely face.
Then hey noney, noney; hey noney, noney.

Canst drink the waters of the crisped spring?
        O sweet Content!
Swim'st thou in wealth, yet sink'st in thine own tears?
        O Punishment!
Then he that patiently Want's burden bears
No burden bears, but is a king, a king.
        O sweet Content, O sweet, O sweet Content!

Work apace, apace, etc.

LULLABY.

[From *Patient Grissil.*]

Golden slumbers kiss your eyes,
Smiles awake you when you rise.
Sleep, pretty wantons, do not cry,
And I will sing a lullaby.
Rock them, rock them, lullaby.

Care is heavy, therefore sleep you.
You are care, and care must keep you.
Sleep, pretty wantons, do not cry,
And I will sing a lullaby,
Rock them, rock them, lullaby.

The Praise of Fortune.

[From *Old Fortunatus.*]

Fortune smiles, cry holiday!
Dimples on her cheek do dwell.
Fortune frowns, cry well-a-day!
Her love is Heaven, her hate is Hell.
Since Heaven and Hell obey her power,
Tremble when her eyes do lower.
Since Heaven and Hell her power obey,
When she smiles cry holiday!
 Holiday with joy we cry,
 And bend and bend, and merrily
 Sing Hymns to Fortune's deity,
 Sing Hymns to Fortune's deity.

Chorus.

Let us sing merrily, merrily, merrily,
With our songs let Heaven resound.
Fortune's hands our heads have crowned
Let us sing merrily, merrily, merrily.

Rustic Song.

[From *the Sun's Darling.*]

Haymakers, rakers, reapers, and mowers,
 Wait on your Summer-Queen!
Dress up with musk-rose her eglantine bowers,
 Daffodils strew the green!
  Sing, dance, and play,
  'Tis holiday!
 The Sun does bravely shine
 On our ears of corn.
  Rich as a pearl
  Comes every girl.
 This is mine, this is mine, this is mine.
Let us die ere away they be borne.

Bow to our Sun, to our Queen, and that fair one
  Come to behold our sports :
Each bonny lass here is counted a rare one,
   As those in princes' courts.
      These and we
      With country glee,
  Will teach the woods to resound,
  And the hills with echoes hollow.
      Skipping lambs
      Their bleating dams
  'Mongst kids shall trip it round ;
For joy thus our wenches we follow.

Wind jolly huntsmen, your neat bugles shrilly,
  Hounds make a lusty cry ;
Spring up, you falconers, partridges freely
  Then let your brave hawks fly !
      Horses amain,
      Over ridge, over plain,
  The dogs have the stag in chase :
 'Tis a sport to content a king.
      So ho ! ho ! through the skies
      How the proud bird flies,
  And sousing, kills with a grace !
Now the deer falls ; hark ! how they ring.

JOHN FORD.

[JOHN FORD belonged to a Devonshire family. He was born in 1586, and his last work was published in 1639. In his younger days, while practising as a barrister, he took part with professional playmakers, Webster, Dekker, Rowley, in the composition of various occasional stage productions. He first appeared in print as a dramatic author with *The Lover's Melancholy*, in 1628. His subsequent plays were published at intervals up to 1639.]

Ford was not one of the herd of playwrights, and he lost no opportunity of letting the world know that he 'cared not to please many.' His poetry was the 'fruit of leisure moments'; he wrote for his own satisfaction, and the enjoyment of his equals in condition. Genial expansive sentiment, joyful presentation of the ordinary virtues, the exaltation of common ideals, was not to be expected in plays that bore upon their title-pages such an avowal of proud reserve. Ford would not walk in beaten dramatic paths ; his pride lay in searching out strange freaks of tragic passion. The heart is not purified and ennobled by his tragedies ; it is surprised, stunned, perplexed. Passion speaks in his verse with overpowering force ; but though he shows profound art in tracing the most monstrous aberrations of love, jealousy, and revenge to a natural origin in strangeness of temper, the sense of strangeness is left predominant. In the preface to *The Broken Heart* the names of the *dramatis personae* are explained as being 'fitted to their qualities,' and from this one might carelessly rush to the conclusion that the strangeness of Ford's characters is due to their being extravagant personifications of single attributes, and not types of real men and women. But his art was much too profound, his mastery of thought and emotion much too living for any such mechanical superficiality. His creations are not inanimate figures; the pulse of life beats in them. The secret of their strangeness seems to lie in a certain intensity and concentration of nature, a hardness and strength of fibre which will not relax where once it has taken hold. The kinship of passion to insanity is strongly suggested by Ford's plays. We seem to have before us men and women with a fixed delusion on some one point, impressed upon them not by the force of overmastering circumstances, but by some vicious warp in their own nature. In Shakespeare's plays men are driven into tragic error by the conspiracy of forces outside themselves ; in Ford's plays fatal false steps are made from mere waywardness of character. In the one case, we are struck with the nearness of the victims of misleading passion to our common humanity; in the other their remoteness from common motives is bewildering. The strangeness of the passions which Ford brings into conflict mars the effect of his two great tragedies as artistic wholes ; we do not turn from them with awestruck hearts, full of subdued fear and wonder—they leave us dissatisfied, tortured, bewildered. If these plays were all that were left to us by which to judge of the Elizabethan age they would justify all that M. Taine has said about its ferocity of spirit. In the play that bears the harsh and mocking title *'Tis Pity She's a Whore*, we feel as if we were present at a hellish carnival of passion. There is no relief to its horrors, except the rapturous exultation of brother and sister in their guilty love. The revolting coarseness of the low-comedy scenes is not a relief but a sickening addition to the chaos.

Ford is not a poet who appears to advantage in quotations. Charles Lamb says truly of him that 'he sought for sublimity, not by parcels, in metaphors or visible images, but directly where she has her full residence in the heart of man.' The sublimity to which his own gloomy austere temper directed him was the sublimity of demoniac resolution, the heroism of unyielding will. Even his heroines are not of the soft and tender type which his contemporaries delighted to paint ; they are as firm and resolute in their purposes as the men whom they love. The sorrowful Penthea, though she bends to her brother's will so far as to marry a husband of his choice, resists all the prayers of her discarded lover to prove unfaithful, and with silent and secret determination starves herself to death. Calantha, his 'flower of beauty,' bears stroke after stroke of appalling misfortune without betraying to the vulgar world one sign of the grief which is breaking her heart ; she falls dead without a tear, when she has set the affairs of her kingdom in order. It is on the supreme force and patient completeness with which he has displayed such stern and passionate natures, that Ford's title to a high place among poets must rest. There is no great intrinsic charm in his verse : it is an admirable vehicle for the expression of intense restrained passion, word following word with severe clear-cutting emphasis ; but without a knowledge of the character and situation one cannot feel the force by which it is animated. Even in his songs, with all the softness of their music, we are conscious of the same severely regulating taste. All his few songs are of a sad strain, but they are not filled with the ecstasy of grief ; their music is chastened and subdued.

W. MINTO.

PENTHEA'S DYING SONG.

[From *the Broken Heart.*]

Oh no more, no more, too late
    Sighs are spent ; the burning tapers
Of a life as chaste as fate,
    Pure as are unwritten papers,
Are burnt out ; no heat, no light
Now remains ; 'tis ever night.
      Love is dead ; let lovers' eyes,
      Locked in endless dreams,
      Th' extremes of all extremes,
      Ope no more, for now Love dies.
Now Love dies—implying
Love's martyrs must be ever, ever dying.

CALANTHA'S DIRGE.

[From *the Broken Heart.*]

Glories, pleasures, pomps, delights and ease,
    Can but please
Outward senses, when the mind
Is untroubled, or by peace refined.
Crowns may flourish and decay,
Beauties shine, but fade away.
Youth may revel, yet it must
Lie down in a bed of dust.
Earthly honours flow and waste,
Time alone doth change and last.
Sorrows mingled with contents prepare
    Rest for care ;
Love only reigns in death ; though art
Can find no comfort for a Broken Heart.

Awakening Song.

[From *the Lover's Melancholy*.]

Fly hence, shadows, that do keep
Watchful sorrows, charmed in sleep!
Though the eyes be overtaken,
Yet the heart doth ever waken
Thoughts chained up in busy snares
Of continual woes and cares:
Love and griefs are so exprest,
As they rather sigh than rest.
Fly hence, shadows, that do keep
Watchful sorrows, charmed in sleep.

WILLIAM BROWNE.

[WILLIAM BROWNE was born at Tavistock in 1588, and died, probably, in the year 1643. He went to Oxford as a member of Exeter College; entered the Inner Temple in 1612; published his elegy on Prince Henry in a volume along with another by his friend Christopher Brooke in 1613; the first book of his *Britannia's Pastorals* in the same year; his *Shepherd's Pipe* in 1614; and the second book of his *Pastorals* in 1616, the year of the death of Shakspeare. The third book of his *Britannia's Pastorals* was unknown till 1851, when it was published for the Percy Society from a manuscript in the Cathedral Library at Salisbury. The most complete edition of Browne is that published in the Roxburghe Library by Mr. W. Carew Hazlitt in 1868.]

Browne was fortunate in his friends. His life at the Inner Temple brought him into contact not only with his intimate friend Wither and Charles Brooke, but also with such a man as Selden, who wrote commendatory verses to the first book of his *Pastorals*. He was too, apparently, one of that knot of brilliant young men who called themselves the 'sons' of Ben Jonson, and there are some interesting verses, of warm yet not extravagant praise, prefixed by Ben Jonson to the second book of the same poem. With Drayton he appears to have been on cordial and intimate terms. Some verses by Browne are prefixed to the second edition of the *Polyolbion*, and some of the most charming commendatory verses that were ever written were penned by Drayton in honour of *Britannia's Pastorals*. Chapman too 'the learned Shepherd of fair Hitching Hill,' was, as more than one indication sufficiently proves, intimate with our poet, and Browne was not only familiar with his friend's Iliad and Odyssey, but also, we may be very sure, knew well that golden book of poetry, the *Hero and Leander*.

With such contemporary influences, and with the fullest know
ledge of and reverence for such of his predecessors as Sidney anc
Spenser, Browne had every advantage given to his genius, and
every help to enable him to float in the full and central stream of
poetic tradition.

Browne was apparently a diligent student of our early poetry.
In his *Shepherd's Pipe* he gives in full a long story from Occleve,
a poet about whom probably, at the time he wrote, no one but
himself knew anything whatever. He also, though he nowhere
refers to him by name, had undoubtedly studied Chaucer to some
purpose. The following passage—

> 'As when some malefactor judged to die
> For his offence, his execution nigh,
> Casteth his sight on states unlike to his
> And weighs his ill by other's happiness,'

reveals its origin at once to anyone familiar with the *Knightes
Tale*. The description of the Cave of Famine, again, is trans-
parently studied from Chaucer's description of the temple of Mars ;
though Browne's poverty in what the critics of the last century
called 'invention' makes him compare ill with his prototype in
passages of this kind. Still more familiar to Browne than the
Canterbury Tales were Shakspeare's plays and poems. Reminis-
cences of Shakspeare might easily be pointed out in his heroic
verse, and a still closer study is apparent in certain of the songs
scattered about his *Britannia's Pastorals*. The two poets, how-
ever, to whom Browne owed most, and whose praises he has most
gratefully recorded are Spenser and Sidney. The influence of the
former's *Aeglogues* as well as of the *Faerie Queene* upon Browne's
style and manner is very perceptible. For Sidney he had that
enthusiastic and affectionate reverence which was commonly felt
by all the poets of that time for the poet and the author of the
Defence of Poesie. The passages on Spenser and Sidney are,
besides their literary interest, of poetic value in themselves, and
will therefore be found among the following selections. Between
Browne and Wither there existed a very intimate friendship, and
in Wither's youth their work ran to a certain extent upon the
same lines. The hand of the author of the *Shepherd's Hunting*
can apparently be traced in several passages of the *Shepherd's
Pipe*, and in his own poems Wither speaks in the most affec-
tionate and respectful terms of the 'singer of the Western main.'

Of Browne's possible relation to Milton it is unnecessary to speak at length. Milton certainly had read Browne's poems and read them carefully, and it is interesting to compare the *Inner Temple Masque* with *Comus* and the elegies contained in the *Pastorals* and the *Shepherd's Pipe* with *Lycidas.* The little song entitled the *Charme* in the former poem bears a strong likeness, as Warton has pointed out, to a well-known passage in *Comus,* and the general design of the two poems is similar enough to excite attention. But while it is right to think of Milton as a friendly reader of our poet, it would be a mistake to ascribe to Browne any great share in his poetic development. What is certain is that both poets felt and showed in their different ways the combined and contending influences of classical and Puritan feeling. Browne is at once a pagan and a Protestant.

There is another English poet of a later day with whom Browne may fairly be brought into some sort of comparison. That poet is Keats[1]. It is unnecessary to say that Browne is a poet of a quite different and lower rank ; but he is like Keats in being before all things an artist, he has the same intense pleasure in a fine line or a fine phrase for its own sake, and he further resembles Keats in possessing very little pure constructive or narrative power. One thinks of Keats passing a fine phrase over his mental palate with an almost sensual pleasure ; 'I look upon fine phrases like a lover,' he himself says in one passage ; and in a lesser degree one can fancy much the same of Browne. There is one passage which is here quoted, the value of which depends almost wholly on the masterly use of proper names. Their beauty of sound and delicate appropriateness to the place they occupy in the line— alliteration and such like expedients being freely employed—help out the historical and literary associations which make such names as Coos or Cilicia in themselves poetical. So in what may be called a 'colour-passage,' a rare control of the resources of our tongue and a rare feeling for and discrimination in shades of colour go to make up a description of real beauty and power. Browne is something of a literary epicure, and however feeble or disconnected may be his narrative of events, he rarely gives us a line which has not been tried and allowed by a taste far more delicate than common. It is consistent with this that he should be a warm defender of poetry.

---

[1] Keats prefixes a quotation from *Britannia's Pastorals* to his own *Epistles.*

> ' 'Tis not the rancour of a cankered heart
> That can debase the excellence of art,'

he says in one passage ; and how easily one might fancy Keats,
transplanted to the age of James I, the author of these most
characteristic lines :—

> ' In lieu of hounds that make the wooded hills
> Talk in a thousand voices to the rills,
> *I like the pleasing cadence of a line,*
> *Struck by the consort of the sacred Nine.'*

Browne's natural tendency is to be copious and glowing in
description, and his warm fancy is always tending to run away
with him.   He wants to be luscious and sweet.   So he appeals to
the 'blessed Muses':—

> 'Dwell on my lines, and, till the last sand fall,
> Run hand in hand with my weak pastoral ;
> Cause every coupling cadence flow in blisses,
> And fill the world with envy of such kisses.
> Make all the rarest beauties of our clime,
> That deign a sweet look on my younger rhyme,
> To linger on each line's enticing graces
> As on their lover's lips and chaste embraces.'

But with all this he feels strongly the force of the flowing
Puritan tide, and spoils his poetry here and there, as Keats never
does, by his resolution to improve the occasion.   Browne is a
staunch Protestant, and uses plain language about nuns and
nunneries, Spain and Rome.   All this does his poetry no good.
We can imagine him passionate and powerful enough if he had
lived a generation earlier.   As it is, one has the feeling in reading
him that he is living between two worlds of poetry without vital
hold on either.   His is neither the ardent muse of the young
Shakspeare, nor the pure august muse of the great Puritan poet
who was to follow him.

The rare qualities of Browne's work cannot blind us to the fact
that he is almost destitute of constructive or narrative power.   As a
narrative poem *Britannia's Pastorals* is deplorable.   The reader is
perpetually passing from the woes of one fair one to those of another,
and has great difficulty in making it clear to himself at any given
time whether he is reading about Marina or Idya or Celia.

The third book ends without any particular conclusion, and there is no reason why Browne should not have gone on in the same strain for half a dozen books more. On the other hand, as pastoral poetry, the work is not without peculiar excellences. It is true that the attempts to keep up the pastoral illusion are sometimes of a desperate character,—as for instance when the poet addresses his readers as 'swaines,'—but Browne's very accurate knowledge of his native county, and his loving enthusiasm for it, give his work a special value, and stamp much of it with the character of a direct personal impression. The allusions to Devonshire are innumerable. Browne had a peculiar love for his native streams, and the waters of his own Tavy are ever murmuring musically through his song. Just as Wordsworth said that he had made thousands of verses as he strolled by his beloved Rotha, so Browne speaks of

> 'Tavy's voiceful stream, to whom I owe
> More strains than from my pipe can ever flow.'

The little tributary Walla has inspired some of his most charming lines. He abounds in old local words like *Berry* and *trend,* and he calls the Tavy trout

> 'The *shoats* with whom is Tavy frought.'

He is enthusiastic about the Devonshire heroes. His knowledge of the country is inbred, and he reveals himself as passing, like Wordsworth, a 'dedicated' youth :—

> 'Nor could I wish those golden hours unspent
> Wherein my fancy led me to the woods,
> And tuned soft lays of rural merriment,
> Of shepherd's love, and never-resting floods.'

We owe to this knowledge and love of the country those pictures of the shepherd wending his early way to his day's work, of the shepherd boy sitting alone on the fell top and piping as he watches his sheep,—a charming mixture, the whole passage, of literal fact and classical reminiscence ;—of the country maid straying through the fields to make her nosegay, of the boys searching the woods for bird's eggs or hunting the squirrel from tree to tree. It is in such pictures that the reader of *Britannia's Pastorals* finds his chief pleasure. Browne cannot be said to have victoriously overcome the inherent difficulties of pastoral poetry, but his genuine delight in country sights and sounds makes him less unreal than any other English poet—if we except perhaps Ramsay,—who has tried this form of composition. He, again like Wordsworth, must be read in selections, if he is to be read with unmixed enjoyment ; but in his best passages—and they are not few—he will send to the listener wafts of pure and delightful music as the young figure steps across the moors,

> δοχμιᾶν διὰ κλιτύων
> ποιμνίτας ὑμεναίους
> συρίζων.

W. T. ARNOLD.

Britannia's Pastorals.

BOOK I.   SONG I.

Marina and the river-god.

The fall of her did make the god below,
Starting, to wonder whence that noise should grow:
Whether some ruder clown in spite did fling
A lamb, untimely fall'n, into his spring :
And if it were, he solemnly then swore
His spring should flow some other way : no more
Should it in wanton manner e'er be seen
To writhe in knots, or give a gown of green
Unto their meadows, nor be seen to play,
Nor drive the rushy-mills, that in his way
The shepherds made : but rather for their lot
Send them red water that their sheep should rot.
And with such moorish springs embrace their field
That it should nought but moss and rushes yield.
Upon each hillock where the merry boy
Sits piping in the shades his notes of joy,
He 'd show his anger by some flood at hand
And turn the same into a running sand.

*   *   *   *   *   *   *   *   *

Thus spake the god : but when as in the water
The corpse came sinking down, he spied the matter,
And catching softly in his arms the maid
He brought her up, and having gently laid
Her on his bank, did presently command
Those waters in her to come forth : at hand
They straight came gushing out, and did contest
Which chiefly should obey their god's behest.
This done, her then pale lips he straight did ope
And from his silver hair let fall a drop
Into her mouth, of such an excellence,
That called back life, which grieved to part from thence
Being for troth assur'd that than this one
She ne'er possess'd a fairer mansion.

Then did the god her body forwards steep,
And cast her for a while into a sleep;
Sitting still by her did his full view take
Of nature's master-piece. Here for her sake
My pipe in silence as of right shall mourn,
Till from the watering we again return.

BOOK I.   SONG 2.

The scented grove.

Then walked they to a grove but near at hand,
Where fiery Titan had but small command,
Because the leaves conspiring kept his beams,
For fear of hurting, when he's in extremes,
The under-flowers, which did enrich the ground
With sweeter scents than in Arabia found.
The earth doth yield, which they through pores exhale,
Earth's best of odours, th' aromatical:
Like to that smell which oft our sense descries
Within a field which long unplowed lies,
Somewhat before the setting of the sun;
And where the rainbow in the horizon
Doth pitch her tips: or as when in the prime,
The earth being troubled with a drought long time,
The hand of heaven his spongy clouds doth strain,
And throws into her lap a shower of rain;
She sendeth up, conceived from the sun,
A sweet perfume and exhalation.
Not all the ointments brought from Delos isle;
Nor from the confines of seven-headed Nile;
Nor that brought whence Phenicians have abodes,
Nor Cyprus' wild vine-flowers, nor that of Rhodes,
Nor roses' oil from Naples, Capua,
Saffron confected in Cilicia;
Nor that of quinces nor of marjoram
That ever from the isle of Coos came.
Nor these, nor any else, though ne'er so rare,
Could with this place for sweetest smells compare.

The music lesson.

As when a maid taught from her mother wing,
To tune her voice unto a silver string,
When she should run, she rests ; rests when should run,
And ends her lesson having now begun :
Now misseth she her stop, then in her song,
And doing of her best she still is wrong,
Begins again, and yet again strikes false,
Then in a chafe forsakes her virginals,
And yet within an hour she tries anew,
That with her daily pains, Art's chiefest due,
She gains that charming skill : and can no less
Tame the fierce walkers of the wilderness,
Than that Œagrian harpist, for whose lay,
Tigers with hunger pined and left their prey.
So Riot, when he gan to climb the hill,
Here maketh haste and there long standeth still,
Now getteth up a step, then falls again,
Yet not despairing all his nerves doth strain
To clamber up anew, then slide his feet,
And down he comes : but gives not over yet,
For, with the maid, he hopes a time will be
When merit shall be linked with industry.

The hunted squirrel.

Then as a nimble squirrel from the wood,
Ranging the hedges for his filbert-food,
Sits pertly on a bough his brown nuts cracking,
And from the shell the sweet white kernel taking,
Till with their crooks and bags a sort of boys,
To share with him, come with so great a noise
That he is forced to leave a nut nigh broke,
And for his life leap to a neighbour oak,

Thence to a beech, thence to a row of ashes ;
Whilst through the quagmires and red water plashes
The boys run dabbling thorough thick and thin,
One tears his hose, another breaks his shin,
This, torn and tatter'd, hath with much ado
Got by the briars ; and that hath lost his shoe :
This drops his band ; that headlong falls for haste ;
Another cries behind for being last :
With sticks and stones, and many a sounding hollow,
The little fool with no small sport they follow,
Whilst he from tree to tree, from spray to spray,
Gets to the wood, and hides him in his dray.

BOOK I.   SONG 5.

A metamorphosis.

And as a lovely maiden, pure and chaste,
With naked ivory neck and gown unlaced,
Within her chamber, when the day is fled,
Makes poor her garments to enrich her bed :
First, puts she off her lily-silken gown,
That shrinks for sorrow as she lays it down ;
And with her arms graceth a waistcoat fine,
Embracing her as it would ne'er untwine.
Her flaxen hair, ensnaring the beholders,
She next permits to wave about her shoulders,
And though she cast it back, the silken slips
Still forward steal, and hang upon her lips :
Whereat she sweetly angry, with her laces
Binds up the wanton locks in curious traces,
Whilst, twisting with her joints, each hair long lingers
As loth to be enchained but with her fingers.
Then on her head a dressing like a crown ;
Her breasts all bare, her kirtle slipping down,
And all things off which rightly ever be
Called the foul-fair marks of our misery,
Except her last, which enviously doth seize her
Lest any eye partake with it in pleasure,

Prepares for sweetest rest, while silvans greet her,
And longingly the down-bed swells to meet her:
So by degrees his shape all brutish wild
Fell from him as loose skin from some young child
In lieu whereof a man-like shape appears,
And gallant youth scarce skilled in twenty years,
So fair, so fresh, so young, so admirable
In every part, that since I am not able
In words to shew his picture, gentle swains,
Recall the praises in my former strains;
And know if they have graced any limb,
I only lent it those, but stole't from him.

BOOK I. SONG 5.

The poet's ambition.

A truer love the Muses never sung,
Nor happier names e'er graced a golden tongue:
O! they are better fitting his sweet stripe,
Who[1] on the banks of Ancor tuned his pipe:
Or rather for that learned swain[2], whose lays
Divinest Homer crowned with deathless bays;
Or any one sent from the sacred well
Inheriting the soul of Astrophell[3]:
These, these in golden lines might write this story,
And make these loves their own eternal glory:
Whilst I, a swain, as weak in years as skill,
Should in the valley hear them on the hill.
Yet when my sheep have at the cistern been
And I have brought them back to shear the green,
To miss an idle hour, and not for meed,
With choicest relish shall mine oaten reed
Record their worths: and though in accents rare
I miss the glory of a charming air,
My Muse may one day make the courtly swains
Enamoured on the music of the plains,
And as upon a hill she bravely sings
Teach humble dales to weep in crystal springs.

[1] Drayton. [2] Chapman. [3] Sidney.

BOOK II.   SONG I.

The praise of Spenser.

All their pipes were still,
And Colin Clout began to tune his quill
With such deep art that every one was given
To think Apollo, newly slid from Heaven,
Had ta'en a human shape to win his love,
Or with the western swains for glory strove.
He sung th' heroic knights of Faiery-land
In lines so elegant, of such command,
That had the Thracian played but half so well,
He had not left Eurydice in Hell.
But ere he ended his melodious song
An host of angels flew the clouds among,
And rapt this swan from his attentive mates,
To make him one of their associates
In Heaven's fair quire : where now he sings the praise
Of Him that is the first and last of days
Divinèst Spenser, heaven-bred, happy Muse !
Would any power into my brain infuse
Thy worth, or all that poets had before,
I could not praise till thou deserv'st no more.

BOOK II.   SONG I.

A lament for his friend.

Glide soft, ye silver floods,
    And every spring.
Within the shady woods
    Let no bird sing !
Nor from the grove a turtle dove
Be seen to couple with her love.
But silence on each dale and mountain dwell,
Whilst Willy bids his friend and joy farewell.

But of great Thetis' train
Ye mermaids fair
That on the shores do plain
Your sea-green hair,
As ye in trammels knit your locks
Weep ye ; and so enforce the rocks
In heavy murmurs through the broad shores tell,
How Willy bade his friend and joy farewell.

Cease, cease, ye murmuring winds,
To move a wave ;
But if with troubled minds
You seek his grave,
Know 'tis as various as yourselves
Now in the deep, then on the shelves,
His coffin tossed by fish and surges fell,
Whilst Willy weeps, and bids all joy farewell.

Had he, Arion like
Been judged to drown,
He on his lute could strike
So rare a sown,
A thousand dolphins would have come
And jointly strive to bring him home.
But he on shipboard died, by sickness fell,
Since when his Willy paid all joy farewell.

'Great Neptune, hear a swain !
His coffin take,
And with a golden chain
For pity make
It fast unto a rock near land !
Where ev'ry calmy morn I 'll stand,
And ere one sheep out of my fold I tell,
Sad Willy's pipe shall bid his friend farewell.

BOOK II.   SONG **2.**

The praise of Sydney.

Ere their arrival ˉAstrophell had done
His shepherd's lay, yet equalized of none.
The admired mirror, glory of our isle,
Thou far far more than mortal man, whose style
Struck more men dumb to hearken to thy song
Than Orpheus' harp, or Tully's golden tongue.
To him, as right, for wit's deep quintessence,
For honour, valour, virtue, excellence,
Be all the garlands, crown his tomb with bay,
Who spake as much as e'er our tongue can say.

*   *   *   *   *   *   *   *   *

He sweetly touchèd what I harshly hit,
Yet thus I glory in what I have writ;
Sidney began, and,—if a wit so mean
May taste with him the dews of Hippocrene,—
I sung the pastoral next; his Muse my mover;
And on the plains full many a pensive lover
Shall sing us to their loves, and praising be
My humble lines the more for praising thee.
Thus we shall live with them, by rocks, by springs,
As well as Homer by the deaths of kings.

BOOK II.   SONG **3.**

A colour passage.

As in the rainbow's many-coloured hue,
Here see we watchet deepened with a blue;
There a dark tawny with a purple mixt,
Yellow and flame, with streaks of green betwixt,
A bloody stream into a blushing run,
And ends still with the colour which begun;
Drawing the deeper to a lighter stain,
Bringing the lightest to the deep'st again,
With such rare art each mingleth with his fellow,
The blue with watchet, green and red with yellow;

Like to the changes which we daily see
About the dove's neck with variety,
Where none can say, though he it strict attends,
Here one begins, and there the other ends :
So did the maidens with their various flowers
Deck up their windows, and make neat their bowers ;
Using such cunning as they did dispose
The ruddy piny with the lighter rose,
The monk's-hoods with the bugloss, and entwine
The white, the blue, the flesh-like columbine
With pinks, sweet-williams : that far off the eye
Could not the manner of their mixtures spy.

BOOK II.   SONG 3.

The description of Walla.

A green silk frock her comely shoulders clad,
And took delight that such a seat it had,
Which at her middle gathered up in pleats
A love-knot girdle willing bondage threats.
Nor Venus' ceston held a braver piece,
Nor that which girt the fairest flower of Greece.
Down to her waist her mantle loose did fall
Which Zephyr, as afraid, still played withal,
And then tuck'd up somewhat below the knee
Showed searching eyes where Cupid's columns be.
The inside lined with rich carnation silk,
And in the midst of both lawn white as milk,
Which white beneath the red did seem to shroud,
As Cynthia's beauty through a blushing cloud.
About the edges curious to behold
A deep fringe hung of rich and twisted gold ;
So on the green marge of a crystal brook
A thousand yellow flowers at fishes look,
And such the beams are of the glorious sun
That through a tuft of grass dispersed run.
Upon her leg a pair of buskins white
Studded with orient pearl and chrysolite,

And, like her mantle, stitch'd with gold and green,
(Fairer yet never wore the forest's queen)
Knit close with ribands of a party hue,
A knot of crimson and a tuft of blue,
Nor can the peacock in his spotted train
So many pleasing colours show again ;
Nor could there be a mixture with more grace,
Except the heavenly roses in her face.
A silver quiver at her back she wore,
With darts and arrows for the stag and boar ;
But in her eyes she had such darts again,
Could conquer gods, and wound the hearts of men.
Her left hand held a knotty Brazil bow,
Whose strength, with tears, she made the red deer know.
So clad, so armed, so dressed to win her will
Diana never trod on Latmus hill.
Walla, the fairest nymph that haunts the woods
Walla, beloved of shepherds, fauns, and floods,
Walla, for whom the frolic satyrs pine,
Walla, with whose fine foot the flowerets twine,
Walla, of whom sweet birds their ditties move,
Walla, the earth's delight, and Tavy's love.

BOOK II.   SONG 3.

The song of Tavy.

As careful merchants do expecting stand
    (After long time and merry gales of wind)
Upon the place where their brave ship must land,
    So wait I for the vessel of my mind.

Upon a great adventure is it bound
    Whose safe return will valued be at more
Than all the wealthy prizes which have crowned
    The golden wishes of an age before.

Out of the East jewels of wealth she brings.
    Th' unvalu'd diamond of her sparkling eye
Wants in the treasure of all Europe's kings ;
    And were it mine they nor their crowns should buy.

The sapphires ringed on her panting breast
  Run as rich veins of ore about the mould,
And are in sickness with a pale possest
  So true, for them I should disvalue gold.

The melting rubies on her cherry lip
  Are of such power to hold ; that as one day
Cupid flew thirsty by, he stooped to sip,
  And fastened there could never get away.

The sweets of Candie are no sweets to me,
  When hers I taste ; nor the perfumes of price,
Robb'd from the happy shrubs of Araby,
  As her sweet breath, so powerful to entice.

Oh hasten then, and if thou be not gone
  Unto that wished traffic through the main,
My powerful sighs shall quickly drive thee on,
  And then begin to draw thee back again.

If in the mean rude waves have it opprest
It shall suffice, I ventured at the best.

BOOK II. SONG 4.

The complaint of Pan.

What boot is it though I am said to be
The worthy son of winged Mercury?
That I with gentle nymphs in forests high
Kissed out the sweet time of my infancy?
And when more years had made me able grown,
Was through the mountains as their leader known?
That high-browed Mænalus where I was bred,
And stony hills not few have honoured
Me as protector by the hands of swains,
Whose sheep retire there from the open plains?
That I in shepherd's cups—rejecting gold—
Of milk and honey measures eight times told
Have offered to me, and the ruddy wine
Fresh and new pressed from the bleeding vine?

That gleesome hunters pleased with their sport
With sacrifices due have thanked me for 't ?
That patient anglers standing all the day
Near to some shallow stickle or deep bay,
And fishermen whose nets have drawn to land
A shoal so great it wellnigh hides the sand,
For such success some promontory's head
Thrust at by waves, hath known me worshipped ?
But to increase my grief, what profits this,
'Since still the loss is as the loser is ?'

BOOK III. SONG I.

The song of Celadyne.

Marina's gone and now sit I
  As Philomela on a thorn,
Turned out of nature's livery,
  Mirthless, alone, and all forlorn :
Only she sings not, while my sorrows can
Breathe forth such notes as suit a dying swan

So shuts the marigold her leaves
  At the departure of the sun ;
So from the honey-suckle sheaves
  The bee goes when the day is done ;
So sits the turtle when she is but one,
And so all woe, as I, since she is gone.

To some few birds kind Nature hath
  Made all the summer as one day ;
Which once enjoy'd, cold winter's wrath,
  As night, they sleeping pass away.
Those happy creatures are, they know not yet
The pain to be deprived, or to forget.

I oft have heard men say there be
  Some, that with confidence profess
The helpful Art of Memory ;
  But could they teach forgetfulness,
I'd learn, and try what further art could do
To make me love her and forget her too.

Sad melancholy, that persuades
  Men from themselves, to think they be
Headless, or other body's shades,
  Hath long and bootless dwelt with me.
For could I think she some idea were
I still might love, forget, and have her here.

But such she is not ; nor would I
  For twice as many torments more,
As her bereaved company
  Hath brought to those I felt before ;
For then no future time might hap to know
That she deserv'd, or I did love her so.

Ye hours then, but as minutes be !
  Though so I shall be sooner old,
Till I those lovely graces see,
  Which, but in her, can none behold.
Then be an age ! that we may never try
More grief in parting, but grow old and die.

BOOK III. SONG 2.

A comparison.

As when a woodman on the greeny lawns,
  Where daily chants the sad-sweet nightingale,
Would count his herd, more bucks, more prickets, fawns
  Rush from the copse and put him from his tale ;
Or some way-faring man, when morning dawns,
  Would tell the sweet notes in a joysome vale,
At every foot a new bird lights and sings,
And makes him leave to count their sonnettings.

So when my willing muse would gladly dress
  Her several graces in immortal lines,
Plenty empoors her ; every golden tress,
  Each little dimple, every glance that shines
As radiant as Apollo, I confess
  My skill too weak for so admired designs ;
For whilst one beauty I am close about,
Millions do newly rise and put me out.

Song.

[From *Minor Poems.*]

Welcome, welcome do I sing
    Far more welcome than the spring:
He that parteth from you never
    Shall enjoy a spring for ever.

Love, that to the voice is near
    Breaking from your ivory pale,
Need not walk abroad to hear
    The delightful nightingale.

    Welcome, welcome then I sing
        Far more welcome than the spring
    He that parteth from you never
        Shall enjoy a spring for ever.

Love, that looks still on your eyes,
    Tho' the winter have begun
To benumb our arteries,
    Shall not want the summer's sun.

    Welcome, welcome, &c.

Love, that still may see your cheeks,
    Where all rareness still reposes,
Is a fool if ere he seeks
    Other lilies, other roses.

    Welcome, welcome, &c.

Love, to whom your soft lip yields,
    And perceives your breath in kissing,
All the odours of the fields
    Never, never shall be missing.

    Welcome, welcome, &c.

Love, that question would anew
    What fair Eden was of old,
Let him rightly study you,
    And a brief of that behold.

    Welcome welcome &c.

THE INNER TEMPLE MASQUE.

The Charm.

Son of Erebus and night
Hie away; and aim thy flight
Where consort none other fowl
Than the bat and sullen owl;
Where upon thy limber grass
Poppy and mandragoras
With like simples not a few
Hang for ever drops of dew.
Where flows Lethe without coil
Softly like a stream of oil.
Hie thee hither gentle sleep:
With this Greek no longer keep.
Thrice I charge thee by my wand,
Thrice with moly from my hand
Do I touch Ulysses eyes,
And with the jaspis: then arise
Sagest Greek.

SONNET.

Fairest, when by the rules of palmistry
You took my hand to try if you could guess,
By lines therein, if any wight there be
Ordained to make me know some happiness;
I wished that those characters could explain,
Whom I will never wrong with hope to win;
Or that by them a copy might be seen,
By you, O love, what thoughts I had within.
But since the hand of Nature did not set
(As providently loth to have it known)
The means to find that hidden alphabet,
Mine eyes shall be th' interpreters alone;
  By them conceive my thoughts, and tell me, fair,
  If now you see her that doth love me there?

GEORGE WITHER.

[GEORGE WITHER was born at Brentworth in Hampshire, June 11, 1588, and died in the year 1667; his literary achievement, both in verse and prose, being proportioned to his length of years. The dates of his chief works are as follows: 1612, the *Elegy on Prince Henry;* 1613, *Epithalamia;* 1613, *Abuses Stript and Whipt;* 1615, *Fidelia* and *Shepherd's Hunting.* To the same year must also be ascribed his share in Browne's *Shepherd's Pipe;* 1618, *the Motto;* 1622, *the Mistress of Philarete;* 1623, *the Hymns and Songs of the Church;* 1628, *Britain's Remembrancer;* 1634, *Emblems;* 1641, *Halle-lujah.*

The above list is very far indeed from exhausting the complete catalogue of Wither's voluminous works. He was an ardent politician, and in the stirring times of the Civil War was perpetually pouring forth songs and broadsheets in justification of the cause he had taken up. Probably no library in England possesses an absolutely complete collection of Wither's works. Certainly the British Museum and the Bodleian do not. The Rev. T. Corser, of Stand, near Manchester, is said to have had the fullest collection in existence, but that has been since dispersed. The poems have been collected by the Spenser Society, but it is a matter for regret that they are not to be had in a more generally accessible form. It is one of the most striking blemishes of Chalmers' collection that Wither is absolutely ignored in it. Of modern editors of portions of his works the chief is Sir Egerton Brydges, who republished the *Shepherd's Hunting* and the *Fidelia* at the beginning of this century, and also gave long extracts from Withers' other poems in his *Censura Literaria.* The *Hymns and Songs of the Church,* and the *Hallelujah* were republished for Russell Smith in 1856 and 1857.]

Wither resembles Wordsworth in having written almost all his good work within a period of a few years. That period is from 1613 to 1623. The great exception is the *Hallelujah*—a collection of sacred poems, in which are some beautiful things written as late as 1641. On the whole, however, the collection of Wither's poems entitled *Juvenilia* contains nearly all his best writing. The enthusiasm with which he threw himself into politics damaged his genius. His nature was not large enough to pour itself with equal power into the two channels of art and practical life. He became an eager partisan and sectary, retaining that moral elevation and dignity which ever honourably distinguishes him, but losing all sense of form and measure, perhaps indeed deliberately neglecting them as things indifferent. It is then to the early part of his life that we have to attend ; and here we must remember his two years at Oxford, where he was a member of Magdalen College : two happy years, he himself has told us, which were unfortunately cut short by his sudden withdrawal from the University. In 1605, he went up to Lincoln's Inn, and there became acquainted with Browne, who was at that time a member of the Inner Temple. The friendship was a very important one for Wither. The two wrote in friendly rivalry, and often in intimate co-partnership, and we shall hardly err in laying great stress upon Browne's influence during the first period of Wither's poetry. Browne was a born artist, if ever there was one, and his example wooed the naturally ascetic and polemical genius of Wither into pleasanter paths for a while. Wither in later life expresses most unnecessary repentance for his early poems. He had no such reason for feelings of the kind as perhaps Chaucer had. Not a single line of his poetry is really corrupt or dishonourable to the writer. But he was young then, and could write of love and the beauty of nature and the beauty of woman, with a facile pen and an ardent delight in the fulness of his life and the power of his art, which seemed no doubt profane and dangerous trifling to the Puritan captain of the Civil War. But even in his youth life did not altogether smile upon him. His very harmless satires, published under the title *Abuses Stript and Whipt* in 1613, were rewarded by imprisonment in the Marshalsea. As Lamb says, it is wonderful that such perfectly general denunciations of the ordinary vices of Gluttony, Avarice, Vanity, and the rest of it in the abstract should have seemed offensive to any human being. But the cap fitted some one in high place, and Wither had to expiate his plain spokenness by a rigorous confinement. After his liberation he renewed more intimately than ever his friendship with Browne, and in 1615 wrote in conjunction with him the *Shepherd's Pipe*. His own *Shepherd's Hunting*, which he wrote in prison (see the extract here given) and which contains perhaps his very best work, appeared in the same year. To this date also must be assigned the first edition of his *Fidelia*, a poetical epistle from a forsaken fair one to her inconstant lover. At the end of this first edition of *Fidelia* is printed that famous song—'Shall I, wasting in despaire?'—which will always keep Wither's memory green, even if all else of his poetry is forgotten. The *Motto* followed in 1618, and met at once with great success. The poem is an amusingly egotistical performance, but the egotism is, as Charles Lamb said, of a sort which no one can resent. The motto is 'Nec habeo, nec careo, nec curo,' and the poem is divided into three parts, one treating of 'nec habeo,' another of 'nec careo,' and the third of 'nec curo.' In a preface addressed to 'Anybody,' he makes a statement which perhaps no one would wish to gainsay. 'The language is but indifferent, for I affected matter rather than words ; the method is none at all : for I was loath to make a business of a recreation.' It is worth noticing that in the preface he alludes to the episode which, in spite of its uncouthness and exaggeration, is perhaps the most amusing part of his satires, in very uncomplimentary terms. 'The foolish Canterbury Tale in my Scourge of Vanity (which I am now almost ashamed to read over) even that hath been by some praised for a witty passage.' Whenever Wither gives himself liberty and has his fling, he is sure not long afterwards to repent. In 1623 appeared his first serious attempt at sacred poetry in the shape of his *Hymns and Songs of the Church*. Great part of this collection consists of metrical paraphrases of the Psalms and Song of Solomon, but there are also some hymns the inspiration of which is due to no one but Wither himself. Such are the *Hymn for All Saints Day* and the *Hymn for the Author*, which are not only interesting in themselves but because a close comparison with the form in which these same poems appeared in the collection entitled *Hallelujah* nearly twenty years afterwards reveals the notable fact that Wither was one of the very few poets who improved his work by retouching it, and that his second thoughts were always his best. I give nothing from his *Britain's Remembrancer* (1628) or from his *Emblems* (1634). The former seems to me a rather tedious political poem, and the latter is merely a collection written to order as text for a certain number of Dutch engravings. It is true that there are one or two of these latter poems which show qualities of thought and diction not to be disregarded, but on the whole I do not think he reaches his best anywhere in the collection. *Hallelujah* (1641) shows that great part of his old power still survives. The versification is flexible and musical in a very high degree, clothing the thought sometimes, as in the poem on *All Saints' Day*, in a form of subtle beauty and strangeness ; in other poems, as in the verses *For those at Sea*, moving with a grand lilt and rapidity which fitly symbolize the theme. The verses on *A Dear Friend Deceased* are of exquisite tenderness and beauty. They are written from the heart and to the heart, and affect us as they must have affected the writer himself. Wither has the same rare power of pathos that was possessed also by his friend Browne.

The limits of our space prevent us quoting even all of the few poems that we have specially named ; but it is hoped that our selection will still be fairly representative of a poet who is certainly much less known than he deserves to be. Braithwaite wrote in 1615—

> 'And long may England's Thespian springs be known
> By lovely Wither and by bonny Browne.'

But the wish has hardly been fulfilled, and there are few readers who would not be a little surprised by the epithet here applied to the Puritan poet. No real lover of poetry will however grudge it him. He is one of the few masters of octosyllabic verse in our language. Lamb has dwelt lovingly on its curious felicities, and for compass and variety it would not be easy to name its superior. It is the one form of verse pre-eminently suited to Wither, who has achieved no such triumphs with the heroic couplet. But it is not only for beauty of poetic form that Wither deserved Braithwaite's enthusiastic epithet. Like the Charmides of Plato's dialogue, he has 'what is much more important, a beautiful soul.' Never was there a purer or more honourable spirit, or one which kept closer to the best it knew, and as Wither has revealed himself in his works in a way in which few poets have done, it is natural to read him not only with admiration but with sympathy.

W. T. Arnold.

WEAKNESS.

[From *Abuses Stript and Whipt.*]

This in defence of poesie to say
I am compelled because that of this day
Weakness and ignorance have wronged it sore;
But what need any man therein speak more
Than divine Sidney hath already done?
For whom, though he deceased ere I begun,
I have oft sighed, and bewailed my fate,
That brought me forth so many years too late
To view that worthy; and now think not you
O Daniel, Drayton, Johnson, Chapman, how
I long to see you with your fellow peers,
Sylvester matchless, glory of these years;
I hitherto have only heard your fames,
And know you yet but by your works and names:
The little time I on the earth have spent
Would not allow me any more content:
I long to know you better, that's the truth,
I am in hope you'll not disdain my youth:
For know you, Muses' darlings, I'll not crave
A fellowship amongst you for to have.
Oh, no; for though my ever willing heart
Have vowed to love and praise you and your art,
And though that I your style do now assume,
I do not, nor I will not so presume;
I claim not that too worthy name of Poet;
It is not yet deserved by me, I know it;
Grant me I may but on your Muses tend,
And be enrolled their servant or their friend;
And if desert hereafter worthy make me,
Then for a fellow, if it please you, take me.

ECLOGUE 4.

[From *The Shepherd's Hunting.*]

Philarete.

Never did the Nine impart
The sweet secrets of their art
Unto any that did scorn
We should see their favours worn.
Therefore unto those that say,
Were they pleas'd to sing a lay,
They could do 't, and will not tho';
This I speak, for this I know:
None e'er drunk the Thespian spring,
And knew how, but he did sing.
For, that once infus'd in man
Makes him shew 't, do what he can.
Nay, those that do only sip,
Or but e'en their fingers dip,
In that sacred fount, poor elves,
Of that brood will shew themselves:
Yea, in hope to get them fame,
They will speak, though to their shame.
Let those then at thee repine
That by their wits measure thine;
Needs those songs must be thine own,
And that one day will be known.
That poor imputation, too,
I myself do undergo:
But it will appear, ere long,
That 'twas Envy sought our wrong:
Who at twice ten have sung more
Than some will do at fourscore.
Cheer thee, honest Willy, then,
And begin thy song again.

Willy.

Fain I would, but I do fear
When again my lines they hear,

If they yield they are my rhymes,
They will feign some other crimes ;
And 'tis no safe vent'ring by,
Where we see Detraction lie :
For, do what I can, I doubt,
She will pick some quarrel out ;
And I oft have heard defended—
Little said, is soon amended.

Philarete.

See'st thou not, in clearest days,
Oft thick fogs cloud Heaven's rays ;
And that vapours which do breathe
From the earth's gross womb beneath,
Seem not to us with black steams
To pollute the sun's bright beams,
And yet vanish into air,
Leaving it, unblemish'd, fair ?
So, my Willy, shall it be
With Detraction's breath on thee ?
It shall never rise so high,
As to stain thy Poesy.
As that sun doth oft exhale
Vapours from each rotten vale ;
Poesy so sometime drains
Gross conceits from muddy brains ;
Mists of envy, fogs of spite,
'Twixt men's judgments and her light :
But so much her power may do,
That she can dissolve them too.
If thy verse do bravely tower,
As she makes wing she gets power ;
Yet the higher she doth soar,
She's affronted still the more :
Till she to the high'st hath past,
Then she rests with fame at last.
Let nought therefore thee affright,
But make forward in thy flight :

For, if I could match thy rhyme,
To the very stars I'd climb:
There begin again, and fly
Till I reach'd eternity.
But, alas! my Muse is slow;
For thy place she flags too low:
Yea, the more's her hapless fate,
Her short wings were clipt of late:
And poor I, her fortune rueing,
Am myself put up a mewing:
But if I my cage can rid,
I'll fly where I never did:
And though for her sake I'm crost,
Though my best hopes I have lost,
And knew she would make my trouble
Ten times more than ten times double:
I should love and keep her too
Spite of all the world could do.
For, though banish'd from my flocks,
And confin'd within these rocks,
Here I waste away the light,
And consume the sullen night,
She doth for my comfort stay,
And keeps many cares away.
Though I miss the flowery fields,
With those sweets the springtide yields,
Though I may not see those groves,
Where the shepherd's chant their loves,
And the lasses more excel
Than the sweet voic'd Philomel;
Though of all those pleasures past,
Nothing now remains at last,
But Remembrance, poor relief,
That more makes than mends my grief:
She's my mind's companion still,
Maugre Envy's evil will;
(Whence she should be driven, too,
Were't in mortal's power to do.)

She doth tell me where to borrow
Comfort in the midst of sorrow :
Makes the desolatest place
To her presence be a grace ;
And the blackest discontents
To be pleasing ornaments.
In my former days of bliss,
Her divine skill taught me this,
That from everything I saw,
I could some invention draw :
And raise pleasure to her height,
Through the meanest object's sight,
By the murmur of a spring,
Or the least boughs rustlëing ;
By a daisy, whose leaves spread
Shut when Titan goes to bed ;
Or a shady bush or tree,
She could more infuse in me,
Than all Nature's beauties can
In some other wiser man.
By her help I also now
Make this churlish place allow
Some things that may sweeten gladness,
In the very gall of sadness.
The dull loneness, the black shade,
That these hanging vaults have made,
The strange music of the waves,
Beating on these hollow caves,
This black den which rocks emboss
Overgrown with eldest moss :
The rude portals that give light
More to Terror than Delight :
This my chamber of Neglect,
Wall'd about with Disrespect ;
From all these and this dull air,
A fit object for despair,
She hath taught me by her might
To draw comfort and delight.

Therefore, thou best earthly bliss,
I will cherish thee for this.
Poesy! thou sweet'st content
That e'er heaven to mortals lent:
Though they as a trifle leave thee,
Whose dull thoughts cannot conceive thee,
Though thou be to them a scorn,
That to nought but earth are born,
Let my life no longer be
Than I am in love with thee,
Though our wise ones call thee madness,
Let me never taste of gladness,
If I love not thy mad'st fits
More than all their greatest wits.
And though some, too, seeming holy,
Do account thy raptures folly,
Thou dost teach me to contemn
What makes knaves and fools of them.

The Author's Resolution in a Sonnet.

Shall I, wasting in despaire
Dye, because a woman's fair?
Or make pale my cheeks with care
Cause anothers Rosie are?
    Be she fairer than the Day
    Or the flowry Meads in May,
    If she thinke not well of me,
    What care I *how* faire she be?

Shall my seely heart be pin'd
Cause I see a woman kind?
Or a well disposed Nature
Joyned with a lovely feature?
    Be she Meeker, Kinder than
    Turtle-dove or *Pellican*:
    If she be not so to me,
    What care I how kind she be?

Shall a woman's Vertues move
Me to perish for her Love?
Or her wel deservings knowne
Make me quite forget mine own?
    Be she with that Goodness blest
    Which may merit name of best:
    If she be not such to me,
    What care I how Good she be?

Cause her *Fortune* seems too high
Shall I play the fool and die?
She that beares a Noble mind,
If not outward helpes she find,
    Thinks what with them he wold do,
    That without them dares her woe.
    And unlesse that *Minde* I see
    What care I how great she be?

Great, or Good, or Kind, or Faire
I will ne're the more despaire:
If she love me (this beleeve)
I will Die ere she shall grieve.
    If she slight me when I woe,
    I can scorne and let her goe,
    For if she be not for me
    What care I for whom she be?[1]

---

[1] I have transcribed this song *verbatim et literatim* (for it is too precious not to be given exactly as it first saw the light) from the original edition of *Fidelia* in which it first appeared. Mr. W. C. Hazlitt in his *Handbook to Early English Literature* assumes the existence of an edition in 1617, before the well-known second edition in the later part of the same year; but adds:—' This first edition is supposed to have been privately printed. No copy is at present known.' There is, however, a copy of this treasure in the Bodleian Library. As I write, the title page of it is before me:—*Fidelia*, London, Printed by Nicholas Okes, 1615.

LOVE-POEMS.

[From *The Mistress of Philarete.*]

I.

And her lips (that shew no dulness)
Full are, in the meanest fulness :
Those, the leaves be, whose unfolding
Brings sweet pleasures to beholding :
For, such pearls they do disclose,
Both the Indies match not those :
Yet are so in order placed,
As their whiteness is more graced.
Each part is so well disposed,
And her dainty mouth composed,
So, as there is no distortion
Misbeseems that sweet proportion.
When her ivory teeth she buries,
Twixt her two enticing cherries,
There appear such pleasures hidden,
As might tempt what were forbidden.
If you look again the whiles
She doth part those lips in smiles,
'Tis as when a flash of light
Breaks from heaven to glad the night.

2.

Oft have the Nymphs of greatest worth,
　Made suit my songs to hear ;
As oft (when I have sighed forth
　Such notes as saddest were)
'Alas !' said they, 'poor gentle heart,
　Whoe'er that shepherd be :'
But, none of them suspects my smart,
　Nor thinks, it meaneth me.

When I have reached so high a strain
　Of passion in my song,
That they have seen the tears to rain
　And trill my cheek along :

Instead of sigh, or weeping eye,
    To sympathise with me ;
'Oh, were he once in love,' they cry,
    'How moving would he be l'

Oh pity me, you powers above,
    And take my skill away ;
Or let my hearers think I love,
    And fain not what I say.
For, if I could disclose the smart,
    Which I unknown do bear ;
Each line would make them sighs impart,
    And every word, a tear.

3.

Her true beauty leaves behind,
Apprehensions in my mind,
Of more sweetness than all art
Or inventions can impart ;
Thoughts too deep to be exprest,
And too strong to be supprest ;
Which oft raiseth my conceits,
To so unbelieved heights,
That (I fear) some shallow brain,
Thinks my muses do but feign.
Sure, he wrongs them if he do :
For, could I have reached to
So like strains as these you see ;
Had there been no such as she ?
Is it possible that I,
Who scarce heard of Poesy,
Should a mere Idea raise
To as true a pitch of praise
As the learned poets could,
Now, or in the times of old,
All those real beauties bring,
Honoured by their sonneting ?
(Having arts and favours too
More t'encourage what they do)

No ; if I had never seen
Such a beauty ; I had been
Piping in the country shades,
To the homely dairy maids,
For a country fiddler's fees ;
Clouted cream, and bread and cheese.
　　I no skill in numbers had,
More than every shepherd's lad,
Till she taught me strains that were
Pleasing to her gentle ear.
Her fair splendour and her worth
From obscureness drew me forth.
And, because I had no Muse,
She herself deigned to infuse
All the skill by which I climb
To these praises in my rhyme.
Which, if she had pleased to add,
To that art sweet Drayton had,
Or that happy swain that shall
Sing Britannia's Pastoral ;
Or to theirs, whose verse set forth
Rosalind, and Stella's worth ;
They had doubled all their skill,
Gained on Apollo's Hill :
And as much more set her forth
As I 'm short of them in worth.
They had unto heights aspired,
Might have justly been admired ;
And, in such brave strains had moved
As of all had been approved.

A Christmas Carol.

So now is come our joyfulst feast ;
　　Let every man be jolly,
Each room with ivy leaves is drest
　　And every post with holly.

Though some churls at our mirth repine,
Round your foreheads garlands twine,
Drown sorrow in a cup of wine,
   And let us all be merry.

   *   *   *   *   *

Now every lad is wondrous trim,
   And no man minds his labour;
Our lasses have provided them
   A bag-pipe and a tabor.
Young men and maids and girls and boys
Give life to one another's joys,
And you anon shall by their noise
   Perceive that they are merry.

Rank misers now do sparing shun,
   Their hall of music soundeth ;
And dogs thence with whole shoulders run,
   So all things here aboundeth.
The country folk themselves advance,
For Crowdy-mutton's come out of France,
And Jack shall pipe, and Jill shall dance,
   And all the town be merry.

Ned Swash hath fetched his bands from pawn,
   And all his best apparel ;
Brisk Nell hath bought a ruff of lawn
   With droppings of the barrel.
And those that hardly all the year
Had bread to eat or rags to wear,
Will have both clothes and dainty fare
   And all the day be merry.

   *   *   *   *   *

The wenches with their wassail-bowls
   About the street are singing,
The boys are come to catch the owls,
   The wild-mare in is bringing.

Our kitchen-boy hath broke his box,
And to the dealing of the ox
Our honest neighbours come by flocks,
   And here they will be merry.

   *   *   *   *   *

Then wherefore in these merry days
   Should we I pray be duller?
No let us sing our roundelays
   To make our mirth the fuller;
And whilest thus inspired we sing
Let all the streets with echoes ring:
Woods, and hills, and every-thing
   Bear witness we are merry.

WHEN WE ARE UPON THE SEAS.

[From *Hallelujah.*]

1 On those great waters now I am,
   Of which I have been told,
That whosoever thither came
   Should wonders there behold.
In this unsteady place of fear,
   Be present, Lord, with me;
For in these depths of water here
   I depths of danger see.

2 A stirring courser now I sit,
   A headstrong steed I ride,
That champs and foams upon the bit
   Which curbs his lofty pride.
The softest whistling of the winds
   Doth make him gallop fast;
And as their breath increased he finds
   The more he maketh haste.

3 Take Thou, oh Lord! the reins in hand,
   Assume our Master's room;
Vouchsafe Thou at our helm to stand,
   And pilot to become.

Trim Thou the sails, and let good speed
　　Accompany our haste ;
Sound Thou the channels at our need,
　　And anchor for us cast.

4 A fit and favourable wind
　　To further us provide ;
And let it wait on us behind,
　　Or lackey by our side.
From sudden gusts, from storms, from sands,
　　And from the raging wave ;
From shallows, rocks, and pirates' hands,
　　Men, goods, and vessel save.

5 Preserve us from the wants, the fear,
　　And sickness of the seas ;
But chiefly from our sins, which are
　　A danger worse than these.
Lord ! let us also safe arrive
　　Where we desire to be ;
And for Thy mercies let us give
　　Due thanks and praise to Thee.

FOR SUMMER TIME.

1 Now the glories of the year
May be viewed at the best,
And the earth doth now appear
In her fairest garments dress'd :
　　Sweetly smelling plants and flowers
　　Do perfume the garden bowers ;
Hill and valley, wood and field,
Mixed with pleasure profits yield.

2 Much is found where nothing was,
Herds on every mountain go,
In the meadows flowery grass
Makes both milk and honey flow ;
　　Now each orchard banquets giveth,
　　Every hedge with fruit relieveth ;
And on every shrub and tree
Useful fruits or berries be.

3 Walks and ways which winter marr'd
By the winds are swept and dried;
Moorish grounds are now so hard
That on them we safe may ride:
  Warmth enough the sun doth lend us,
  From his heat the shades defend us;
And thereby we share in these
Safety, profit, pleasure, ease.

4 Other blessings, many more,
At this time enjoyed may be,
And in this my song therefore
Praise I give, O Lord! to Thee:
  Grant that this my free oblation
  May have gracious acceptation,
And that I may well employ
Everything which I enjoy.

THE PRAYER OF OLD AGE.

[Third part of *Hallelujah*.]

As this my carnal robe grows old,
Soil'd, rent, and worn by length of years,
Let me on that by faith lay hold
Which man in life immortal wears:
  So sanctify my days behind,
  So let my manners be refined,
That when my soul and flesh must part,
There lurk no terrors in my heart.

So shall my rest be safe and sweet
When I am lodgèd in my grave;
And when my soul and body meet,
A joyful meeting they shall have;
  Their essence then shall be divine,
  This muddy flesh shall starlike shine,
And God shall that fresh youth restore
Which will abide for evermore.

GILES FLETCHER.

[BORN about 1588, died 1623. *Christ's Victory and Triumph in Heaven and Earth over and after Death* was published in 1640.]

Giles, the brother of Phineas, and cousin of John Fletcher, is one of the chief poets of what may be called the Spenserian School, which 'flourished' in the first quarter of the seventeenth century. Spenser and Chaucer were the supreme names in non-dramatic poetry till Milton arose ; and in the Jacobean period the Plantagenet poet was eclipsed by the Elizabethan ; and thus it was to Spenser that the lesser poetic spirits of the age looked up to as their master, and upon their writings his influence is deeply impressed. Amongst these retainers of 'Colin' must be counted Milton when young, before he had developed his own style and become himself an original power, himself a master ; and not the least of the interests that distinguish Giles Fletcher and his fellow Spenserians is that Milton extended to them the study and attention which he gave with no ordinary sympathy to 'our sage and serious Spenser, whom I dare be known to think a better teacher than Scotus and Aquinas.'

These words of Milton's suggest some leading characteristics of the Spenserian school. It too proposed to be 'sage and serious.' It inclined indeed to be didactic. In that notorious production, 'The Purple Island,' we have in fact a lecture on Anatomy. More commonly its purpose was directly ethical ; and it must be allowed that the artist is at times lost in the moralist.

Giles Fletcher is eminently a religious poet—in the technical sense of the word, as happily also in the more general sense. He deals with Christian themes : 'Christ's Victory in Heaven,' 'Christ's Victory on Earth,' 'Christ's Triumph over Death,' 'Christ's Triumph after Death'; and it is his special distinction, that in handling such themes he does not sink into a mere rhyming dogmatist, but writes with a genuine enthusiasm and joy. For certainly what has commonly been written for 'religious' poetry has been 'religious' rather than poetical. Its orthodoxy may have been unimpeachable ; but no less so its prosiness. How few hymns are worthy of the name of poems ! The cause of this frequent failure is probably to be looked for in the writer's relation to his subject. It is not, and cannot be, one of sufficient freedom. His mind is in a sense subdued and fettered by the very conditions of the case. He is dealing with a certain definite interpretation of profound mysteries ; and the mysteries themselves are such as to overpower and paralyse the free movement of his intelligence. How can he sing at ease ? He is like one with a lesson set him, which he must reproduce as best he may. It is rather his faith and his memory that are called into action than his imagination. At all events his imagination has an inferior part assigned her ; she is not to create but rather to decorate and glorify what is created. To worship and adore and love—these are real move-ments and impulses of the poet's mind, and may have and have had their expression in lyrics that may be fully styled divine ; but, when the details of a creed are celebrated, then for the most part the sweet enthusiasm dies away out of the poet's eyes, the rapture chills and freezes, and we are reminded of the Thirty-nine Articles rather than of the Beatific Vision.

Giles Fletcher's success as a 'religious' poet, so far as he succeeds, is due first to the selection of themes which he makes, and secondly to the genuine religious ardour that inspired him. He delighted to contemplate the career of the central Hero of his Christian faith and love—His ineffable self-sacrifice, His leading captivity captive, His complete and irreversible triumph. That career he conceived and beheld vividly and intensely with a pure unalloyed acceptance ; it thrilled and inspired him with a real passion of worship and delight. So blissfully enthralled and enraptured, what else could he sing of ? His heart was hot within him ; while he was musing, the fire burned ; then spake he with his tongue.

It was the tongue of one highly cultured and accomplished, of a rich and clear imagination, with a natural gift of eloquence, with a fine sense of melody, and metrical skill to express it.

JOHN W. HALES.

CHRIST'S VICTORY IN HEAVEN.

But Justice had no sooner Mercy seen
Smoothing the wrinkles of her Father's brow,
But up she starts, and throws her self between:
As when a vapour, from a moory slough,
Meeting with fresh Eoüs, that but now
   Open'd the world, which all in darknesse lay,
   Doth heav'n's bright face of his rayes disarray,
And sads the smiling Orient of the springing day.

She was a Virgin of austere regard;
Not as the world esteems her, deaf and blind;
But as the eagle, that hath oft compar'd
Her eye with Heav'n's, so, and more brightly shin'd
Her lamping sight; for she the same could wind
   Into the solid heart, and with her ears
   The silence of the thought loud speaking hears,
And in one hand a paire of even scales she wears.

No riot of affection revel kept
Within her brest, but a still apathy
Possessèd all her soule, which softly slept
Securely, without tempest; no sad cry
Awakes her pity, but wrong'd poverty,
   Sending her eyes to heav'n swimming in tears,
   With hideous clamours ever struck her ears,
Whetting the blazing sword, that in her hand she bears.

The wingèd lightning is her Mercury,
And round about her mighty thunders sound:
Impatient of himself lies pining by
Pale Sickness with his kercher'd head upwound,
And thousand noisome plagues attend her round;
   But if her cloudy brow but once grow foul,
   The flints do melt, and rocks to water roll,
And airy mountaines shake, and frighted shadows howl.

Famine, and bloodless Care, and bloody War,
Want, and the want of knowledge how to use
Abundance; Age, and Fear that runs afar
Before his fellow Grief, that aye pursues
His wingèd steps; for who would not refuse
 Grief's company, a dull and rawboned sprite,
 That lanks the cheeks, and pales the freshest sight,
Unbosoming the cheerful breast of all delight?

Before this cursed throng goes Ignorance,
That needs will lead the way he cannot see:
And, after all, Death doth his flag advance,
And, in the midst, Strife still would roguing be,
Whose ragged flesh and clothes did well agree:
 And round about amazèd Horror flies,
 And ouer all, Shame veils his guilty eyes,
And underneath, Hell's hungry throat still yawning lies.

Upon two stony tables, spread before her,
She lean'd her bosom, more than stony hard;
There slept th' unpartial Judge, and strict restorer
Of wrong or right, with pain or with reward;
There hung the score of all our debts, the card
 Where good, and bad, and life, and death were painted:
 Was never heart of mortal so untainted,
But when that scroll was read, with thousand terrors fainted.

Witness the thunder that mount Sinai heard,
When all the hill with fiery clouds did flame,
And wandering Israel, with the sight afeard,
Blinded with seeing, durst not touch the same,
But like a wood of shaking leaves became.
 On this dead Justice, she, the Living Law,
 Bowing herself with a majestic awe,
All heav'n, to hear her speech, did into silence draw.

SIR HENRY WOTTON.

[Born 1568, died 1639. 'How happy is he born and taught,' said to have been printed in 1614; see *Courtly Poets*, ed. Hannah, 1875. It was quoted to Drummond by Ben Jonson in 1618 or 1619: 'Sir Edward [Henry] Wotton's verses of a happy life he hath by heart.' 'You meaner beauties of the night,' printed with music in Est's *Sixth Set of Books*, 1624. It was probably written a few years before. In 1651, *Reliquiae Wottonianae*.]

Sir Henry Wotton, a highly accomplished gentleman and distinguished diplomatist in his day, is now best known to us personally through the affectionate memoir of his humble friend and fellow angler Isaac Walton, and the kindly interest he showed in Milton, whose *Comus* had excited his warm admiration. He was well born, well bred, and one of the most cultivated men of his time. But, immersed in politics and society, he found but little leisure for the studies he loved till his appointment to the Provostship of Eton in 1624, when he was some 56 years of age. All the middle period of his life from 1595 he was occupied with affairs, not without peril, as when he was one of the secretaries of the Earl of Essex (his fellow secretary, Cuffe, was hanged), not without much vexation, as when his famous definition of an ambassador, public attention being called to it eight years after it was entered in Flecamon's 'albo' at Augsburg, brought him for a time into disgrace with James I.

Of poetry he wrote but little; but of that little two pieces at least have obtained a permanent place in English literature, his *Character of a Happy Life*, written probably circ. 1614; and the lines, *On his mistress the Queen of Bohemia*, circ. 1620. Of the apophthegm 'the style is of the man,' it would be difficult to find better illustrations. As in a mirror, they reflect the high refined nature of one who, living in the world, and a master of its ways and courtesies, was yet never of it—was never a worldling.

JOHN W. HALES.

THE CHARACTER OF A HAPPY LIFE.

How happy is he born and taught
   That serveth not another's will ;
Whose armour is his honest thought,
   And simple truth his utmost skill ;

Whose passions not his masters are ;
   Whose soul is still prepared for death,
Untied unto the world by care
   Of public fame or private breath ;

Who envies none that chance doth raise,
   Nor vice ; who never understood
How deepest wounds are given by praise ;
   Nor rules of state, but rules of good ;

Who hath his life from rumours freed ;
   Whose conscience is his strong retreat ;
Whose state can neither flatterers feed,
   Nor ruin make oppressors great ;

Who God doth late and early pray
   More of his grace than gifts to lend ;
And entertains the harmless day
   With a religious book or friend.

This man is freed from servile bands
   Of hope to rise or fear to fall :
Lord of himself, though not of lands,
   And, having nothing, yet hath all.

ON HIS MISTRESS, THE QUEEN OF BOHEMIA.

You meaner beauties of the night,
   That poorly satisfy our eyes
More by your number than your light ;
   You common people of the skies ;
   What are you when the moon shall rise ?

You curious chanters of the wood,
  That warble forth Dame Nature's lays,
Thinking your passions understood
    By your weak accents ; what's your praise,
    When Philomel her voice shall raise?

You violets that first appear,
  By your pure purple mantles known
Like the proud virgins of the year,
    As if the spring were all your own ;
    What are you when the rose is blown?

So, when my mistress shall be seen
  In form and beauty of her mind,
By virtue first, then choice, a Queen,
    Tell me if she were not designed
    The eclipse and glory of her kind?

Upon the Death of Sir Albertus Morton's Wife.

He first deceased ; she for a little tried
To live without him, liked it not, and died.

THOMAS CAREW.

[THOMAS CAREW, Sewer in Ordinary to Charles I, was born about 1589, and died in 1639. He published *Coelum Brittanicum*, 1633, and *Poems*, 1640.]

Among the Royalist lyrists of the seventeenth century Carew takes a foremost place. In genius he is surpassed by Herrick only, and in age he is the first of that gallant band of cavalier song-writers of whom Rochester is the last. Born in the flush of the Elizabethan summer, when the whole garden of English poetry was ablaze with blossom, he lived to hand down to his followers a tradition of perfume and dainty form, that vivified the autumn of the century with a little Martin's summer of his own. The lyrists of the school of Carew preserved something of the brave Shakspearean tradition when the dramatists of the school of Shirley had completely lost it, and the transition from romanticism to classicism was more gently made in this order of writing than in any other. It is the special glory of Carew that he formularised the practice of writing courtly amorous poetry. Strains very similar to his own had appeared in the works of older poets, as in *The Forest* of Ben Jonson and in the plays of Fletcher, but always casually; it was Carew who seized this floating improvisation, and made an art of it. As there were Anacreontic poets before Anacreon, so there were octosyllabic addresses to Julia or Celia before Carew; yet we grant to him the praise of the invention, since he gave his best work, and not, as others had done, his lightest to it.

In his elegiac lines on Donne, Carew joins the chorus of eulogy with more than customary earnestness, and claims for that great man the title of king among the English poets. Yet no one of Donne's contemporaries was less injuriously affected by the presence of that most crabbed and eccentric genius than Carew,

whose sweet and mellow Muse neither rises into the dangerous
heights nor falls into the terrible pitfalls haunted by her audacious
sister. A certain tendency to conceit was the sin not of one
school but of the age, and Carew's trivialities have none of the
vehemence or intellectual perversity of Donne's. In company
with Herrick, this thoroughly sensual poet draws his pet concetti
from the art of the kitchen, and offends us most by being reminded
of his dinner as he walks abroad ;—

> 'No more the frost
> Candies the grass, or casts an icy cream
> Upon the silver lake or crystal stream,'

are phrases that justly excite our ridicule, but they are far re-
moved from the heavy machinery of symbolism with which
Donne, and a whole host of imitators after him, sought to involve
their simplest fancies in sublimity. Carew was far too indolent
to trouble himself with the rhetoric of the schools or to speculate
upon the conduct of the mind. He loved wine, and roses, and
fair florid women, to whom he could indite joyous or pensive
poems about their beauty, adoring it while it lasted, regretting it
when it faded. He has not the same intimate love of detail as
Herrick ; we miss in his poems those realistic touches that give
such wonderful freshness to the verses of the younger poet ; nor
does he indulge in the same amiable pedantry. But the habit of the
two men's minds was very similar ; both were pagans and given
up to an innocent hedonism ; neither was concerned with much
beyond the eternal commonplaces of bodily existence, the attrac-
tion of beauty, the mutability of life, the brevity and sweetness of
enjoyment. In the hands of the disciples the strings of the lyre
became tenser, the garlands less luxuriant, and when we reach
Sedley and Rochester we find little trace left of Herrick and
Carew save the brisk, elegant versification, and the courtly turn of
compliment.

It is unfortunate that Carew was never persuaded to attempt a
long poem. His masque of *Coelum Brittannicum*, which was
undertaken in company with Inigo Jones to grace a royal visit,
has the customary faults of pieces of this kind. It is abstract in
interest, fragmentary in form, and the separate passages of verse
have little charm of fancy. The best poem of Carew, *The Rapture*,
is also the longest, yet does not reach the length of two hundred
lines. Unhappily its beauties are presented to us with so much

enthusiasm and with so little reticence, that no adequate citation from it can be laid before the general reader. But it gives the student a finer impression of Carew's powers than he would gain from any other piece, and betrays narrative and descriptive qualities that would have risked nothing in competition with Browne or with Giles Fletcher. It is, of course, by his lyrics alone that Carew is known to the ordinary reader of poetry. His songs are extremely mellifluous and well-balanced ; he has an unusual art of sustaining his flight through an entire lyric, so that his poems are not strings of more or less pretty stanzas, but organic structures. It is in this that he excels Habington, Lovelace, and even Suckling, whose separate stanzas are often as graceful as his, but who rarely succeed in maintaining the same elegance of language throughout. It would seem that this admirable instinct for form led Carew to compose with great care, and to polish his verses assiduously. Sir John Suckling upbraids him with the 'trouble and pain' with which his muse brought forth children, and hazards the criticism that a laureate poet should be easy and free. We can only wish that Suckling himself had been a more conscientious artist, and a less free and easy rhymester ; but the remark is interesting as showing us the stumbling-block on which the later Cavalier lyrists fell. They were such fine gentlemen that they disdained to cultivate their art and live laborious days, and we suffer as we search here and there for gems of spontaneous song amid the rubbish-heap that their carelessness has bequeathed us. To Carew, as to Webster before him, the impertinence of his contemporaries can have mattered little in comparison with the satisfaction he must have felt in his work as an artist.

The claim of Carew to a place among the artificers of our language must not be overlooked. In his hands English verse took a smooth and flexible character that had neither the splendours nor the discords of the great Elizabethan school, but formed an admirable medium for gentle thought and florid reverie. The praise that Voltaire gave to Waller might be transferred to Carew if it were not that to give such praise to any one writer is uncritical. But Waller might never have written, and the development of English verse would be still unbroken, whereas Carew is a necessary link between the Elizabethans and Prior. He represents the main stream of one of the great rivers of poetic influence proceeding from Ben Jonson, and he contrived to do so much because he remained so close to that master and yet in his

particular vein excelled him.   He is sometimes strangely modern.
Such verses as those beginning—

> As Celia rested in the shade
> With Cleon by her side,'

have all the character of the eighteenth century.   Carew is thus a
transitional figure.   He holds Shakspeare with one hand and
Congreve with the other, and leads us down the hill of the seven-
teenth century by a path more flowery and of easier incline than
any of his compeers.   Yet we must never forget, in considering
his historical position, that his chief merit lies, after all, in his
fresh colouring and sincere and tender passion.

EDMUND W. GOSSE.

Song.

Ask me no more where Jove bestows,
When June is past, the fading rose,
For in your beauty's orient deep
These flowers, as in their causes, sleep.

Ask me no more whither do stray
The golden atoms of the day,
For, in pure love, heaven did prepare
Those powders to enrich your hair.

Ask me no more whither doth haste
The nightingale when May is past,
For in your sweet dividing throat
She winters and keeps warm her note.

Ask me no more where those stars light
That downwards fall in dead of night,
For in your eyes they sit, and there
Fixëd become as in their sphere.

Ask me no more if east or west
The Phœnix builds her spicy nest,
For unto you at last she flies,
And in your fragrant bosom dies.

A Prayer to the Wind.

Go, thou gentle whispering wind,
Bear this sigh, and if thou find
Where my cruel fair doth rest,
Cast it in her snowy breast,
So, enflamed by my desire,
It may set her heart a-fire.
Those sweet kisses thou shalt gain
Will reward thee for thy pain ;
Boldly light upon her lip,
There suck odours, and thence skip

To her bosom; lastly fall
Down, and wander over all;
Range about those ivory hills,
From whose every part distils
Amber dew,—there spices grow,
There pure streams of nectar flow;
There perfume thyself, and bring
All those sweets upon thy wing;
As thou return'st, change by thy power
Every weed into a flower,
Turn each thistle to a vine,
Make the bramble eglantine!
For so rich a booty made,
Do but this, and I am paid.
Thou canst with thy powerful blast
Heat apace, and cool as fast;
Thou canst kindle hidden flame,
And again destroy the same;
Then, for pity, either stir
Up the fire of love in her,
That alike both flames may shine,
Or else quite extinguish mine.

THE CRUEL MISTRESS.

We read of kings and gods that kindly took
A pitcher filled with water from the brook,
But I have daily tendered without thanks
Rivers of tears that overflow their banks;
A slaughtered bull will appease angry Jove,
A horse the Sun, a lamb the god of love,
But she disdains the spotless sacrifice
Of a pure heart that at her altar lies.
Vesta is not displeased if her chaste urn
Do with repairèd fuel ever burn,
But my saint frowns, though to her honoured name,
I consecrate a never-dying flame.
The Assyrian king did none i' the furnace throw
But those that to his image did not bow,—

With bended knees I daily worship her,
Yet she consumes her own idolater.
Of such a goddess no times leave record,
That burned the temple where she was adored.

A Deposition from Love.

I was foretold your rebel sex
    Nor love, nor pity knew,
And with what scorn you use to vex
    Poor hearts that humbly sue ;
Yet I believed, to crown our pain,
    Could we the fortress win,
The happy lover sure should gain
    A paradise within.
I thought Love's plagues, like dragons, sate,
Only to fright us at the gate.

But I did enter and enjoy
    What happy lovers prove,
For I could kiss, and sport and toy,
    And taste those sweets of love,
Which, if they had a lasting state,
    Or if in Celia's breast
The force of love might not abate,
    Jove were too mean a guest.
But now her breach of faith far more
Afflicts, than did her scorn before.

Hard fate ! to have been once possessed
    As victor of a heart,
Achieved with labour and unrest,
    And then forced to depart ;
If the stout foe will not resign,
    When I besiege a town,
I lose but what was never mine,
    But he that is cast down
From enjoyed beauty, feels a woe
Only deposèd kings can know.

DISDAIN RETURNED.

He that loves a rosy cheek,
    Or a coral lip admires,
Or from star-like eyes doth seek
    Fuel to maintain his fires,
As old Time makes these decay,
So his flames must waste away.

But a smooth and steadfast mind,
    Gentle thoughts and calm desires,
Hearts, with equal love combined,
    Kindle never-dying fires ;
Where these art not, I despise
Lovely cheeks or lips or eyes.

No tears, Celia, now shall win,
    My resolved heart to return ;
I have searched thy soul within
    And find nought but pride and **scorn ;**
I have learned thy arts, and now
Can disdain as much as thou !

CELIA SINGING.

You that think love can convey
    No other way,
But through the eyes, into the heart,
    His fatal dart,
Close up those casements and but hear
    This siren sing,
    And on the wing
Of her sweet voice it shall appear
That love can enter at the ear.

Then unveil your eyes, behold
    The curious mould
Where that voice dwells, and as we **know,**
    When the cocks crow,

We freely may
Gaze on the day,
So may you, when the music's done,
Awake and see the rising sun.

THE LADY TO HER INCONSTANT SERVANT.

When on the altar of my hand,
    Bedewed with many a kiss and tear,
Thy now revolted heart did stand
    An humble martyr, thou didst swear
    Thus, and the God of Love did hear :—
By those bright glances of thine eye,
Unless thou pity me, I die!

When first those perjured lips of thine,
    Bepaled with blasting sighs, did seal
Their violated faith on mine,
    From the soft bosom that did heal
    Thee, thou my melting heart didst steal;
My soul, enflamed with thy false breath,
Poisoned with kisses, sucked in death.

Yet I nor hand nor lip will move
    Revenge or mercy to procure
From the offended god of love;
    My curse is fatal, and my pure
    Love shall beyond thy scorn endure;
If I implore the gods, they'll find
Thee too ungrateful, me too kind.

A PASTORAL DIALOGUE.

Shepherd. Nymph. Chorus.

She. This mossy bank they pressed. *Nym.* That aged oak
        Did canopy the happy pair
        All night from the damp air.
Cho. Here let us sit, and sing the words they spoke,
    Till the day, breaking, their embraces broke.

Shep. See, Love, the blushes of the morn appear,
　　　　And now she hangs her pearly store,
　　　　Robbed from the eastern shore,
　　In the cowslip's bell and roses rare ;
　　Sweet, I must stay no longer here !

Nym. Those streaks of doubtful light usher not day,
　　　　But show my sun must set ; no morn
　　　　Shall shine till thou return ;
　　The yellow planets and the grey
　　Dawn shall attend thee on thy way.

Shep. If thine eyes gild my paths, they may forbear
　　　　Their useless shine. *Nym.* My tears will quite
　　　　Extinguish their faint light.

Shep. Those drops will make their beams more clear,
　　Love's flames will shine in every tear.

Cho. They kissed and wept, and from their lips and eyes,
　　　　In a mixed dew, of briny sweet
　　　　Their joys and sorrows meet ;
　　But she cries out. *Nym.* Shepherd, arise,
　　The sun betrays us else to spies.

Shep. The winged hours fly fast whilst we embrace,
　　　　But when we want their help to meet,
　　　　They move with leaden feet.

Nym. Then let us pinion time, and chase
　　The day forever from this place.

Shep. Hark ! *Nym.* Ay me ! stay ! *Shep.* Forever : *Nym.* No !
　　　　arise !
　　　　We must be gone ! *Shep.* My nest of spice !
　　Nym. My soul ! *Shep.* My Paradise !

Cho. Neither could say farewell, but through their eyes
　　Grief interrupted speech with tears' supplies.

FROM 'THE RAPTURE.'

Meanwhile the bubbling stream shall court the shore,
The enamoured chirping wood-choir shall adore
In varied tunes the deity of Love,
The gentle blasts of western winds shall move

The trembling leaves, and through their close boughs breathe
Still music, while we rest ourselves beneath
Their dancing shade, till a soft murmur, sent
From souls entranced in amorous languishment,
Rouse us, and shoot into our veins fresh fire,
Till we in their sweet extasy expire.

*   *   *   *   *   *   *   *

Daphne hath broke her bark, and that swift foot,
Which th' angry gods had fastened with a root
To the fixed earth, doth now unfettered run
To meet the embraces of the youthful Sun ;
She hangs upon him, like his Delphic lyre,
Her kisses blow the old, and breathe new fire,
Full of her god, she sings inspirëd lays,
Sweet odes of love, such as deserve the bays
Which she herself was.   Next her, Laura lies
In Petrarch's learned arms, drying those eyes,
That did in such sweet smooth-paced numbers flow
As made the world enamoured of his woe.
These, and ten thousand beauties more, that died
Slave to the tyrant, now, enlarged, deride
His cancelled laws, and, for their time misspent,
Pay into Love's exchequer double rent.

EPITAPH ON THE LADY MARY VILLERS.

The Lady Mary Villers lies
Under this stone ; with weeping eyes
The parents that first gave her birth,
And their sad friends, laid her in earth.
If any of them, reader, were
Known unto thee, shed a tear ;
Or if thyself possess a gem
As dear to thee as this to them,
Though a stranger to this place,
Bewail in theirs thy own hard case,
For thou, perhaps, at thy return
May'st find thy darling in an urn.

SONG.

Would you know what's soft? I dare
Not bring you to the down, or air,
Nor to stars to show what's bright,
Nor to snow to teach you white;

Nor, if you would music hear,
Call the orbs to take your ear;
Nor, to please your sense, bring forth
Bruisëd nard, or what's more worth;

Or on food were your thoughts placed,
Bring you nectar for a taste;
Would you have all these in one,
Name my mistress, and 'tis done!

THE PROTESTATION.

No more shall meads be decked with flowers,
Nor sweetness dwell in rosy bowers,
Nor greenest buds on branches spring,
Nor warbling birds delight to sing,
Nor April violets paint the grove,
If I forsake my Celia's love.

The fish shall in the ocean burn,
And fountains sweet shall bitter turn,
The humble oak no flood shall know
When floods shall highest hills o'erflow,
Black Lethe shall oblivion leave,
If ere my Celia I deceive.

Love shall his bow and shaft lay by,
And Venus' doves want wings to fly,
The Sun refuse to show his light,
And day shall then be turned to night,
And in that night no star appear,
If once I leave my Celia dear.

Love shall no more inhabit earth,
Nor lovers more shall love for worth,
Nor joy above in heaven dwell,
Nor pain torment poor souls in hell,
Grim death no more shall horrid prove,
If ere I leave bright Celia's love.

IN PRAISE OF HIS MISTRESS.

You that will a wonder know,
  Go with me ;
Two suns in a heaven of snow
  Both burning be,—
All they fire that do but eye them,
Yet the snow's unmelted by them.

Leaves of crimson tulips met
  Guide the way
Where two pearly rows be set,
  As white as day;
When they part themselves asunder
She breathes oracles of wonder.

All this but the casket is
  Which contains
Such a jewel, as to miss
  Breeds endless pains,—
That's her mind, and they that know it
May admire, but cannot show it.

ROBERT HERRICK.

[ROBERT HERRICK was born in Cheapside, in August 1594, and died at Dean-Prior, in Devonshire, on the 15th of October, 1674. He published one volume, containing He perides, dated 1648, and Noble Numbers, dated 1647.]

Among the English pastoral poets, Herrick takes an undisputed precedence, and as a lyrist generally he is scarcely excelled, except by Shelley. No other writer of the seventeenth century approached him in abundance of song, in sustained exercise of the purely musical and intuitive gifts of poetry. Shakspeare, Milton, and perhaps Fletcher, surpassed him in the passion and elevated harmony of their best lyrical pieces, as they easily excelled him in the wider range of their genius and the breadth of their accomplishment. But while these men exercised their art in all its branches, Herrick confined himself very narrowly to one or two, and the unflagging freshness of his inspiration, flowing through a long life in so straitened a channel, enabled him to amass such a wealth of purely lyrical poetry as no other Englishman has produced. His level of performance was very high ; he seems to have preserved all that he wrote, and the result is that we possess more than twelve hundred of his little poems, in at least one out of every three of which we may find something charming or characteristic. Of all the Cavalier lyrists Herrick is the only one that followed the bent of his genius undisturbed, and lived a genuine artist's life. Consequently, while we have to lament, in the case of Lovelace or Suckling, a constant waste of energy, and unthrifty drain of poetic power, in Herrick all is wisely husbanded, and we feel satisfied that we possess the best that he could produce. His life was an ideal one so far as quiet and retirement went ; to fourteen years of seclusion at Cambridge there succeeded twenty years of unbroken Arcadian repose in a Devonshire vicarage, and it was not till the desire to rhyme had left him that the poet was brought rudely face to face with the clamour and vexation of political feud. Thus he was preserved from that public riot and constant disturbance of the common-wealth which did its best to drown the voice of every poet from Carew to Dryden, which drove Crashaw away to madness and death, which made harsh the liquid melodies of Milton, which be-lied the promise of Davenant and broke the heart of Cowley. From all this disturbance and discord Herrick was fortunately free, and we may look in vain through his pastoral elegies and jets of amorous verse to discover a trace of the frantic times he lived in.

The one book which Herrick has bequeathed to us is filled with short poems, thrown together without any attempt at arrangement either of subject or time of composition. They range between odes and epithalamia of five or six pages, and epigrams of a single couplet. In preparing the *Hesperides* for the press it would seem as though the English poet took for his model the works of the Latin epigrammatist Martial. There is, however, a deeper resemblance between the two writers than is to be found in the mere outward arrangement of their works. The successive editors of Herrick have noted what they conceive to be his likeness to Catullus, but this is hardly critical. The prominent qualities of Herrick's verse are not passion so much as sensuous reverie, not fire so much as light, not the music of the lyre so much as of the flute and fiddle. In all these respects he is far enough from resembling Catullus, but very near to Martial, who, moreover, alone among the Latin poets has that minute picturesqueness of detail and delight in the accessories of life which we admire in Herrick. Moreover, it must be frankly admitted, that in his tendency to obscene and unsavoury jest, and in his radical in-delicacy of fancy the English poet follows, happily at a great distance, the foulest of the ancients. But Herrick was not in-debted solely to Martial or to Catullus; his imagination was steeped in antique literature, and whether he was a Greek scholar or no, he contrived to assimilate into his work more of the temper of Theocritus and of the lyrists of the Anthology than any English writer of the century. The atmosphere is Greek, though we find little that shows direct study; perhaps, with the tact of a poet, he extracted the odour and flavour of ancient verse without under-standing it very well, just as Petrarch, dreaming above the MS. of Homer that he could not read, divined the place that Greek was destined to take in the revival of culture.

Herrick was a Pagan and a hedonist, and it was natural that

his mind should revert with extreme longing to the primitive civilisation of Europe. He dreamed himself to be a priest in some past age of Sicily or Tuscany, earnestly partaking in the ceremonial of a god that could be wreathed with flowers or invoked in a libation of wine, and he was quietly contented with the physical fulness of life around him, without caring to define with much antiquarian exactitude what the age was or what the worship. So little had he of the pedant in his constitution, that he brought these genial rites in fancy to the doors of his Devonian vicarage, and raised the thyrsus underneath his clerical roof, while the roses reigned around, and his puritan locks were shining with galbanum and storax. There were quintals at Dean-Prior, wakes and wassailings, and Herrick gaily assimilated to his antique dream these pleasant pastoral survivals, ribbanding the may-pole as though it were the cone-tipped rod of Dionysus, and pouring over the clumsy morris-dances of his parishioners the ideal grace of some Dorian round of nymphs and shepherds. His classic fancy is brighter, and his sensuous vision more amply sustained than in the poems of those of his contemporaries who affected the same sentimental paganism. Even Ben Jonson, when he was most Latin, was but a burly Londoner masquerading in a toga; but Herrick, if not born a Greek, as Keats was, might yet claim to be the compatriot of those Italian lyrists of the early renaissance, who completely divested themselves of all trace of Christendom. In saying this, no harsh judgment is passed upon Herrick's performance of those duties, ceremonial or poetical, which his position as a clerk of the English Church demanded from him. He preached sermons or wrote ' Noble Numbers ' with zeal and sincerity, but these were not the product of the native spirit of the man. He was an exile from Arcadia all his days, walking through our sober modern life without revolt or passion, but always conscious that he had seen more glorious sights, and walked through a land much more eminent for luxury and beauty. In Herrick the sense of bodily loveliness was perilously acute, but his good sense and artistic tact sufficed to restrain it within bounds ; and, thus confined, it simply served to redeem his verse from the tasteless errors of his contemporaries, and to interpenetrate it with melody and colour.

What Herrick did not learn from the ancients, he gathered at the feet of Ben Jonson. He was the greatest and the most reverential in the group of youths of genius who formed the school and boasted of being the 'sons' of the great tragic master. But in temper and bent of mind few writers could naturally have less in common than Jonson and Herrick, and it is therefore not surprising that we find but one section of the older poet's work exercising an influence over the younger. How wide and versatile was the genius of Ben Jonson is but little known to those who study him only as a dramatist. His masques, and the beautiful collection called *The Forest*, display him to us as one of the most graceful and original of lyrists ; and it was at this point that Herrick fell under his inspiration. It has been conjectured that Herrick first became acquainted with the author of *The Alchemist* on the memorable occasion of the first performance of that comedy in 1610, when the young man was in his nineteenth year. It was in that same year that Jonson published *Oberon, the Fairy Prince*, a masque peopled by the gay assemblage of fays and elves, which Herrick afterwards adopted as his own peculiar property, and full of classical allusions and strains of light versification in the spirit of the *Hesperides*. It is here, and in the other masques and songs of Jonson, that we must look for the immediate inspiration of much that Herrick afterwards adorned, intensified, and made his own.

There is not a sunnier book in the world than the *Hesperides*. To open it is to enter a rich garden on a summer afternoon, and to smell the perfume of a wealth of flowers and warm herbs and ripening fruits. The poet sings, in short flights of song, of all that makes life gay and luxurious, of the freshness of a dewy field, of the fecundity and heat of harvest, of the odour and quietude of an autumn orchard. All the innocent pastimes of the people find a laureate in him, his Muse disdains no circumstance of rural holiday, and is more than ready to accompany him to country wakes and races, to the riot of the hay-field and the may-pole, to the village bridal and to the crowning of the hock-cart. She presides with him at the mixing of a wedding-cake or of a spicy wassail-bowl, and lends her presence to the celebration of the humblest rites of rural superstition. Herrick has summed up the subject of his book very neatly in its opening lines—which also form the prelude to our present selection. But his verse is not all so objective as he pretends ; to the observation of nature and the praise of enjoyment in others he adds copious reflection on the construction of his own mind and body, and discusses his experiences with a charming candour. No more garrulous egotist is to be found in literature ;

he prattles away with child-like simplicity, about his hopes of
pleasure and his fears of death, his loves and his companions,
even about his food and the various creature comforts of his
vicarage. He tells us that he is anxious for fame, and, again, that
he is confident of securing it. He gives us a list of his domestic
pets, and we see them pass before us, his goose, his lamb, his
spaniel, his cat, his learned pig. We sit with him beside the fire
so quietly that we see the brisk mouse come out to feed herself
with crumbs, till 'Prewdence Baldwin' or 'the green-eyed kitling
comes.' It is this happy realism and personal frankness which, in
conjunction with that Doric fancy of which we have already spoken,
combine to give the poetry of Herrick such an intimate charm, at
once strange and familiar, like that of the more dramatic passages
in Theocritus. There is no strain on the feelings, no rage or
fervour, all is quiet, picturesque and penetrating, and the poet is
so circumstantial in describing his Arcadia, that it seems to us
while we listen to him, that we have lived there all our lives. The
deceptive air of reality which clothes the landscapes of Herrick
should, by analogy, make his biographers careful in accepting too
exactly all that he says about himself. Little can be gained by
analysing his various loves, or by attempting to disentangle Silvia
from Perilla, or Corinna from Anthea. These nymphs were
probably mere artist's studies, for which some primrose-gatherer
or milk-maid of Dean-Prior sat quite unconsciously. Only in the
description of Julia we may detect more individuality and personal
presence, and the poems which are dedicated to her probably date
from the years preceding the poet's acceptance of holy orders.
We must not forget that before he left Cambridge he was thirty-
eight years of age, the first fever of the blood was allayed, and
without doubt the warmest verses of the *Hesperides*, his 'wild
unbaptisëd rhymes,' were the production of his youth.

The sacred poetry of Herrick is weak, as might be expected,
from a theological point of view, and attains success rather in spite
of the author's aim than through it. He is very genuine in his
devotion, as far as it goes, but his pagan temperament leaves him
rather callous, and we have none of the spiritual elevation of
Vaughan, none of the conscience-searching and holy aspiration of
Herbert. Herrick sings lustily in church, but he sings to the old
heathen tunes, and, even at his prayers, his spirit is mundane and
not filled with heavenly things. He succeeds best where he permits
himself to adorn a celestial theme with the picturesque detail of his

secular poems; he is happy if he be allowed to crown the infant Saviour with daffadils or pin a rose into His stomacher. His longer odes and elegies owe their interest to no divine fervour, but to the bright and fantastic touches, to the introduction of flowers and odours, and to the luxury and pomp of ceremonial. Herrick must ever be regarded as an alien in the choir of divine singers, which the seventeenth century produced; he has something of their technical character, but in spirit he is divided from them by a barrier that neither a genuine piety nor a desire to edify could over-step. His best religious pieces are *The Litany*, *The Dirge of Jephthah's Daughter* (both of them given in our selection), and *The Dirge of Dorcas*, a poem containing some grotesque passages, but many of extraordinary lyric felicity.

We have no means of discovering, or even of conjecturing, by what steps Herrick arrived at the mastery over the technical part of poetry which we discover in the *Hesperides*. It was characteristic of the fashion of the day to invent verse-forms of great intricacy and difficulty, the beauty of which was of less import to the writer than the oddity. Donne had set the example of these fantastic eccentricities, and the wanton way in which they were employed soon drove men of taste to the rigid use of the heroic couplet only. Herrick, however, avoided this capital offence against artistic harmony. His measures are many of them his own, and show great ingenuity, but they are all, or almost all, justified by their inherent beauty. He attempted a great variety of experiments, mainly with a view to intensifying and sustaining the pleasurable recurrence of rhyme; some of these are scarcely successful, because the language is not pliant enough for such *tours-de-force*, but the experiments themselves are not contrary to the principles of versification. The lyrics of Herrick are very luscious and liquid in their flow of language; he is not a passionate writer, and we always miss, even in his best work, that mounting and piercing melody which goes straight to the heart, and which Burns and Shelley give us, each in his own way. In his verse-music, as in everything else, Herrick is excessively mundane, too easily satisfied with the sincere and exquisite expression of a common thought to care about the uncommon; and hence it is that with all his wonderful art and skill he is never named among the few English poets of the first class, but always as pre-eminent among those of the second class.

EDMUND W. GOSSE.

THE ARGUMENT OF THE HESPERIDES.

I sing of brooks, of blossoms, birds, and bowers,
Of April, May, of June, and July-flowers;
I sing of May-poles, hock-carts, wassails, wakes,
Of bride-grooms, brides, and of their bridal-cakes.
I write of Youth, of Love;—and have access
By these, to sing of cleanly wantonness;
I sing of dews, of rains, and, piece by piece,
Of balm, of oil, of spice, and ambergris.
I sing of times trans-shifting; and I write
How roses first came red, and lilies white.
I write of groves, of twilights, and I sing
The court of Mab, and of the Fairy King.
I write of Hell; I sing, and ever shall
Of Heaven,—and hope to have it after all.

WHEN HE WOULD HAVE HIS VERSES READ.

In sober mornings, do not thou rehearse
The holy incantation of a verse;
But when that men have both well drunk, and fed,
Let my enchantments then be sung or read.
When laurel spirts i' th' fire, and when the hearth
Smiles to itself, and gilds the roof with mirth;
When up the Thyrse is raised, and when the sound
Of sacred orgies, flies around, around;
When the rose reigns, and locks with ointments shine,
Let rigid Cato read these lines of mine.

CORINNA'S GOING A MAYING.

Get up, get up for shame! the blooming morn
Upon her wings presents the god unshorn.
  See how Aurora throws her fair
  Fresh-quilted colours through the air:
  Get up, sweet slug-a-bed, and see
  The dew bespangling herb and tree.

Each flower has wept, and bow'd toward the east,
Above an hour since ; yet you not drest,
    Nay ! not so much as out of bed ?
    When all the birds have matins said,
    And sung their thankful hymns : 'tis sin,
    Nay, profanation, to keep in,—
Whenas a thousand virgins on this day,
Spring, sooner than the lark, to fetch in May.

Rise ; and put on your foliage, and be seen
To come forth, like the Spring-time, fresh and green,
    And sweet as Flora. Take no care
    For jewels for your gown, or hair :
    Fear not ; the leaves will strew
    Gems in abundance upon you :
Besides, the childhood of the day has kept,
Against you come, some orient pearls unwept :
    Come, and receive them while the light
    Hangs on the dew-locks of the night :
    And Titan on the eastern hill
    Retires himself, or else stands still
Till you come forth. Wash, dress, be brief in praying ·
Few beads are best, when once we go a Maying.

Come, my Corinna, come ; and coming, mark
How each field turns a street ; each street a park
    Made green, and trimm'd with trees : see how
    Devotion gives each house a bough
    Or branch : each porch, each door, ere this,
    An ark, a tabernacle is
Made up of white-thorn neatly interwove ;
As if here were those cooler shades of love.
    Can such delights be in the street,
    And open fields, and we not see 't ?
    Come, we'll abroad : and let's obey
    The proclamation made for May :
And sin no more, as we have done, by staying ;
But, my Corinna, come, let's go a Maying.

There's not a budding boy, or girl, this day,
But is got up, and gone to bring in May.
    A deal of youth, ere this, is come
    Back, and with white-thorn laden home.
    Some have dispatch'd their cakes and cream,
    Before that we have left to dream :
And some have wept, and woo'd, and plighted troth,
And chose their priest, ere we can cast off sloth :
    Many a green gown has been given ;
    Many a kiss, both odd and even :
    Many a glance, too, has been sent
    From out the eye, love's firmament :
Many a jest told of the keys betraying
This night, and locks pick'd :—yet we're not a Maying.

—Come, let us go, while we are in our prime ;
And take the harmless folly of the time !
    We shall grow old apace, and die
    Before we know our liberty.
    Our life is short ; and our days run
    As fast away as does the sun :—
And as a vapour, or a drop of rain
Once lost, can ne'er be found again :
    So when or you or I are made
    A fable, song, or fleeting shade ;
    All love, all liking, all delight
    Lies drown'd with us in endless night.
—Then while time serves, and we are but decaying,
Come, my Corinna ! come, let's go a Maying.

THE ROCK OF RUBIES.

    Some ask'd me where the Rubies grew :
      And nothing I did say,
    But with my finger pointed to
      The lips of Julia.
    Some ask'd how Pearls did grow, and where :
      Then spoke I to my girl,
    To part her lips, and shew me there
      The quarrelets of Pearl.

CANDLEMAS EVE.

Down with the rosemary and bays,
  Down with the misletoe ;
Instead of holly, now up-raise
  The greener box, for show.

The holly hitherto did sway ;
  Let box now domineer,
Until the dancing Easter-day,
  Or Easter's eve appear.

Then youthful box, which now hath grace
  Your houses to renew,
Grown old, surrender must his place
  Unto the crispèd yew.

When yew is out, then birch comes in,
  And many flowers beside,
Both of a fresh and fragrant kin,
  To honour Whitsuntide.

Green rushes then, and sweetest bents,
  With cooler oaken boughs,
Come in for comely ornaments,
  To re-adorn the house.
Thus times do shift ; each thing his turn does hold ;
New things succeed, as former things grow old.

THE NIGHT PIECE.

Her eyes the glow-worm lend thee,
The shooting stars attend thee ;
    And the elves also,
    Whose little eyes glow
Like the sparks of fire, befriend thee.

No Will-o'th'-Wisp mis-light thee,
Nor snake or slow-worm bite thee ;
    But on, on thy way,
    Not making a stay,
Since ghost there's none to affright thee.

Let not the dark thee cumber;
What though the moon does slumber?
    The stars of the night
    Will lend thee their light,
Like tapers clear, without number.

Then, Julia, let me woo thee,
Thus, thus to come unto me;
    And when I shall meet
    Thy silvery feet,
My soul I'll pour into thee.

TO THE VIRGINS.

Gather ye rose-buds while ye may:
    Old Time is still a-flying;
And this same flower that smiles to-day,
    To-morrow will be dying.

The glorious lamp of heaven, the Sun,
    The higher he's a-getting,
The sooner will his race be run,
    And nearer he's to setting.

That age is best, which is the first,
    When youth and blood are warmer;
But being spent, the worse, and worst
    Times, still succeed the former.

—Then be not coy, but use your time,
    And while ye may, go marry;
For having lost but once your prime,
    You may for ever tarry.

TO BLOSSOMS.

Fair pledges of a fruitful tree,
    Why do ye fall so fast?
    Your date is not so past,
But you may stay yet here a-while,
    To blush and gently smile;
        And go at last.

What, were ye born to be
    An hour or half's delight;
    And so to bid good-night?
'Twas pity Nature brought ye forth,
    Merely to show your worth,
      And lose you quite.

But you are lovely leaves, where we
    May read how soon things have
    Their end, though ne'er so brave:
And after they have shown their pride,
    Like you, a-while,—they glide
      Into the grave.

To Primroses filled with Morning Dew.

Why do ye weep, sweet babes? can tears
    Speak grief in you,
    Who were but born
  Just as the modest morn
  Teem'd her refreshing dew?
Alas, you have not known that shower
    That mars a flower,
    Nor felt th' unkind
  Breath of a blasting wind,
  Nor are ye worn with years;
    Or warp'd as we,
  Who think it strange to see,
Such pretty flowers, like to orphans young,
To speak by tears, before ye have a tongue.

Speak, whimp'ring younglings, and make known
    The reason why
    Ye droop and weep;
  Is it for want of sleep,
  Or childish lullaby?
Or that ye have not seen as yet
    The violet?
    Or brought a kiss
  From that Sweet-heart, to this?
  —No, no, this sorrow shown

By your tears shed,
Would have this lecture read,
That things of greatest, so of meanest worth,
Conceived with grief are, and with tears brought forth.

To Daffadils.

Fair Daffadils, we weep to see
 You haste away so soon ;
As yet the early-rising sun
 Has not attain'd his noon.
  Stay, stay,
 Until the hasting day
  Has run
 But to the even-song ;
And, having pray'd together, we
 Will go with you along.

We have short time to stay, as you ;
 We have as short a spring ;
As quick a growth to meet decay,
 As you, or any thing.
  We die
 As your hours do, and dry
  Away,
 Like to the summer's rain ;
Or as the pearls of morning's dew,
 Ne'er to be found again.

To Meadows.

Ye have been fresh and green,
 Ye have been fill'd with flowers ;
And ye the walks have been
 Where maids have spent their hours.

You have beheld how they
 With wicker arks did come,
To kiss and bear away
 The richer cowslips home.

You've heard them sweetly sing,
    And seen them in a round;
Each virgin, like a spring,
    With honeysuckles crown'd.

But now, we see none here,
    Whose silvery feet did tread,
And with dishevell'd hair
    Adorn'd this smoother mead.

Like unthrifts, having spent
    Your stock, and needy grown,
You're left here to lament
    Your poor estates alone.

A Thanksgiving to God.

Lord, thou hast given me a cell,
        Wherein to dwell;
A little house, whose humble roof
        Is weather proof;
Under the spars of which I lie
        Both soft and dry;
Where thou, my chamber for to ward,
        Hast set a guard
Of harmless thoughts, to watch and keep
        Me, while I sleep.
Low is my porch, as is my fate;
        Both void of state;
And yet the threshold of my door
        Is worn by th' poor,
Who thither come, and freely get
        Good words, or meat.
Like as my parlour, so my hall
        And kitchen's small;
A little buttery, and therein
        A little bin,
Which keeps my little loaf of bread
        Unchipt, unflead;

Some brittle sticks of thorn or briar
 Make me a fire,
Close by whose living coal I sit,
 And glow like it.
Lord, I confess too, when I dine,
 The pulse is thine,
And all those other bits that be
 There placed by thee ;
The worts, the purslain, and the mess
 Of water-cress,
Which of thy kindness thou hast sent ;
 And my content
Makes those, and my belovèd beet,
 To be more sweet.
'Tis thou that crown'st my glittering hearth
 With guiltless mirth,
And giv'st me wassail bowls to drink,
 Spiced to the brink.
Lord, 'tis thy plenty-dropping hand
 That soils my land,
And giv'st me, for my bushel sown,
 Twice ten for one ;
Thou mak'st my teeming hen to lay
 Her egg each day ;
Besides, my healthful ewes to bear
 Me twins each year ;
The while the conduits of my kine
 Run cream, for wine :
All these, and better, thou dost send
 Me, to this end,—
That I should render, for my part,
 A thankful heart ;
Which, fired with incense, I resign,
 As wholly thine ;
—But the acceptance, that must be,
 My Christ, by Thee.

The Mad Maid's Song.

Good morrow to the day so fair ;
　　Good morning, sir, to you ;
Good morrow to mine own torn hair,
　　Bedabbled with the dew.

Good morning to this primrose too ;
　　Good morrow to each maid ;
That will with flowers the tomb bestrew
　　Wherein my Love is laid.

Ah ! woe is me, woe, woe is me,
　　Alack and well-a-day !
For pity, sir, find out that bee,
　　Which bore my Love away.

I'll seek him in your bonnet brave ;
　　I'll seek him in your eyes ;
Nay, now I think they've made his grave
　　I' th' bed of strawberries.

I'll seek him there ; I know, ere this,
　　The cold, cold earth doth shake him ;
But I will go, or send a kiss
　　By you, sir, to awake him.

Pray hurt him not ; though he be dead,
　　He knows well who do love him ;
And who with green turfs rear his head,
　　And who do rudely move him.

He's soft and tender, pray take heed,
　　With bands of cowslips bind him,
And bring him home ;—but 'tis decreed
　　That I shall never find him.

Upon Julia's Clothes.

Whenas in silks my Julia goes,
Till, then, methinks, how sweetly flows
That liquefaction of her clothes !

Next, when I cast mine eyes, and see
That brave vibration each way free ;
O how that glittering taketh me !

DELIGHT IN DISORDER.

A sweet disorder in the dress
Kindles in clothes a wantonness ;
A lawn about the shoulders thrown
Into a fine distraction ;
An erring lace, which here and there
Enthrals the crimson stomacher ;
A cuff neglectful, and thereby
Ribbons to flow confusedly ;
A winning wave, deserving note,
In the tempestuous petticoat ;
A careless shoe-string, in whose tie
I see a wild civility ;—
Do more bewitch me, than when art
Is too precise in every part.

ART ABOVE NATURE.

When I behold a forest spread
With silken trees upon thy head ;
And when I see that other dress
Of flowers set in comeliness ;
When I behold another grace
In the ascent of curious lace,
Which, like a pinnacle, doth shew
The top, and the top-gallant too ;
Then, when I see thy tresses bound
Into an oval, square, or round,
And knit in knots far more than I
Can tell by tongue, or True-love tie ;
Next, when those lawny films I see
Play with a wild civility ;

And all those airy silks to flow,
Alluring me, and tempting so—
I must confess, mine eye and heart
Dotes less on nature than on art.

CHERRY-RIPE.

Cherry-ripe, ripe, ripe, I cry,
Full and fair ones ; come, and buy :
If so be you ask me where
They do grow ? I answer, there
Where my Julia's lips do smile ;—
There's the land, or cherry-isle ;
Whose plantations fully show
All the year where cherries grow.

THE BRIDE-CAKE.

This day, my Julia, thou must make
For Mistress Bride the wedding-cake :
Knead but the dough, and it will be
To paste of almonds turn'd by thee ;
Or kiss it thou but once or twice,
And for the bride-cake there'll be spice.

HIS PRAYER TO BEN JONSON.

When I a verse shall make,
    Know I have pray'd thee,
For old religion's sake,
    Saint Ben, to aid me.

Make the way smooth for me,
    When, I, thy Herrick,
Honouring thee on my knee
    Offer my Lyric.

Candles I'll give to thee,
　And a new altar ;
And thou, Saint Ben, shalt be
　Writ in my psalter.

AN ODE FOR BEN JONSON.

Ah Ben !
Say how or when
Shall we, thy guests,
Meet at those lyric feasts,
Made at the Sun,
The Dog, the Triple Tun ;
Where we such clusters had,
As made us nobly wild, not mad ?
And yet each verse of thine
Out-did the meat, out-did the frolic wine.

My Ben !
Or come again,
Or send to us
Thy wit's great overplus;
But teach us yet
Wisely to husband it,
Lest we that talent spend ;
And having once brought to an end
That precious stock,—the store
Of such a wit the world should have no more.

TO ANTHEA.

Bid me to live, and I will live
　Thy Protestant to be ;
Or bid me love, and I will give
　A loving heart to thee.

A heart as soft, a heart as kind,
　A heart as sound and free
As in the whole world thou canst find,
　That heart I'll give to thee.

'Bid that heart stay, and it will stay
　　To honour thy decree ;
Or bid it languish quite away,
　　And 't shall do so for thee.

Bid me to weep, and I will weep,
　　While I have eyes to see ;
And having none, yet I will keep
　　A heart to weep for thee.

Bid me despair, and I'll despair,
　　Under that cypress tree ;
Or bid me die, and I will dare
　　E'en death, to die for thee.

—Thou art my life, my love, my heart,
　　The very eyes of me ;
And hast command of every part,
　　To live and die for thee.

To Anthea.

Now is the time when all the lights wax dim ;
And thou, Anthea, must withdraw from him
Who was thy servant : Dearest, bury me
Under that holy-oak, or gospel-tree ;
Where, though thou see'st not, thou may'st think upon
Me, when thou yearly go'st procession ;
Or, for mine honour, lay me in that tomb
In which thy sacred reliques shall have room ;
For my embalming, Sweetest, there will be
No spices wanting, when I'm laid by thee.

To Perilla.

Ah, my Perilla ! dost thou grieve to see
Me, day by day, to steal away from thee ?
Age calls me hence, and my gray hairs bid come,
And haste away to mine eternal home ;
'Twill not be long, Perilla, after this,
That I must give thee the supremest kiss :—

Dead when I am, first cast in salt, and bring
Part of the cream from that religious spring,
With which, Perilla, wash my hands and feet ;
That done, then wind me in that very sheet
Which wrapt thy smooth limbs, when thou didst **implore**
The Gods' protection, but the night before ;
Follow me weeping to my turf, and there
Let fall a primrose, and with it a tear :
Then lastly, let some weekly strewings be
Devoted to the memory of me ;
Then shall my ghost not walk about, but keep
Still in the cool and silent shades of sleep.

THE WAKE.

Come, Anthea, let us two
Go to feast, as others do :
Tarts and custards, creams and cakes,
Are the junkets still at wakes ;
Unto which the tribes resort,
Where the business is the sport :
Morris-dancers thou shalt see,
Marian, too, in pageantry :
And a mimic to devise
Many grinning properties.
Players there will be, and those
Base in action as in clothes ;
Yet with strutting they will please
The incurious villages.
Near the dying of the day
There will be a cudgel-play,
Where a coxcomb will be broke,
Ere a good word can be spoke :
But the anger ends all here,
Drench'd in ale, or drown'd in beer.
—Happy rustics ! best content
With the cheapest merriment ;
And possess no other fear,
Than to want the Wake next year.

To Robin Red-breast.

Laid out for dead, let thy last kindness be
With leaves and moss-work for to cover me ;
And while the wood-nymphs my cold corpse inter,
Sing thou my dirge, sweet-warbling chorister !
For epitaph, in foliage, next write this :
Here, here the tomb of Robin Herrick is !

To the Lark.

Good speed, for I this day
Betimes my matins say,
Because I do
Begin to woo,
Sweet singing Lark,
Be thou the clerk,
And know thy when
To say Amen.
And if I prove
Blest in my love,
Then thou shalt be
High Priest to me,
At my return
To incense burn,
And so to solemnise
Love's and my sacrifice.

To the Rose.

Song.

Go, happy Rose, and interwove
With other flowers, bind my Love.
Tell her, too, she must not be
Longer flowing, longer free,
That so oft has fetter'd me.

Say, if she's fretful, I have bands
Of pearl and gold, to bind her hands ;
 Tell her, if she struggle still,
 I have myrtle rods at will,
 For to tame, though not to kill.

Take thou my blessing thus, and go
And tell her this,—but do not so !—
 Lest a handsome anger fly-
 Like a lightning from her eye,
 And burn thee up, as well as I !

The Bag of the Bee.

About the sweet bag of a bee
 Two Cupids fell at odds ;
And whose the pretty prize should be
 They vow'd to ask the Gods.

Which Venus hearing, thither came,
 And for their boldness stript them ;
And taking thence from each his flame,
 With rods of myrtle whipt them.

Which done, to still their wanton cries,
 When quiet grown she'd seen them,
She kiss'd and wiped their dove-like eyes,
 And gave the bag between them.

To the Duke of York.

 May his pretty Duke-ship grow
 Like to a rose of Jericho,
 Sweeter far than ever yet
 Showers or sunshine could beget ;
 May the Graces and the Hours
 Strew his hopes and him with flowers
 And so dress him up with love
 As to be the chick of Jove ;

May the thrice three Sisters sing
Him the sovereign of their spring,
And entitle none to be
Prince of Helicon but he ;
May his soft foot, where it treads,
Gardens thence produce and meads,
And those meadows full be set
With the rose and violet ;
May his ample name be known
To the last succession,
And his actions high be told
Through the world, but writ in gold.

THE LITANY.

In the hour of my distress,
When temptations me oppress,
And when I my sins confess,
  Sweet Spirit, comfort me !

When I lie within my bed,
Sick in heart, and sick in head,
And with doubts discomforted,
  Sweet Spirit, comfort me !

When the house doth sigh and weep,
And the world is drown'd in sleep,
Yet mine eyes the watch do keep,
  Sweet Spirit, comfort me !

When the artless doctor sees
No one hope, but of his fees,
And his skill runs on the lees,
  Sweet Spirit, comfort me !

When his potion and his pill,
Has, or none, or little skill,
Meet for nothing but to kill,
  Sweet Spirit, comfort me !

When the passing-bell doth toll,
And the furies in a shoal
Come to fright a parting soul,
    Sweet Spirit, comfort me !

When the tapers now burn blue,
And the comforters are few,
And that number more than true,
    Sweet Spirit, comfort me !

When the priest his last hath pray'd,
And I nod to what is said,
'Cause my speech is now decay'd,
    Sweet Spirit, comfort me !

When, God knows, I'm tost about,
Either with despair or doubt ;
Yet, before the glass be out,
    Sweet Spirit, comfort me !

When the tempter me pursu'th
With the sins of all my youth,
And half damns me with untruth,
    Sweet Spirit, comfort me !

When the flames and hellish cries
Fright mine ears, and fright mine eyes,
And all terrors me surprise,
    Sweet Spirit, comfort me !

When the Judgment is reveal'd,
And that open'd which was seal'd ;
When to Thee I have appeal'd,
    Sweet Spirit, comfort me !

GRACE FOR A CHILD.

Here, a little child, I stand,
Heaving up my either hand :
Cold as paddocks though they be,
Here I lift them up to thee,
For a benison to fall
On our meat, and on our all.   Amen.

The Dirge of Jephthah's Daughter.

O thou, the wonder of all days !
O paragon, and pearl of praise !
O Virgin-martyr, ever blest
      Above the rest
Of all the maiden-train ! We come,
And bring fresh strewings to thy tomb.

Thus, thus, and thus, we compass round
Thy harmless and unhaunted ground ;
And as we sing thy dirge, we will
      The daffadil,
And other flowers, lay upon
The altar of our love, thy stone.

Thou wonder of all maids, liest here,
Of daughters all, the dearest dear ;
The eye of virgins ; nay, the queen
      Of this smooth green,
And all sweet meads, from whence we get
The primrose and the violet.

Too soon, too dear did Jephthah buy,
By thy sad loss, our liberty ;
His was the bond and cov'nant, yet
      Thou paid'st the debt ;
Lamented Maid ! he won the day :
But for the conquest thou didst pay.

Thy father brought with him along
The olive branch and victor's song ;
He slew the Ammonites, we know,
      But to thy woe ;
And in the purchase of our peace,
The cure was worse than the disease.

For which obedient zeal of thine,
We offer here, before thy shrine,
Our sighs for storax, tears for wine ;
   And to make fine
And fresh thy hearse-cloth, we will here
Four times bestrew thee every year.

Receive, for this thy praise, our tears ;
Receive this offering of our hairs ;
Receive these crystal vials, fill'd
   With tears, distill'd
From teeming eyes ; to these we bring,
Each maid, her silver filleting,

To gild thy tomb ; besides, these cauls,
These laces, ribbons, and these falls,
These veils, wherewith we use to hide
   The bashful bride,
When we conduct her to her groom ;
All, all we lay upon thy tomb.

No more, no more, since thou art dead,
Shall we e'er bring coy brides to bed;
No more, at yearly festivals,
   We, cowslip balls,
Or chains of columbines shall make,
For this or that occasion's sake.

No, no ; our maiden pleasures be
Wrapt in the winding-sheet with thee ;
'Tis we are dead, though not i' th' grave ;
   Or if we have
One seed of life left, 'tis to keep
A Lent for thee, to fast and weep.

Sleep in thy peace, thy bed of spice,
And make this place all paradise ;
May sweets grow here, and smoke from hence
   Fat frankincense ;
Let balm and cassia send their scent
From out thy maiden-monument.

May no wolf howl, or screech owl stir
A wing about thy sepulchre!
No boisterous winds or storms come hither,
  To starve or wither
Thy soft sweet earth; but, like a spring,
Love keep it ever flourishing.

May all shy maids, at wonted hours,
Come forth to strew thy tomb with flowers ·
May virgins, when they come to mourn,
  Male-incense burn
Upon thine altar; then return,
And leave thee sleeping in thy urn.

ODE TO ENDYMION PORTER.

Not all thy flushing suns are set,
  Herrick, as yet;
Nor doth this far-drawn hemisphere
Frown and look sullen everywhere;
Days may conclude in nights, and suns may rest
  As dead within the West,
Yet the next morn regild the fragrant East.

Alas! for me! that I have lost
  E'en all, almost!
Sunk is my sight, set is my sun,
And all the loom of life undone;
The staff, the elm, the prop, the sheltering wall
  Whereon my vine did crawl,
Now, now blown down; needs must the old stock fall.

Yet, Porter, while thou keep'st alive,
  In death I thrive,
And like a Phoenix re-aspire
From out my nard and funeral fire,
And as I prime my feathered youth, so I
  Do marvell how I could die
When I had thee, my chief preserver, by.

I'm up, I'm up, and bless that hand,
        Which makes me stand
Now as I do, and, but for thee,
I must confess, I could not be ;
The debt is paid, for he who doth resign
        Thanks to the generous Vine,
Invites fresh grapes to fill his press with wine.

WHAT LOVE IS.

Love is a circle, that doth restless move
In the same sweet eternity of Love.

UPON PREW HIS MAID.

In this little urn is laid
Prewdence Baldwin, once my maid,
From whose happy spark here let
Spring the purple violet.

THE WHITE ISLAND.

In this world, the Isle of Dreams,
While we sit by sorrow's streams,
Tears and terrors are our themes,
        Reciting :

But when once from hence we fly,
More and more approaching nigh
Unto young eternity,
        Uniting

In that whiter Island, where
Things are evermore sincere ;
Candour here, and lustre there,
        Delighting :—

There no monstrous fancies shall
Out of hell an horror call,
To create, or cause at all
        Affrighting.

There, in calm and cooling sleep,
We our eyes shall never steep,
But eternal watch shall keep,
          Attending

Pleasures such as shall pursue
Me immortalized, and you ;
And fresh joys, as never too
          Have ending.

MUSIC.

Charm me asleep, and melt me so
    With thy delicious numbers,
That being ravish'd, hence I go
    Away in easy slumbers.
        Ease my sick head,
        And make my bed,
    Thou Power that canst sever
        From me this ill ;—
        And quickly still,
        Though thou not kill
          My fever.

Thou sweetly canst convert the same
    From a consuming fire,
Into a gentle-licking flame,
    And make it thus expire.
        Then make me weep
        My pains asleep,
    And give me such reposes,
        That I, poor I,
        May think, thereby,
        I live and die
          'Mongst roses.

Fall on me like a silent dew,
    Or like those maiden showers,
Which, by the peep of day, do strew
    A baptism o'er the flowers.

Melt, melt my pains
With thy soft strains ;
That having ease me given,
With full delight,
I leave this light,
And take my flight
For Heaven.

OBERON'S FEAST.

Shapcot ! to thee the Fairy State
I with discretion dedicate :
Because thou prizest things that are
Curious and unfamiliar,
Take first the feast ; these dishes gone,
We'll see the Fairy-court anon.

A little mushroom-table spread,
After short prayers, they set on bread,
A moon-parch'd grain of purest wheat,
With some small glitt'ring grit, to eat
His choice bits with ; then in a trice
They make a feast less great than nice.
But all this while his eye is served,
We must not think his ear was sterved ;
But that there was in place to stir
His spleen, the chirring grasshopper,
The merry cricket, puling fly,
The piping gnat for minstrelsy.
And now, we must imagine first,
The elves present, to quench his thirst,
A pure seed-pearl of infant dew,
Brought and besweeten'd in a blue
And pregnant violet ; which done,
His kitling eyes begin to run
Quite through the table, where he spies
The horns of papery butterflies,
Of which he eats ; and tastes a little
Of that we call the cuckoo's spittle ;

A little fuz-ball pudding stands
By, yet not blessèd by his hands,
That was too coarse ; but then forthwith
He ventures boldly on the pith
Of sugar'd rush, and eats the sagge
And well-bestrutted bees' sweet bag ;
Gladding his palate with some store
Of emmet's eggs ; what would he more ?
But beards of mice, a newt's stew'd thigh,
A bloated earwig, and a fly;
With the red-capt worm, that 's shut
Within the concave of a nut,
Brown as his tooth. A little moth,
Late fatten'd in a piece of cloth ;
With wither'd cherries, mandrakes' ears,
Moles' eyes : to these the slain stag's tears ;
The unctuous dew-laps of a snail,
The broke-heart of a nightingale
O'ercome in music ; with a wine
Ne'er ravish'd from the flattering vine,
But gently prest from the soft side
Of the most sweet and dainty bride,
Brought in a dainty daisy, which
He fully quaffs up, to bewitch
His blood to height ; this done, commended
Grace by his priest ; The feast is ended.

To Phillis.

Live, live with me, and thou shalt see
The pleasures I'll prepare for thee :
What sweets the country can afford
Shall bless thy bed, and bless thy board.
The soft sweet moss shall be thy bed,
With crawling woodbine over-spread :
By which the silver-shedding streams
Shall gently melt thee into dreams.
Thy clothing next, shall be a gown
Made of the fleeces' purest down.

The tongues of kids shall be thy meat ;
Their milk thy drink ; and thou shalt eat
The paste of filberts for thy bread
With cream of cowslips butterèd :
Thy feasting-table shall be hills
With daisies spread, and daffadils ;
Where thou shalt sit, and Red-breast by,
For meat, shall give thee melody.
I 'll give thee chains and carcanets
Of primroses and violets.
A bag and bottle thou shalt have,
That richly wrought, and this as brave ;
So that as either shall express
The wearer's no mean shepherdess.
At shearing-times, and yearly wakes,
When Themilis his pastime makes,
There thou shalt be ; and be the wit,
Nay more, the feast, and grace of it.
On holydays, when virgins meet
To dance the heys with nimble feet,
Thou shalt come forth, and then appear
The Queen of Roses for that year.
And having danced ('bove all the best)
Carry the garland from the rest,
In wicker-baskets maids shall bring
To thee, my dearest shepherdling,
The blushing apple, bashful pear,
And shame-faced plum, all simp'ring there.
Walk in the groves, and thou shalt find
The name of Phillis in the rind
Of every straight and smooth-skin tree ;
Where kissing that, I'll twice kiss thee.
To thee a sheep-hook I will send,
Be-prank'd with ribbands, to this end,
This, this alluring hook might be
Less for to catch a sheep, than me.
Thou shalt have possets, wassails fine,
Not made of ale, but spicèd wine ;
To make thy maids and self free mirth,

All sitting near the glitt'ring hearth.
Thou shalt have ribbands, roses, rings,
Gloves, garters, stockings, shoes, and strings
Of winning colours, that shall move
Others to lust, but me to love.
—These, nay, and more, thine own shall be,
If thou wilt love, and live with me.

WILLIAM HABINGTON.

[WILLIAM HABINGTON was born at Hindlip Hall, near Worcester, in 1605, and died 1654. His *Castara* alone preserves his name from oblivion, but he also wrote a tragi-comedy entitled *The Queene of Arragon*, acted in 1640, and completed a *History of Edward IV*, which had been set in hand by his father. The first edition of *Castara* was published in 1634, the second in 1635, and the third, enlarged and in the form in which we now possess the poems, in 1640. The poems have been reprinted by Chalmers in 1810, Gutch in 1812, Mr. Arber in 1870.]

The centre alike of Habington's life and of his poetry is the lady whom he has sung under the fanciful name of Castara. She was Lucy, daughter of William, Lord Powis, rather above her lover in rank and wealth, as his own verses plainly show, but, as is not less obvious, at no time indifferent to his courtship. What obstacles were interposed by her parents and relatives yielded to their mutual constancy, and Habington was allowed to carry off his bride to his country-house at Hindlip, in Worcestershire, a house which, as he tells her,

> 'doth not want extent
> Of roome, (though not magnificent)
> To give free welcome to content.'

There they seem to have lived a happy equable life together. Habington devotes as many of his poems to his wife, as to his mistress, and in them reaches a higher level of poetic accomplishment than he elsewhere attains. It is pleasant to contemplate the happy course of this pure and honourable affection, and it is impossible not to feel a kind of liking for so constant a wooer, so good a friend, and so upright a man. We must not complain if, like Evelyn, Habington seems to have gone through the Civil War without taking a decided part one way or the other. The man was no hero, nor born to shine in public life. What political sympathies his writings reveal were strongly Royalist ; he himself came of an old Catholic stock, and was educated at St. Omer ; and we may be sure that as far as he took any side at all, he took part against those whom he would regard as rebels and schismatics. Habington—as revealed to us by his own verses—was something of a dreamer, something of an ascetic, something even of a bigot. His was just the sort of life and character which could live through, as not of them, the din and turmoil and passion of those stirring years. He was not of those who are great among the sons of men ; nevertheless the interest that his work arouses is likely rather to increase than diminish, for though narrow in scope it is intense in feeling, and though in parts feeble and one-sided, it is as a whole made vital by the impress of a distinct and original personality.

It is not altogether easy to gather from Habington's poems in what relation he stood to previous or contemporary singers. The one indubitable fact is his devotion to Sidney, a sentiment he shares in common with all the poets of that time, on whom the Astrophel and Stella sonnets made the most marked impression. Of his few references to other poets the first occurs in a poetical account of his own youthful years, which he gives in *The Holy Man* :—

> 'Grown elder I admired
> Our poets, as from Heaven inspired ;
> What obelisks decreed I fit
> For Spenser's art and Sydney's wit !
> But waxing sober, soon I found
> Fame but an idle sound.'

Another mention of Sidney occurs in a sonnet commemorating Ovid's Corinna and Petrarch's Laura—

> 'while our famous Thames
> Doth whisper Sidney's Stella to her streams.'

There are also two passing mentions of Drayton and Spenser, and an interesting allusion to ' Chapman's reverend ashes ' lying ' rudely mingled in the vulgar dust.' There are no allusions to such poets as Herbert, whose genius was in some respects akin to his own, but this is easily explained by the difference between the two men's religious opinions.

Castara is divided into three, by some editors into four parts. There are at any rate four distinct themes—the Mistress, the Wife,

the Friend, and the Holy Man. It is by his love verses that
Habington is best known, though some of his most powerful and
deeply-felt work is to be found in the other sections. A feature
which strikes the reader of these verses is their almost exaggerated
purity of tone. Habington is never tired of assuring us of the
chastity of his affection, and the reader wearies of the monotony
of assertions which might very well be taken for granted. In one
passage he says scornfully of other poets—

> 'You who are earth and cannot rise
>   Above your sense,
> Boasting the envied wealth which lies
> Bright in your mistress' lips or eyes,
>   Betray a pitied eloquence.'

It is only fair however to say that, all deductions made, Habington's
love poems are often sweet and tunable enough, and show real
warmth of feeling and delicacy of sentiment. The verses on his
friend and kinsman Talbot, a nephew of the Earl of Shrewsbury,
who died young, also contain some fine passages ; but more charac-
teristic and less agreeable features of the writer's mind come out in
The Holy Man. There are some exceedingly powerful and sombre
verses in this collection, but the tone of them is more than Catholic ;
in parts is revealed an almost Calvinistic relentlessness of bigotry.
Habington speaks, as in duty bound, as a good Catholic, and
assumes that the Holy Man is necessarily of his own creed.
'Catholique faith is the foundation on which he erects religion ;
knowing it a ruinous madnesse to build in the ayre of a private
spirit or on the sands of any new schisme.' This is as it should
be ; one admires him for his sturdy maintenance of unpopular
opinions ; but it is not easy equally to sympathise with his de-
scription of his God, who 'without passion didst provide to punish
treason racks and death in hell,' and who

> 'when he as your judge appears
> In vain you'll tremble and lament,
> And hope to soften him with teares,
> To no advantage penitent.'

But gloomy as his theology may be, it is yet the natural outcome
of that intense and narrow spirit, and some of the lines in this
section have a searching penetrating power such as is not often
found in Herbert or other religious poets more widely famous.
Habington is terribly in earnest ; he has forgotten his love for his

mistress and his friend ; as he draws on in life the ascetic element which betrayed itself in him from the first, gains in strength, he throws this life scornfully behind him, and his thoughts fasten themselves more and more exclusively upon death and immortality.

From a purely literary point of view, Habington only rarely reaches high water mark in poetry. There are no glaring faults in his verse, and few conceits. The mass of his work is fluent, ingenious, tolerable poetry. It does not often attain to the inner music which can only proceed from a born singer, or to the flawless expression of a noble thought. Perfect literary tact Habington does not possess ; he will follow up a fine stanza with a lame and halting one, apparently without sense of the incongruity. It takes a strong *furor poeticus* to uplift him wholly, and keep him at a high level throughout an entire poem, however short. He excels greatly sometimes in single lines or couplets. He now and then surprises us with expressions like 'the weeping magic of my verse'; or so sonorous a line as

> 'and keep
> *Strayed honour in the true magnificke way*';

or a delicious commencement of a poem which falls off as it proceeds, such as

> 'Where sleepes the north wind when the south inspires
> Life in the spring, and gathers into quires
> The scattered nightingales';

or a strange and impressive thought like that comparison of virtue, which, lost to the world by his friend Talbot's death, only lives still in some solitary hermit's cell—

> ' So 'mid the ice of the far northern sea
> A star about the arctic circle may
> Than ours yield clearer light, yet that but shall
> Serve at the frozen pilot's funeral.'

It is quite consistent with this that the couplets which terminate a poem are with him sometimes extraordinarily vigorous and happy. In more than one case this final line or couplet constitutes the entire value of the poem. Take this, for instance :—

> ' And thus there will be left no bird to sing
> Farewell to the waters, welcome to the spring' ;

or this—

> ' All her vows religious be
> And her love she vows to me';

or this—

> 'But virtuous love is one sweet endless fire;'

or this—

> 'The bad man's death is horror; but the just
> Keeps something of his glory in his dust.'

But his inadequate sense of poetic form does not allow him often to attain to a perfect whole. He is too fond of awkward elisions, and endeavours to force more into a line than it will fairly hold. His sonnets, one or two of which rank among the best efforts, are formally speaking, not sonnets at all, but strings of seven rhyming couplets. He does not sufficiently know, he has not sufficiently laboured at, the technical business of his art. 'Quoi qu'on en puisse dire, la poésie est un art qui s'apprend, qui a ses méthodes, ses formules, ses arcanes, son contre point et son travail harmonique. L'inspiration doit trouver sous ses mains un clavier parfaitement juste, auquel ne manque aucune corde.' Habington is one of the many English poets whose imperfect realisation of this aspect of the truth has left their achievement inferior to their talent.

W. T. ARNOLD.

To Roses in the Bosom of Castara.

Ye blushing virgins happy are
In the chaste nunnery of her breasts,
For he'd profane so chaste a fair,
Who e'er should call them Cupid's nests.

Transplanted thus how bright ye grow,
How rich a perfume do ye yield?
In some close garden cowslips so
Are sweeter than i' th' open field.

In those white cloisters live secure
From the rude blasts of wanton breath,
Each hour more innocent and pure,
Till you shall wither into death.

Then that which living gave you room
Your glorious sepulchre shall be :
There wants no marble for a tomb,
Whose breast has marble been to me.

To Cupid, upon a Dimple in Castara's cheek.

Nimble boy, in thy warm flight
What cold tyrant dimmed thy sight?
Had'st thou eyes to see my fair,
Thou would'st sigh thyself to air,
Fearing, to create this one,
Nature had herself undone.
But if you, when this you hear,
Fall down murdered through your ear,
Beg of Jove that you may have
In her cheek a dimpled grave.
Lily, rose, and violet
Shall the perfumed hearse beset ;
While a beauteous sheet oᶠ lawn
O'er the wanton corpse is drawn :
And all lovers use this breath ;
        'Here lies Cupid blest in death.'

THE DESCRIPTION OF CASTARA.

Like the violet which alone
Prospers in some happy shade;
My Castara lives unknown,
To no looser eye betrayed,
    For she's to her self untrue,
    Who delights i' th' public view.

Such is her beauty as no arts
Have enriched with borrowed grace;
Her high birth no pride imparts,
For she blushes in her place.
    Folly boasts a glorious blood,
    She is noblest, being good.

Cautious, she knew never yet
What a wanton courtship meant;
Nor speaks loud to boast her wit,
In her silence eloquent:
    Of her self survey she takes
    But 'tween men no difference makes.

She obeys with speedy will
Her grave parents' wise commands;
And so innocent that ill
She nor acts nor understands;
    Women's feet run still astray
    If once to ill they know the way.

She sails by that rock, the court,
Where oft honour splits her mast:
And retiredness thinks the port,
Where her fame may anchor cast:
    Virtue safely cannot sit,
    Where vice is enthroned for wit.

She holds that day's pleasure best
Where sin waits not on delight;
Without mask, or ball, or feast,
Sweetly spends a winter's night:
    O'er that darkness, whence is thrust
    Prayer and sleep, oft governs lust.

She her throne makes reason climb,
While wild passions captive lie;
And each article of time
Her pure thoughts to Heaven fly:
    All her vows religious be,
    And her love she vows to me.

To Castara, in a Trance.

Forsake me not so soon; Castara, stay,
And as I break the prison of my clay
I 'll fill the canvas with my expiring breath,
And sail with thee o'er the vast main of Death.
Some cherubin thus, as we pass, shall play:
'Go, happy twins of love!'—the courteous sea
Shall smooth her wrinkled brow; the winds shall sleep,
Or only whisper music to the deep;
Every ungentle rock shall melt away,
The sirens sing to please, not to betray;
The indulgent sky shall smile; each starry quire
Contend, which shall afford the brighter fire.
    While Love, the pilot, steers his course so even
    Ne'er to cast anchor till we reach at Heaven.

To Castara, upon the Death of a Lady.

Castara weep not, tho' her tomb appear
Sometime thy grief to answer with a tear:
The marble will but wanton with thy woe.
Death is the sea, and we like rivers flow
To lose ourselves in the insatiate main,
Whence rivers may, she ne'er, return again.

Nor grieve this crystal stream so soon did fall
Into the ocean ; since she perfum'd all
The banks she past, so that each neighbour field
Did sweet flowers cherish'd by her watering yield,
Which now adorn her hearse. The violet there
On her pale cheek doth the sad livery wear,
Which Heaven's compassion gave her : and since she
'Cause clothed in purple, can no mourner be,
As incense to the tomb she gives her breath,
And fading on her lady waits in death :
Such office the Ægyptian handmaids did
Great Cleopatra, when she dying chid
The asp's slow venom, trembling she should be
By fate robb'd even of that black victory.
The flowers instruct our sorrows. Come, then, all
Ye beauties, to true beauty's funeral,
And with her to increase death's pomp, decay.
Since the supporting fabric of your clay
Is fallen, how can ye stand? How can the night
Show stars, when Fate puts out the day's great light?

AGAINST THEM WHO LAY UNCHASTITY TO THE SEX OF WOMEN.

They meet but with unwholesome springs,
    And summers which infectious are ;
They hear but when the mermaid sings,
    And only see the falling star,
            Who ever dare
    Affirm no woman chaste and fair.

Go, cure your fevers ; and you 'll say
    The dog-days scorch not all the year ;
In copper mines no longer stay,
    But travel to the west, and there
            The right ones see,
    And grant all gold's not alchemy.

What madman, 'cause the glow-worm's flame
    Is cold, swears there 's no warmth in fire?
'Cause some make forfeit of their name,
    And slave themselves to man's desire,
        Shall the sex, free
From guilt, damn'd to the bondage be?

Nor grieve, Castara, though t' were frail ;
    Thy virtue then would brighter shine,
When thy example should prevail,
    And every woman's faith be thine:
        And were there none,
'Tis majesty to rule alone.

To Castara. Of true delight.

Why doth the ear so tempt the voice
That cunningly divides the air?
Why doth the palate buy the choice
Delights o' th' sea, to enrich her fare?

As soon as I my ear obey,
The echo 's lost even with the breath ;
And when the sewer takes away,
I 'm left with no more taste than death.

Be curious in pursuit of eyes
To procreate new loves with thine ;
Satiety makes sense despise
What superstition thought divine.

Quick fancy ! how it mocks delight !
As we conceive, things are not such ;
The glowworm is as warm as bright,
Till the deceitful flame we touch.

When I have sold my heart to lust,
And bought repentance with a kiss ;
I find the malice of my dust,
That told me hell contained a bliss.

The rose yields her sweet blandishment
Lost in the fold of lovers' wreaths ;
The violet enchants the scent,
When early in the spring she breathes.

But winter comes, and makes each flower
Shrink from the pillow where it grows ;
Or an intruding cold hath power
To scorn the perfume of the rose.

Our senses, like false glasses, show
Smooth beauty, where brows wrinkled are,
And makes the cozen'd fancy glow ;
Chaste virtue's only true and fair.

NOX NOCTI INDICAT SCIENTIAM.

When I survey the bright
    Celestial sphere :
So rich with jewels hung, that night
Doth like an Ethiop bride appear :

My soul her wings doth spread
    And heaven-ward flies,
The Almighty's mysteries to read
In the large volumes of the skies.

For the bright firmament
    Shoots forth no flame
So silent, but is eloquent
In speaking the Creator's name.

No unregarded star
    Contracts its light,
Into so small a character,
Remov'd far from our human sight,

But if we steadfast look
    We shall discern
In it as in some holy book,
How man may heavenly knowledge learn.

It tells the conqueror,
    That far-stretched power,
Which his proud dangers traffic for,
Is but the triumph of an hour.

That from the farthest north
    Some nation may
Yet undiscovered issue forth,
And o'er his new got conquest sway.

Some nation yet shut in
    With hills of ice,
May be let out to scourge his sin,
Till they shall equal him in vice.

And then they likewise shall
    Their ruin have;
For as yourselves your empires fall,
And every kingdom hath a grave.

Thus those celestial fires,
    Though seeming mute,
The fallacy of our desires
And all the pride of life, confute.

For they have watched since first
    The world had birth:
And found sin in itself accursed,
And nothing permanent on earth.

SIR JOHN SUCKLING.

[Suckling was born at Twickenham in 1608-9, and committed suicide in Paris in 1642. He published during his life-time the drama of *Aglaura* in 1638 and the *Ballad of a Wedding* in 1640. His other works were first collected posthumously in 1648, under the title of *Fragmenta Aurea*.]

It is impossible to consider the poems of Suckling without regard to his career. No English poet has lived a life so public, so adventurous and so full of vicissitude as his. Nothing short of an irresistible bias towards the art of poetry could have induced so busy and so fortunate a man to write in verse at all. Beautiful and vigorous in body, educated in all the accomplishments that grace a gentleman, endowed from earliest youth with the prestige of a soldier and a popular courtier, his enormous wealth enabled him to indulge every whim that a fondness for what was splendid or eccentric in dress, architecture and pageantry could devise. Such a life could present no void which literary ambition could fill, and Suckling's scorn for poetic fame was well known to his contemporaries. At the age of nineteen he went away to the continent, and wandered through France, Italy, Germany and Spain for four years, seeking adventure. He offered his sword to the King of Sweden, fought in command of a troop in front of Glogau and of Magdeburg, performed astounding feats of prowess in Silesia, and returned before the battle of Lützen simply because his imperious fancy began to find the great war a tedious pastime. He proceeded to London, and lived for six years in a style of such gorgeous profusion that at last he contrived to cripple one of the amplest fortunes of that age. He retired for a while, ostentatiously enough, into a literary seclusion at Bath, taking the obsequious Davenant with him as a sort of amanuensis. During this brief time, no doubt, his tragedies were composed. The King, however, fretted for his return, and he emerged as the leader of the Royalist party in its earliest troubles. After the crisis, Suckling fled to France, and thence to Spain ; at Madrid he fell into the clutches of the Inquisition, and underwent horrible tortures. He escaped to Paris, with a mind probably unstrung by these torments, for he poisoned himself in his thirty-fourth year. Such was the career of a man whose light verses, carelessly thrown off and half forgotten, have outlived the pomp and public glitter of his famous adventures, by which he now seems to us rather dwarfed and injured than exalted.

Written under such circumstances, and preserved in a fragment-ary state by friends, it would be surprising if the poems of Suckling presented any great finish or completeness. In point of fact, they display to us but the ruins of his genius. A ballad of wonderful brightness and sweetness, half-a-dozen songs full of the most aery and courtly grace, these alone of all he has left behind him are in any sense worthy of their author's splendid fame. His contem-poraries, and the men of the next generation, remembering his shining qualities of personal presence, his wit, his fluent fancy and, perhaps, many fine poems that we shall never see, spoke of him as an epoch making writer, in terms that we reserve for Herrick, of whom they never speak. His name still lives in the popular ear, as the names of poets far greater than he will never live. His figure takes a place in poetic literature which the student fresh from his pages is apt to consider unduly high, and which his 'golden fragments' scarcely seem to justify. But the instinct of the people, in this as in so many other cases, is probably right, and though the imperfections of his poems may cloud it, there is no doubt that his genius existed. It shows itself even more in his disciples than in himself ; his manner of writing affected the course of English literature, and showed its strength less in his own lyrics, than in the fact that for the next fifty years no one could write a good love-song without more or less reminding the reader of Suckling. To the very end of the century 'natural, easy Suckling' was the type of literary elegance to the Millamants and Lady Froths of fashion.

His existing works consist of a slender collection of lyrical and complimentary poems, and of four plays, one of them incomplete. Suckling, who had a creditable adoration for Shakespeare, in-herited none of his dramatic genius. A worse playwright is scarcely to be found, even in that miserable period, among the Gomersalls,

Lowers, and Killigrews. *Aglaura*, a monster of tedious pageantry, was arranged with a tragic and a comic ending, according to choice : but this was not so unique as has been supposed, for we find the same silly contrivance in Howard's *Vestal Virgin* and in the *Pandora* of Sir William Killigrew.

The only drama of Suckling's which is at all readable is *Brenno-ralt,* which is incoherent enough, but does contain some fine tragic writing. The only real merit of these plays however consists in the beautiful songs they harbour.

The lyrical pieces of Suckling's which were collected under the title of *Fragmenta Aurea* present considerable difficulty to the critic. Never was a volume of poems so unequal in merit presented to the public. Side by side with songs that will be enjoyed as long as the English language exists, we find stanzas which it is impossible either to scan or to construe, and which would disgrace the Poet's Corner of a provincial newspaper. The famous *Session of the Poets*, one of those pieces which were most admired in the age that saw its production, is full of laxities of style that fairly astonish the modern reader. Such a stanza, for instance, as that dedicated to Jonson, limps and waddles along with a strangely gouty gait :—

> ' The first that broke silence was good old Ben,
> Prepared before with Canary wine,
> And he told them plainly he deserved the bays,
> For his were called works, while others were but plays.'

In the case of other poems, in which we find awkward and confused passages, we may suppose that Suckling left the verse confused or incomplete, and that the text suffers from inartistic revision, but *The Session of the Poets* is one of the few pieces published in his life-time, and we are therefore inclined to suppose that he was but little affected by errors of style that are palpable to us. When, however, he is at his best, he throws off all awkwardness and obscurity ; his versification becomes liquid and nimble, and in one instance, the famous *Ballad upon a Wedding*, he has contrived to keep up his tone of airy vivacity through twenty-two incomparable verses. But as a rule his lyric flights are brief. His songs owe their special charm to their gallantry and impudence, their manly ardour and their frivolous audacity. The temper expressed in ' Why so pale and wan, fond lover ?' was in sympathy with the age, and gave a delight which seems to us extravagant ; Suckling's admiration for Shakespeare not preventing him from being one of the chief heralds of the poetry of the Restoration. He sings like a royalist gentleman ; he leaves the weaving of conceits to learned contemporaries, such as Cowley and Lovelace ; he inaugurates a simpler, most straightforward expression of inflamed fancy and amorous discontent. This is in his songs only ; in his moral pieces, such as that beginning

> 'My dearest rival, lest our love
> Should with eccentric motion move,'

he is as quaint and conceited, if not so ingenious, as the best of the poets once called Metaphysical. His great praise is his manliness : after all the rhymesters who for a century had been sonneting their mistress' eyebrow, and avowing the most abject deference, the attitude of Suckling strutting with his impudent smiling face through the galaxy of ladies, struck the contemporary mind as refreshing, and a new fashion in gallantry set in. What had been good sense in Suckling, soon however became effrontery in Sedley, and cynicism in Congreve, and the base sensual feast to which the poets of the Restoration sat down we feel to have been a sorry exchange for the Arcadian diet of the Elizabethans. Even here also there was some brisk music of a gallantry not wholly base, and for this we have to thank Suckling and his sprightly mood.

EDMUND W. GOSSE.

A Ballad upon a Wedding [1].

I tell thee, Dick, where I have been,
Where I the rarest things have seen;
   O, things without compare!
Such sights again cannot be found
In any place on English ground,
   Be it at wake or fair.

At Charing-Cross, hard by the way,
Where we (thou know'st) do sell our hay,
   There is a house with stairs;
And there did I see coming down
Such folk as are not in our town,
   Forty at least, in pairs.

Amongst the rest, one pest'lent fine
(His beard no bigger though than thine)
   Walked on before the rest:
Our landlord looks like nothing to him:
The King (God bless him) 'twould undo him,
   Should he go still so drest.

At Course-a-Park, without all doubt,
He should have first been taken out
   By all the maids i'th' town:
Though lusty Roger there had been,
Or little George upon the Green,
   Or Vincent of the Crown.

But wot you what? the youth was going
To make an end of all his wooing;
   The parson for him stay'd:
Yet by his leave (for all his haste)
He did not so much wish all past
   (Perchance), as did the maid.

[1] The wedding was that of Roger Boyle, Lord Broghill (afterwards Earl of Orrery), with Lady Margaret Howard. Mr. Hazlitt thinks that the Ballad is addressed to Lovelace.

The maid (and thereby hangs a tale),
For such a maid no Whitsun-ale
    Could ever yet produce :
No grape, that 's kindly ripe, could be
So round, so plump, so soft as she,
    Nor half so full of juice.

Her finger was so small, the ring,
Would not stay on, which they did bring,
    It was too wide a peck :
And to say truth (for out it must)
It looked like the great collar (just)
    About our young colt's neck.

Her feet beneath her petticoat,
Like little mice, stole in and out,
    As if they fear'd the light :
But O she dances such a way !
No sun upon an Easter-day
    Is half so fine a sight.

Her cheeks so rare a white was on,
No daisy makes comparison,
    (Who sees them is undone),
For streaks of red were mingled there
Such as are on a Catherine pear
    The side that 's next the sun.

Her lips were red, and one was thin,
Compar'd to that was next her chin
    (Some bee had stung it newly) ;
But, Dick, her eyes so guard her face ;
I durst no more upon them gaze
    Than on the sun in July.

Her mouth so small, when she does speak,
Thou 'dst swear her teeth her words did break,
    That they might passage get ;
But she so handled still the matter,
They came as good as ours, or better,
    And are not spent a whit.

Just in the nick the cook knocked thrice,
And all the waiters in a trice
    His summons did obey;
Each serving-man, with dish in hand,
Marched boldly up, like our trained band,
    Presented, and away.

When all the meat was on the table,
What man of knife or teeth was able
    To stay to be intreated?
And this the very reason was,
Before the parson could say grace,
    The company was seated.

The business of the kitchen 's great,
For it is fit that men should eat ;
    Nor was it there denied :
Passion o' me, how I run on !
There 's that that would be thought upon
    (I trow) besides the bride.

Now hats fly off, and youths carouse ;
Healths first go round, and then the house,
    The bride's came thick and thick :
And when 'twas nam'd another's health,
Perhaps he made it hers by stealth ;
    And who could help it, Dick ?

On the sudden up they rise and dance ;
Then sit again and sigh, and glance :
    Then dance again and kiss :
Thus several ways the time did pass,
Whilst ev'ry woman wished her place,
    And every man wished his.

Truth in Love.

Of thee, kind boy, I ask no red and white,
      To make up my delight:
       No odd becoming graces,
Black eyes, or little know-not-whats in faces;
Make me but mad enough, give me good store
Of love for her I court:
       I ask no more,
'Tis love in love that makes the sport.

There's no such thing as that we beauty call,
      It is mere cosenage all;
       For though some long ago
Liked certain colours mingled so and so,
That doth not tie me now from choosing new;
If I a fancy take
       To black and blue,
That fancy doth it beauty make.

'Tis not the meat, but 'tis the appetite
      Makes eating a delight,
       And if I like one dish
More than another, that a pheasant is;
What in our watches, that in us is found,—
So to the height and nick
       We up be wound,
No matter by what hand or trick.

The Dance.

Love, Reason, Hate, did once bespeak
Three mates to play at barley-break;
Love Folly took; and Reason, Fancy;
And Hate consorts with Pride; so dance they.
Love coupled last, and so it fell,
That Love and Folly were in hell.

They break, and Love would Reason meet,
But Hate was nimbler on her feet;
Fancy looks for Pride, and thither
Hies, and they two hug together:
Yet this new coupling still doth tell,
That Love and Folly were in hell.

The rest do break again, and Pride
Hath now got Reason on her side;
Hate and Fancy meet, and stand
Untouched by Love in Folly's hand;
Folly was dull, but Love ran well;
So Love and Folly were in hell.

ORSAMES' SONG IN 'AGLAURA.'

Why so pale and wan, fond lover?
  Prithee, why so pale?
Will, when looking well can't move her,
  Looking ill prevail?
  Prithee, why so pale?

Why so dull and mute, young sinner?
  Prithee, why so mute?
Will, when speaking well can't win her,
  Saying nothing do 't?
  Prithee, why so mute?

Quit, quit, for shame, this will not move:
  This cannot take her.
If of herself she will not love,
  Nothing can make her:
  The devil take her!

Song.

I prithee send me back my heart,
  Since I cannot have thine :
For if from yours you will not part,
  Why then shouldst thou have mine?

Yet now I think on 't, let it lie,
  To find it were in vain,
For th' hast a thief in either eye
  Would steal it back again.

Why should two hearts in one breast lie
  And yet not lodge together?
O love, where is thy sympathy,
  If thus our breasts thou sever?

But love is such a mystery,
  I cannot find it out :
For when I think I 'm best resolv'd,
  I then am in most doubt.

Then farewell care, and farewell woe,
  I will no longer pine :
For I 'll believe I have her heart,
  As much as she hath mine.

The Lute Song in 'The Sad One.'

Hast thou seen the down in the air,
    When wanton blasts have tossed it?
Or the ship on the sea,
    When ruder winds have crossed it?
Hast thou marked the crocodile's weeping,
    Or the fox's sleeping?
Or hast viewed the peacock in his pride,
    Or the dove by his bride,
    When he courts for his lechery?
O, so fickle, O, so vain, O, so false, so false is she!

N 2

CONSTANCY.

Out upon it, I have loved
　　Three whole days together ;
And am like to love three more,
　　If it prove fair weather.

Time shall moult away his wings,
　　Ere he shall discover
In the whole wide world again
　　Such a constant lover.

But the spite on 't is, no praise
　　Is due at all to me :
Love with me had made no stays,
　　Had it any been but she.

Had it any been but she,
　　And that very face,
There had been at least ere this
　　A dozen dozen in her place.

RICHARD LOVELACE.

[RICHARD LOVELACE was born at Woolwich in 1618; he died in Gun-powder Alley, near Shoe Lane, London, in April 1658. His *Lucas'a* was published in 1649 and his *Posthume Poems* in 1659. He was the author of *The Scholar*, a comedy, written in 1634, and of *The Soldier*, a tragedy, written in 1640, but these dramas are lost.]

It may safely be said that of all the Royalist lyrists Lovelace has been overestimated the most, as Carew has been the most neglected. The reason of this is not hard to find. Carew was a poet of great art and study, whose pieces reach a high but com-paratively uniform standard, while Lovelace was an improvisatore who wrote two of the best songs in the language by accident, and whose other work is of much inferior quality. A more slovenly poet than Lovelace it would be difficult to find; his verses have reached us in the condition of unrevised proofs sent out by a careless compositor; but it is plain that not to the printer only is due the lax and irregular form of the poems. It did not always occur to Lovelace to find a rhyme, or to persist in a measure, and his ear seems to have been singularly defective. To these technical faults he added a radical tastelessness of fancy, and an excess of the tendency of all his contemporaries to dwell on the surroundings of a subject rather than on the subject itself. His verses on 'Ellinda's Glove' must have been remarkable even in an age of *concetti*. The poet commences by calling the glove a snowy farm with five tenements; he has visited there to pay his daily rents to the white mistress of the farm, who has gone into the meadows to gather flowers and hearts. He then changes his image, and calls the glove an ermine cabinet, whose alabaster lady will soon come home, since any other tenant would eject himself, by finding the rooms too narrow to contain him. The poet, therefore, leaves his rent, five kisses, at the door, observing, with another change of figure, that though the lute is too high for him, yet, like a servant, he is allowed to fiddle with the case. Such trivialities as these were brought into fashion by the wayward genius of Donne, and continued in vogue long enough to betray the youth of Dryden. In Lovelace we find the fashion in its most insipid extravagance.

Yet there are high qualities in the verses of Lovelace, though he rarely allows us to see them unalloyed. His language has an heroic ring about it ; he employs fine epithets and gallant phrases, two at least of which have secured the popular ear, and become part of our common speech. 'Going to the Wars,' his best poem, contains no line or part of a line that could by any possibility be improved[1]; 'To Althea' is less perfect, but belongs to a higher order of poetry. The first and fourth stanzas of this exquisite lyric would do honour to the most illustrious name, and form one of the treasures of our literature. It is surprising that a poet so obscure could for once be so crystalline, and that the weaver of gossamer conceits could contrive to be so tenderly sincere. The romantic circumstances under which Lovelace wrote these lines have given to them a popular charm. The imprisonment under which he was suffering was brought upon him in the unselfish performance of duty. He had been chosen by the whole body of the county of Kent to deliver the Kentish petition to the House of Commons ; the result was, doubtless, what he expected, the petition being burned by the Common Hangman, and he himself, on the 30th of April, 1642, thrown into the Gatehouse Prison.

The romantic career of Lovelace must be taken into consideration when we blame the defects of his poems. He was born to wealth and station, he was generously educated, and he became a favourite with the royal family while he was but a youth. During the brief period of his prosperity he lived the life of a spoiled child. He was the handsomest man of his generation, he was addressed under the name of Adonis, and he spent his time in reading Greek poetry, in playing and singing, and in feats of arms. His manners were, we are told 'incomparably graceful.' Yet, born into that iron age, his career closed in the most tragic way. It being reported that he was killed, his betrothed married another man ; and after wasting all his substance in the recklessness of despair, this darling of the Graces died in extreme want, and in a cellar. A life of only

---

[1] It is curious, however, that the beautiful figure of the first stanza is to be found in Habington's, 'To Roses in the bosom of Castara.' See p. 163.

forty years spent in such vicissitudes gave little opportunity for that retirement from the world which scholarship and art require. His hasty verses were thrown off at a heat, and the genius in them is often rather a spark than a steady flame. In the curious verses entitled *The Grasshopper*, of which we shall presently quote all that is intelligible, we seem to possess an instance of his hurried and jejune mode of composition. He commences by addressing the grasshopper, in lines of unusual dignity and pregnancy, but he presently forgets this, and, without any sign of transition, recommences 'Thou best of men and friends,' this time plainly addressing the friend, Charles Cotton, to whom the ode was sent. It is difficult to believe that he ever himself read over his lines, for it could not fail to occur to him, had he done so, that the same object could not be spoken to as ' Poor verdant fool ' and as ' Thou best of men and friends.' But when we consider with what nonchalance the lyrical poets of the seventeenth century composed and then neglected their effusions, the surprising thing is not that these have reached us in so inaccurate and fragmentary a form, but that they have reached us at all.

EDMUND W. GOSSE.

GOING TO THE WARS.

Tell me not, sweet, I am unkind,
  That from the nunnery
Of thy chaste breast and quiet mind
  To war and arms I fly.

True, a new mistress now I chase,
  The first foe in the field,
And with a stronger faith embrace
  A sword, a horse, a shield.

Yet this inconstancy is such
  As you too shall adore,—
I could not love thee, dear, so much,
  Loved I not honour more.

THE ROSE.

Sweet, serene, sky-like flower,
Haste to adorn her bower,
    From thy long cloudy bed
    Shoot forth thy damask head.

New-startled blush of Flora,
The grief of pale Aurora
    (Who will contest no more),
    Haste, haste to strew her floor!

Vermilion ball that's given
From lip to lip in heaven,
    Love's couch's coverled,
    Haste, haste to make her bed.

Dear offspring of pleased Venus
And jolly plump Silenus,
    Haste, haste to deck the hair
    O' the only sweetly fair!

See! rosy is her bower,
Her floor is all this flower,
    Her bed a rosy nest
    By a bed of roses pressed!

To Althea from Prison.

When love with unconfined wings
  Hovers within my gates,
And my divine Althea brings
  To whisper at the grates;
When I lie tangled in her hair,
  And fettered to her eye,
The birds that wanton in the air
  Know no such liberty.

When flowing cups run swiftly round
  With no allaying Thames,
Our careless heads with roses bound,
  Our hearts with loyal flames;
When thirsty grief in wine we steep,
  When healths and draughts go free,
Fishes that tipple in the deep
  Know no such liberty.

When, like committed linnets, I
  With shriller throat shall sing
The sweetness, mercy, majesty,
  And glories of my King;
When I shall voice aloud, how good
  He is, how great should be,
Enlarged winds that curl the flood
  Know no such liberty.

Stone walls do not a prison make,
  Nor iron bars a cage;
Minds innocent and quiet take
  That for an hermitage;
If I have freedom in my love,
  And in my soul am free,
Angels alone, that soar above,
  Enjoy such liberty.

The Grasshopper.

[Ode: to Mr. Charles Cotton.]

Oh ! thou that swingst upon the waving ear
    Of some well-fillèd oaten beard,
Drunk every night with a delicious tear,
    Dropt thee from heaven, where thou wert reared ;

The joys of earth and air are thine entire,
    That with thy feet and wings dost hop and fly,
And, when thy poppy works, thou dost retire
    To thy carved acorn-bed to lie.

Up with the day, the Sun thou welcomest then,
    Sport'st in the gilt plaits of his beams,
And all these merry days mak'st merry men,
    Thyself, and melancholy streams.

But ah ! the sickle ! Golden ears are cropped ;
    Ceres and Bacchus bid good night ;
Sharp frosty fingers all your flowers have topped,
    And what scythes spared, winds shave off quite.

Thou best of men and friends ! we will create
    A genuine summer in each other's breast,
And spite of this cold time and frozen fate,
    Thaw us a warm seat for our rest.

Our sacred hearths shall burn eternally,
    As vestal flames ; the North Wind, he
Shall strike his frost-stretched wings, dissolve and fly
    This Ætna in epitome.

Night, as clear Hesper, shall our tapers whip
    From the light casements where we play,
And the dark hag from her black mantle strip,
    And stick there everlasting day.

Thus richer than untempted kings are we,
    That asking nothing, nothing need ;
Though lord of all that seas embrace, yet he
    That wants himself is poor indeed.

To Lucasta.

Lucasta, frown, and let me die !
 But smile, and, see, I live !
The sad indifference of your eye
 Both kills and doth reprieve ;
You hide our fate within its screen ;
 We feel our judgment, e'er we hear ;
So in one picture I have seen
 An angel here, the devil there !

LORD HERBERT

OF CHERBURY.

[EDWARD HERBERT, Lord Herbert of Cherbury, elder brother of the poet
George Herbert, was born in 1581, and closed a life full of incident and
interest in Queen Street, London, August 20, 1648.]

The world has long done justice to Lord Herbert's famous
treatise *De Veritate*, to his admirable *Life of Henry VIII*, to his
singularly interesting Autobiography; but no one has yet been
found to vindicate his claim to a place among English poets. His
poems first appeared in a little volume which was published in
1665, nearly eighteen years after his death; and, as we gather
from the preface, were collected by Henry Herbert, uncle to the
second Lord Herbert of Cherbury, to whom they are dedicated.
They consist of Sonnets, Epitaphs, Satires, Madrigals, and Odes
in various measures. Herbert is, like his more distinguished
brother, a disciple of the Metaphysical School, though his poems,
unlike those of George, are not of a religious character. With
much of that extravagance which deforms the lyric poetry of his
contemporaries, Lord Herbert has in a large measure grace,
sweetness, and originality. He never lacks vigour and freshness.
His place is, with all his faults, beside Donne and Cowley. His
versification is indeed as a rule far superior to theirs. It is uni-
formly musical, and his music is often at once delicate and subtle.
Though he did not invent the metre, he certainly discovered the
melody of that stanza with which Tennyson's great poem has
familiarised us, and he has as certainly anticipated some of its
most beautiful effects. He is never likely to hold the same place
among English poets as his brother, but we do not hesitate to say
that no collection of representative English poets should be con-
sidered complete which does not contain the poetical works of
Lord Herbert of Cherbury.

J. CHURTON COLLINS.

AN ODE UPON A QUESTION MOVED WHETHER LOVE SHOULD CONTINUE FOR EVER.

Having interr'd her Infant-birth
  The watery ground that late did mourn
  Was strew'd with flowers for the return
Of the wish'd bridegroom of the earth.

The well-accorded birds did sing
  Their hymns unto the pleasant time,
  And in a sweet consorted chime
Did welcome in the cheerful spring.

To which, soft whistles of the wind,
  And warbling murmurs of a brook,
  And varied notes of leaves that shook,
An harmony of parts did bind.

When with a love none can express
  That mutually happy pair,
  Melander and Celinda fair,
The season with their loves did bless.

Long their fix'd eyes to Heaven bent
  Unchanged, they did never move ;
  As if so great and pure a love
No glass but it could represent.

When with a sweet though troubled look
  She first brake silence, saying, 'Dear friend,
  O that our love might take no end,
Or never had beginning took.'

    *   *   *   *   *

Then with a look, it seem'd, denied
  All earthly power but hers, yet so
  As if to her breath he did owe
This borrow'd life, he thus replied :

'O no, Belov'd, I am most sure
    These vertuous habits we acquire
    As being with the soul entire
Must with it evermore endure.

Else should our souls in vain elect,
    And vainer yet were Heaven's laws,
    When to an everlasting cause
They give a perishing effect.

Nor here on earth then, nor above,
    One good affection can impair;
    For where God doth admit the fair,
Think you that He excludeth Love?

These eyes again thine eyes shall see,
    These hands again thine hand enfold,
    And all chaste blessings can be told
Shall with us everlasting be.

For if no use of sense remain
    When bodies once this life forsake,
    Or they could no delight partake,
Why should they ever rise again?

And if every imperfect mind
    Make love the end of knowledge here,
    How perfect will our love be where
All imperfection is refin'd.

Let then no doubt, Celinda, touch,
    Much less your fairest mind invade;
    Were not our souls immortal made,
Our equal loves can make them such.

So when from hence we shall be gone,
    And be no more, nor you, nor I;
    As one another's mystery
Each shall be both, yet both but one.

Upon Combing her Hair.

Breaking from under that thy cloudy veil,
  Open and shine yet more, shine out more clear,
  Thou glorious, golden beam of darling hair,
Even till my wonder-stricken senses fail.

Shine out in light, and shine those rays on far,
  Thou much more fair than is the Queen of Love
  When she doth comb her on her sphere above,
And from a planet turns a blazing star.

Nay, thou art greater too, more destiny
  Depends on thee, than on her influence;
  No hair thy fatal hand doth now dispense
But to some one a thread of life must be.

While gracious unto me, thou both dost sunder
  Those glories which, if they united were,
  Might have amazed sense, and shew'st each hair
Which if alone had been too great a wonder.

But stay, methinks new beauties do arise
  While she withdraws these glories which were spread;
  Wonder of beauties, set thy radiant head,
And strike out day from thy yet fairer eyes.

SANDYS, HERBERT, CRASHAW, VAUGHAN.

[GEORGE SANDYS, son of Archbishop Sandys, was born 1577, and died 1643. Set out for the East 1616. Published translation of Ovid 1626; the Psalms 1636 ; other paraphrases 1638 and 1641.]

[GEORGE HERBERT, born 1592-3, died 1634. He was Public Orator at Cambridge from 1619 to 1627, and was Rector of Bemerton in Wiltshire in 1631. His poems were first published 1633.]

[RICHARD CRASHAW, born 1615 (?); expelled from Cambridge 1644; became a Roman Catholic. Published *Steps to the Altar* 1646, and died canon of Loretto 1650.]

[HENRY VAUGHAN, born 1621-2, died 1695. Published *Secular Poems* 1646; *Olor Iscanus* 1651; *Silex Scintillans*, part 1, 1650, part 2, 1656; *Thalia Rediviva* 1678.]

Poets are never independent of circumstances : Sandys, the only one of the four whose names stand at the head of this section who escaped the epidemic of conceits which ran its course in the first half of the seventeenth century, was the only one who had a full and successful life. He too was the only one who could write smooth, clear and vigorous verse, an accomplishment which requires perfect self-possession, or overmastering inspiration, or good models. Sandys wrote before Waller and Denham as well as the average versifiers who came after Dryden. His classical translations are not equal to his scriptural paraphrases, and if he had finished the Æneid Dryden would have left it alone. Like Dryden he did his best work late : he was fifty-nine when he published the Psalms. It does not do to compare Sandys with the authorised version of the Bible. Wherever the original is peculiarly striking he is disappointing : he gives his reader no such compensation for his temerity as Sternhold's version of the Theophany in the 18th Psalm or the close of the 24th, or as Watts's equally well-known paraphrase of the 90th. Even Tate and Brady at their best, as in the 139th Psalm, come very near to Sandys' highest level ; but he is much more equable ; he never subsides, like Sternhold and Hopkins, into doggerel ; he never subsides, like Tate and Brady, into diffuse platitudes. He always grasps the meaning for himself ; he seems to work, if not always from the Hebrew, from an ancient version, and he sometimes exhibits a really masterly power of condensation, as in the 119th and the 150th Psalms. Apart from the strictly relative praise due to the versification, the paraphrase on Job is appal- lingly tame.

The sacred poetry of Sandys was the dignified amusement of the evening of a successful life, whose morn had been spent in eastern travel and in colonial enterprise, without a trace of the internal struggles which form the staple of the poetry of Herbert. *The Temple* is the enigmatical history of a difficult resignation ; it is full of the author's baffled ambition and his distress, now at the want of a sphere for his energies, now at the fluctuations of spirit, the ebb and flow of intellectual activity, natural to a temper- ament as frail as it was eager. There is something a little feverish and disproportioned in his passionate heart-searchings. The facts of the case lie in a nutshell. Herbert was a younger son of a large family ; he lost his father early, and his mother, a devout, tender, imperious woman, decided, partly out of piety and partly out of distrust of his power to make his own way in the world, that he should be provided for in the Church. When he was twenty-six he was appointed Public Orator at Cambridge, and hoped to make this position a stepping-stone to employment at court. After eight years his patrons and his mother were dead, and he made up his mind to settle down with a wife on the living of Bemerton, where he died after a short but memorable incumbency of three years. The flower of his poetry seems to belong to the two years of acute crisis which preceded his installation at Bemerton or to the Indian summer of content when he imagined that his failure as a courtier was a prelude to his success in the higher character of a country parson. The well-known poem on Sunday, which he sang to his lute so near the end, and the quaint poem on the ideal priest, which we extract, may date from Bemerton. The Quip and The Collar may date from the years of crisis. Still, much, like the poems on

Employment, of which we insert a specimen, dates from the years of hopeful ambition. There are no traces of consecration or defeat in the *Church Porch*, where Herbert, like a precocious Polonius, frames a rule of life for himself and other pious courtiers. Herbert, who had thought much of national destiny, and decided that religion and true prosperity were to take flight for America, considered that England was 'full of sin, but most of sloth.'

The plain truth is, that after the defeat of the Spanish Armada, the submission of the chieftains of Ulster, and the tardy pacification of the Netherlands, the English gentry were for the first time since the Field of the Cloth of Gold without a rational object of public concern. Poets were left for the first time to feed idly on their own fancies and feelings : that all kinds of enterprise were feasible, as Herbert repeatedly urged, was of little avail in the absence of motive power. The excitement without impulse which characterises Herbert is the explanation of the old criticism that he has 'enthusiasm without sublimity.' He was, it may be, too fastidious to have succeeded in the best of times. The ascetic temper shows early—

> 'Look on meat, think it dirt, then eat a bit,
> And say withal—"earth to earth I commit";

and more pleasantly—

> 'Welcome dear feast of Lent. Who loves not thee
> He loves not temperance or authority.
>
> . . . . . .
>
> Beside the cleanness of sweet abstinence
> Quick thoughts and motions at a small expense,
> A face not fearing light.'

He thinks thrift and cleanness go well together, and likes strictness and method for their own sake. The worldling's false pride in licence offends him from the first. There is more self-complacency than penitence in a poem like *The Size*. From the first he is preoccupied with the thought of death, and hungers for eternity. Only at first the feeling is that he holds of God for two lives, and hopes to make improvement in both : it is affliction that convinces him that he must sacrifice everything in the present life. To the last his piety lacks wings : he is always tormenting himself that he does not love as he should ; his fastidious imagination cannot stop short of the highest good, and then he finds that the imagination cannot carry the affections with it in its flight. He tries vainly to chide and argue himself into fervour : when the mood of fanciful exaltation becomes unattainable he trembles under a sense of deserved displeasure : he feels the pathos of his own ingratitude more keenly than he feels the majesty or the generosity of the Being he is trying to love. He is far too ingenious for the contagious passion of the great mystics : he moves us most when he subsides into meek wistful yearning, and then he is more interesting for himself than for his subject.

The intellectual interest is decidedly stronger in him than in two writers who in a sense belong to his school. Crashaw looks up to him as Faber looked up to Keble. Vaughan was still more strongly and directly influenced by him. Crashaw cannot be said to imitate Herbert, he only is encouraged by the example of a distinguished Cambridge man who had achieved a court and academical reputation as a sacred poet ; Vaughan on the contrary is converted by Herbert, and, as we shall see, imitates him copiously. Either of them is perhaps more musically pious by nature than Herbert : at their best either excels him : Vaughan's clear intensity and Crashaw's glowing impetuosity alike make the laboured crabbed ingenuity of Herbert seem tame. And yet Herbert has always kept a larger place as a poet in the eyes of the public than Crashaw or Vaughan : he owes much of course to Walton's charming life, much to his own *Country Parson*, but after all *The Temple* is a book in a sense that *Steps to the Temple* or *Silex Scintillans* are not. The Williams MS. proves that Herbert corrected himself more severely in MS. than Vaughan in print, for the only change on the second edition of *Silex Scintillans* is the removal of a few crude naïvetés from one poem. Even Herbert tolerates much in style and metre that we wish away. Crashaw is smoother because more fluent, but Herbert's poems have always a plan and substance, which those of his successors often lack. Crashaw is full of diffuseness and repetition ; in the Wishes for his Mistress he puts in every fantastic way possible the hope that she will not paint ; often the variations are so insignificant that he can hardly have read the poem through before sending it to press As Pope observed, he wrote like a gentleman for his own amusement, and he wrote most at his ease when he was paraphrasing. Marino is his master, while Herbert is his patron and example ; but though Marino was the Coryphaeus of that literature of conceits which travelled over Europe, his poem on the Massacre of the Innocents is continually surpassed by Crashaw, who always introduces a fancy when Marino is content for a moment to be plain.

Here are one or two specimens from those collected by Wilmott and Grosart :—

> 'He saw Heav'n blossom with a new-born light,
> On which as on a glorious stranger gazed
> The golden eyes of night,'

literally in Marino

> 'He sees also shining from heaven,
> With beauteous ray, the wondrous star.'

When Alecto rises

> 'The fields' fair eyes saw her and said no more,
> But shut their flowery lids for ever;'

in Marino

> 'The flowers all round and the verdure appears
> To feel the strength of the plague, the anger of winter.'

Such imagery does not tax invention : one can put eyes everywhere and turn eyes into everything. We have only to turn to *The Weeper*, a poem upon St. Mary Magdalen which Pope read with interest. The saint's eyes are

> 'Heavens of ever falling stars.'

Again,

> 'Angels with crystal vials come
> And draw from those full eyes of thine
> Their Master's water, their own wine.'

Again,

> 'When sorrow would be seen
> In her brightest majesty
> (For she is a Queen),
> Then is she drest by none but thee.
> Then and only then she wears
> Her proudest pearls: I mean, thy tears.'

In the next stanzas we get something better :—

> 'Nowhere but here did ever meet
> Sweetness so sad, sadness so sweet.'

> 'Gladness itself would be more glad
> To be made so sweetly sad.'

Even Crashaw meant these for alternatives, but he likes to linger ; he spins the 23rd psalm into three dozen couplets. The Stabat Mater is very far from being the severest of mediæval hymns, but there is an appropriateness in Crashaw's own tit'e for his paraphrase 'A Pathetical descant on the devout Plain Song of the Church,' as though he were a pianist performing variations upon a classical air. He extemporises at ease in his rooms at Peterhouse, then the ritualistic college of Cambridge. Like Herbert he was a piece of a courtier, but he did not go to court to seek his fortune, he found nothing there but materials for a sketch of the supposed mistress who never disturbed his pious vigils. Of the three he is the only one who seems to have known no inward struggles ; he passes from Peterhouse to Loretto as pilgrims pass from one chapel to another in the Church of the Holy Sepulchre. There is no substantial difference between the tone of the poem to St. Theresa, written before his change of profession, and the two which he wrote after. If anything, the earlier poem is more serious and reverent. The wonderful close of the poem on the Flaming Heart is more wonderful because it comes after an atrocious and prolonged conceit to the effect that the saint's heart would not be inflamed by the arrow of the seraph, but was fit to inflame that and all creatures beside.

Vaughan only began to be a poet when Crashaw's career was over ; and he did not continue to be a poet to any purpose long. Everything he wrote before or after the two parts of *Silex Scintillans* might be spared. He is a mystic, as Herbert is an ascetic and Crashaw a devotee. Herbert's temptation is the world, Vaughan's temptation is the flesh ; the special service that Herbert does him is to lift his mind from profane love to sacred. He is quite pathetic in the preface to *Silex Scintillans* about his early loose love-poetry. He suppressed the worst of it, and adjures his reader to leave the sufficiently harmless collection which escaped him unread. When he was seven and twenty years older (he would not have thought wiser) he collected some more of his love verses equally innocent and rather insignificant. Amoret and Etesia are less interesting than Saccharissa and Althea and Castara. Perhaps Etesia's name implies that she was good to love for a year and no longer. The long interval of twenty-two years between the second part of *Silex Scintillans* and *Thalia Rediviva*, is filled mainly by little translations of works of edification and a few original prayers The prayers are rather too like sermons, and the title *Silex Scintillans* implies that his heart was a stone from which sparks might be struck now and then. He is as full as Herbert of the fluctuations of his own feelings, and as ready to interpret any failure of power as a judgment, as ready too to lecture upon his spiritual experience for the instruction of his reader. In both the lesson is the same, that external disappointments are good for the inner life. For Vaughan too rebelled against his circumstances : after Oxford and a riotous holiday in London, it was dull to settle down at Brecknock : the world had not promissed so much to him as to Herbert, but it performed even less. *The Mutiny* reminds us of *The Collar,* as *Rules and Maxims* remind us of *The Church Porch.* *The Tempest* recalls *Providence,* and in *Sundays* the coincidence is even closer : again, *The ' Queer,'* as we should now say *The Riddle,* is obviously suggested by *The Quip.* Even the complaint that men inflame themselves with a scarf or glove is borrowed from Herbert, who knew the world better than Vaughan, and gives pointed counsel and criticism, where Vaughan grumbles at the poverty of poets or the weight of a cloak. On the other hand, he knows nature much better. Herbert has no feeling for anything but the sweetness of flowers and sunshine, Vaughan feels the awe of the freshness of morning among the Welsh mountains. It is in morning walks that he meets God ; early rising is the one original recommendation in *Rules and Maxims.* The sanctity and insight of childhood are more to him than even to Wordsworth. Many religious writers speak of this life as an exile, Vaughan carries the metaphor through : we are exiles not only from the home we seek but from the home we have left. He even suspects the stars may have something to do with the uncompensated misfortune of birth into a world of time and sense. His twin brother Thomas studied alchemy not as a means to the transmutation of metals, but as a key to the hidden unity of nature. In his own translations Henry Vaughan uses Neoplatonists quite as familiarly as Jesuits. His prose is rich and musical ; his few Latin poems mostly insignificant, more pointless than Herbert's and quite without the airy grace of Crashaw's Bubble, of which Mr. Grosart has made a very pretty English poem. His translations from Ovid and Juvenal are rough and cumbrous ; he writes decasyllabics very badly compared not only with Sandys but with Crashaw, whose description of a Religious House contains one line, ' Obedient slumbers that can wake and weep,' worthy of Pope. His translations in octosyllabics from Casimir and Boethius are excellent, especially the poem on the Golden Age from Boethius.

G. A. SIMCOX.

SANDYS.

From the 'Paraphrase upon Luke I.'

O praise the Lord, his wonders tell,
Whose mercy shines in Israel,
At length redeem'd from sin and hell.

The crown of our salvation,
Deriv'd from David's royal throne,
He now hath to His people shown.

This to His prophets did unfold,
By all successively foretold,
Until the infant world grew old.

That He our wrongs would vindicate,
Save from our foes' inveterate hate,
And raise our long depress'd estate.

To ratify His ancient deed,
His promis'd grace, by oath decreed,
To Abraham and his faithful seed.

That we might our Preserver praise,
Walk purely in His perfect ways,
And fearless serve Him all our days.

His path Thou shalt prepare, sweet Child,
And run before the Undefil'd,
And Prophet of th' Almighty styl'd.

Our knowledge to inform, from whence
Salvation springs : from penitence,
And pardon of each foul offence.

Through mercy, O how infinite !
Of our Great God, Who clears our sight,
And from the Orient sheds His light.

A leading Star t' enlighten those
Whom night and shades of death inclose,
Which that high track to glory shows.

HERBERT.

THE COLLAR.

I struck the board, and cry'd, 'No more;
   I will abroad!
What, sha'l I ever sigh and pine?
My lines and life are free; free as the road,
 Loose as the wind, as large as store.
    Shall I be still in suit?
 Have I no harvest but a thorn
 To let me blood, and not restore
What I have lost with cordial fruit?
    Sure there was wine
 Before my sighs did dry it; there was corn
  Before my tears did drown it;
 Is the year only lost to me?
 Have I no bays to crown it,
No flowers, no garlands gay? all blasted,
    All wasted?
 Not so, my heart; but there is fruit,
    And thou hast hands.
 Recover all thy sigh-blown age
On double pleasures; leave thy cold dispute
Of what is fit and not; forsake thy cage,
    Thy rope of sands
Which petty thoughts have made; and made to thee
 Good cable, to enforce and draw,
    And be thy law,
 While thou didst wink and wouldst not see.
    Away! take heed;
    I will abroad.
Call in thy death's-head there, tie up thy fears;
    He that forbears
   To suit and serve his need
    Deserves his load.'

But as I rav'd, and grew more fierce and wild
  At every word,
Methought I heard one calling, 'Child';
  And I reply'd, 'My Lord.'

AARON.

Holiness on the head,
  Light and perfections on the breast,
Harmonious bells below, raising the dead
  To lead them unto life and rest:
    Thus are true Aarons drest.

Profaneness in my head,
  Defects and darkness in my breast,
A noise of passions ringing me for dead
  Unto a place where is no rest:
    Poor priest, thus am I drest.

Only another head
  I have, another heart and breast,
Another music, making live, not dead,
  Without Whom I could have no rest:
    In Him I am well drest.

Christ is my only head,
  My alone-only heart and breast,
My only music striking me ev'n dead,
  That to the old man I may rest,
    And he in Him new-drest.

So holy in my head,
  Perfect and light in my dear breast,
My doctrine tun'd by Christ, Who is not dead,
  But lives in me while I do rest,
    Come, people; Aaron's drest.

The Quip.

The merry World did on a day
With his train-bands and mates agree
To meet together where I lay,
And all in sport to jeer at me.

First Beauty crept into a rose,
Which when I pluckt not, 'Sir,' said she,
'Tell me, I pray, whose hands are those?'
But Thou shalt answer, Lord, for me.

Then Money came, and chinking still,
'What tune is this, poor man?' said he:
'I heard in Music you had skill;'
But Thou shalt answer, Lord, for me.

Then came brave Glory puffing by
In silks that whistled, who but he!
He scarce allow'd me half an eye;
But Thou shalt answer, Lord, for me.

Then came quick Wit and Conversation,
And he would needs a comfort be,
And, to be short, make an oration:
But Thou shalt answer, Lord, for me.

Yet when the hour of Thy design
To answer these fine things shall come,
Speak not at large; say, I am Thine,
And then they have their answer home.

Misery.

Lord, let the angels praise Thy name:
Man is a foolish thing, a foolish thing;
Folly and sin play all his game;
His house still burns, and yet he still doth sing—
Man is but grass,
He knows it—Fill the glass!

*   *   *   *   *   *   *

Man cannot serve Thee : let him go
And serve the swine—there, there is his delight :
　He doth not like this virtue, no ;
Give him his dirt to wallow in all night :
　　　　These preachers make
　　　　His head to shoot and ache.

＊　＊　＊　＊　＊　＊　＊　＊

Indeed, at first Man was a treasure,
A box of jewels, shop of rarities,
　A ring whose posy was ' My pleasure ';
He was a garden in a Paradise ;
　　　　Glory and grace
　　　　Did crown his heart and face.

But sin hath fool'd him ; now he is
A lump of flesh, without a foot or wing
　To raise him to a glimpse of bliss ;
A sick-toss'd vessel, dashing on each thing,
　　　　Nay, his own shelf ;
　　　　My God, I mean myself.

LOVE.

Thou art too hard for me in Love ;
There is no dealing with Thee in that Art,
　That is Thy Masterpiece, I see.
When I contrive and plot to prove
Something that may be conquest on my part,
　Thou still, O Lord, outstrippest me.

Sometimes, when as I wash, I say,
And shrewdly as I think, Lord, wash my soul,
　More spotted than my flesh can be !
But then there comes into my way
Thy ancient baptism, which when I was foul
　And knew it not, yet cleansèd me.

I took a time when Thou didst sleep,
Great waves of trouble combating my breast:
  I thought it brave to praise Thee then;
  Yet then I found that Thou didst creep
Into my heart with joy, giving more rest
  Than flesh did lend Thee back again.

  Let me but once the conquest have
Upon the matter, 'twill Thy conquest prove:
  If Thou subdue mortality,
  Thou dost no more than doth the grave;
Whereas if I o'ercome Thee and Thy love,
  Hell, Death, and Devil come short of me.

THE PULLEY.

  When God at first made man,
Having a glass of blessing standing by;
Let us (said he) pour on him all we can:
Let the world's riches which dispersed lie
  Contract into a span.

  So strength first made a way;
Then beauty flow'd, then wisdom, honour, pleasure;
When almost all was out, God made a stay,
Perceiving that alone, of all his treasure,
  Rest in the bottom lay.

  For if I should (said he)
Bestow this jewel also on my creature,
He would adore my gifts instead of me,
And rest in Nature, not the God of Nature;
  So both should losers be.

  Yet let him keep the rest,
But keep them with repining restlessness:
Let him be rich and weary, that at least,
If goodness lead him not, yet weariness
  May toss him to my breast.

EMPLOYMENT.

He that is weary, let him sit ;
      My soul would stir
And trade in courtesies and wit ;
      Quitting the fur
To cold complexions needing it.

Man is no star, but a quick coal
      Of mortal fire :
Who blows it not, nor doth control
      A faint desire,
Lets his own ashes choke his soul.

    *   *   *   *   *   *

Oh that I were an orange-tree,
      That busy plant !
Then should I ever laden be,
      And never want
Some fruit for him that dressèd me.

But we are still too young or old ;
      The man is gone
Before we do our wares unfold ;
      So we freeze on,
Until the grave increase our cold.

THE WORLD.

Love built a stately house, where Fortune came ;
And spinning fancies, she was heard to say
That her fine cobwebs did support the frame,
Whereas they were supported by the same ;
But Wisdom quickly swept them all away.

Then Pleasure came, who, liking not the fashion,
Began to make balconies, terraces,
Till she had weaken'd all by alteration ;
But rev'rend laws, and many a proclamation,
Reformed all at length with menaces.

Then enter'd Sin, and with that sycamore
Whose leaves first shelt'red man from drought and dew,
Working and winding slily evermore,
The inward walls and sommers cleft and tore ;
But Grace shor'd these, and cut that as it grew.

Then Sin combin'd with Death in a firm band
To rase the building to the very floor :
Which they effected, none could them withstand ;
But Love took Grace and Glory by the hand,
And built a braver palace than before.

CRASHAW.

WISHES. TO HIS SUPPOSED MISTRESS.

Whoe'er she be,
That not impossible she
That shall command my heart and me ;

Where'er she lie,
Lock'd up from mortall eye,
In shady leaves of Destiny;

Till that ripe birth
Of studied Fate stand forth,
And teach her fair steps tread our Earth ;

Till that divine
Idea, take a shrine
Of crystal flesh, through which to shine ;

Meet you her, my wishes,
Bespeak her to my blisses,
And be ye call'd, my absent kisses.

I wish her, beauty
That owes not all its duty
To gaudy tire or glistring shoe tie.

*   *   *   *   *   *

A face that's best
By its own beauty drest,
And can alone commend the rest.

* * * * * *

A cheek where Youth,
And blood, with pen of Truth
Write, what their reader sweetly ru'th.

* * * * * * *

Lips, where all day
A lover's kiss may play,
Yet carry nothing thence away.

* * * * *

Eyes, that displace
The neighbour diamond, and out-face
That sunshine, by their own sweet grace

Tresses, that wear
Jewels, but to declare
How much themselves more precious are,

* * * * * *

Days, that need borrow,
No part of their good morrow,
From a forespent night of sorrow.

* * * * * *

Life, that dares send
A challenge to his end,
And when it comes say, Welcome friend !

* * * * * *

I wish her store
Of worth may leave her poor
Of wishes ; and I wish—no more.

Now if Time knows
That her, whose radiant brows
Weave them a garland of my vows ;

Her that dares be,
What these lines wish to see :
I seek no further : it is she.

The Flaming Heart.

[Upon the book and picture of the Seraphical Saint Theresa, as she is
usually expressed with a Seraphim beside her.]

* * * * * * * *

O thou undaunted daughter of desires !
By all thy dower of lights and fires ;
By all the eagle in thee, all the dove ;
By all thy lives and deaths of love ;
By thy large draughts of intellectual day,
And by thy thirsts of love more large than they ;
By all thy brim-fill'd bowls of fierce desire,
By thy last morning's draught of liquid fire ;
By the full kingdom of that final kiss
That seiz'd thy parting soul, and seal'd thee His ;
By all the Heav'n thou hast in Him
(Fair sister of the seraphim !)
By all of Him we have in thee ;
Leave nothing of myself in me.
Let me so read thy life, that I
Unto all life of mine may die.

Description of a Religious House.

No roofs of gold o'er riotous tables shining
Whole days and suns, devour'd with endless dining ;
No sails of Tyrian silk, proud pavements sweeping,
Nor ivory couches costlier slumber keeping ;
False lights of flaring gems ; tumultuous joys ;
Halls full of flattering men and frisking boys ;
Whate'er false shows of short and slippery good
Mix the mad sons of men in mutual blood.
But walks, and unshorn woods ; and souls, just so
Unforc'd and genuine ; but not shady though.
Our lodgings hard and homely as our fare,
That chaste and cheap, as the few clothes we wear.

Those, coarse and negligent, as the natural locks
Of these loose groves ; rough as th' unpolish't rocks.
A hasty portion of prescribèd sleep ;
Obedient slumbers, that can wake and weep,
And sing, and sigh, and work, and sleep again ;
Still rolling a round sphere of still-returning pain.
Hands full of hasty labours ; pains that pay
And prize themselves ; do much, that more they may,
And work for work, not wages ; let to-morrow's
New drops wash off the sweat of this day's sorrows.
A long and daily-dying life, which breathes
A respiration of reviving deaths.
But neither are there those ignoble stings
That nip the blossom of the world's best things,
And lash Earth-labouring souls . . . . .
No cruel guard of diligent cares, that keep
Crown'd woes awake, as things too wise for sleep :
But reverent discipline, and religious fear,
And soft obedience, find sweet biding here ;
Silence, and sacred rest ; peace, and pure joys ;
Kind loves keep house, lie close, and make no noise ;
And room enough for monarchs, while none swells
Beyond the kingdoms of contentful cells.
The self-remembring soul sweetly recovers
Her kindred with the stars ; not basely hovers
Below : but meditates her immortal way
Home to the original source of Light and intellectual day.

VAUGHAN.

THE RETREAT.

Happy those early days, when I
Shin'd in my angel-infancy!
Before I understood this place
Appointed for my second race,
Or taught my soul to fancy ought
But a white, celestial thought;
When yet I had not walk'd above
A mile or two, from my first love,
And looking back—at that short space—
Could see a glimpse of His bright face;
When on some gilded cloud or flower
My gazing soul would dwell an hour,
And in those weaker glories spy
Some shadows of eternity;
Before I taught my tongue to wound
My conscience with a sinful sound,
Or had the black art to dispense,
A sev'ral sin to ev'ry sense,
But felt through all this fleshly dress
Bright shoots of everlastingness.
O how I long to travel back,
And tread again that ancient track!
That I might once more reach that plain,
Where first I left my glorious train;
From whence th' enlightened spirit sees
That shady city of palm trees.
But ah! my soul with too much stay
Is drunk, and staggers in the way!
Some men a forward motion love,
But I by backward steps will move;
And when this dust falls to the urn,
In that state I came, return.

The Burial of an Infant.

Blest infant bud, whose blossom-life
Did only look about, and fall
Wearied out in a harmless strife
Of tears, and milk, the food of all;

Sweetly didst thou expire : thy soul
Flew home unstain'd by his new kin;
For ere thou knew'st how to be foul,
Death wean'd thee from the world, and sin.

Softly rest all thy virgin-crumbs
Lapt in the sweets of thy young breath,
Expecting till thy Saviour comes
To dress them, and unswaddle death!

The World.

I saw Eternity the other night,
Like a great ring of pure and endless light,
    All calm, as it was bright ;
And round beneath it, Time in hours, days, years,
    Driv'n by the spheres
Like a vast shadow mov'd ; in which the world
    And all her train were hurl'd.
The doting lover in his quaintest strain
    Did there complain ;
Near him, his lute, his fancy, and his slights,
    Wit's sour delights,
With gloves, and knots, the silly snares of pleasure,
    Yet his dear treasure,
All scatter'd lay, while he his eyes did pour
    Upon a flower.

The darksome statesman, hung with weights and woe,
Like a thick midnight-fog, mov'd there so slow,
    He did not stay, nor go ;
Condemning thoughts—like sad eclipses—scowl
    Upon his soul,
And clouds of crying witnesses without
    Pursued him with one shout.
Yet digg'd the mole, and lest his ways be found,
    Worked under ground,
Where he did clutch his prey ; but one did see
    That policy ;
Churches and altars fed him ; perjuries
    Were gnats and flies ;
It rain'd about him blood and tears, but he
    Drank them as free.

The fearful miser on a heap of rust
Sate pining all his life there, did scarce trust
    His own hands with the dust,
Yet would not place one piece alone, but lives
    In fear of thieves.
Thousands there were as frantic as himself,
    And hugg'd each one his pelf ;
The downright epicure plac'd heav'n in sense,
    And scorn'd pretence ;
While others, slipt into a wide excess,
    Said little less ;
The weaker sort, slight, trivial wares enslave,
    Who think them brave ;
And poor despised Truth sate counting by
    Their victory.

Yet some, who all this while did weep and sing,
And sing, and weep, soar'd up into the ring ;
    But most would use no wing.
O fools—said I—thus to prefer dark night
    Before true light !

To live in grots, and caves, and hate the day
    Because it shews the way,
The way, which from this dead and dark abode
    Leads up to God ;
A way where you might tread the sun, and be
    More bright than he !
But as I did their madness so discuss
    One whisper'd thus,
'This ring the Bridegroom did for none provide,
    But for His bride.'

BEYOND THE VEIL.

They are all gone into the world of light !
    And I alone sit lingering here ;
Their very memory is fair and bright,
    And my sad thoughts doth clear.

It glows and glitters in my cloudy breast,
    Like stars upon some gloomy grove,
Or those faint beams in which this hill is drest,
    After the sun's remove.

I see them walking in an air of glory,
    Whose light doth trample on my days :
My days, which are at best but dull and hoary,
    Mere glimmering and decays.

O holy Hope ! and high Humility,
    High as the heavens above !
These are your walks, and you have shew'd them me,
    To kindle my cold love.

Dear, beauteous Death ! the jewel of the just,
    Shining no where, but in the dark ;
What mysteries do lie beyond thy dust ;
    Could man outlook that mark !

He that hath found some fledg'd birds' nest, may know
　　At first sight, if the bird be flown ;
But what fair well or grove he sings in now,
　　That is to him unknown.

And yet as angels in some brighter dreams
　　Call to the soul, when man doth sleep :
So some strange thoughts transcend our wonted themes
　　And into glory peep.

If a star were confin'd into a tomb,
　　The captive flames must needs burn there ;
But when the hand that lock'd her up, gives room,
　　She 'll shine through all the sphere.

O Father of eternal life, and all
　　Created glories under Thee !
Resume thy spirit from this world of thrall
　　Into true liberty.

Either disperse these mists, which blot and fill
　　My perspective—still—as they pass :
Or else remove me hence unto that hill,
　　Where I shall need no glass.

JAMES SHIRLEY.

[SHIRLEY was born in London about the year 1596, and lived through the Civil War and Commonwealth into the Restoration, dying in 1667. His copious dramatic activity began in 1625, in which year he produced the comedy entitled *Love's Tricks*. Before this, in 1618, he had published an imitation of *Venus and Adonis* under the title of *Echo*. His plays were produced in rapid succession up to 1641. In 1646 he published a volume of poems, chiefly erotic, and two small volumes of Masques etc. in 1653 and 1659.]

Shirley was essentially an imitative not an original genius. His claim to a place among the great poets of his age rests solely upon his wonderful manipulative dexterity, his power of assimilating and reshaping the creations of his great predecessors. Towards the close of a grand period, perhaps even while its leading spirits are in full creative swing, two distinct tendencies manifest themselves. Men of independent mind separate themselves from the main current, and cast about for fields which the masters have left unoccupied. Men of more pliant and docile intellect follow humbly in the footsteps of the masters, and seize freely upon the wealth which they have accumulated. Shirley belonged to the latter class. He did not try to invent new types, or to say what had not been said before ; but stored his mind with the thoughts and the imagery of his predecessors, and reproduced them with joyous facility. We may admire the fluency, the elegance, and the force of Shirley's verse, the ease and naturalness of his dramatic situations, but the attentive reader of his predecessors is never called upon to admire anything new. Fletcher was his chief model and exemplar, but he laid them all freely under contribution. The chief critical pleasure in reading him is the pleasure of memory.

W. MINTO.

A LULLABY.

[From *The Triumph of Beauty*, a Masque, 1646.]

Cease, warring thoughts, and let his brain
No more discord entertain,
But be smooth and calm again.
Ye crystal rivers that are nigh,
As your streams are passing by
Teach your murmurs harmony.
Ye winds that wait upon the Spring
And perfumes to flowers do bring,
Let your amorous whispers here
Breathe soft music to his ear.
Ye warbling nightingales repair
From every wood, to charm this air,
And with the wonders of your breast
Each striving to excel the rest,
When it is time to wake him, close your parts,
And drop down from the tree with broken hearts.

THE GARDEN.

[From *Poems*, 1646.]

This garden does not take my eyes,
Though here you show how art of men
Can purchase nature at such price
Would stock old Paradise again.

These glories while you dote upon,
I envy not your spring nor pride ;
Nay boast the summer all your own,
My thoughts with less are satisfied.

Give me a little plot of ground,
Where might I with the sun agree,
Though every day he walk the round
My garden he should seldom see.

Those tulips that such wealth display
To court my eye, shall lose their name,
Though now they listen, as if they
Expected I should praise their flame.

But I would see myself appear
Within the violet's drooping head,
On which a melancholy tear
The discontented morn hath shed.

Within their buds let roses sleep
And virgin lilies on their stem,
Till sighs from lovers glide and creep
Into their leaves to open them.

I' th' centre of my ground compose
Of bays and yew my summer-room,
Which may, so oft as I repose,
Present my arbour and my tomb.

No woman here shall find me out,
Or if a chance do bring one hither,
I'll be secure, for round about
I'll moat it with my eyes' foul weather.

No birds shall live within my pale,
To charm me with their shames of art,
Unless some wandering nightingale
Come here to sing and break her heart;

Upon whose death I'll try to write
An epitaph, in some funeral stone,
So sad and true, it may invite
Myself to die, and prove mine own.

THE MIGHT OF DEATH.

[From *Cupid and Death*, a Masque, 1653.]

Victorious men of earth, no more
  Proclaim how wide your empires are;
Though you bind in every shore,
  And your triumphs reach as far
    As night or day,

Yet you, proud monarchs, must obey,
And mingle with forgotten ashes when
Death calls ye to the crowd of common men.

Devouring Famine, Plague, and War,
  Each able to undo mankind,
Death's servile emissaries are;
  Nor to these alone confined
    He hath at will
More quaint and subtle ways to kill;
A smile or kiss, as he will use the art,
Shall have the cunning skill to break a heart.

A DIRGE.

[From *The Contention of Ajax and Ulysses*, printed 1659.]

The glories of our blood and state
  Are shadows, not substantial things;
There is no armour against fate;
  Death lays his icy hand on kings:
    Sceptre and crown
    Must tumble down,
  And in the dust be equal made
  With the poor crooked scythe and spade.

Some men with swords may reap the field,
  And plant fresh laurels where they kill;
But their strong nerves at last must yield;
  They tame but one another still:
    Early or late
    They stoop to fate,
  And must give up their murmuring breath,
  When they, poor captives, creep to death.

The garlands wither on your brow,
  Then boast no more your mighty deeds;
Upon Death's purple altar now
  See, where the victor-victim bleeds:
    Your heads must come
    To the cold tomb,
  Only the actions of the just
  Smell sweet and blossom in their dust.

THOMAS RANDOLPH.

[THOMAS RANDOLPH was born in the summer of 1605, at Dodford, in Northamptonshire, and died at Blatherwick, in the same county, in March 163⅘. His drama of *The Jealous Lovers* was printed in 1632; the remainder of his works appeared posthumously in 1638.]

It seems probable that in the premature death of Randolph, English literature underwent a very heavy loss. He died unexpectedly when he was only twenty-nine, leaving behind him a mass of writing at once very imperfect and very promising. The patronage of Ben Jonson, it would seem, rather than any very special bias to the stage, led him to undertake dramatic composition, and though he left six plays behind him, it is by no means certain that he would have ended as a dramatist. His knowledge of stage requirements is very small indeed; it would be impossible to revive any of his pieces on the modern boards on account of the essential uncouthness of the movement, the length of the soliloquies, and the thinness of the plot. His three best dramas are distinguished by a vigorous directness and buoyancy of language, and by frequent passages of admirable rhetorical quality, but they are hardly plays at all, in the ordinary sense. His master-piece, *The Muses' Looking Glass*, is a moral essay in a series of dialogues, happily set in a framework of comedy; the *Jealous Lovers* is full, indeed, of ridiculous stratagems and brisk humorous transitions, but it has no sanity of plot; while *Amyntas* is a beautiful holiday dream, aery and picturesque, and ringing with peals of faery laughter, but not a play that any mortal company of actors could rehearse. Intellect and imagination Randolph possessed in full measure, but as he does not seem to have been born to excel in play-writing or in song-writing, and as he died too early to set his own mark on literature, we are left to speculate down what groove such brilliant and energetic gifts as his would finally have proceeded. Had he lived longer his massive intelligence might have made him a dangerous rival or a master to Dryden, and as he shows no inclination towards the French manner of poetry, he might have delayed or altogether warded off the influx of the classical taste. He showed no precocity of genius; he was gradually gathering his singing-robes about him, having already studied much, yet having still much to learn. There is no poet whose works so tempt the critic to ask, 'what was the next step in his development?' He died just too soon to impress his name on history.

Besides his dramas, Randolph composed a considerable number of lyrics and occasional poems. Of these the beautiful *Ode to Master Anthony Stafford to hasten him into the country* is the best. In this he is more free and graceful in his Latinism than usual. He was a deep student of the Roman poets, and most of his non-dramatic pieces are exercises, performed in a hard though stately style, after Ovid, Martial and Claudian. It cannot be said that these have much charm, except to the technical student of poetry, who observes, with interest, the zeal and energy with which Randolph prepared himself for triumphs which were never to be executed. In pastoral poetry he had attained more ease than in any other, and some of his idyls are excellently performed. The glowing verses entitled *A Pastoral Courtship* remind the reader of the twenty-seventh idyl of Theocritus, on which they were probably modelled. The *Cotswold Eclogue*, which originally appeared in a very curious book entitled *Annalia Dubrensia*, 1636, is one of the best pastorals which we possess in English. But in reviewing the fragments of the work of Randolph, the critic is ever confronted by the imperfection of his growing talent, the insufficiency of what exists to account for the personal weight that Randolph carried in his lifetime, and for the intense regret felt at his early death. Had he lived he might have bridged over, with a strong popular poetry, the abyss between the old romantic and the new didactic school, for he had a little of the spirit of each. As it is, he holds a better place in English literature than Dryden, or Gray, or Massinger would have held had they died before they were thirty.

EDMUND W. GOSSE.

ODE TO MASTER ANTHONY STAFFORD.

Come, spur away,
I have no patience for a longer stay,
But must go down,
And leave the chargeable noise of this great town;
I will the country see,
Where old simplicity,
Though hid in grey,
Doth look more gay
Than foppery in plush and scarlet clad.
Farewell, you city wits, that are
Almost at civil war;
'Tis time that I grow wise, when all the world grows mad.

More of my days
I will not spend to gain an idiot's praise;
Or to make sport
For some slight puisne of the Inns-of-Court.
Then, worthy Stafford, say,
How shall we spend the day?
With what delights
Shorten the nights?
When from this tumult we are got secure,
Where mirth with all her freedom goes,
Yet shall no finger lose;
Where every word is thought, and every thought is pure.

There from the tree
We 'll cherries pluck, and pick the strawberry;
And every day
Go see the wholesome country girls make hay,
Whose brown hath lovelier grace
Than any painted face,
That I do know
Hyde Park can show.
Where I had rather gain a kiss than meet
(Though some of them in greater state
Might court my love with plate)
The beauties of the Cheap, and wives of Lombard Street.

But think upon
Some other pleasures : these to me are none.
Why did I prate
Of women, that are things against my fate?
I never mean to wed
That torture to my bed.
My muse is she
My love shall be.
Let clowns get wealth and heirs ; when I am gone,
And the great bugbear, grisly death,
Shall take this idle breath,
If I a poem leave, that poem is my son.

Of this no more ;
We 'll rather taste the bright Pomona's store.
No fruit shall 'scape
Our palates, from the damson to the grape.
Then (full) we 'll seek a shade,
And hear what music's made ;
How Philomel
Her tale doth tell,
And how the other birds do fill the quire :
The thrush and blackbird lend their throats
Warbling melodious notes ;
We will all sports enjoy which others but desire.

Ours is the sky,
Whereat what fowl we please our hawk shall fly:
Nor will we spare
To hunt the crafty fox or timorous hare ;
But let our hounds run loose
In any ground they 'll choose,
The buck shall fall,
The stag, and all :
Our pleasures must from their own warrants be,
For to my muse, if not to me,
I'm sure all game is free :
Heaven, earth, all are but parts of her great royalty.

And when we mean
To taste of Bacchus' blessings now and then,
And drink by stealth
A cup or two to noble Barkley's health,
I 'll take my pipe and try
The Phrygian melody ;
Which he that hears,
Lets through his ears
A madness to distemper all the brain.
Then I another pipe will take
And Doric music make,
To civilise with graver notes our wits again.

FROM THE 'COTSWOLD ECLOGUE.'

Colin. Early in May up got the jolly rout,
Call'd by the lark, and spread the fields about :
One, for to breathe himself, would coursing be
From this same beech to yonder mulberry,
A second leap'd his supple nerves to try ;
A third was practising his melody ;
This a new jig was footing, others were
Busied at wrestling, or to throw the bar,
Ambitious which should bear the bell away,
And kiss the nut-brown lady of the May.
This stirr'd 'em up ; a jolly swain was he,
Whom Peg and Susan after victory
Crown'd with a garland they had made, beset
With daisies, pinks, and many a violet,
Cowslip, and gilliflower. Rewards, though small,
Encourage virtue, but if none at all
Meet her, she languisheth, and dies, as now
Where worth's deni'd the honour of a bough.
And, Thenot, this the cause I read to be
Of such a dull and general lethargy.
Thenot. Ill thrive the lout that did their mirth gainsay !
Wolves haunt his flocks that took those sports away !

Colin. Some melancholy swains about have gone
To teach all zeal their own complexion:
Choler they will admit sometimes, I see,
But phlegm and sanguine no religions be.
These teach that dancing is a Jezebel,
And barley-break the ready way to hell;
The morrice-idols, Whitsun-ales, can be
But profane relics of a jubilee!
These, in a zeal t'express how much they do
The organs hate, have silenc'd bagpipes, too,
And harmless Maypoles, all are rail'd upon,
As if they were the towers of Babylon.
Some think not fit there should be any sport
I' th' country, 'tis a dish proper to th' Court.
Mirth not becomes 'em; let the saucy swain
Eat beef and bacon, and go sweat again.
Besides, what sport can in the pastimes be,
When all is but ridiculous foppery?

FROM 'A PASTORAL COURTSHIP.'

Behold these woods, and mark, my sweet,
How all the boughs together meet?
The cedar his fair arms displays,
And mixes branches with the bays!
The lofty pine deigns to descend,
And sturdy oaks do gently bend.
One with another subtly weaves
Into one loom their various leaves,
As all ambitious were to be
Mine and my Phyllis' canopy.
Let's enter and discourse our loves;
These are, my dear, no tell-tale groves!
There dwell no pies nor parrots there,
To prate again the words they hear,
Nor babbling echo, that will tell
The neighbouring hills one syllable.

*　　*　　*　　*　　*　　*　　*

Now let me sit, and fix mine eyes
On thee, that art my paradise.
Thou art my all ; my spring remains
In the fair violets of thy veins ;
And that you are my summer's day,
Ripe cherries in thy lips display.
And when for autumn I would seek,
'Tis in the apples of thy cheek.
But that which only moves my smart,
Is to see winter in thy heart.
Strange, when at once in one appear
All the four seasons of the year !
I 'll clasp that neck, where should be set
A rich and orient carcanet.
But swains are poor ; admit of, then,
More natural chains—the arms of men.

To Ben Jonson.

I was not born to Helicon, nor dare
Presume to think myself a Muse's heir.
I have no title to Parnassus Hill
Nor any acre of it by the will
Of a dead ancestor, nor could I be
Ought but a tenant unto poetry.
But thy adoption quits me of all fear,
And makes me challenge a child's portion there.
I am akin to heroes, being thine,
And part of my alliance is divine,
Orpheus, Musæus, Homer too, beside
Thy brothers by the Roman mother's side ;
As Ovid, Virgil, and the Latin lyre
That is so like thee, Horace ; the whole quire
Of poets are, by thy adoption, all
My uncles ; thou hast given me power to call
Phœbus himself my grandsire ; by this grant
Each sister of the Nine is made my aunt.

Go, you that reckon from a large descent
Your lineal honours, and are well content
To glory in the age of your great name,
Though on a herald's faith you build the same :
I do not envy you, nor think you blest
Though you may bear a Gorgon on your crest
By direct line from Perseus ; I will boast
No further than my father ; that's the most
I can, or should be proud of ; and I were
Unworthy his adoption, if that here
I should be dully modest.

WILLIAM CARTWRIGHT.

[Born, according to one authority, at Burford in Oxfordshire, August 16th, 1615 ; according to another, at Northway in Gloucestershire, in September 1611. From 1628 he chiefly resided at Oxford. where he died of the 'camp disease' November 29th, 1643. His plays and poems were collected and published in 1651.]

Cartwright, whom his academical and literary contemporaries regarded as a phenomenon, is to us chiefly interesting as a type. If it be allowable to regard as extravagant the tendencies represented by him in both his life and his poetry, he may justly be remembered by a sufficiently prominent title among English poets —that of the typically extravagant Oxford resident of his period. He was a most enthusiastic royalist in the most royalist city and community of the kingdom ; and, in a sense, he died a martyr to his political sentiment. In an age of 'florid and seraphical preachers,' this designation was attached distinctively to the youthful succentor of Salisbury Cathedral and junior proctor of the University. It is therefore but natural that among the panegyrical poets of an age given to panegyric, Cartwright's efforts in this direction should have remained unsurpassed. His muse devoted herself with that unshrinking courtliness which has often characterised our old Universities to singing the praises of the King, the Queen, their 'fourth child,' their 'sixth child,' and all the royal family, as occasion might demand, invite or suggest. When 'our happy Charles' recovered from the terrible epidemic of his times, Cartwright, in the first of the poems given here, was at hand with an exercise of flattery, which in its central conceit was afterwards imitated, but hardly equalled, by the youthful Dryden. Other events belonging to the sphere of the Court chronicler prompted longer and loftier strains : returns from journeys across the border or abroad, marriages, and above all occasions sacred to Lucina, the favourite deity, and indeed the satest inspiration, of panegyrical poets. In default of these, there were the deaths of noblemen and gentlewomen, and the advents of promising Vice-Chancellors to be sung, or the merits of brother dramatists past or present, a Fletcher or a Killigrew, to be extolled, and there was the living 'Father of Poets,' Ben Jonson, to be venerated *coram publico* by his pious son.

And yet Ben Jonson himself, among whose foibles it was not to overpraise even friends and followers, was not in error when he proclaimed of 'his son Cartwright' that he 'wrote all like a man.' Cartwright, though his study of Horace and Martial had failed to teach him the grace of simplicity, was a sure and a ripe scholar; and he moves among classical illustrations and allusions with an almost alarming ease. His conceits, fetched from far and near, and jostling one another in their superabundance, mark him out as a genuine member of the Fantastic School of poets. In his lines *To the Memory of Ben Jonson*, he blames his fellow-playwrights,

> 'who into one piece do
> Throw all that they can say, and their friends too,
> Pumping themselves for one term's noise so dry
> As if they made their wills in poetry.'

Among non-dramatic poets at all events, Cartwright is as amenable to this very charge of too visible effort as any other member of the school to which he belongs.

Of the higher imaginative power and tenderer grace to be found in some of the members of that school Cartwright has but few traces. But he possessed a real rhetorical inventiveness, and an extraordinary felicity of expression. These gifts he was able to display on occasions of the most opposite and diverse character, great and small, public and private,—from the occurrence of an unexampled frost to the publication of a treatise on the art of vaulting. Yet even with a panegyrical poet of the Fantastic School the relations between his theme and his own tastes and sentiments are of the highest importance. In ingenuity Cartwright can hardly be said to have elsewhere surpassed the longest of the three following pieces, congenial to himself in its subject, though elaborately singular in treatment. For it may safely be asserted that this Ordination poem achieves its object of being altogether unique, without being altogether inappropriate. On the other hand, there could be no more common theme for elegiac verse than a premature death; but the lines on an occasion of the kind here reprinted are out of the common, though by no means unpleasing. Whether, had Cartwright lived beyond early manhood, he would have fulfilled or exceeded the promise of his youth, it is useless to enquire. He was more genuinely successful as a writer of occasional lyrics and elegies than as a dramatist. Perhaps the seriousness of the epoch at the opening of which he died might have turned his efforts to religious poetry, in which the Fantastic School of English poetry achieved its noblest results, and to which this academical preacher's and poet's mind must have had a natural bias. What he actually accomplished in this direction was but little, though not altogether unworthy of being associated with the music of Milton's friend and favourite composer.

A. W. WARD.

On His Majesty's Recovery from the Small-Pox, 1633.

I do confess, the over-forward tongue
Of public duty turns into a wrong,
And after-ages, which could ne'er conceive
Our happy CHARLES so frail as to receive
Such a disease, will know it by the noise
Which we have made in shouting forth our joys;
And our informing duty only be
A well-meant spite, or loyal injury.
Let then the name be alter'd; let us say
They were small stars fix'd in a Milky-way,
Or faithful turquoises, which Heaven sent
For a discovery, not a punishment;
To show the ill, not make it; and to tell
By their pale looks the bearer was not well.
Let the disease forgotten be, but may
The joy return us yearly as the day;
Let there be new computes, let reckoning be
Solemnly made from His recovery;
Let not the Kingdom's Acts hereafter run
From His (though happy) Coronation,
But from His Health, as in a better strain.
That plac'd Him on His throne; This makes Him reign.

A NEW YEAR'S GIFT TO BRIAN LORD BISHOP OF SARUM UPON
THE AUTHOR'S ENTERING INTO HOLY ORDERS, 1638.

Now that the village reverence doth lie hid,
  As Egypt's Wisdom did,
In birds and beasts, and that the tenant's soul
  Goes with his New-year's fowl ;
   So that the cock and hen speak more
   Now, than in fables heretofore ;
    And that the feather'd things
    Truly make love have wings :
Though we no flying present have to pay,
A quill yet snatch'd from thence may sign the day.

But, being the Canon bars me wit and wine,
  Enjoining the true Vine,
Being the bays must yield unto the Cross,
  And all be now one loss ;
   So that my raptures are to steal
   And knit themselves in one pure zeal,
    And that my each day's breath
    Must be a daily death :
Without all strain or fury I must than[1]
Tell you this New-year brings you a new man.

New, not as th' year, to run the same course o'er
  Which it hath run before,
Lest in the man himself there be a round,
  As in his humour's[2] found,
   And that return seem to make good
   Circling of actions, as of blood.
    Motion, as in a mill,
    Is busy standing still ;
And by such wheeling we but thus prevail,
To make the serpent swallow his own tail.

   [1] then.   [2] moisture, i. e. the blood.

Nor new by solemnising looser toys,
    And erring with less noise,
Taking the flag and trumpet from the sin,
    So to' offend within ;
    As some men silence loud perfumes
    And draw them into shorter rooms :
      This will be understood
      More wary, not more good.
Sins too may be severe, and so, no doubt,
The vice but only sour'd, not rooted out.

But new, by th' using of each part aright,
    Changing both step and sight ;
That false direction come not from the eye,
    Nor the foot tread awry ;
    That neither *that* the way aver
    Which doth toward fame, or profit, err,
      Nor *this* tread that path which
      Is not the right, but rich ;
That thus the foot being fix'd, thus led the eye,
I pitch my walk low, but my prospect high.

New too, to teach my opinions not t' submit
    To favour, or to wit ;
Nor yet to walk on edges, where they may
    Run safe in broader way;
    Nor to search out for new paths, where
    Nor tracks nor footsteps do appear,
      Knowing that deeps are ways
      Where no impression stays ;
Nor servile thus, nor curious, may I then
Approve my faith to Heaven, my life to men.

---

[1] so as to.

But I who thus present myself as new,
    Am thus made new by you.
Had not your rays dwelt on me, one long night
    Had shut me up from sight.
    Your beams exhale me from among
    Things tumbling in the common throng.
      Who thus with your fire burns,
      Now gives not, but returns.
To others then be this a day of thrift :
They do receive ; but you, sir, make the gift.

On a Virtuous young Gentlewoman that died
SUDDENLY.

When the old flaming Prophet climb'd the sky,
Who, at one glimpse, did vanish, and not die,
He made more preface to a death than this :
So far from sick, she did not breathe amiss.
She, who to Heaven more heaven doth annex,
Whose lowest thought was above all our sex,
Accounted nothing death but t' be repriev'd,
And died as free from sickness as she liv'd.
Others are dragg'd away, or must be driven,
She only saw her time and stepp'd to Heaven,
Where Seraphims view all her glories o'er
As one return'd, that had been there before.
For while she did this lower world adorn,
Her body seem'd rather assum'd than born :
So rarefied, advanc'd, so pure and whole,
That body might have been another's soul ;
And equally a miracle it were,
That she could die or that she could live here.

ABRAHAM COWLEY.

[ABRAHAM COWLEY was the posthumous son of a London stationer, and was born in the latter part of the year 1618. He was educated at Westminster School and Trinity College, Cambridge, where he remained from 1636 to 1643. He took the royalist side during the Civil War, and helped the King's cause both at Oxford and afterwards as Secretary to the Queen in her exile in Paris. In 1655 he returned to England, where he remained under strict surveillance till Cromwell's death; then he rejoined his friends in France At the Restoration he came back, and lived in retirement at Barnes and Chertsey till his death in 1667. His poems were published in the following order: *Poetical Blossomes*, 1633; *Love's Riddle*, a comedy, 1638; *The Mistress*, 1647; *The Guardian* (surreptitiously published), 1650: the first folio edition of the *Works*, 1656; other editions of the same followed with the addition of such new poems and essays as he produced from time to time. The most complete editions of his works are those which appeared in 1708 and 1721.]

The history of Cowley's reputation offers an easy text for a discourse on the variations of the standard of taste. A marvel of precocity, widely known as a poet at fifteen; the poetical wonder of Cambridge; so famous at thirty that pirates and forgers made free with his name on their title-pages while he was serving the exiled queen; issuing in self-defence, at thirty-eight, a folio of his poems which was destined to pass through eight editions in a generation; accepted by his literary contemporaries, men of cultivated intelligence, as not only the greatest among themselves, but greater than all that had gone before; buried in state at Westminster by the side of Chaucer and Spenser, and ranked by his biographer, a sober critic, as equal not only to them but to 'the authors of that true antiquity, the best of the Greeks and Romans'; —in thirty years he had sunk out of notice and his name had become a mere memory, mentioned *honoris causa* but no more. 'Though he must always be thought a great poet, he is no longer esteemed a good writer,' said Dryden in 1700. Addison praised him with even more discrimination. Two editions of his works appeared early in the eighteenth century, but in 1737 Pope was able to ask 'Who now reads Cowley?' Then followed Johnson's celebrated Life, which has eclipsed for almost every one the works of its subject. Except for a few students like Lamb and Sir Egerton Brydges, Cowley's verse is in this century unread and unreadable. Not even the antiquarian curiosity of an age which reprints Brathwaite and Crowne has yet availed to present him in a new edition. The reasons of this extraordinary decline in a poetical reputation are not difficult to find ; Dryden absorbed all that was best in Cowley, and superseded him for the readers of the eighteenth century, and the nineteenth century, which reads Dryden little, naturally reads Cowley less. Yet criticism has to justify great names. There must be something in a man who was regarded by his age, and that an age which boasted of having outgrown all illusions, as the most profound and ingenious of its writers. A rapid review of Cowley's work will help us to judge between the estimate of his time and the estimate of posterity.

With the volume of *Poetical Blossomes* which he published at fifteen, when he was a schoolboy at Westminster, we are not further concerned than to note its vast superiority to the verses of most clever boys. If Cowley, like Chatterton, had died before manhood, these verses might perhaps have kept his name alive ; but as it is he soon outdid them, and in his mature writings he valued them justly as 'commendable extravagance in a boy,' but declined to give them a place in the permanent collection of his poems. Some stanzas from *The Wish* he excepted, quoting them in his pleasant essay *Of Myself* as verses of which ' I should hardly now be ashamed.' He wrote them at thirteen, he says ; and our extracts may fairly begin with them. But in the main we shall be right in confining ourselves to the mature poems of the Folio of 1656, with the additions that were made to it during his lifetime. He meant it to be a definitive edition of his poems ; he excluded much from it deliberately, and he intended to add nothing to it. In 1656, as he says in his most interesting Preface—a class of writing which he raised to a new importance— in 1656 he felt in no mood for making poetry. The times were against it, his own health of body and mind were against it. ' A warlike, various, and tragical age is best to write *of*, but worst to write *in.*' Living as a political *suspect,* with scanty means and no prospects, he had no encouragement to write. 'The soul must be filled with bright and delightful ideas when it undertakes to communicate delight to others, which is the main end of poesy.' He was seriously turning his thoughts away from Cromwell's England; planning an 'obscure retreat' in the American plantations; and the book was to be a legacy to the world to which he would soon be dead. As every one knows, times changed, and he did not go to America. The Restoration brought him, not success indeed—his failure to obtain the Mastership of the Savoy was pathetically bewailed by him—but relief from all pressing necessities, and a quiet home first at Barnes and then at Chertsey, not beyond the reach of visits from Evelyn and Dean Sprat and other appreciative friends. In such surroundings he made his peace with the Muse and wrote during the years that remained to him some of his best poems.

The divisions of the Folio are (1) *Miscellanies,* including *Anacreontiques*; (2) *The Mistress,* a collection of love poems; (3) *Pindarique Odes*; (4) *Davideis,* an heroic poem of the troubles of David; and, in the later issues, (5) *Verses on various occasions,* and (6) *Several Discourses by way of Essays in verse and prose.* The *Miscellanies,* he tells us, are poems preserved by chance from a much larger number—some of them the works of his early youth, and some, like the celebrated Elegy on Crashaw, belonging to his best years. What we notice in these pages, as in all that Cowley published, is his curious inability to distinguish good from bad; he prints rubbish, like the intolerable Ode 'Here's to thee Dick,' side by side with the touching verses on the death of his friend Mr. William Hervey; he mars poem after poem with some scholastic absurdity or comparison drawn from a science that has nothing to do with poetry. The fine lines on Falkland, for example—lines that we should prize if only as a memorial of the friendship between two such interesting men—these lines are ruined, poetically speaking, by Cowley's science. Falkland is gone on the expedition against the Scots, and the poet addresses the North :—

> 'Great is thy charge, O North ! be wise and just:
> England commits her Falkland to thy trust;
> Return him safe; Learning would rather choose
> Her Bodley or her Vatican to lose.
> All things that are but writ or printed there
> In his unbounded breast engraven are.'

So far the conceit may pass ; but what are we to say of the illustrations by which Cowley would show us the order that reigns in the crowded mind of his hero?

> 'So thousand divers species fill the air,
> Yet neither crowd nor mix confusedly there.'

What are we to say of the political image under which, with elephantine humour, he pretends to complain of Falkland's too great learning?

> 'How could he answer 't, if the State saw fit
> *To question a monopoly of wit?*'

It is a painful but inevitable thought that Cowley was better pleased with his 'species' and his 'monopoly' than with the noble lines which follow—lines whose force, condensation, dignity and rhythm have hardly been surpassed by Dryden himself :—

> 'Such is the man whom we require the same
> We lent the North, untouched as is his fame.
> He is too good for war, and ought to be
> As far from danger as from fear he's free.
> Those men alone (and they are useful too)
> Whose valour is the only art they know
> Were for sad war and bloody battles born :
> Let them the state defend, and he adorn!

The Mistress (which had been printed in 1647) is a collection of about a hundred love-poems, explained by the author in the preface to the Folio as being mere feigned addresses to some fair creature of the fancy. 'So it is that Poets are scarce thought Freemen of the Company without paying some duties and obliging themselves to be true to Love.' The apology, even if true, was hardly required even by Puritan strictness ; for with two or three exceptions the poems are as cold as icy conceits can make them. Johnson's characteristic judgment is hardly too severe : 'the compositions are such as might have been written for penance by a hermit, or for hire by a philosophical rhymer who had only heard of another sex.' It is as though in the course of a hundred years the worst fancies which Wyatt had borrowed from Petrarch had become fossilized, and were yet brought out by Cowley to do duty for living thoughts. What is love? he seems to ask : it is an interchange of hearts, a flame, a worship, a river to be frozen by disdain—he has a hundred such physical and psychological images of it ; and the poetry consists in taking the images one by one and developing them in merciless disregard of taste and truth of feeling. Is love

fire ? (we may give two or three of his illustrations even after
Addison's page-long summary) :—

> ' Another from my mistress' door
>   Saw me with eyes all watery come ;
>   Nor could the hidden cause explore,
>   But thought some smoke was in the room :—
>   Such ignorance from unwounded learning came ;
>   He knew tears made by smoke, but not by flame !'

The lover writes his love-letters in lemon-juice, that the fire of his
mistress' eyes may bring the letters to light. At another time he
pictures his heart as not inflammable only, but explosive :—

> ' Woe to her stubborn heart if once mine come
>   Into the selfsame room !
> ' Twill tear and blow up all within,
>   Like a grenado shot into a magazine.'

At another, the story of his love cut in the bark has burnt and
withered up the tree. Again, if love is worship, his mistress, who
has proved unfaithful, is like the idolators of old who sinned against
light :—

> ' So the vain Gentiles, when they left t' adore
>   One Deity, could not stop at thousands more . . .
>   Ah, fair Apostate ! could'st thou think to flee
>   From Truth and Goodness, yet keep Unity ? '

Or again ; is his mistress dressed out for conquest? Then her
beauty, which had been a civil government before, becomes a
tyranny. But we have said enough : *The Mistress*, Cowley's
most elaborate and sustained effort, is clearly a failure. Nothing
of what we require of love-poetry is there—neither grace nor glow
nor tenderness nor truth. The passion is neither deeply felt
nor lightly uttered.

We cannot judge so simply the *Pindarique Odes*, a form of
composition of which Cowley was the inventor, and which found
universal favour in England down to the time of Gray. He was
well aware that in writing in this way, which he thought to be an
imitation of Pindar, he was making a questionable innovation.
' I am in great doubt,' he says, ' whether they will be understood
by most readers ; nay even by very many who are well enough
acquainted with the common roads and ordinary tracks of poesy.
. . . The digressions are many and sudden, and sometimes long,
according to the fashion of all lyrics, and of Pindar above all men
living. The figures are unusual and bold, even to temerity, and

such as I durst not have to do withal in any other kind of poetry; the numbers are various and irregular, and sometimes, especially some of the long ones, seem harsh and uncouth if the just measures and cadences be not observed in the pronunciation. So that almost all their sweetness and numerosity (which is to be found, if I mistake not, in the roughest, if rightly repeated) lies in a manner wholly at the mercy of the reader.' For himself, however, he had no doubts about the value of the new style of poetry; nay, he found a pleasure in comparing the 'liberty' of the ode with the moral liberty of which he was always a votary :—

> ' If Life should a well-ordered poem be
>   (In which he only hits the white
> Who joins true profit with the best delight)
> The more heroic way let others take,
>   Mine the Pindaric way I'll make.
> The matter shall be garve, the numbers loose and free.'

But the analogy was a very imperfect one with him ; for while the moral liberty which he enjoyed led him to a life of great simplicity, unworldliness and charm, his liberty of verse led him too often into mere intellectual athleticism and display. 'That for which I think this inequality of number is chiefly to be preferred,' says Dr. Sprat with great artlessness, 'is its affinity with prose'; and that no doubt was the reason which induced the Flatmans and the Samuel Wesleys of the next generation to choose that mode of dress for their platitudes. But with Cowley the attractiveness of the Ode seems to have been the wealth of opportunity which it afforded for what he called 'bold figures,' that is, for imagery such as could and would have occurred to no one else than to himself. Only Cowley, and only in an Ode, could have paused in the midst of a solemn address to the Muse and bidden her 'rein her Pindaric Pegasus closely in'—for

> ' 'Tis an unruly and a hard-mouthed horse.'

Only Cowley, and only in an Ode, could have set the same Muse in her chariot, with Eloquence and Wit and Memory and Invention in the traces and the 'airy footmen' of Conceits to run by her side, and then have suddenly turned to compare this Muse with the Creator : —

> ' Where never yet did pry
>   The busy Morning's curious eye,
> The wheels of thy bold Coach pass quick and free,
>   And all 's an open road to thee.

> Whatever God did say
> Is all thy plain and smooth uninterrupted way.
> Nay, even beyond his works thy voyages are known,
>   Thou 'st thousand worlds too of thine own.
> Thou speak'st, Great Queen, in the same style as he,
> And a new world leaps forth when thou say'st, Let it be!'

The very apparatus of notes with which it was permissible to issue the Odes enlarged the poet's opportunities. In the *Praise of Pindar*, for example, we have—

> 'So Pindar does new words and figures roll
> Down his impetuous dithyrambic tide.
>   Which in no channel deigns to abide,
>   Which neither banks nor dikes control;'

on which the note is, '*Banks*, natural; *Dikes*, artificial. It will neither be bounded nor circumscribed by nature nor by art.' With such a means of interpretation at hand, what limit need the poet set on his invention?

And yet, when the subject is one that interests him, Cowley has something to say that we should not wish unsaid or said differently. Sonorousness counts for something, after all, in the treatment of such themes as the future of knowledge or the fate of a hero and a cause. The two odes which we have chosen for quotation—that *To Mr. Hobbes* and that called *Brutus*—are rightly grandiose, and are therefore successful. Like the other leading spirits of his age, Cowley looked across the passing troubles of the day to the new world to which Bacon had pointed, and which Bacon's followers were hastening to occupy; and of this feeling the *Ode to Mr. Hobbes* is the best expression. Again, the dominant fact in contemporary history (the Odes were published in 1656) was the success of the new Cæsar, Cromwell. Conscientious royalists like Cowley, such at least as were men of contemplation not of action, threw themselves back on history and philosophy, and if they could not explain the evil they paralleled it with other evils from which good had seemed to flow. Brutus, the slayer of Cæsar, the avenger of his country's murder, is himself slain; but what then? Virtue is for all that not an idol or a name :—

> 'Hold, noble Brutus, and restrain
> The bold voice of thy generous disdain.
>   These mighty gulfs are yet
>   Too deep for all thy judgment and thy wit.'

The two odes are brilliant examples of what Cowley could do when he left what he was conventionally expected to feel for what he really felt.

About the *Davideis*, the epic of whose twelve books fortunately only four came to the birth, perhaps the less said the better. We do not altogether wish it away, on account of the vigorous pages which it inspired in the preface ; the pages which contain Cowley's eloquent and almost Miltonic plea for sacred poetry :—

'It is not without grief and indignation that I behold that divine science employing all her inexhaustible riches of wit and eloquence, either in the wicked and beggarly flattery of great persons, or the unmanly idolizing of foolish women, or the wretched affectation of scurril laughter, or at best on the confused antiquated dreams of senseless fables and meta- morphoses. Amongst all holy and consecrated things which the devil ever stole and alienated from the service of the deity; as altars, temples, sacrifices, prayers, and the like ; there is none that he so universally, and so long usurped as poetry It is time to recover it out of the tyrant's hands, and to restore it to the kingdom of God who is the Father of it. It is time to baptize it in Jordan, for it will never become clean by bathing in the water of Dama cus.'

But if we ask how Cowley realised his aspirations, how he succeeded in 'elevating poesy' rather than 'abasing divinity,' the answer must be disappointing. The *Davideis* is a school exercise, no more. It is at least no injustice to take as a specimen the most famous of the descriptive passages, the picture of Hell :—

'Beneath the silent chambers of the earth,
Where the sun's fruitful beams give metals birth,
Where he the growth of fatal gold doth see,
Gold which above more influence has than he;
Beneath the dens where unfledged tempests lie,
And infant winds their tender voices try ;
Beneath the mighty ocean's wealthy caves,
Beneath th' eternal fountain of all waves,
Where their vast court the mother-waters keep,
And undisturb'd by moons in silence sleep ;
There is a place deep, wondrous deep below,
Which genuine night and horror does o'erflow ;
No bound controls th' unwearied space, but hell
Endless as those dire pains that in it dwell.
Here no dear glimpse of the sun's lovely face
Strikes through the solid darkness of the place;

No dawning morn does her kind reds display ;
One slight weak beam would here be thought the day.
No gentle stars with their fair gems of light
Offend the tyrannous and unquestion'd night.
Here Lucifer the mighty captive reigns,
Proud, 'midst his woes, and tyrant in his chains.'

We are driven in sheer despair to Milton :—

'He views
The dismal situation waste and wild ;
A dungeon horrible on all sides round
As one great furnace flamed : yet from those flames
No light, but rather darkness visible,
Served only to discover sights of woe,
Regions of sorrow, doleful shades—'

Here are two nearly contemporary pictures : the one full of gloom, profundity, terror, all coming directly from Milton's simple handling of simple elements. Fire and darkness—these are the physical materials of his hell, and they are left to produce their effect upon the reader by their own intensity and vastness, while the spiritual side of hell is presented in that ceaseless note of woe, 'Regions of sorrow, doleful shades.' In Milton, in effect, we have that 'union of simplicity with greatness' that marks the true epic. But Cowley's hell is shown to us as lying piled with imaginary cosmical lumber, under the caverns where metals are bred, under the nests of the callow crying tempests, under the court of the waters. He cannot take us to it except through a labyrinth of details, on each of which he would dwell for a moment, losing sight of the end. 'Infant winds,' 'tender voices,' 'the vast court of the mother waters,' the influence of gold, the cause of tides and tidelessness—what have these to do with hell, that is, with the deepest conception of dread and darkness which the mind can form ? But it is a consolation to be able to believe that Cowley was dissatisfied with the *Davideis*, and that in his maturity he regarded it as merely indicating to others the poetical capabilities of the Bible history. 'I shall be ambitious of no other fruit from this weak and imperfect attempt of mine,' he says at the end of the preface, 'but the opening of a way to the courage and industry of some other persons, who may be better able to perform it throughly and successfully.' Eleven years after these words were written appeared *Paradise Lost.*

The subsequent editions of the folio contain other writings, both verse and prose, that Cowley published in his later years, and some of the verse we give in our selections. There are no general features however by which we can distinguish these poems from the rest of his work : sometimes, as in the beautiful stanzas which we quote from the *Hymn to Light,* or in the verses which close the *Essay on Solitude,* or in the *Ode on the Royal Society,* he rises to his highest point ; sometimes, as in what he wrote on the death of 'the matchless Orinda,' and in the poem on *The Garden,* he sinks to his lowest.

Addison's Essay [1] and Johnson's Life have said the last word on Cowley's 'mixed wit,' 'metaphysics,' or 'conceits'; and we need hardly dwell at any greater length on what is the first, most obvious, and most disastrous quality of his muse. He owes to it his poetical effacement with posterity, as he owed to it his first success with his contemporaries ; and it would be ungracious as well as uncritical to fasten our attention solely upon that canker of his style. He lived at the end of one intellectual epoch and at the beginning of another ; he held of both, and he was marred by the vices of the decadence as much as, but no more than, he was glorified by the dawning splendours of the new age. What had been the extravagance of a young and uncontrolled imagination in Lyly and Sidney became the pedantry of ingenuity in the sane and learned Cowley, the master of two or three positive sciences and of all the literatures of Europe. But this pedantry was not all. 'I cannot conclude this head of mixed wit,' says Addison, 'without owning that the admirable poet out of whom I have taken the examples of it had as much true wit as any author that ever writ, and indeed all other talents of an extraordinary genius.' Not, perhaps, all other talents of an extraordinary genius, but knowledge, reflection, calmness and clearness of judgment ; in a word, the gifts of the age of science and of prose which set in with the Restoration ; and with these a rhetorical and moral fervour that made him a power in our literature greater, for the moment, than any that had gone before.

EDITOR.

[1] *Spectator, no. 62.*

I.

A WISH.

[First printed in *Poetical Blossomes*, 2nd edition.]

This only grant me, that my means may lie
Too low for envy, for contempt too high.
    Some honour I would have
Not from great deeds, but good alone.
The unknown are better than ill known ;
    Rumour can ope the grave.
Acquaintance I would have, but when 't depends
Not on the number, but the choice of friends.

Books should, not business, entertain the light,
And sleep, as undisturb'd as death, the night.
    My house a cottage, more
Than palace, and should fitting be,
For all my use, not luxury.
    My garden painted o'er
With nature's hand, not art's ; and pleasures yield,
Horace might envy in his Sabine field.

Thus would I double my life's fading space,
For he that runs it well, twice runs his race.
    And in this true delight,
These unbought sports, this happy state,
I would not fear nor wish my fate,
    But boldly say each night,
To-morrow let my sun his beams display,
Or in clouds hide them ; I have liv'd to-day.

2.

[From *The Miscellanies.*]

ODE OF WIT.

Tell me, O tell, what kind of thing is wit,
    Thou who master art of it !
For the first matter loves variety less ;
Less women love 't, either in love or dress.
    A thousand different shapes it bears,
    Comely in thousand shapes appears.
Yonder we saw it plain ; and here 'tis now,
Like spirits in a place, we know not how.

London that vents of false ware so much store,
    In no ware deceives us more.
For men led by the colour, and the shape,
Like Zeuxis' birds fly to the painted grape ;
    Some things do through our judgment **pass**
    As through a multiplying glass ;
And sometimes, if the object be too far,
We take a falling meteor for a star.

Hence 'tis a wit, that greatest word of fame,
    Grows such a common name ;
And wits by our creation they become,
Just so, as titular Bishops made at Rome.
    'Tis not a tale, tis not a jest
    Admir'd with laughter at a feast,
Nor florid talk which can that title gain ;
The proofs of wit for ever must remain.

'Tis not to force some lifeless verses meet
    With their five gouty feet.
All everywhere, like man's, must be the soul,
And reason the inferior powers control.
    Such were the numbers which could call
    The stones into the Theban wall.
Such miracles are ceas'd ; and now we see
No towns or houses rais'd by poetry.

Yet 'tis not to adorn, and gild each part;
    That shows more cost, than art.
Jewels at nose and lips but ill appear;
Rather than all things wit, let none be there.
    Several lights will not be seen.
    If there be nothing else between.
Men doubt, because they stand so thick i' th' sky,
If those be stars which paint the galaxy.

'Tis not when two like words make up one noise,
    Jests for Dutch men, and English boys.
In which who finds out wit, the same may see
In anagrams and acrostics poetry.
    Much less can that have any place
    At which a virgin hides her face;
Such dross the fire must purge away; 'tis just
The author blush, there where the reader must.

'Tis not such lines as almost crack the stage,
    When Bajazet begins to rage.
Nor a tall metaphor in the bombast way,
Nor the dry chips of short-lung'd Seneca;
    Nor upon all things to obtrude,
    And force some odd similitude.
What is it then, which like the power divine
We only can by negatives define?

In a true piece of wit all things must be,
    Yet all things there agree.
As in the ark, join'd without force or strife,
All creatures dwelt; all creatures that had life.
    Or as the primitive forms of all
    (If we compare great things with small)
Which without discord or confusion lie,
In that strange mirror of the Deity.

But love that moulds one man up out of two,
    Makes me forget and injure you.
I took you for myself sure when I thought
That you in anything were to be taught.
    Correct my error with thy pen ;
    And if any ask me then,
What thing right wit, and height of genius is,
I'll only shew your lines, and say, 'Tis this.

ON THE DEATH OF MR. WILLIAM HERVEY.

It was a dismal and a fearful night,
Scarce could the Morn drive on th' unwilling light,
When sleep, death's image, left my troubled breast,
    By something more like death possest.
My eyes with tears did uncommanded flow,
    And on my soul hung the dull weight
    Of some intolerable fate.
What bell was that? Ah me ! Too much I know.

My sweet companion, and my gentle peer,
Why hast thou left me thus unkindly here,
Thy end for ever, and my life to moan?
    O thou hast left me all alone !
Thy soul and body when death's agony
    Besieg'd around thy noble heart,
    Did not with more reluctance part
Than I, my dearest friend, do part from thee.

My dearest friend, would I had died for thee !
Life and this world henceforth will tedious be,
Nor shall I know hereafter what to do
    If once my griefs prove tedious too.
Silent and sad I walk about all day,
    As sullen ghosts stalk speechless by
    Where their hid treasures lie ;
Alas, my treasure's gone, why do I stay?

He was my friend, the truest friend on earth;
A strong and mighty influence join'd our birth;
Nor did we envy the most sounding name
    By friendship giv'n of old to fame.
None but his brethren he, and sisters knew,
      Whom the kind youth preferr'd to me;
      And ev'n in that we did agree,
For much above myself I lov'd them too.

Say, for you saw us, ye immortal lights,
How oft unwearied have we spent the nights?
Till the Ledaean stars, so fam'd for love,
    Wondered at us from above.
We spent them not in toys, in lusts, or wine;
      But search of deep philosophy,
      Wit, eloquence, and poetry,
Arts which I lov'd, for they, my friend, were thine.

Ye fields of Cambridge, our dear Cambridge, say,
Have ye not seen us walking every day?
Was there a tree about which did not know
    The love betwixt us two?
Henceforth, ye gentle trees, for ever fade,
      Or your sad branches thicker join,
      And into darksome shades combine,
Dark as the grave wherein my friend is laid.

Henceforth no learned youths beneath you sing,
Till all the tuneful birds t' your boughs they bring;
No tuneful birds play with their wonted cheer,
    And call the learned youths to hear;
No whistling winds through the glad branches fly,
      But all with sad solemnity,
      Mute and unmoved be,
Mute as the grave wherein my friend does lie.

To him my muse made haste with every strain
Whilst it was new, and warm yet from the brain,
He lov'd my worthless rhymes, and like a friend
    Would find out something to commend.

Hence now, my muse, thou canst not me delight;
　　Be this my latest verse
　　With which I now adorn his hearse,
And this my grief without thy help shall write.

Had I a wreath of bays about my brow
I should contemn that flourishing honour now,
Condemn it to the fire, and joy to hear
　　It rage and crackle there.
Instead of bays, crown with sad cypress me;
　　Cypress which tombs does beautify;
　　Not Phoebus griev'd so much as I
For him, who first was made that mournful tree.

Large was his soul; as large a soul as e'er
Submitted to inform a body here;
High as the place 'twas shortly in heav'n to have,
　　But low, and humble as his grave;
So high that all the virtues there did come
　　As to their chiefest seat
　　Conspicuous, and great;
So low that for me too it made a room.

He scorn'd this busy world below, and all
That we, mistaken mortals, pleasure call;
Was filled with innocent gallantry and truth,
　　Triumphant o'er the sins of youth.
He like the stars, to which he now is gone,
　　That shine with beams like flame,
　　Yet burn not with the same,
Had all the light of youth, of the fire none.

Knowledge he only sought, and so soon caught,
As if for him knowledge had rather sought;
Nor did more learning ever crowded lie
　　In such a short mortality.
When e'er the skilful youth discours'd or writ,
　　Still did the notions throng
　　About his eloquent tongue,
Nor could his ink flow faster than his wit.

So strong a wit did nature to him frame,
As all things but his judgment overcame;
His judgment like the heav'nly moon did show,
    Temp'ring that mighty sea below.
Oh had he lived in learning's world, what bound
      Would have been able to control
      His overpowering soul?
We have lost in him arts that not yet are found.

His mirth was the pure spirits of various wit,
Yet never did his God or friends forget.
And when deep talk and wisdom came in view,
    Retir'd and gave to them their due.
For the rich help of books he always took,
      Though his own searching mind before
      Was so with notions written o'er
As if wise nature had made that her book.

So many virtues join'd in him, as we
Can scarce pick here and there in history,
More than old writers' practice e'er could reach,
    As much as they could ever teach.
These did religion, queen of virtues, sway,
      And all their sacred motions steer,
      Just like the first and highest sphere
Which wheels about, and turns all heav'n one way.

With as much zeal, devotion, piety,
He always liv'd, as other saints do die.
Still with his soul severe account he kept,
    Weeping all debts out ere he slept.
Then down in peace and innocence he lay,
      Like the sun's laborious light,
      Which still in water sets at night,
Unsullied with his journey of the day.

Wondrous young man, why wert thou made so good,
To be snatched hence ere better understood?
Snatched before half of thee enough was seen!
    Thou ripe, and yet thy life but green!

Nor could thy friends take their last sad farewell,
    But danger and infectious death
    Maliciously seiz'd on that breath
Where life, spirit, pleasure always us'd to dwell.

But happy thou, ta'en from this frantic age,
Where ignorance and hypocrisy does rage !
A fitter time for heaven no soul ere chose,
    The place now only free from those.
There 'mong the blest thou dost for ever shine,
    And wheresoe'er thou cast thy view
    Upon that white and radiant crew,
See'st not a soul cloth'd with more light than thine.

And if the glorious saints cease not to know
Their wretched friends who fight with life below ,
Thy flame to me does still the same abide,
    Only more pure and rarified.
There whilst immortal hymns thou dost rehearse,
    Thou dost with holy pity see
    Our dull and earthly poesy,
Where grief and misery can be joined with verse.

THE CHRONICLE. A BALLAD.

Margarita first possest,
    If I remember well, my breast,
    Margarita first of all ;
But when awhile the wanton maid
With my restless heart had played,
    Martha took the flying ball.

Martha soon did it resign
    To the beauteous Catharine.
    Beauteous Catharine gave place
(Though loth and angry she to part
With the possession of my heart)
    To Elisa's conquering face.

Elisa till this hour might reign
    Had she not evil counsels ta'en.
    Fundamental laws she broke,
And still new favourites she chose,
Till up in arms my passions rose,
    And cast away her yoke.

Mary then and gentle Ann
    Both to reign at once began.
    Alternately they sway'd,
And sometimes Mary was the fair,
And sometimes Ann the crown did wear,
    And sometimes both I obey'd.

Another Mary then arose
    And did rigorous laws impose.
    A mighty tyrant she !
Long, alas, should I have been,
Under that iron-sceptered Queen,
    Had not Rebecca set me free.

When fair Rebecca set me free,
    'Twas then a golden time with me.
    But soon those pleasures fled,
For the gracious Princess died
In her youth and beauty's pride,
    And Judith reigned in her stead.

One month, three days, and half an hour
    Judith held the sovereign power.
    Wondrous beautiful her face,
But so weak and small her wit,
That she to govern was unfit,
    And so Susanna took her place.

But when Isabella came
    Arm'd with a resistless flame
    And th' artillery of her eye ;
Whilst she proudly marched about
Greater conquests to find out,
    She beat out Susan by the by.

But in her place I then obeyed
 Black-ey'd Bess, her viceroy-maid,
 To whom ensu'd a vacancy,
Thousand worse passions then possest
The interregnum of my breast.
 Bless me from such an anarchy!

Gentle Henriette then
 And a third Mary next began,
 Then Joan, and Jane, and Audria.
And then a pretty Thomasine,
And then another Katharine,
 And then a long et cætera.

But should I now to you relate,
 The strength and riches of their state,
 The powder, patches, and the pins,
The ribbons, jewels, and the rings,
The lace, the paint, and warlike things
 That make up all their magazines;

If I should tell the politic arts
 To take and keep men's hearts,
 The letters, embassies, and spies,
The frowns, and smiles, and flatteries,
The quarrels, tears, and perjuries,
 Numberless, nameless mysteries!

And all the little lime-twigs laid
 By Matchavil the waiting-maid;
 I more voluminous should grow
(Chiefly if I like them should tell
All change of weathers that befell)
 Than Holinshed or Stow.

But I will briefer with them be,
 Since few of them were long with me.
 An higher and a nobler strain
My present Emperess dost claim,
Heleonora, first o' the name;
 Whom God grant long to reign!

On the Death of Mr. Crashaw.

Poet and Saint! to thee alone are given
The two most sacred names of earth and Heaven,
The hard and rarest union which can be
Next that of godhead with humanity.
Long did the muses banish'd slaves abide,
And built vain pyramids to mortal pride;
Like Moses thou (though spells and charms withstand)
Hast brought them nobly home back to their Holy Land.

    Ah wretched we, poets of earth! but thou
Wert living the same poet which thou 'rt now.
Whilst angels sing to thee their airs divine,
And joy in an applause so great as thine,
Equal society with them to hold,
Thou need'st not make new songs, but say the old.
And they (kind spirits!) shall all rejoice to see
How little less than they, exalted man may be.
Still the old heathen gods in numbers dwell,
The heavenliest thing on earth still keeps up hell.
Nor have we yet quite purg'd the Christian land;
Still idols here like calves at Bethel stand.
And though Pan's death long since all oracles broke,
Yet still in rhyme the fiend Apollo spoke:
Nay with the worst of heathen dotage we
(Vain men!) the monster woman deify;
Find stars, and tie our fates there in a face,
And paradise in them, by whom we lost it, place.
What different faults corrupt our muses thus?
Wanton as girls, as old wives fabulous!

    Thy spotless muse, like Mary, did contain
The boundless godhead; she did well disdain
That her eternal verse employed should be
On a less subject than eternity;
And for a sacred mistress scorn'd to take
But her whom God himself scorn'd not his spouse to make.
It (in a kind) her miracle did do;
A fruitful mother was, and virgin too,

How well, blest swan, did fate contrive thy death;
And make thee render up thy tuneful breath
In thy great mistress' arms, thou most divine
And richest offering of Loretto's shrine[1]
Where like some holy sacrifice t' expire
A fever burns thee, and love lights the fire
Angels (they say) brought the famed chapel there,
And bore the sacred load in triumph through the air
'Tis surer much they brought thee there, and they,
And thou, their charge, went singing all the way.

Pardon, my mother church, if I consent
That angels led him when from thee he went,
For even in error sure no danger is
When join'd with so much piety as his.
Ah, mighty God, with shame I speak 't, and grief,
Ah that our greatest faults were in belief!
And our weak reason were even weaker yet,
Rather than thus our wills too strong for it.
His faith perhaps in some nice tenents might
Be wrong ; his life, I 'm sure, was in the right.
And I myself a Catholic will be,
So far at least, great saint, to pray to thee.

Hail, bard triumphant ! and some care bestow
On us, the poets militant below !
Opposed by our old enemy, adverse chance,
Attacked by envy, and by ignorance,
Enchain'd by beauty, tortured by desires,
Expos'd by tyrant-love to savage beasts and fires.
Thou from low earth in nobler flames didst rise,
And like Elijah, mount alive the skies.
Elisha-like (but with a wish much less,
More fit thy greatness, and my littleness)
Lo here I beg (I whom thou once didst prove
So humble to esteem, so good to love)
Not that thy spirit might on me doubled be,
I ask but half thy mighty spirit for me ;
And when my muse soars with so strong a wing,
'Twill learn of things divine, and first of thee to sing.

[1] Crashaw became a Roman Catholic, and died a canon of Loretto, 1650.

3.

[*Anacreontiques.*]

DRINKING.

The thirsty earth soaks up the rain,
And drinks, and gapes for drink again,
The plants suck in the earth, and are
With constant drinking fresh and fair.
The sea itself, which one would think
Should have but little need of drink,
Drinks ten thousand rivers up,
So fill'd that they oerflow the cup.
The busy sun (and one would guess
By its drunken fiery face no less)
Drinks up the sea, and when he's done,
The moon and stars drink up the sun.
They drink and dance by their own light,
They drink and revel all the night.
Nothing in nature's sober found,
But an eternal health goes round.
Fill up the bowl then, fill it high,
Fill all the glasses there, for why
Should every creature drink but I,
Why, man of morals, tell me why?

THE SWALLOW.

Foolish prater, what dost thou
So early at my window do
With thy tuneless serenade?
Well't had been had Tereus made
Thee as dumb as Philomel;
There his knife had done but well.
In thy undiscovered nest,
Thou dost all the winter rest,
And dreamest o'er thy summer joys
Free from the stormy season's noise:
Free from th' ill thou'st done to me,
Who disturbs or seeks out thee?

Hadst thou all the charming notes
Of the wood's poetic throats,
All thy art could never pay
What thou'st ta'en from me away ;
Cruel bird, thou'st ta'en away
A dream out of my arms to-day,
A dream that ne'er must equall'd be
By all that waking eyes may see.
Thou this damage to repair,
Nothing half so sweet or fair,
Nothing half so good canst bring,
Though men say, thou bring'st the spring.

4.

[From *The Mistress.*]

THE SPRING.

Though you be absent here, I needs must say
The trees as beauteous are, and flowers as gay,
    As ever they were wont to be ;
    Nay the birds' rural music too
    Is as melodious and free,
    As if they sung to pleasure you :
I saw a rose-bud ope this morn ; I'll swear
The blushing morning open'd not more fair.

How could it be so fair, and you away?
How could the trees be beauteous, flowers so gay?
    Could they remember but last year,
    How you did them, they you delight,
    The sprouting leaves which saw you here,
    And call'd their fellows to the sight,
Would, looking round for the same sight in vain,
Creep back into their silent barks again.

Where'er you walk'd trees were as reverend made,
As when of old gods dwelt in every shade.
    Is't possible they should not know,
    What loss of honour they sustain,
    That thus they smile and flourish now,
    And still their former pride retain?
Dull creatures! 'tis not without cause that she,
Who fled the god of wit, was made a tree.

In ancient times sure they much wiser were,
When they rejoic'd the Thracian verse to hear;
    In vain did nature bid them stay,
    When Orpheus had his song begun,
    They call'd their wondering roots away,
    And bade them silent to him run.
How would those learned trees have followed you?
You would have drawn them, and their poet too.

But who can blame them now? for, since you're gone,
They're here the only fair, and shine alone.
    You did their natural rights invade;
    Where ever you did walk or sit,
    The thickest boughs could make no shade,
    Although the Sun had granted it:
The fairest flowers could please no more, near you,
Than painted flowers, set next to them, could do.

When e'er then you come hither, that shall be
The time, which this to others is, to me.
    The little joys which here are now,
    The name of punishments do bear,
    When by their sight they let us know
    How we depriv'd of greater are.
'Tis you the best of seasons with you bring;
This is for beasts, and that for men the spring.

THE WISH.

Well then ; I now do plainly see,
This busy world and I shall ne'er agree ;
The very honey of all earthly joy
    Does of all meats the soonest cloy,
    And they, methinks, deserve my pity,
Who for it can endure the stings,
The crowd, and buzz, and murmurings
    Of this great hive, the city.

Ah, yet, ere I descend to th' grave
May I a small house and large garden have !
And a few friends, and many books, both true,
    Both wise, and both delightful too !
    And since love ne'er will from me flee,
A mistress moderately fair,
And good as guardian-angels are,
    Only belov'd, and loving me !

O fountains, when in you shall I
Myself, eased of unpeaceful thoughts, espy?
O fields ! O woods ! when, when shall I be made
    The happy tenant of your shade?
    Here's the spring-head of pleasure's flood ;
Where all the riches lie, that she
    Has coin'd and stamp'd for good.

Pride and ambition here,
Only in far-fetched metaphors appear ;
Here nought but winds can hurtful murmurs scatter,
    And nought but echo flatter.
    The gods, when they descended, hither
From heav'n did always choose their way ;
And therefore we may boldly say,
    That 'tis the way too thither.

How happy here should I,
And one dear she live, and embracing die !
She who is all the world, and can exclude
    In deserts solitude.
  I should have then this only fear,
Lest men, when they my pleasures see,
Should hither throng to live like me,
    And make a city here.

5.

[From *Pindarique Odes.*]

To Mr. Hobbes.

Vast bodies of philosophy
    I oft have seen, and read,
    But all are bodies dead,
      Or bodies by art fashioned ;
I never yet the living soul could see,
    But in thy books and thee.
  'Tis only God can know
Whether the fair idea thou dost show
Agree entirely with his own or no ;
    This I dare boldly tell,
'Tis so like truth 'twill serve our turn as well.
Just as in nature thy proportions be,
As full of concord their variety,
As firm the parts upon their centre rest,
And all so solid are that they, at least
As much as nature, emptiness detest.

Long did the mighty Stagirite retain
The universal intellectual reign,
Saw his own country's short-lived leopard[1] slain ;
The stronger Roman eagle did outfly,
Oftener renewed his age, and saw that die ;
Mecca itself, in spite of Mahomet possessed,
And chas'd by a wild deluge from the east,
His monarchy new planted in the west.

[1] The Macedonian empire. See the commentators on Daniel, ch. 7.

But as in time each great imperial race
Degenerates, and gives some new one place,
    So did this noble empire waste,
    Sunk by degrees from glories past,
And in the school-men's hands it perished quite at last.
    Then nought but words it grew,
    And those all barbarous too.
    It perished, and it vanished there,
The life and soul breath'd out became but empty air.

The fields which answer'd well the ancients' plough,
Spent and outworn return no harvest now,
In barren age wild and unglorious lie,
    And boast of past fertility,
The poor relief of present poverty.
      Food and fruit we now must want
      Unless new lands we plant.
We break up tombs with sacrilegious hands;
      Old rubbish we remove;
To walk in ruins, like vain ghosts, we love,
    And with fond divining wands
      We search among the dead
      For treasures buried,
    Whilst still the liberal earth does hold
So many virgin mines of undiscovered gold.

The Baltic, Euxine, and the Caspian,
And slender-limbed Mediterranean,
Seem narrow creeks to thee, and only fit
For the poor wretched fisher-boats of wit.
Thy nobler vessel the vast ocean tries,
    And nothing sees but seas and skies,
    Till unknown regions it descries,
Thou great Columbus of the golden lands of new philosophies!
    Thy task was harder much than his,
    For thy learn'd America is
    Not only found out first by thee,
And rudely left to future industry,
    But thy eloquence and thy wit
Has planted, peopled, built, and civiliz'd it.

I little thought before,
(Nor, being my own self so poor,
Could comprehend so vast a store)
That all the wardrobe of rich eloquence,
Could have afforded half enough,
Of bright, of new, and lasting stuff,
To clothe the mighty limbs of thy gigantic sense.
Thy solid reason like the shield from heaven
To the Trojan hero given,
Too strong to take a mark from any mortal dart,
Yet shines with gold and gems in every part,
And wonders on it grav'd by the learn'd hand of art ;
A shield that gives delight
Even to the enemies' sight,
Then when they're sure to lose the combat by't.

Nor can the snow which now cold age does shed
Upon thy reverend head
Quench or allay the noble fires within,
But all which thou hast been
And all that youth can be thou'rt yet,
So fully still dost thou
Enjoy the manhood, and the bloom of wit,
And all the natural heat, but not the fever too.
So contraries on Ætna's top conspire,
Here hoary frosts, and by them breaks out fire.
A secure peace the faithful neighbours keep,
Th' emboldened snow next to the flame does sleep.
And if we weigh, like thee,
Nature, and causes, we shall see
That thus it needs must be :
To things immortal time can do no wrong,
And that which never is to die, for ever must be young.

BRUTUS.

Excellent Brutus, of all human race
The best till nature was improved by grace,
Till men above themselves faith raised more
      Than reason above beasts before ;
Virtue was thy life's centre, and from thence
Did silently and constantly dispense
      The gentle vigorous influence
To all the wide and fair circumference :
And all the parts upon it lean'd so easily,
Obey'd the mighty force so willingly,
That none could discord or disorder see
      In all their contrariety ;
Each had his motion natural and free,
And the whole no more moved than the whole world could be.

From thy strict rule some think that thou didst swerve
(Mistaken honest men) in Caesar's blood ;
What mercy could the tyrant's life deserve,
From him who kill'd himself rather than serve ?
Th' heroic exaltations of good
      Are so far from understood,
We count them vice : alas, our sight's so ill,
That things which swiftest move seem to stand still.
We look not upon virtue in her height,
On her supreme idea, brave and bright,
      In the original light :
    But as her beams reflected pass
Through our own nature or ill custom's glass.
      And 'tis no wonder so,
      If with dejected eye
    In standing pools we seek the sky,
That stars so high above should seem to us below.

Can we stand by and see
Our mother robb'd, and bound, and ravish'd be,
Yet not to her assistance stir,
Pleas'd with the strength and beauty of the ravisher?
Or shall we fear to kill him, if before
The cancell'd name of friend he bore?
Ungrateful Brutus do they call?
Ungrateful Caesar who could Rome enthrall!
An act more barbarous and unnatural
(In th' exact balance of true virtue tried)
Than his successor Nero's parricide!
There's none but Brutus could deserve
That all men else should wish to serve,
And Caesar's usurped place to him should proffer;
None can deserve 't but he who would refuse the offer.

Ill fate assumed a body thee t' affright,
And wrapped itself i' th' terrors of the night,
I'll meet thee at Philippi, said the sprite;
I'll meet thee there, saidst thou,
With such a voice, and such a brow,
As put the trembling ghost to sudden flight,
It vanished as a taper's light
Goes out when spirits appear in sight.
One would have thought 't had heard the morning crow,
Or seen her well-appointed star
Come marching up the eastern hill afar.
Nor durst it in Philippi's field appear,
But unseen attacked thee there.
Had it presumed in any shape thee to oppose,
Thou wouldst have forced it back upon thy foes:
Or slain 't like Cæsar, though it be
A conqueror and a monarch mightier far than he.

What joy can human things to us afford,
When we see perish thus by odd events,
Ill men, and wretched accidents,
The best cause and best man that ever drew a sword?

When we see
The false Octavius, and wild Antony,
  Godlike Brutus, conquer thee?
What can we say but thine own tragic word,
That virtue, which had worshipped been by thee
As the most solid good, and greatest deity,
  By this fatal proof became
   An idol only, and a name?
 Hold, noble Brutus, and restrain
The bold voice of thy generous disdain :
  These mighty gulfs are yet
Too deep for all thy judgment and thy wit.
The time's set forth already which shall quell
Stiff reason, when it offers to rebel ;
  Which these great secrets shall unseal,
  And new philosophies reveal.
A few years more, so soon hadst thou not died,
Would have confounded human virtue's pride,
  And shew'd thee a God crucified.

6.

[From *Verses written on Several Occasions.*]

STANZAS FROM THE 'HYMN TO LIGHT.'

Thou in the moon's bright chariot proud and gay
  Dost thy bright wood of stars survey ;
  And all the year dost with thee bring
Of thousand flow'ry lights thine own nocturnal spring.

 Thou Scythian-like dost round thy lands above
  The sun's gilt tent for ever move,
  And still as thou in pomp dost go
The shining pageants of the world attend thy show.

Nor amidst all these triumphs dost thou scorn
  The humble glow-worms to adorn,
  And with those living spangles gild
(O greatness without pride !) the bushes of the field.

Night, and her ugly subjects thou dost fright,
    And sleep, the lazy owl of night ;
    Ashamed and fearful to appear
They screen their horrid shapes with the black hemisphere.

With them there hastes, and wildly takes the alarm,
    Of painted dreams a busy swarm,
    At the first opening of thine eye,
The various clusters break, the antic atoms fly.

The guilty serpents, and obscener beasts,
    Creep conscious to their secret rests :
    Nature to thee does reverence pay,
Ill omens and ill sights removes out of thy way.

At thy appearance, grief itself is said
    To shake his wings, and rouse his head,
    And cloudy care has often took
A gentle beamy smile reflected from thy look.

At thy appearance, fear itself grows bold ;
    Thy sunshine melts away his cold.
    Encourag'd at the sight of thee,
To the cheek colour comes, and firmness to the knee.

When, goddess, thou lift'st up thy waken'd head
    Out of the morning's purple bed,
    Thy quire of birds about thee play,
And all the joyful world salutes the rising day.

    All the world's bravery that delights our eyes
        Is but thy sev'ral liveries,
        Thou the rich dye on them bestowest,
Thy nimble pencil paints this landscape as thou goest.

    A crimson garment in the rose thou wear'st ;
        A crown of studded gold thou bear'st,
        ·The virgin lilies in their white,
Are clad but with the lawn of almost naked light !

From the 'Ode to the Royal Society.'

From words, which are but pictures of the thought,
(Though we our thoughts from them perversely drew)
To things, the mind's right object, he[1] it brought.
Like foolish birds to painted grapes we flew ;
He sought and gather'd for our use the true ;
And when on heaps the chosen bunches lay,
He prest them wisely the mechanic way,
Till all their juice did in one vessel join,
Ferment into a nourishment divine,
   The thirsty soul's refreshing wine.
Who to the life an exact piece would make,
Must not from others' work a copy take ;
   No, not from Rubens or Vandyke ;
Much less content himself to make it like
Th' ideas and the images which lie
In his own fancy, or his memory.
   No, he before his sight must place
   The natural and living face ;
   The real object must command
Each judgment of his eye, and motion of his hand.

From these and all long errors of the way,
In which our wandering predecessors went,
And like th' old Hebrews many years did stray
   In deserts but of small extent,
Bacon, like Moses, led us forth at last.
   The barren wilderness he past,
   Did on the very border stand
   Of the blest promis'd land,
And from the mountain's top of his exalted wit,
   Saw it himself, and shew'd us it.
But life did never to one man allow
Time to discover worlds, and conquer too ;
Nor can so short a line sufficient be
To fathom the vast depths of nature's sea :

[1] Lord Bacon.

The work he did we ought t' admire,
And were unjust if we should more require
From his few years, divided 'twixt th' excess
Of low affliction and high happiness.
For who on things remote can fix his sight,
That's always in a triumph, or a fight?

7.

[From the *Discourses by Way of Essays.*]

ON SOLITUDE.

Hail, old patrician trees, so great and good!
 Hail ye plebeian underwood!
 Where the poetic birds rejoice,
And for their quiet nests and plenteous food,
 Pay with their grateful voice.

Hail, the poor muse's richest manor seat!
 Ye country houses and retreat,
 Which all the happy gods so love,
That for you oft they quit their bright and great
 Metropolis above.

Here nature does a house for me erect,
 Nature the wisest architect,
 Who those fond artists does despise
That can the fair and living trees neglect,
 Yet the dead timber prize.

Here let me careless and unthoughtful lying,
 Hear the soft winds above me flying
 With all their wanton boughs dispute,
And the more tuneful birds to both replying,
 Nor be myself too mute.

A silver stream shall roll his waters near,
 Gilt with the sunbeams here and there,
 On whose enamel'd bank I'll walk,
And see how prettily they smile, and hear
 How prettily they talk.

Ah wretched, and too solitary he
  Who loves not his own company!
  He 'll feel the weight of 't many a day
Unless he call in sin or vanity
  To help to bear 't away.

O Solitude, first state of human-kind!
  Which blest remain'd till man did find
  Even his own helper's company.
As soon as two (alas!) together join'd,
  The serpent made up three.

The god himself, through countless ages thee
  His sole companion chose to be,
  Thee, sacred Solitude alone,
Before the branchy head of number's tree
  Sprang from the trunk of one.

Thou (though men think thine an unactive part)
  Dost break and tame th' unruly heart,
  Which else would know no settled pace,
Making it more well manag'd by thy art
  With swiftness and with grace.

Thou the faint beams of reason's scatter'd light,
  Dost like a burning-glass unite,
  Dost multiply the feeble heat,
And fortify the strength, till thou dost bright
  And noble fires beget.

Whilst this hard truth I teach, methinks, I see
  The monster London laugh at me,
  I should at thee too, foolish city,
If it were fit to laugh at misery,
  But thy estate I pity.

Let but thy wicked men from out thee go,
  And all the fools that crowd thee so,
  Even thou who dost thy millions boast,
A village less than Islington wilt grow,
  A solitude almost.

EDMUND WALLER.

[EDMUND WALLER was born, March 3, 1605, at Coleshill in Warwick shire. At seventeen years of age he was elected member of parliament for Agmondesham. He married early, and lost his wife soon; after her death he paid court to Lady Dorothy Sidney, daughter of the Earl of Leicester. He protracted his unsuccessful suit, celebrating the lady under the title of Sacharissa, until in 1639 she married the Earl of Sunderland. In 1640 he entered parliament again, and made himself remarkable by his opposition to the King's measures, but when the Civil War became imminent he took the Royalist side. In 1643 he was arrested as one of the leaders of a plot against the Parliament, and having with difficulty preserved his life, proceeded to France on his release. After some years he returned to England and made his peace with Cromwell; at the Restoration he eagerly laid his homage at the feet of Charles II. He was made Provost of Eton, and sat in several parliaments after the Restoration. He died of dropsy at Beaconsfield, in Buckinghamshire, on the 21st of October, 1687. His poems, first published in 1645, were very frequently reprinted during his life-time, and always with additions.]

The reputation of Waller has suffered greater fluctuation of fortune than that of any other English poet. In his youth, he was outshone by the last great Elizabethans, his contemporaries ; during the Civil Wars he gradually rose to be considered second only to Cowley. After the Restoration, and when that writer was in his grave, Waller found himself still more popular, and when he died, at a very great age, the wits and critics, with Thomas Rymer at their head, exalted him to the first place in the English Parnassus. Until the end of the century it was tacitly admitted that Waller was the greatest English poet. The juster sense of Addison and of Pope curtailed these extravagant honours, while leaving to Waller the praise of unrivalled sweetness. In the hands of Gray, Johnson and Cowper, Waller sank gradually back into the rank and file of poets, while the critics of the beginning of our century went further still, and denied him all lyrical merit. Of late even his historical position has been assailed, and there is perhaps no famous writer at the present moment so little read or considered as Waller. But the scale has certainly descended too far on the side of dispraise, and it is time to insist on the part filled by this poet in the progress of our literature.

It was Dryden who, with his usual nice discrimination, first observed the quality in which Waller differed from all the writers of his time. In the preface to *The Rival Ladies*, 1664, that great critic remarks : ' the excellence and dignity of rhyme were never fully known till Mr. Waller taught it ; he first made writing easily an art, first showed us to conclude the sense, most commonly, in distichs, which in the verse of those before him runs on for so many lines together, that the reader is out of breath to overtake it.' Half a century later, Voltaire paraphrased and enlarged this criticism of Dryden's in language which has become more famous, but which is far from being so pithy or so exact. It is not true, as Voltaire would teach us, that sweetness of versification, the art of liquid numbers, was invented by Waller, but it is true, as Dryden noted, that Waller was the first English poet to adopt the French fashion of writing in couplets, instead of enjambments. He seems to have been born as neat a poet as he died ; his complimentary piece, called *His Majesty's Escape at St. Andrews*, has the full character of Augustan verse, and was written as early as 1623. We have given an extract from this poem in our selection, not on account of its intrinsic merit so much as on account of its extraordinary interest as the first note of classicism in English poetry. From this piece, through Denham, Dryden, Pope, Johnson, Darwin, the chain of heroic distich-writing passes unbroken down to *English Bards an l Scotch Reviewers*, a progress of nearly two hundred years. It was long before Waller gained a single imitator, and the old system of enjambments continued in fashion until the Restoration, with its tide of thought setting from France, swept it away. The *Pharonnida* of Chamberlayne, 1659, and the *Thealma and Clearchus* of Chalkhill, 1683, were the last heroic poems in the old style, and Waller, who had for years written alone in the French manner, lived to see his experiment universally adopted. If we consider this fact, and moreover the satisfaction with which the new mechanic art of rhyming was regarded, we shall not wonder at the immense reputation of Waller. It is, moreover, only fair to note that he persevered twenty years in his new versification before he gained his first disciple, Denham.

Waller continued to polish his verses, and to add to them, foɪ nearly sixty years, yet they remained a slender collection to the last. If we except his absurd dramatic efforts, a travesty of the *Maid's Tragedy* in rhyme, and a certain share in the holiday task, set by Orinda to the wits, of translating a play by Corneille, the body of his poems does not much exceed five thousand lines. In his youth he wrote a florid epic about the Bermudas, which he proposed to visit, but did not ; this is *The Battle of the Summer's Islands;* towards the close of his life he composed six very serious cantos *Of Divine Love*, in the didactic manner afterwards to become so fashionable. Of the remainder of his verse, half is occupied with love-ditties addressed to Sacharissa, the poetic name under which, between the years 1629 and 1639 he courted Lady Dorothy Sidney, who finally married the Earl of Sunderland. Waller married and was left a widower very early in life ; he was a man of fortune, a country gentleman, and a member of parliament, staunch on the royalist side, at least at that time, and some of his biographers have wondered that he did not secure the hand of Lady Dorothy. But the reader who studies the Sacharissa poems will doubt whether he was really very anxious to do so ; the love-making is extremely elegant and ingenious, but without passion, and the ambition to be remembered through Sacharissa as Petrarch through Laura is a little too obvious. But Waller's love-verses, though frigid, are more manly than those of Cowley, and if they do not take the heart by storm, they beleaguer it with great strategic art, and an infinite show of patience.

The ingenuity of Waller is entirely distinct from that 'meta-physical' wit for which his contemporaries were famous. He does not strive to dazzle and bewilder the mind with paradox, like Donne, or to deck out one poor thought in gaudy raiment of conceits, like the school of Donne. He is scholastic in a politer sense ; he balances his thoughts, as he does his syllables, and in him first we detect that see-saw of phraseology, now up, now down, which was to become the crowning sin of the classic poetry. His powers of antithesis, though trifling in comparison with those of Dryden and Pope, and in his own last days equalled by such inferior writers as Roscommon and Aphra Behn, were the wonder of his earlier con-temporaries, and chiefly led to his great reputation for wit. Charles I., amcng whose faults neglect of polite letters has never been included, early became aware of the polished style of Waller, and welcomed him to Whitehall that he might secure his poetical services. The poet proved only too easy a courtier, and his poems, as published in his own lifetime, display a singularly cynical indifference to political rectitude, for a 'Panegyric upon Oliver Cromwell' immediately precedes a piece on the 'Death of the late usurper O. C.' He appears, however, to have conceived a sincere regard for Cromwell, and even in calling him a usurper, he cannot refrain from eulogy.

The poetry of Waller can never again be popular, even with students. It is hard, dry, and insignificant, it fails to touch the heart, and requires laborious attention to be understood, not because it is obscure, but because the argument lies outside the track of human interest. From this condemnation all the world exempts the celebrated song to a Rose, and the careful reader will also exempt a few little pieces scarcely inferior to this in sincerity and simplicity. English poetry is studded with the names of those who have possessed imagination and warmth of fancy, but who have failed to survive, in popular estimation, through their lack of style. Waller, on the other hand, is a signal example of the converse law, that a writer cannot subsist on style alone. The decay of reputation seems in the latter case to be less rapid, but it is in the end more fatal, for it is beyond the hope of reparation.

EDMUND W. GOSSE.

ON A GIRDLE.

That which her slender waist confined,
Shall now my joyful temples bind ;
No monarch but would give his crown
His arms might do what this has done.

It was my heaven's extremest sphere,
The pale which held that lovely deer,
My joy, my grief, my hope, my love,
Did all within this circle move.

A narrow compass, and yet there
Dwelt all that's good and all that's fair ;
Give me but what this ribband bound,
Take all the rest the sun goes round.

SONG.

Go, lovely Rose,
Tell her that wastes her time and me,
That now she knows
When I resemble her to thee
How sweet and fair she seems to be.

Tell her that's young,
And shuns to have her graces spied,
That had'st thou sprung
In deserts where no men abide,
Thou must have uncommended died.

Small is the worth
Of beauty from the light retired ;
Bid her come forth,
Suffer herself to be desired,
And not blush so to be admired.

Then die, that she
The common fate of all things rare
May read in thee,
How small a part of time they share
Who are so wondrous sweet and fair.

FROM 'HIS MAJESTY'S ESCAPE AT ST. ANDREWS.'

While to his harp divine Arion sings
The loves and conquests of our Albion kings ;
Of the fourth Edward was his noble song,
Fierce, goodly, valiant, beautiful and young ;
He rent the crown from vanquished Henry's head,
Raised the white rose, and trampled on the red,
Till love triumphing o'er the victor's pride,
Brought Mars and Warwick to the conquered side,—
Neglected Warwick, whose bold hand like fate,
Gives and resumes the sceptre of our state,
Wooes for his Master, and with double shame,
Himself deluded, mocks the princely dame,—
The Lady Bona, whom just anger burns,
And foreign war with civil rage returns ;
Ah ! spare your sword, where beauty is to blame,
Love gave the affront, and must repair the same,
When France shall boast of her, whose conquering eyes
Have made the best of English hearts their prize,
Have power to alter the decrees of fate,
And change again the counsels of our state.

TO ONE WHO WROTE AGAINST A FAIR LADY.

What fury has provoked thy wit to dare
    With Diomede to wound the Queen of Love ?
Thy mistress' envy, or thine own despair ?
    Not the just Pallas in thy breast did move ;
So blind a rage with such a different fate,
He honour won, where thou hast purchased hate.

T 2

She gave assistance to his Trojan foe;
  Thou that without a rival thou may'st love,
Dost to the beauty of this lady owe,
  While after her the gazing world does move;
Can'st thou not be content to love alone,
Or is thy mistress not content with one?

Hast thou not read of fairy Arthur's shield,
  Which, but disclosed, amazed the weaker eyes
Of proudest foes, and won the doubtful field?
  So shall thy rebel wit become her prize;
Should thy iambics swell into a book,
All were confuted with one radiant look.

Heaven he obliged that placed her in the skies,
  Rewarding Phoebus for inspiring so
His noble brain, by likening to those eyes
  His joyful beams, but Phoebus is thy foe,
And neither aids thy fancy nor thy sight,
So ill thou rhym'st against so fair a light.

THE BUD.

Lately on yonder swelling bush
  Big with many a coming rose,
This early bud began to blush
  And did but half itself disclose;
I plucked it, though no better grown,
And now you see how full 'tis blown.

Still as I did the leaves inspire,
  With such a purple light they shone
As if they had been made of fire,
And spreading so, would flame anon
All that was meant by air or sun,
To the young flower my breath has done.

If our loose breath so much can do,
　What may the same informed of love,—
Of purest love and music too,—
　When Flavia it aspires to move ;
When that which lifeless buds persuades
To wax more soft, her youth invades.

Thf Marriage of the Dwarfs.

Design or chance makes others wive,
But nature did this match contrive ;
Eve might as well have Adam fled,
As she denied her little bed
To him, for whom Heaven seemed to frame
And measure out this only dame.
Thrice happy is that humble pair,
Beneath the level of all care,
Over whose heads those arrows fly
Of sad distrust and jealousy,
Securèd in as high extreme
As if the world held none but them.
To him the fairest nymphs do show
Like moving mountains topped with snow,
And every man a Polypheme
Doth to his Galatea seem ;
None may presume her faith to prove,
He profers death who profers love.
Ah ! Chloris, that kind nature thus
From all the world had severed us,
Creating for ourselves us two,
As love has me for only you.

From 'The Battle of the Summer's Islands.'

Such is the mould that the blest tenant feeds
On precious fruits, and pays his rent in weeds ;
With candied plantains, and the juicy pine,
On choicest melons and sweet grapes they dine,

And with potatoes fat their wanton swine ;
Nature these cates with such a lavish hand
Poors out among them, that our coarser land
Tastes of that bounty, and does cloth return,
Which not for warmth but ornament is worn ;
For the kind spring which but salutes us here,
Inhabits there and courts them all the year ;
Ripe fruits and blossoms on the same trees live,
At once they promise what at once they give ;
So sweet the air, so moderate the clime,
None sickly lives or dies before his time ;
Heaven sure has kept this spot of earth uncurst
To show how all things were created first.
The tardy plants in our cold orchards placed
Reserve their fruits for the next age's taste,
There a small grain in some few months will be
A firm, a lofty and a spacious tree ;
The Palma Christi and the fair Papaw,
Now but a seed, preventing nature's law,
In half the circle of the hasty year
Project a shade, and lovely fruits do wear ;
And as their trees in our dull region set
But faintly grow and no perfection get,
So in this northern tract our hoarser throats
Utter unripe and ill-constrainèd notes,
Where, the supporter of the poet's style,
Phoebus on them eternally does smile.
O how I long my careless limbs to lay
Under the plantain's shade, and all the day
With amorous airs my fancy entertain,
Invoke the Muses, and improve my vein !
No passion there in my free breast should move,
None but the sweetest, best of passions, love !
There while I sing, if gentle Love be by,
That tunes my lute, and winds the strings so high ;
With the sweet sound of Sacharissa's name,
I 'll make the listening savages grow tame :—
But while I do these pleasing dreams indite,
I am diverted from the promised fight.

SIR JOHN DENHAM.

[SIR JOHN DENHAM was born in Dublin in 1615. He took a prominent part in public affairs, acting for the King in several capacities; and after many vicissitudes of fortune he died at Whitehall on the 10th of April, 1668. He published *The Sophy*, a tragedy, in 1641, and *Cooper's Hill*, anonymously, in the same year.]

Denham was the first writer to adopt the precise manner of versification introduced by Waller. His relation to that poet resembles that taken a century later by Mason with respect to Gray, but Denham is a more original writer than Mason. The names of Waller and Denham were first associated by Dryden, and the critics of the next sixty years were unanimous in eulogizing the sweetness of the one, and the strength of the other. It is quite true that the versification of Denham is vigorous ; it proceeds with greater volume than that of Waller, and produces a stronger impression. But he is a very unequal and irregular writer, and not unfrequently descends to doggerel, and very dull doggerel too. His literary taste was superior to his genius ; he knew what effect he desired to produce, and strove to conquer the difficulties of antithesis, but the result of his effort was rarely classic. He takes the same place in English poetry as is taken in French by Chapelain and other hard versifiers of the beginning of the seventeenth century, who had lost the romantic fervour and had not yet gained the classic grace. But, like those poets, he has his fine flashes of style.

The works of Denham are small in extent. They consist of *The Sophy*, a languid tragedy of Turkish misrule ; *Cooper's Hill*, a topographical poem, *The Destruction of Troy*, an insignificant paraphrase of part of the *Æneid* ; and a selection of miscellaneous pieces. These latter, and *Cooper's Hill*, are all that need attract critical attention. The reputation of the last-mentioned poem rests almost entirely upon its famous quatrain : —

> 'O could I flow like thee, and make thy stream
> My great example, as it is my theme!
> Though deep yet clear, though gentle yet not dull,
> Strong without rage, without o'erflowing full.'

It is a curious fact that this exquisite apostrophe, which is one of the gems of our language, does not occur in the first edition of *Cooper's Hill*. There are no other lines in that poem which approach these in elegance and force, and it occurs to the mind of the present writer that they may possibly have been contributed by Waller. This, however, is unlikely, and it would be unfair, without shadow of proof, to deprive Denham of his chief claim to immortality. The two passages we select give the reader a fair idea of the general manner of this poem, which has certainly been over-praised. The style is obscure and the wit laboured, while it probably contains more errors against the rules of grammar than any other poem in the language ; but Denham is at all times a singularly ungrammatical writer. Of his other long poems, by far the best is the *Elegy on Cowley*, which was written but a very few months before his own death, and after a long attack of insanity. In this poem he is brighter and more easy than in any other long composition, and it contains some interesting critical matter. Denham was highly esteemed for his comical vein, and his lampoons are not devoid of wit, though incredibly brutal and coarse. He is very unlike the amorous poets of his age in this, that he has left behind him not one copy of love-verses ; and his best poem is written in dispraise of love. Among the royalist lyrists there is but one, Cleveland, who forms a connecting link between Denham and the old lyric school. His satires and squibs are closely allied to those of Cleveland, and he has something of the same cynical and defiant attitude of mind. He adored litera-ture with the worship of one who practises it late in life, and without much ease ; his conception of the ideal dignity of the poet's function contrasts oddly with the indecorous matter that he puts forth as comic poetry. There was nothing about him very original, for *Cooper's Hill*, which was destined to inspire *Windsor Forest*, had been itself preceded by Ben Jonson's *Penshurst*. But he forms an important link in the chain of transition, and ranks chronologically second among our Augustan poets.

EDMUND W. GOSSE.

VIEW OF LONDON FROM COOPER'S HILL.

Through untraced ways and airy paths I fly,
More boundless in my fancy than my eye,—
My eye, which swift as thought contracts the space
That lies between, and first salutes the place
Crowned with that sacred pile, so vast, so high,
That whether 'tis a part of earth or sky
Uncertain seems, and may be thought a proud
Aspiring mountain or descending cloud,—
Paul's, the late theme of such a Muse whose flight
Has bravely reached and soared above thy height;
Now shalt thou stand, though sword or time or fire,
Or zeal more fierce than they, thy fall conspire,
Secure, while thee the best of poets sings,
Preserved from ruin by the best of kings.
Under his proud survey the city lies,
And like a mist beneath a hill doth rise,
Whose state and wealth, the business and the crowd,
Seems at this distance but a darker cloud,
And is to him who rightly things esteems
No other in effect but what it seems,
Where, with like haste, though several ways, they run,
Some to undo, and some to be undone;
While luxury and wealth, like war and peace,
Are each the other's ruin and increase;
As rivers lost in seas some secret vein
Thence reconveys, there to be lost again.
O happiness of sweet retired content!
To be at once secure and innocent!

PRAISE OF THE THAMES.

[From *Cooper's Hill.*]

My eye, descending from the hill, surveys
Where Thames amongst the wanton valleys strays ;
Thames, the most loved of all the Ocean's sons,
By his old sire to his embraces runs,
Hasting to pay his tribute to the sea,
Like mortal life to meet eternity ;
Though with those streams he no resemblance hold,
Whose foam is amber, and their gravel gold,
His genuine and less guilty wealth to explore,
Search not his bottom, but survey his shore,
O'er which he kindly spreads his spacious wing,
And hatches plenty for th' ensuing spring ;
Nor then destroys it with too fond a stay,
Like mothers which their infants overlay,
Nor, with a sudden and impetuous wave,
Like profuse kings, resumes the wealth he gave ;
No unexpected inundations spoil
The mower's hopes, nor mock the ploughman's toil,
But godlike his unwearied bounty flows,
First loves to do, then loves the good he does ;·
Nor are his blessings to his banks confined,
But free and common as the sea or wind ;
When he to boast or to disperse his stores,
Full of the tributes of his grateful shores,
Visits the world, and in his flying towers,
Brings home to us, and makes both Indies ours,
Finds wealth where 'tis, bestows it where it wants,
Cities in deserts, woods in cities plants ;
So that to us no thing, no place is strange,
While his fair bosom is the world's exchange.
O could I flow like thee, and make thy stream
My great example, as it is my theme !
Though deep, yet clear, though gentle, yet not dull,
Strong without rage, without o'erflowing full.

Against Love.

Love making all things else his foes
Like a fierce torrent overflows
Whatever doth his course oppose.

This was the cause the poets sung,
Thy Mother from the sea was sprung,
But they were mad to make thee young.

Her father, not her son, art thou ;
From our desires our actions grow,
And from the cause the effect must flow.

Love is as old as place or time ;
'Twas he the fatal tree did climb,
Grandsire of Father Adam's crime.

Love drowsy days and stormy nights
Makes, and breaks friendship, whose delights
Feed, but not glut our appetites.

How happy he, that loves not, lives !
Him neither hope nor fear deceives,
To Fortune who no hostage gives.

How unconcerned in things to come !
If here he frets, he finds at Rome,
At Paris, or Madrid his home.

Secure from low and private ends,
His life, his zeal, his wealth attends
His prince, his country and his friends.

Song.

[From *The Sophy*, Act V.]

Morpheus, the humble god, that dwells
In cottages and smoky cells,
Hates gilded roofs and beds of down,
And though he fears no prince's frown,
Flies from the circle of a crown.

Come, I say, thou powerful god,
And thy leaden charming-rod,
Dipt in the Lethean lake,
O'er his wakeful temples shake,
Lest he should sleep and never wake.

Nature, alas! why art thou so
Obligèd to thy greatest foe?
Sleep that is thy best repast,
Yet of death it bears a taste,
And both are the same thing at last.

From the 'Elegy on Cowley.'

Old Chaucer, like the morning-star,
To us discovers day from far;
His light those mists and clouds dissolved
Which our dark nation long involved;
But he descending to the shades,
Darkness again the age invades.
Next, like Aurora, Spenser rose
Whose purple blush the day foreshows.
The other three, with his own fires,
Phoebus, the poets' god, inspires;
By Shakespeare's, Jonson's, Fletcher's lines
Our stage's lustre Rome's outshines.
These poets near our princes sleep,
And in one grave their mansion keep;
They lived to see so many days,
Till time had blasted all their bays;
But cursed be the fatal hour
That plucked the fairest, sweetest flower
That in the Muses' garden grew,
And amongst withered laurels threw.
Time, which made them their fame outlive,
To Cowley scarce did ripeness give.
Old mother-wit and nature gave
Shakespeare and Fletcher all they have;

In Spenser and in Jonson art
Of slower nature got the start;
But both in him so equal are,
None knows which bears the happiest share;
To him no author was unknown,
Yet what he wrote was all his own.
He melted not the ancient gold,
Nor, with Ben Jonson, did make bold
To plunder all the Roman stores
Of poets and of orators.
Horace's wit and Virgil's state
He did not steal, but emulate,
And when he would like them appear,
Their garb, but not their clothes, did wear;
He not from Rome alone, but Greece,
Like Jason brought the golden fleece;
To him that language, though to none
Of th' others, as his own was known.
On a stiff gale, as Flaccus sings,
The Theban swan extends his wings,
When through the ethereal clouds he flies,
To the same pitch our swan doth rise.
Old Pindar's flights by him are reached,
When on that gale his wings are stretched.
His fancy and his judgment such,
Each to the other seemed too much,
His severe judgment, giving law,
His modest fancy, kept in awe,
As rigid husbands jealous are
When they believe their wives too fair.

THOMAS STANLEY.

[THOMAS STANLEY was born at Cumberlow, in Hertfordshire, in 1625, and died in Suffolk Street, London, on the 12th of April, 1678. His translations appeared in 1649 and his original poems in 1651.]

Eminent among the scholars of the Restoration as the historian of Philosophy and the expounder of Aeschylus, Stanley had dedicated his youth to studies less severe, and is now principally remembered as the last of the old school of lyrists. Born into a younger generation than that of Waller and Denham, he really belongs, as a poet, to the age before them, and in him the series of writers called 'Metaphysical' closes. Stanley is without the faults or the merits of his predecessors. His conceits are never violent or crude, though often insipid : but he has no flashes of music or sudden inspired felicities. He is a tamer and duller Herrick, resembling that writer in his versification, and following him at a distance in temperament and tone. Stanley was a very delicate and poetical translator ; and he had the originality to select the authors from whom he translated according to his own native bias. He delighted in Moscnus and Ausonius among the ancients, and in Joannes Secundus and Ronsard among the moderns ; the world in which his fancy loved to wander was one of refined Arcadian beauty, rather chilly and autumnal, but inhabited by groups of nymphs and shepherds, who hung garlands of flowers on votive urns, or took hands in stately pensive dances. In no poet of the century is the negative quality of shrinking from ugliness and coarseness so defined as in Stanley. He constantly sacrifices strength to it, not as Habington sometimes did, from instinctive reticence and modesty of fancy, but from sheer over-refinement. Stanley makes a strange figure among the rough prosaic writers of the Restoration, and no poems of his have been preserved, except those of his youth. He probably ceased to write, and gave his intellect to less shifting studies, when he found the whole temper of the nation obstinately set against his inclination. He died in middle life, just when Lee and Otway were at the height of their vogue, and a few weeks before another great tradition in English poetry ceased at the death of Marvell.

EDMUND W. GOSSE.

CELIA SINGING.

Roses in breathing forth their scent,
Or stars their borrowed ornament,
Nymphs in the watery sphere that move,
Or angels in their orbs above,
The wingèd chariot of the light,
Or the slow silent wheels of night,
The shade which from the swifter sun
Doth in a circular motion run,
Or souls that their eternal rest do keep,
Make far less noise than Celia's breath in sleep.

But if the Angel, which inspires
This subtle flame with active fires,
Should mould this breath to words, and those
Into a harmony dispose,
The music of this heavenly sphere
Would steal each soul out at the ear,
And into plants and stones infuse
A life that Cherubim would choose,
And with new powers invert the laws of fate,
Kill those that live, and dead things animate.

THE TOMB.

When, cruel fair one, I am slain
    By thy disdain,
And, as a trophy of thy scorn,
    To some old tomb am borne,
Thy fetters must their power bequeath
    To those of Death ;
Nor can thy flame immortal burn,
Like monumental fires within an urn ;
Thus freed from thy proud empire, I shall prove
There is more liberty in Death than Love.

And when forsaken lovers come
  To see my tomb,
Take heed thou mix not with the crowd
  And, as a victor, proud
To view the spoils thy beauty made
  Press near my shade,
Lest thy too cruel breath or name
Should fan my ashes back into a flame,
And thou, devoured by this revengeful fire,
His sacrifice, who died as thine, expire.

But if cold earth or marble must
  Conceal my dust,
Whilst hid in some dark ruins, I
  Dumb and forgotten lie,
The pride of all thy victory
  Will sleep with me;
And they who should attest thy glory,
Will, or forget, or not believe this story.
Then to increase thy triumph, let me rest,
Since by thine eye slain, buried in thy breast.

SIR WILLIAM DAVENANT.

[SIR WILLIAM DAVENANT was born at Oxford, in February 1605, and died in Lincoln's Inn Fields, April 17, 1668. His epic poem of *Gondibert* was printed in 1651.]

There is not a more hopelessly faded laurel on the slopes of the English Parnassus than that which once flourished so bravely around the grotesque head of Davenant. The enormous folio edition of his works, brought out in 1673 in direct emulation of Ben Jonson, is probably the most deplorable collection of verses anywhere to be found, dead and dusty beyond the wont of forgotten classics. The critic is inclined to say that everything is spurious about Davenant, from the legend that connects his blood with Shakespeare's to the dramatic genius that his latest contemporaries praised so highly. He is not merely a ponderous, he is a nonsensical writer, and having begun life by writing meaningless romantic plays in imitation of Massinger, and insipid masques in the school of Ben Jonson, he closed his long and busy career by parodying the style of Dryden. But he really deserves to be classed with none of these authors, but with Sir William Killigrew and Sir Robert Stapleton, the dullest crew of pedants and poetasters which our literature has seen. From this wide condemnation of the writings of Davenant, his romantic epic of *Gondibert* must be excepted. It is a poem of chivalry, the scene of which is laid in Lombardy, but which the author grew tired of before it had occurred to him to construct a plot. It is, accordingly, nothing but an incoherent, rambling fragment, through which the reader toils, as if through a quicksand, dragging his steps along, and rewarded every now and then by a firmer passage containing some propriety of thought or a beautiful single line. The form of *Gondibert* is borrowed from the *Nosce Teipsum* of Sir John Davies, and was soon afterwards employed again by Dryden for his *Annus Mirabilis.*

EDMUND W. GOSSE.

From 'Gondibert,' Book I. Canto 6.

Soon they the palace reached of Astragon,
  Which had its beauty hid by envious night,
Whose cypress curtain, drawn before the sun,
  Seemed to perform the obsequies of light.

Yet light's last rays were not entirely spent,
  For they discerned their passage through a gate,
Whose height and space showed ancient ornament,
  And ancients there in careful office sate.

Who by their weights and measures did record
  Such numerous burdens as were thither brought
From distant regions, to their learned lord,
  On which his chymics and distillers wrought.

But now their common business they refrain,
  When they observe a quiet sullenness
And bloody marks in such a civil train,
  Which showed at once their worth and their distress.

The voice of Ulfin they with gladness knew,
  Whom to this house long neighbourhood ende?red :
Approaching torches perfected their view,
  And taught the way till Astragon appeared.

Who soon did Ulfin cheerfully embrace ;
  The visit's cause by whispers he received,
Which first he hoped was meant him as a grace,
  But being known, with manly silence grieved.

And then, with gestures full of grave respect,
  The Duke he to his own apartment led ;
To each distinct retirement did direct,
  And all the wounded he ordained to bed.

Then thin digestive food he did provide,
  More to enable fleeting strength to stay,
To wounds well-searched he cleansing wines applied,
  And so prepared his ripening balsam's way.

Balm of the warrior ! herb Hypernicon !
  To warriors, as in use, in form decreed,
For, through the leaves, transparent wounds are shown,
  And rudely touched, the golden flower doth bleed.

For sleep they juice of pale Nymphæa took,
  Which grows, to show that it for sleep is good,
Near sleep's abode in the soft murmuring brook,
  This cools, the yellow flower restrains the blood.

And now the weary world's great medicine, Sleep,
  This learned host dispensed to every guest,
Which shuts those wounds where injured lovers weep,
  And flies oppressors to relieve the opprest.

It loves the cottage and from court abstains,
  It stills the seaman though the storm be high,
Frees the grieved captive in his closest chains,
  Stops Want's loud mouth, and blinds the treacherous spy.

SONG.

  The lark now leaves his watery nest,
    And climbing shakes his dewy wings,
  He takes your window for the east,
    And to implore your light, he sings ;
  Awake, awake, the moon will never rise,
  Till she can dress her beauty at your eyes.

  The merchant bows unto the seaman's star,
    The ploughman from the sun his season takes ;
  But still the lover wonders what they are,
    Who look for day before his mistress wakes :
  Awake, awake, break through your veils of lawn !
  Then draw your curtains and begin the dawn.

U 2

ON THE CAPTIVITY OF THE COUNTESS OF ANGLESEY.

O whither will you lead the fair
  And spicy daughter of the morn?
Those manacles of her soft hair,
  Princes, though free, would fain have worn.

What is her crime? what has she done?
  Did she, by breaking beauty, stay,
Or from his course mislead the sun,
  So robbed your harvest of a day?

Or did her voice, divinely clear,
  Since lately in your forest bred,
Make all the trees dance after her,
  And so your woods disforested?

Run, run! pursue this gothic rout,
  Who rudely love in bondage keep;
Sure all old lovers have the gout,
  The young are overwatched and sleep!

JOHN MILTON.

[JOHN MILTON (1608–1674) was born in Bread Street, Cheapside, 9 Dec. 1608. Educated at St. Paul's School, and Christ's College, Cambridge, he was destined by his family for the Church. From this however. he was diverted, partly by his strong Puritan bias, partly by an ambition which possessed him from a very early period, to compose a great work which should bring honour to his country, and to the English language. Full of this lofty purpose, he retired to his father's country residence at Horton. in the county of Bucks. Here he gave himself up to study, and poetical meditation, in preparation for the work to which he had resolved to devote his life. He looked upon himself as a man dedicated to a high purpose, and framed his life accordingly. He thought that ' he who would not be frustrated of his hope to write well hereafter in laudable things, ought himself to be a true poem, ... not presuming to sing high praises of heroic men or famous cities, unless he have in himself the experience and practice of all that which is praiseworthy.'

This residence at Horton constitutes Milton's first poetic period, 1632–1638. During these six years he wrote L'Allegro and Il Penseroso, Arcades, Comus, and Lycidas. All these were thrown off by their author as occasional pieces, exercises for practice, preluding to the labour of his life, which he was all the while meditating.

A journey to Italy, 1638-9, was undertaken as a portion of the poet's education which he was giving himself He was recalled from his tour by the lowering aspect of public affairs at home. For the next twenty years his thoughts were diverted from poetry by the absorbing interest of the civil struggle. His time was occupied, partly by official duties as Latin secre- tary to the Council of the Commonwealth, partly by the voluntary share he took in the controversies of the time.

The public cause to which he had devoted himself being lost. and the ruin of his party consummated in 1660, Milton reverted to his long cherished poetical scheme. During the twenty years of political agitation this scheme had never been wholly banished from his thoughts. After much hesitation, 'long choosing and beginning late,' both subject and form had been decided on. The poem was to be an epic. and was to treat of the fall and recovery of man. He had begun to compose on this theme as early as 1658, and in 1665 Paradise Lost was completed. Owing to the Plague and the Fire, it was not published till August, 1667. It was originally in ten books, which were afterwards made into twelve, as the normal epical number by subdividing books 7 and 10. The subject of the recovery of man had been dropped out of the plan at an early stage, and was afterwards made the subject of a second poem, *Paradise Regained*, on a hint given by Milton's young quaker friend. Ellwood. These years of disaster and distress, 1665-6, were specially prolific, if, as is probable, both *Paradise Regained*, and *Samson Ago-nistes* were written during them. The two poems came out in 1 vol. in 1671, and closed Milton's second poetic period. He lived three years longer, during which he occupied himself with carrying through the press a new edition of his *Poems* (the 1st ed. was 1645) as well as several compilations, which furnished mental occupation without requiring inventive power. He died 8 Nov. 1674.]

I.

Our earliest specimen of Milton is a little poem which was first printed among the commendatory verses prefixed, according to a custom then prevailing, to the Shakspeare folio of 1632, where it is headed, *An epitaph on the admirable dramatick poet, W. Shak-spere*. It was written in 1630, æt. 22. Though not Milton's earliest effort, it is the first piece of which it can be said that its merit does not lie chiefly in its promise. What he had written before this date, was, besides college exercises, an ode *On the morning of Christ's nativity, Upon the circumcision, The Passion, On the death of a fair infant*, &c. In all these early pieces is discernible in germ that mental quality which became in his mature production his poetic characteristic. This quality, which the poverty of our language tries to express by the words solemnity, gravity, majesty, nobility, loftiness, and which, name it as we may, we all feel in reading *Paradise Lost*, is already conspicuous in the sixteen lines of the epitaph on Shakspeare. This sublimity does not reside in the thesis which is logically enunciated, nor in the image presented. These are, as often in Milton, commonplace enough. The elevation is communicated to us not by the dogma or deliverance, but by sympathy. We catch the contagion of the poet's mental attitude. He makes us bow with him before the image of Shakspeare, though there is not a single discriminating epithet to point out in what the greatness which we are made to feel consists. An eighteenth century poet would have offered some clever analysis, or judicious criticism. 'Avant donc que d'écrire, apprenez à penser,' was the precept of that age for prose and poetry alike. To be sensible of the sudden decadence of poetry after 1660 we have only to compare, with this Miltonic tribute to Shakespeare, Dryden's lines on Milton himself prefixed to the first folio of 1688 :—

> ' Three poets, in three distant ages born,' &c.

In Milton's sixteen lines the lofty tone is so independent of the thought presented, that we overlook the inadequacy of the thought itself. Were we to suppress the feeling, and look only at the logical sentence, as Johnsonian criticism used to do, we should be obliged to say that the residuum is a frigid conceit in the style of Marini. We, the readers, are turned into marble monuments to the memory of Shakespeare—a farfetched fancy, which deadens, instead of excites, awe and admiration.

2.

The dates of the two pieces headed *L'Allegro* and *Il Penseroso* can only be approximately given. They are with great probability assigned to the early years of Milton's residence at Horton, 1632 and following. The Italian titles show that they were written at a time when Milton had already begun to learn Italian, while the incorrect form 'penseroso' shows that he was only beginning. *L'Allegro* = 'the cheerful man'; *Il Penseroso* is intended to mean 'the thoughtful man.' But from 'pensiero' the adjectival form is 'pensieroso.' There was an old form 'pensero,' but the Italian dictionaries do not acknowledge any adjective 'penseroso' as derived from it. Petrarch, with whom Milton must have been early acquainted, habitually uses 'pensoso,' but always with the connotation of 'sadness,' 'melancholy.'

The two Odes, taken together, present contrasted views of the scholar's life. It is what the rhetoricians call an antiperistasis, or development of an idea by its opposite. Or we may rather regard them as alternating moods, buoyant spirits and solemn recollected-ness succeeding and displacing each other, as in life. They are Milton's own moods, and might be employed as autobiography, depicting his studious days in those years when he was forming his mind and hiving wisdom. But they are ideally and not literally true, just as the landscape of the odes is ideally, but not literally, that of the neighbourhood of Horton. The joyous mood is the mood of daytime, beginning with the first flight of the lark before dawn, and closing with music inducing sleep. The thoughtful mood is that of the same scholar studying through the night, or meditating in his solitary moonlight walk. For the country life of these idylls is not the life of the native of the country, peasant or proprietor, but of the scholar to whose emotions all the country objects are subordinated. Milton does not set himself to tell us what rural objects are like, but indicates them by their bearing on the life lived among them by his studious youth. Whereas in Browne's *Britannia's Pastorals* (1613-16), with which Milton was well acquainted, there is generally the faintest possible breath of human interest, in Milton, town and country are but scenery to the moods of the human agent. Milton, like all poets of the first order, knew or rather felt, that human action or passion is the only subject of poetry. This is no mere conventional rule established by the critics, or by custom ; it rests upon the truth that poetry must be a vehicle of emotion. Poetry is an address to the feelings and imagination, not to the judgment and the understanding. The world and its cosmical processes, or nature and natural scenery, are in themselves only objects of science. They become matter for the poet only after they have been impregnated with the joys and distresses, the hopes and fears, of man. 'We receive but what we give.' This truth, the foundation of any sufficient 'poetic,' is itself contained in the still wider law, under which colour and form, light itself, are but affections of our human organs of perception.

The doctrine that human action and passion are the only material of poetic fiction was the first theorem of Greek æsthetic. But it had been lost sight of, and was not introduced into modern criticism till its revival by Lessing in 1766. The practice both of our poets, and of our English critics, in the eighteenth century, had forgotten this capital distinction between the art of language, and the art of design. The English versifiers of that century had not the poetic impulse in sufficient intensity to feel the distinction. And the Addison-Johnson criticism, which regarded a poem as made up of images and propositions in verse, could not teach the truth. So the poets went to work to describe scenery. And our collections are filled with verse, didactic and descriptive, which, with many merits of style and thought, has no title to rank as poetry.

Descriptive poetry is in fact a contradiction in terms. A landscape can be represented to the eye by imitative colours laid on a flat surface. But it cannot be presented in words which, being necessarily successive, cannot render juxtaposition in space. To exhibit in space is the privilege of the arts of design. Poetry, whose instrument is language, involves succession in time, and can only present that which comes to pass—*das geschehene*—under one or other of its two forms, action or passion.

Milton was in possession of this secret, not as a trick taught him by the critics, but in virtue of the intensity of human passion which glowed in his bosom. He has exemplified the principle in these two lyrics. In them, as in Wordsworth's best passages, the imagery is not there for its own sake, it is the vehicle of the personal feelings of the Man. The composition derives its unity and its denomination from his mental attitude as spectator.

It is misleading, then, when these odes are spoken of as 'master-pieces of description.' A naturalist discerns at once, in more than one minute touch, that the poet is not an accurate observer of nature, or thoroughly familiar with country life. As a town-bred youth, 'in populous city pent,' Milton missed that intimacy with rural sights and sounds, which belongs, like the mother tongue, to those who have been born and bred among them. But the same want of familiarity which makes his notice of the object inaccurate, intensifies the emotion excited in him by the objects, when he is first brought in contact with them. Nature has for Milton the stimulus of novelty. Like other town poets, he knows nature less, but feels it more. What he does exactly render for us is not objective nature, but its effect upon the emotional life of the lettered student.

If Milton is not ideally descriptive, still less is he the copyist of a given scene. That the locality of Horton suggested the scenery of these odes is one thing; that they describe that locality, that the 'mountains' *are* the Chilterns, and the 'towers and battlements' *are* Windsor, is quite another. It might seem hardly necessary to dwell upon this, but that this confusion of poetical truth with historical truth is so widely spread, even among the educated. While pilgrims are still found endeavouring to identify the Troy sung by Homer with some one Asiatic site, Hissarlik or other, the critic must continue to repeat the trite lesson that poetry feigns, and does not describe. Fact and fiction are contra-dictories, and exclude each other. Truth of poetry may be called philosophical truth ; truth of fact, historical. So beauty in nature is one thing, beauty of a work of art quite another thing. And this is how it is that *L'Allegro* and *Il Penseroso* have the highest beauty as works of art, while they may abound with naturalistic solecism.

3.

Comus, 1634, bears the title of a 'Mask,' and may be described as a lyrical drama. It was written as words to a musical composition by Henry Lawes, and intended to be performed by amateurs, at an entertainment given by the Earl of Bridgwater to celebrate his entry on his office as Lord President of Wales. These shows, in which the dramatic element was subordinated to the pageantry and the music, had been popular at court in the beginning of the century. But the gradual growth of Puritan sentiment throughout the nation was chilling the taste for such entertainments. The 'mask' would have died out but for the publication, in 1633, of a violent and onesided invective against the stage, in Prynne's *Histriomastix*. This overt attack occasioned a reaction in favour of the drama, and there was, for a short time, a spasmodic revival of the 'mask' in cavalier and courtly circles. It was during this brief revival that *Comus* was written, a chance thus making the future Puritan poet the last composer of a cavalier mask. The extract we give from *Comus*, ll. 93–330, comprises, in one continuous scene, specimens of its (1) lyrical measures, (2) its monologue, and (3) its dialogue. For while *Comus* was to be a 'mask,' after the model of those written by the dramatists of the previous age, Milton endeavoured to mould its parts on the pattern of those Greek tragedies, the perfection of whose form his pure taste had already recognised. In 'The star that bids the shepherd fold &c.' we have a close imitation of the dithyrambic monody of Euripides ; as in the brief dialogue between the Lady and Comus (' What chance, good lady, hath bereft you thus ?') we have the Greek stichomythia in single alternate lines exactly reproduced.

4.

Comus (1634) was followed by *Lycidas* (November, 1637), which we give entire. *Lycidas* is an elegiac ode contributed by Milton to a volume of memorial verse, printed at Cambridge on the occasion of the death of one of the Fellows of Christ's College. Edward King had been a contemporary and companion of Milton at Christ's, and in 1630 had been elected to a fellowship in that college, in obedience to a royal mandate, and, as it should seem, over Milton's head. King, who is described to us as a young man of great promise, perished by shipwreck on the passage from

Chester to Dublin in the long vacation of 1637. This piece, unmatched in the whole range of English poetry, and never again equalled by Milton himself, leaves all criticism behind. Indeed so high is the poetic note here reached, that the common ear fails to catch it. *Lycidas* is the touchstone of taste ; the 18th century criticism could not make anything of it. The very form of the poem is a stumbling-block to the common-sense critic. For while the equable and temperate emotion of *L'Allegro* allowed of direct expression in the poet's own person, the burning heat of passion in *Lycidas* has to be transferred into the artificial framework of the conventional pastoral to make it approachable. At the same time it will be observed that this passion is not stirred by personal attachment, such as lends its pathos to *In Memoriam.* It is obvious from the elegy itself that Milton's relation to Edward King was not a specially tender relation. The sorrow for his loss does not go beyond such regret as may have been generally excited at Cambridge by the shock of such a casualty. It is when the poet passes on from the individual bereavement to generalise as to the fortunes of the Church, that he attains to a rapt grandeur of enigmatic denunciation in the lines ' Last came and last did go,' &c. In the suppressed passion of this Cassandra prophecy first emerges the Milton of *Paradise Lost* and *Samson.* The effect of the passage is enhanced by the contrast of the quiet beauty of the pastoral dirge in the preceding part of the poem. *Lycidas* accordingly marks the point of transition from the early Milton, the Milton of mask, pastoral, and idyll, to the quite other Milton, who, after twenty years of hot party struggle, returned to poetry in another vein,—never to the ' woods and pastures ' of which he took a final leave in *Lycidas.*

5.

Between the composition of *Lycidas*, 1637, and the commencement of *Paradise Lost*, 1657, a space of twenty years, the course of Milton's life and thoughts was such as did not admit of the abstraction necessary for a sustained poetical effort. Officially, as Latin secretary to the Commonwealth, and unofficially, as an ardent partisan of the republican movement, he was absorbed in the interests of the day. Occasionally, during this interval, his feeling found vent in a sonnet, 'the Petrarchian stanza,' as he calls it, now first put to martial uses. The sonnets are of two kinds, personal or political. Our selections offer two examples of each kind. The personal sonnets are not the expression of a transitory mood or an occasional sentiment, but of abiding, governing mental states, which pervaded either long periods of the poet's life or the whole of it. The first sonnet, ' How soon hath time, &c.,' written æt. 23, proceeds from the uneasy sense that he himself was idling, while others were already doing. His still preparation of his powers—'growing wings'—the poet's education he was industriously giving himself, was a slow and invisible process. It lasted into manhood. He feels that an apology is due to others,—to his father, to admonitory friends ;—still more is he dissatisfied himself with the progress he has made.

The second sonnet in our selections, ' When I consider, &c.,' continues, aet. 50, the strain of reproach which first found vent, æt. 23, in the foregoing sonnet, with this difference, that in youth he excused himself to his friends, in mature age he is only careful to present 'his true account' to his 'Maker.' This sonnet is remarkable for its direct assertion of the doctrine of 'living' as against that of 'doing.'

The subject of the third sonnet is the massacre, in 1655, of his own subjects by the reigning Duke of Savoy. It gives voice to the horror and indignation which ran through Puritan England when the dreadful tidings reached our shores. Even at this distance of time the passion that dictated them still burns in Milton's lines ; how must they have moved men's minds when the bloody deed was still recent! It is to this sonnet that Wordsworth's lines are specially applicable, 'in his hands

> The thing became a trumpet whence he blew
> Soul-animating strains, alas too few !'

The fourth and last sonnet which we have selected is an appeal to Cromwell in 1652 not to establish a paid ministry, one of the points of public policy on which Milton felt most deeply, and on which he differed from the policy adopted by the Protector.

6.

But all this while Milton never lost sight of his fixed purpose to write a great poem. This life-aim was in abeyance, not relinquished. From a very early date this purpose had taken possession of his mind, and governed his conduct. He educated himself for it, and even during the twenty years of seeming alienation, he was but making himself 'more fit.' In a pamphlet written in 1641 he put in print a public pledge to execute his design of a great poem in English. 'Neither do I think it shame to covenant with any knowing reader, that for some few years yet I may go on trust with him toward the payment of what I am now indebted, as being a work not to be raised from the heat of youth or the vapours of wine, like that which flows at waste from the pen of some vulgar amorist, or the trencher-fury of a riming parasite, nor to be obtained by the invocation of Dame Memory and her Siren daughters, but by devout prayer to that eternal Spirit who can enrich with all utterance and knowledge, and sends out his Seraphim with the hallowed fire of his altar to touch and purify the lips of whom he pleases. To this must be added industriously select reading, steady observation, insight into all seemly and generous arts and affairs—till which in some measure be compassed at mine own peril and cost, I refuse not to sustain this expectation from as many as are not loth to hazard so much credulity upon the best pledges that I can give them.'

It is material to a right judgment on *Paradise Lost* to come to the study of it with this knowledge of its origin. For it is one of the most artificial poems in the world ; having this, among other qualities, in common with the Æneid. It belongs to the class which the Greek critics (and all modern critics have adopted their nomenclature) called 'Epic.' This division of poems into Epic and Dramatic is founded upon a prominent difference in their manner of recital. Both alike present to us a story, or transaction. In the Epic the story is narrated to us by a third person ; in the Drama the personages of the story come themselves before us as speaking and acting. This classification, however, though convenient for the purposes of a catalogue, does not reach the essential poetic qualities of composition in verse. Such a division, founded upon poetic quality, we should obtain, if we divided narrative poems into the 'naive,' and the 'artificial.' The poet may be wholly preoccupied with his story, bent upon preserving the memory of events transmitted to him by tradition. Or the story may be a secondary consideration, and only used by him as a medium of producing a given mental impression, and satisfying by choice of language and rhythm the demands of imagination and taste. *Paradise Lost* is an epic of the latter class. Milton's mind was full to overflowing with vague conceptions of the lofty, the vast, and the sublime, and he cast about for a transaction in which he could embody them. He first thought of some conspicuous event in English history, in which Shakespeare had found his dramatic material. For in order to constitute a national epic, the events narrated must be of general national concernment. They must neither be foreign, nor taken from the byeways of history. Such a topic Milton at first thought he had found in the Arturian legend, the outlines of which are given in Geoffrey of Monmouth's Latin paraphrase of Tysilio. He afterwards abandoned national history in favour of a scriptural subject, as possessing more universality, being every man's property and concernment, and having also the highest guarantee of truth. Among possible scriptural subjects his choice wavered for some time, but settled at last upon the Fall and Restoration of Man, a subject involving the fortunes of the whole human race from before the world began to be. The merits of this material for a work of art are, that its interest extends to every human being, and is perennial ; the struggle of moral freedom against external temptation in combination with fate, or divine decree, presenting the still unsolved problem which is ever urging human speculation to fresh efforts. The form in which Milton adopted the theme, viz. the story as told in Genesis, offers to a poet the further advantage of concreting the eternal conflict of good and evil in two persons, our ancestors, upon whose behaviour the fortunes of us, their descendants, hang trembling in the balance. It is not for Hector or for Dido, that our sympathy is demanded, it is our happiness or misery that is at stake.

The disadvantages of the story for epic treatment are, the paucity of agents, and the want of naturalness or verisimilitude, in the events. There are but two human beings in the twelve books. And they are not entirely human till after the Fall, i. e. till after the tragic catastrophe of the plot. The preponderance of superhuman personages, demoniac or divine, creates a demand upon the imagination greater than what any, but poetic natures, can supply. The supernatural is a necessary ingredient of a fictitious history, but to be in credible proportions it must always be sparingly mingled with the ordinary and probable course of events. In a realistic age constantly fed with fiction which dwells among the realities of domestic life, it becomes difficult to assimilate the deities and devils of *Paradise Lost*, and the heaven and hell, their respective dwelling-places.

The defects of the plot or fable have to be redeemed by poetic ornament, language, harmony. And here Milton is beyond comparison the greatest artist who has yet employed our language in verse. Dr. Guest says he 'diligently tutored an ear which nature had gifted with delicate sensibility . . . . His verse almost ever fits the subject, and so insensibly does poetry blend with this —the last beauty of exquisite versification—that the reader may sometimes doubt whether it be the thought itself, or merely the happiness of its expression, which is the source of a gratification so deeply felt.' If the personages in the two poems are unimaginable, and the situations unnatural, the art of exciting poetic emotion by the employment and collocation of words has never been practised by any English writer with such refinement. Single lines are alive with feeling, and there is a long swell which accompanies us even through the tame and dreary flats of the poem, such as the 5th, 6th, and 7th books. 'There are no such vistas and avenues of verse as Milton's. In reading *Paradise Lost* one has a feeling of spaciousness such as no other poet gives. He showed from the first that larger style which was to be his peculiar distinction. The strain heard in his earlier productions is of a higher mood as regards metrical construction than anything that had thrilled the English ear before, giving no uncertain augury of him who was to show what sonorous metal lay silent, till he touched the keys in the epical organ-pipes of our various language, that have never since felt the strain of such prevailing breath.' (Lowell.)

7.

Paradise Regained was written, in whole, or in part, during the poet's retirement to Chalfont S. Giles' from the Great Plague, 1665 –6. Ellwood, Milton's young quaker friend, tells us that he himself was the person who first suggested this subject. But, without questioning the literal exactness of Ellwood's report of his conversation with Milton, it is probable that Milton originally conceived the subject of his great work—the Fall and Recovery of Man—in one, and only when he came to write, found that the two parts of the drama of humanity must be separately treated. He therefore contented himself with a prophetic reference to the recovery, and the Messiah, in an awkward supplement, Book 12 of *Paradise Lost.* From Ellwood's suggestion, too, Milton has taken no more than the title of his poem. For though he calls it *Paradise Regained*, the subject of the poem is the Temptation ; and this would have been its proper title.

It is observed by the critics that the later epic has, in every country, a tendency to pass into the drama. *Paradise Regained*

cannot be ranked as an epic, as not being full enough of person-
ages or events.   At the same time, it is not a drama, as the one
transaction of which it consists is narrated to us by the poet, and
not performed before us by the only two actors introduced.   The
bulk of the poem consists of dialogue.   It is an astonishing feat of
amplification, that more than 2000 lines should have been con-
structed out of some twenty verses of the synoptical gospels,
without our anywhere having the sense of circumlocution and
weakened effect, which paraphrases ordinarily produce.

   Paradise Regained is undoubtedly inferior in interest to *Paradise
Lost*.   This is owing to its exaggerating the defects of the former
poem, which were too little action, too few agents, and the super-
human character of those few.   The language of the later poem is
also less ornate, less charged with subtle suggestion than was that
of *Paradise Lost*.   But, though barren of human interest, and
denuded of all verbal ornamentation, the patient student of
Paradise Regained will find himself impressed by it with a sense
of power which awes all the more because it is latent.   Phillips
tells us that the poet himself 'could not bear with patience' to
hear that it was inferior to *Paradise Lost*.   Johnson, with his
habitual carelessness, converted this statement into the different
one that 'his last poetical offspring was his favourite.'   This is
not warranted by the authority which Johnson quotes, that of
Phillips.   But it is remarkable that two poets of the early part of
our century, Coleridge and Wordsworth, have each given expression
to a similar opinion.   Wordsworth says : '*Paradise Regained* is the
most perfect in execution of anything written by Milton ;' Coleridge,
that 'in its kind it is the most perfect poem extant, though its
kind may be inferior in interest.'

8.

   With *Samson Agonistes*, written 1667, published 1671, Milton
closed his authorship as poet.   In composing this piece he ful-
filled more than one cherished intention.   *Samson* is a drama, and
though Milton had, after mature deliberation, chosen the epic
form for his chief work, it was not without secretly reserving the
intention to repeat the experiment of a drama, in which the Greek
model should be even more closely adhered to than in *Comus*
Milton's taste had been offended by the want of art and regularity
of the English drama, and he tried to give a specimen of a tragedy
in conformity with the severest type.   In *Samson* not only are the

unities of time and place observed, but dialogue is varied by choral odes ; no division of act or scene is made, but the transitions are managed by the intervention of a chorus of compatriots and sympathisers. How much, in composing this piece, Milton's thoughts were occupied with the question of form, is proved by his choosing to preface it by some remarks with a bearing on that point only. He says nothing, in this preface, which could point the references to his own fate and fortunes. The prefatory remarks are apologetic, and explain why he has adopted the dramatic form, in spite of the objection of religious men to the stage, and why he has modelled his drama after the ancients and Italians.

Besides reviving the more correct form of drama, Milton's intention, in *Samson*, is to offer one which in substance is free from the coarse buffooneries of the Restoration stage. Though taste and friendship both forbade his naming Dryden, or any living dramatist, we see of whom he is thinking, when he ' would vindicate tragedy from the small esteem, or rather infamy, which in the account of many it undergoes at this day, with other common interludes, suffering through the poet's error of intermixing comic stuff with tragic sadness and gravity ; or introducing trivial and vulgar persons ; which by all judicious hath been counted absurd, and brought in without discretion, corruptly to gratify the people.'

Lastly, under the story of *Samson*, as here presented, the poet has adumbrated his own fate—the splendid promise of his God-dedicated youth, in contrast with the tragic close in blind and forsaken age, poor, despised, and if not a prisoner himself, witness of the captivity of his friends, and the triumph of the Philistine foe—all this is distinctly imaged throughout this piece. The resemblance is completed by the scene with Dalila, in which we see how bitter, even at the distance of five and twenty years, is Milton's remembrance of what he suffered in his first marriage with the daughter of a Philistine house. When we remember that the line, ' with fear of change Perplexes monarchs,' in *Paradise Lost* had staggered a not unfriendly censor, we may wonder that the unmistakable allusion in *Samson*—

> ' their carcasses
> To dogs and fowls a prey, or else captiv'd :
> Or to th' unjust tribunals under change of times
> And condemnation of th' ingrateful multitude,'

should have passed unchallenged in 1671.

MARK PATTISON

An Epitaph on the Admirable Dramatic Poet, William Shakespeare.

[1630; æt. 22.]

What needs my Shakespeare for his honour'd bones,
The labour of an age in piled stones?
Or that his hallow'd relics should be hid
Under a star-ypointing pyramid?
Dear son of memory, great heir of fame,
What need'st thou such weak witness of thy name?
Thou, in our wonder and astonishment,
Hast built thyself a livelong monument.
For whilst, to the shame of slow-endeavouring art,
Thy easy numbers flow, and that each heart
Hath, from the leaves of thy unvalued book,
Those Delphic lines with deep impression took,
Then thou, our fancy of itself bereaving,
Dost make us marble with too much conceiving:
And, so sepulchred, in such pomp dost lie,
That kings for such a tomb would wish to die.

L'ALLEGRO.

[1632-4; æt. 24-26.]

Hence, loathed Melancholy,
Of Cerberus and blackest midnight born,
In Stygian cave forlorn,
'Mongst horrid shapes, and shrieks, and sights unholy!
Find out some uncouth cell,
Where brooding Darkness spreads his jealous wings
And the night-raven sings;
There under ebon shades, and low-brow'd rocks,
As ragged as thy locks,
In dark Cimmerian desert ever dwell.

But come, thou goddess fair and free,
In heaven yclep'd Euphrosyne,
And by men, heart-easing Mirth ;
Whom lovely Venus, at a birth,
With two sister Graces more,
To ivy-crowned Bacchus bore :
Or whether (as some sager sing)
The frolic wind that breathes the spring,
Zephyr, with Aurora playing,
As he met her once a-Maying ;
There on beds of violets blue,
And fresh-blown roses wash'd in dew,
Fill'd her with thee a daughter fair,
So buxom, blithe, and debonair.
Haste thee, nymph, and bring with thee
Jest, and youthful jollity,
Quips, and cranks, and wanton wiles,
Nods, and becks, and wreathed smiles,
Such as hang on Hebe's cheek,
And love to live in dimple sleek ;
Sport that wrinkled Care derides,
And Laughter holding both his sides.
Come, and trip it as you go,
On the light fantastic toe ;
And in thy right hand lead with thee
The mountain-nymph, sweet Liberty ;
And, if I give thee honour due,
Mirth, admit me of thy crew,
To live with her, and live with thee,
In unreproved pleasures free ;
To hear the lark begin his flight,
And singing startle the dull night,
From his watch-tower in the skies,
Till the dappled dawn doth rise ;
Then to come, in spite of sorrow,
And at my window bid good-morrow,
Through the sweet-briar, or the vine,
Or the twisted eglantine :

While the cock, with lively din,
Scatters the rear of darkness thin,
And to the stack, or the barn-door,
Stoutly struts his dames before:
Oft listening how the hounds and horn
Cheerly rouse the slumbering morn,
From the side of some hoar hill,
Through the high wood echoing shrill.
  Sometime walking, not unseen,
By hedge-row elms, on hillocks green,
Right against the eastern gate,
Where the great sun begins his state,
Robed in flames and amber light,
The clouds in thousand liveries dight;
While the ploughman, near at hand,
Whistles o'er the furrow'd land,
And the milkmaid singeth blithe,
And the mower whets his scythe,
And every shepherd tells his tale,
Under the hawthorn in the dale.
  Straight mine eye hath caught new pleasures,
While the landscape round it measures;
Russet lawns, and fallows grey,
Where the nibbling flocks do stray;
Mountains, on whose barren breast
The labouring clouds do often rest;
Meadows trim, with daisies pied,
Shallow brooks, and rivers wide;
Towers and battlements it sees
Bosom'd high in tufted trees,
Where perhaps some beauty lies,
The cynosure of neighbouring eyes.
  Hard by, a cottage chimney smokes
From betwixt two aged oaks,
Where Corydon and Thyrsis met,
Are at their savoury dinner set
Of herbs, and other country messes,
Which the neat-handed Phillis dresses;

And then in haste her bower she leaves,
With Thestylis to bind the sheaves ;
Or, if the earlier season lead,
To the tann'd haycock in the mead.
   Sometimes with secure delight
The upland hamlets will invite,
When the merry bells ring round,
And the jocund rebecks sound
To many a youth and many a maid,
Dancing in the chequer'd shade,
And young and old come forth to play
On a sun-shine holy-day,
Till the livelong day-light fail :
Then to the spicy nut-brown ale,
With stories told of many a feat,
How faery Mab the junkets eat ;
She was pinch'd, and pull'd, she said ;
And he, by friar's lantern led,
Tells how the drudging goblin sweat
To earn his cream-bowl duly set,
When in one night, ere glimpse of morn,
His shadowy flail hath thresh'd the corn,
That ten day-labourers could not end ;
Then lies him down the lubber fiend,
And, stretch'd out all the chimney's length,
Basks at the fire his hairy strength ;
And crop-full out of doors he flings,
Ere the first cock his matin rings.
Thus done the tales, to bed they creep,
By whispering winds soon lull'd asleep.
   Tower'd cities please us then,
And the busy hum of men,
Where throngs of knights and barons bold,
In weeds of peace, high triumphs hold,
With store of ladies, whose bright eyes
Rain influence, and judge the prize
Of wit or arms, while both contend
To win her grace, whom all commend.

There let Hymen oft appear
In saffron robe, with taper clear,
And pomp, and feast, and revelry,
With mask and antique pageantry ;
Such sights as youthful poets dream
On summer eves by haunted stream.
Then to the well-trod stage anon,
If Jonson's learned sock be on,
Or sweetest Shakespeare, Fancy's child,
Warble his native wood-notes wild.
   And ever, against eating cares,
Lap me in soft Lydian airs,
Married to immortal verse ;
Such as the meeting soul may pierce,
In notes with many a winding bout
Of linked sweetness long drawn out,
With wanton heed and giddy cunning ;
The melting voice through mazes running,
Untwisting all the chains that tie
The hidden soul of harmony ;
That Orpheus' self may heave his head
From golden slumber on a bed
Of heap'd Elysian flowers, and hear
Such strains as would have won the ear
Of Pluto, to have quite set free
His half-regain'd Eurydice.
   These delights if thou canst give,
Mirth, with thee I mean to live.

IL PENSEROSO.

   Hence, vain deluding joys,
The brood of Folly without father bred !
How little you bested,
      Or fill the fixed mind with all your toys !

Dwell in some idle brain,
   And fancies fond with gaudy shapes possess,
As thick and numberless
As the gay motes that people the sunbeams ;
Or likest hovering dreams,
The fickle pensioners of Morpheus' train.
But hail, thou goddess sage and holy,
Hail, divinest Melancholy !
Whose saintly visage is too bright
To hit the sense of human sight,
And therefore to our weaker view
O'erlaid with black, staid wisdom's hue ;
Black, but such as in esteem
Prince Memnon's sister might beseem,
Or that starr'd Ethiop queen that strove
To set her beauty's praise above
The sea-nymphs, and their powers offended :
Yet thou art higher far descended ;
Thee bright-hair'd Vesta, long of yore,
To solitary Saturn bore ;
His daughter she ; in Saturn's reign
Such mixture was not held a stain :
Oft in glimmering bowers and glades
He met her, and in secret shades
Of woody Ida's inmost grove,
Whilst yet there was no fear of Jove.
   Come, pensive nun, devout and pure,
Sober, steadfast, and demure,
All in a robe of darkest grain,
Flowing with majestic train,
And sable stole of cypress lawn,
Over thy decent shoulders drawn.
Come, but keep thy wonted state,
With even step, and musing gait ;
And looks commercing with the skies,
Thy rapt soul sitting in thine eyes :
There, held in holy passion still,
Forget thyself to marble, till

With a sad leaden downward cast
Thou fix them on the earth as fast ;
And join with thee calm Peace, and Quiet,
Spare Fast, that oft with gods doth diet,
And hears the Muses in a ring
Aye round about Jove's altar sing :
And add to these retired Leisure,
That in trim gardens takes his pleasure.
But first, and chiefest, with thee bring,
Him that yon soars on golden wing,
Guiding the fiery-wheeled throne,
The cherub Contemplation ;
And the mute Silence hist along,
'Less Philomel will deign a song,
In her sweetest saddest plight,
Smoothing the rugged brow of night,
While Cynthia checks her dragon yoke,
Gently o'er the accustom'd oak :
Sweet bird, that shunn'st the noise of folly,
Most musical, most melancholy !
Thee, chantress, oft the woods among
I woo, to hear thy even-song ;
And, missing thee, I walk unseen
On the dry smooth-shaven green,
To behold the wand'ring moon,
Riding near her highest noon,
Like one that had been led astray
Through the heaven's wide pathless way ;
And oft, as if her head she bow'd,
Stooping through a fleecy cloud.
   Oft, on a plat of rising ground,
I hear the far-off curfew sound,
Over some wide water'd shore,
Swinging slow with sullen roar :
Or, if the air will not permit,
Some still removed place will fit,
Where glowing embers through the room
Teach light to counterfeit a gloom ;

Far from all resort of mirth,
Save the cricket on the hearth,
Or the bellman's drowsy charm,
To bless the doors from nightly harm.
  Or let my lamp, at midnight hour,
Be seen in some high lonely tower,
Where I may oft outwatch the Bear,
With thrice-great Hermes, or unsphere
The spirit of Plato, to unfold
What worlds or what vast regions hold
The immortal mind that hath forsook
Her mansion in this fleshly nook:
And of those demons that are found
In fire, air, flood, or under ground,
Whose power hath a true consent
With planet or with element.
Sometime let gorgeous tragedy
In sceptr'd pall come sweeping by,
Presenting Thebes, or Pelops' line,
Or the tale of Troy divine ;
Or what (though rare) of later age
Ennobl'd hath the buskin'd stage.
  But, O sad virgin, that thy power
Might raise Musæus from his bower !
Or bid the soul of Orpheus sing
Such notes as, warbled to the string,
Drew iron tears down Pluto's cheek,
And made hell grant what love did seek :
Or call up him that left half told
The story of Cambuscan bold,
Of Camball, and of Algarsife,
And who had Canace to wife,
That own'd the virtuous ring and glass ;
And of the wondrous horse of brass,
On which the Tartar king did ride :
And if aught else great bards beside
In sage and solemn tunes have sung,
Of turneys, and of trophies hung,

Of forests, and enchantments drear,
Where more is meant than meets the ear.
   Thus, night, oft see me in thy pale career,
Till civil-suited morn appear,
Not trick'd and frounc'd as she was wont
With the Attic boy to hunt,
But kerchieft in a comely cloud,
While rocking winds are piping loud,
Or usher'd with a shower still,
When the gust hath blown his fill,
Ending on the rustling leaves,
With minute drops from off the eaves.
And, when the sun begins to fling
His flaring beams, me, goddess, bring
To arched walks of twilight groves,
And shadows brown, that Sylvan loves,
Of pine, or monumental oak,
Where the rude axe, with heaved stroke,
Was never heard the nymphs to daunt,
Or fright them from their hallow'd haunt.
There in close covert by some brook,
Where no profaner eye may look,
Hide me from day's garish eye,
While the bee with honey'd thigh,
That at her flowery work doth sing,
And the waters murmuring,
With such concert as they keep,
Entice the dewy-feather'd sleep ;
And let some strange mysterious dream
Wave at his wings in airy stream
Of lively portraiture display'd,
Softly on my eyelids laid.
And, as I wake, sweet music breathe
Above, about, or underneath,
Sent by some spirit to mortals good,
Or the unseen genius of the wood.
   But let my due feet never fail
To walk the studious cloister's pale,

And love the high-embowed roof,
With antique pillars massy proof,
And storied windows richly dight,
Casting a dim religious light :
There let the pealing organ blow,
To the full-voiced quire below,
In service high and anthems clear,
As may with sweetness, through mine ear,
Dissolve me into extasies,
And bring all heaven before mine eyes.
　　And may at last my weary age
Find out the peaceful hermitage,
The hairy gown and mossy cell,
Where I may sit and rightly spell
Of every star that heaven doth shew,
And every herb that sips the dew ;
Till old experience do attain
To something like prophetic strain.
　　These pleasures, Melancholy, give,
And I with thee will choose to live.

FROM 'COMUS.'

[1634; æt. 26.]

　Comus. The star that bids the shepherd fold,
Now the top of heaven doth hold ;
And the gilded car of day
His glowing axle doth allay
In the steep Atlantic stream ;
And the slope Sun his upward beam
Shoots against the dusky pole ;
Pacing toward the other goal
Of his chamber in the East.
Meanwhile, welcome joy, and feast,
Midnight shout, and revelry,
Tipsy dance, and jollity,

Braid your locks with rosy twine,
Dropping odours, dropping wine.
Rigour now is gone to bed,
And advice with scrupulous head,
Strict age, and sour severity,
With their grave saws in slumber lie.
We that are of purer fire,
Imitate the starry quire,
Who in their nightly watchful spheres
Lead in swift round the months and years.
The sounds and seas, with all their finny droves,
Now to the moon in wav'ring morrice move;
And, on the tawny sands and shelves,
Trip the pert fairies and the dapper elves;
By dimpled brook and fountain-brim,
The wood-nymphs, deck'd with daisies trim,
Their merry wakes and pastimes keep;
What hath night to do with sleep?
Night hath better sweets to prove,
Venus now wakes, and wakens love.
Come, let us our rites begin,
'Tis only day-light that makes sin,
Which these dun shades will ne'er report.
Hail goddess of nocturnal sport,
Dark-veil'd Cotytto! to whom the secret flame
Of midnight torches burns; mysterious dame
That ne'er art call'd, but when the dragon womb
Of Stygian darkness spits her thickest gloom,
And makes one blot of all the air;
Stay thy cloudy ebon chair,
Wherein thou rid'st with Hecat', and befriend
Us thy vow'd priests; till utmost end
Of all thy dues be done, and none left out;
Ere the blabbing eastern scout,
The nice morn on the Indian steep,
From her cabin'd loophole peep,
And to the tell-tale sun descry
Our conceal'd solemnity.

Come, knit hands, and beat the ground,
In a light fantastic round.

The Measure.

Break off, break off, I feel the different pace
Of some chaste footing near about this ground.
Run to your shrouds, within these brakes and trees;
Our number may affright : some virgin sure
(For so I can distinguish by mine art)
Benighted in these woods.   Now to my charms,
And to my wily trains : I shall ere long
Be well stock'd with as fair a herd as graz'd
About my mother Circe.   Thus I hurl
My dazzling spells into the spongy air,
Of power to cheat the eye with blear illusion,
And give it false presentments ; lest the place
And my quaint habits breed astonishment,
And put the damsel to suspicious flight ;
Which must not be, for that's against my course :
I, under fair pretence of friendly ends,
And well-placed words of glozing courtesy
Baited with reasons not unplausible,
Wind me into the easy-hearted man,
And hug him into snares.   When once her eye
Hath met the virtue of this magic dust,
I shall appear some harmless villager
Whom thrift keeps up about his country gear.
But here she comes ; I fairly step aside,
And hearken, if I may her business hear.

The Lady enters.

Lady. This way the noise was, if mine ear be true,
My best guide now ; methought it was the sound
Of riot and ill-manag'd merriment,
Such as the jocund flute, or gamesome pipe
Stirs up among the loose unletter'd hinds,
When for their teeming flocks and granges full,
In wanton dance they praise the bounteous Pan,

And thank the gods amiss. I should be loth
To meet the rudeness, and swill'd insolence
Of such late wassailers; yet O ! where else
Shall I inform my unacquainted feet
In the blind mazes of this tangled wood?
My brothers, when they saw me wearied out
With this long way, resolving here to lodge
Under the spreading favour of these pines,
Stept, as they said, to the next thicket side
To bring me berries, or such cooling fruit
As the kind hospitable woods provide.
They left me then, when the grey-hooded Even,
Like a sad votarist in palmer's weed,
Rose from the hindmost wheels of Phœbus' wain.
But where they are, and why they came not back,
Is now the labour of my thoughts; 'tis likeliest
They had engaged their wandering steps too far,
And envious darkness, ere they could return,
Had stole them from me ; else O thievish night,
Why shouldst thou, but for some felonious end,
In thy dark lantern thus close up the stars,
That Nature hung in Heaven, and fill'd their lamps
With everlasting oil, to give due light
To the misled and lonely traveller?
This is the place, as well as I may guess,
Whence even now the tumult of loud mirth
Was rife, and perfect in my listening ear;
Yet nought but single darkness do I find.
What might this be? A thousand fantasies
Begin to throng into my memory,
Of calling shapes, and beckoning shadows dire,
And airy tongues that syllable men's names
On sands, and shores, and desert wildernesses.
These thoughts may startle well, but not astound
The virtuous mind, that ever walks attended
By a strong siding champion, conscience.
O welcome, pure-eyed Faith, white-handed Hope,
Thou hov'ring angel girt with golden wings,
And thou, unblemish'd form of Chastity !

I see ye visibly, and now believe
That he, the Supreme Good, to whom all things ill
Are but as slavish officers of vengeance,
Would send a glist'ring guardian, if need were,
To keep my life and honour unassail'd.
Was I deceived, or did a sable cloud
Turn forth her silver lining on the night?
I did not err, there does a sable cloud
Turn forth her silver lining on the night,
And casts a gleam over this tufted grove:
I cannot halloo to my brothers, but
Such noise as I can make to be heard farthest
I 'll venture, for my new enliven'd spirits
Prompt me; and they perhaps are not far off.

Song.

Sweet Echo, sweetest Nymph, that livest unseen
   Within thy airy shell,
  By slow Meander's margent green,
And in the violet-embroider'd vale
   Where the love-lorn nightingale
Nightly to thee her sad song mourneth well:
Canst thou not tell me of a gentle pair
   That likest thy Narcissus are?
    O, if thou have
   Hid them in some flowery cave,
    Tell me but where,
Sweet queen of parley, daughter of the sphere!
So may'st thou be translated to the skies,
And give resounding grace to all Heaven's harmonies.

Enter Comus.

Comus. Can any mortal mixture of earth's mould
Breathe such divine enchanting ravishment?
Sure something holy lodges in that breast,
And with these raptures moves the vocal air
To testify his hidden residence.

How sweetly did they float upon the wings
Of silence through the empty-vaulted night,
At every fall smoothing the raven down
Of Darkness till it smiled ! I have oft heard
My mother Circe with the Sirens three,
Amidst the flowery-kirtled Naiades,
Culling their potent herbs, and baleful drugs ;
Who, as they sung, would take the prison'd soul
And lap it in Elysium ; Scylla wept,
And chid her barking waves into attention,
And fell Charybdis murmur'd soft applause :
Yet they in pleasing slumber lull'd the sense,
And in sweet madness robb'd it of itself ;
But such a sacred, and home-felt delight,
Such sober certainty of waking bliss
I never heard till now.   I 'll speak to her,
And she shall be my queen.   Hail, foreign wonder !
Whom certain these rough shades did never breed :
Unless the goddess that in rural shrine
Dwell'st here with Pan, or Sylvan, by blest song
Forbidding every bleak unkindly fog
To touch the prosperous growth of this tall wood.

Lady. Nay, gentle shepherd, ill is lost that praise
That is address'd to unattending ears ;
Not any boast of skill, but extreme shift
How to regain my sever'd company,
Compell'd me to awake the courteous Echo
To give me answer from her mossy couch.

Comus. What chance, good lady, hath bereft you thus ?

Lady. Dim darkness, and this leafy labyrinth.

Comus. Could that divide you from near-ushering guides ?

Lady. They left me weary on a grassy turf.

Comus. By falsehood, or discourtesy, or why ?

Lady. To seek i' the valley some cool friendly spring.

Comus. And left your fair side all unguarded, lady ?

Lady. They were but twain, and purposed quick return.

Comus. Perhaps forestalling night prevented them.

Lady. How easy my misfortune is to hit!

Comus. Imports their loss, beside the present need?

Lady. No less than if I should my brothers lose.

Comus. Were they of manly prime, or youthful bloom?

Lady. As smooth as Hebe's their unrazor'd lips.

Comus. Two such I saw, what time the labour'd ox
In his loose traces from the furrow came,
And the swink'd hedger at his supper sate;
I saw them under a green mantling vine
That crawls along the side of yon small hill,
Plucking ripe clusters from the tender shoots.
Their port was more than human, as they stood;
I took it for a fairy vision
Of some gay creatures of the element,
That in the colours of the rainbow live,
And play i' the plighted clouds. I was awe-struck,
And as I past, I worshipt; if those you seek,
It were a journey like the path to heaven
To help you find them.

Lady.   Gentle villager,
What readiest way would bring me to that place?

Comus. Due west it rises from this shrubby point.

Lady. To find out that, good shepherd, I suppose,
In such a scant allowance of star-light,
Would overtask the best land-pilot's art,
Without the sure guess of well-practised feet.

Comus. I know each lane, and every alley green,
Dingle, or bushy dell, of this wild wood,
And every bosky bourn from side to side,
My daily walks and ancient neighbourhood:
And if your stray attendance be yet lodged,
Or shroud within these limits, I shall know
Ere morrow wake, or the low-roosted lark
From her thatch'd pallet rouse; if otherwise,
I can conduct you, lady, to a low

But loyal cottage, where you may be safe
Till further quest.

    Lady.   Shepherd, I take thy word,
And trust thy honest-offer'd courtesy,
Which oft is sooner found in lowly sheds
With smoky rafters, than in tapestry halls
In courts of princes, where it first was named
And yet is most pretended : in a place
Less warranted than this, or less secure,
I cannot be, that I should fear to change it.
Eye me, blest Providence, and square my trial
To my proportion'd strength. Shepherd, lead on.   [*Exeunt.*

LYCIDAS.

[1637; æt. 29.]

Yet once more, O ye laurels, and once more
Ye myrtles brown, with ivy never sere,
I come to pluck your berries harsh and crude ;
And, with forced fingers rude,
Shatter your leaves before the mellowing year.
Bitter constraint, and sad occasion dear,
Compels me to disturb your season due :
For Lycidas is dead, dead ere his prime,
Young Lycidas, and hath not left his peer :
Who would not sing for Lycidas ? he knew
Himself to sing, and build the lofty rhyme.
He must not float upon his watery bier
Unwept, and welter to the parching wind,
Without the meed of some melodious tear.
    Begin then, sisters of the sacred well,
That from beneath the seat of Jove doth spring ;
Begin, and somewhat loudly sweep the string ;
Hence with denial vain, and coy excuse :
So may some gentle muse
With lucky words favour my destin'd urn ;
And, as he passes, turn,

And bid fair peace be to my sable shroud.
   For we were nursed upon the self-same hill,
Fed the same flock, by fountain, shade, and rill;
Together both, ere the high lawns appear'd
Under the opening eyelids of the morn,
We drove afield, and both together heard
What time the grey fly winds her sultry horn,
Battening our flocks with the fresh dews of night,
Oft till the star, that rose at evening bright,
Toward heaven's descent had slop'd his westering wheel.
Meanwhile the rural ditties were not mute,
Temper'd to the oaten flute ;
Rough Satyrs danc'd, and fauns with cloven heel
From the glad sound would not be absent long ;
And old Damœtas loved to hear our song.
   But, O the heavy change, now thou art gone,
Now thou art gone, and never must return !
Thee, shepherd, thee the woods, and desert caves,
With wild thyme and the gadding vine o'ergrown,
And all their echoes, mourn :
The willows, and the hazel copses green,
Shall now no more be seen
Fanning their joyous leaves to thy soft lays.
As killing as the canker to the rose,
Or taint-worm to the weanling herds that graze,
Or frost to flowers, that their gay wardrobe wear,
When first the whitethorn blows ;
Such, Lycidas, thy loss to shepherds' ear.
   Where were ye, nymphs, when the remorseless ^
Closed o'er the head of your loved Lycidas?
For neither were ye playing on the steep
Where your old bards, the famous Druids, lie,
Nor on the shaggy top of Mona high,
Nor yet where Deva spreads her wizard stream ;
Ah me ! I fondly dream,
Had ye been there :—for what could that have done?
What could the Muse herself that Orpheus bore,
The Muse herself, for her enchanting son,
Whom universal nature did lament,

When, by the rout that made the hideous roar,
His gory visage down the stream was sent,
Down the swift Hebrus to the Lesbian shore?
  Alas! what boots it with incessant care
To tend the homely, slighted, shepherd's trade,
And strictly meditate the thankless Muse?
Were it not better done, as others use,
To sport with Amaryllis in the shade,
Or with the tangles of Neæra's hair?
Fame is the spur that the clear spirit doth raise
(That last infirmity of noble minds)
To scorn delights and live laborious days:
But the fair guerdon when we hope to find,
And think to burst out into sudden blaze,
Comes the blind Fury with the abhorred shears,
And slits the thin-spun life. 'But not the praise,'
Phœbus replied, and touch'd my trembling ears;
'Fame is no plant that grows on mortal soil,
Nor in the glistering foil
Set off to the world, nor in broad rumour lies:
But lives and spreads aloft by those pure eyes,
And perfect witness of all-judging Jove;
As he pronounces lastly on each deed,
Of so much fame in heaven expect thy meed.'
  O fountain Arethuse, and thou honour'd flood,
Smooth-sliding Mincius, crown'd with vocal reeds!
That strain I heard was of a higher mood:
But now my oat proceeds,
And listens to the herald of the sea,
That came in Neptune's plea;
He ask'd the waves, and ask'd the felon winds,
What hard mishap hath doom'd this gentle swain?
And question'd every gust of rugged wings
That blows from off each beaked promontory:
They knew not of his story;
And sage Hippotades their answer brings,
That not a blast was from his dungeon stray'd:
The air was calm, and on the level brine
Sleek Panope with all her sisters play'd.

It was that fatal and perfidious bark,
Built in the eclipse, and rigg'd with curses dark,
That sunk so low that sacred head of thine.
  Next Camus, reverend sire, went footing slow,
His mantle hairy, and his bonnet sedge,
Inwrought with figures dim, and on the edge
Like to that sanguine flower inscribed with woe.
'Ah! who hath reft,' quoth he, 'my dearest pledge?'
Last came, and last did go,
The pilot of the Galilean lake;
Two massy keys he bore of metals twain
(The golden opes, the iron shuts amain),
He shook his mitred locks, and stern bespake:
'How well could I have spared for thee, young swain,
Enow of such, as for their bellies' sake
Creep, and intrude, and climb into the fold!
Of other care they little reck'ning make,
Than how to scramble at the shearers' feast,
And shove away the worthy bidden guest;
Blind mouths! that scarce themselves know how to hold
A sheep-hook, or have learn'd aught else the least
That to the faithful herdman's art belongs!
What recks it them? What need they? They are sped;
And, when they list, their lean and flashy songs
Grate on their scrannel pipes of wretched straw;
The hungry sheep look up, and are not fed,
But, swoln with wind and the rank mist they draw,
Rot inwardly, and foul contagion spread:
Besides what the grim wolf with privy paw
Daily devours apace, and nothing said:
But that two-handed engine at the door
Stands ready to smite once, and smite no more.
  Return, Alpheus, the dread voice is past,
That shrunk thy streams; return, Sicilian Muse,
And call the vales, and bid them hither cast
Their bells and flowerets of a thousand hues.
Ye valleys low, where the mild whispers use
Of shades, and wanton winds, and gushing brooks,
On whose fresh lap the swart star sparely looks;

Throw hither all your quaint enamell'd eyes,
That on the green turf suck the honey'd showers,
And purple all the ground with vernal flowers.
Bring the rathe primrose that forsaken dies,
The tufted crow-toe, and pale jessamine,
The white pink, and the pansy freak'd with jet,
The glowing violet,
The musk-rose, and the well-attired woodbine,
With cowslips wan that hang the pensive head,
And every flower that sad embroidery wears:
Bid amaranthus all his beauty shed,
And daffodillies fill their cups with tears,
To strew the laureat hearse where Lycid lies.
For, so to interpose a little ease,
Let our frail thoughts dally with false surmise;
Ah me! whilst thee the shores and sounding seas
Wash far away, where'er thy bones are hurl'd,
Whether beyond the stormy Hebrides,
Where thou perhaps, under the whelming tide,
Visit'st the bottom of the monstrous world;
Or whether thou, to our moist vows denied,
Sleep'st by the fable of Bellerus old,
Where the great vision of the guarded mount
Looks toward Namancos and Bayona's hold;
Look homeward, angel, now, and melt with ruth:
And, O ye dolphins, waft the hapless youth.

   Weep no more, woful shepherds, weep no more,
For Lycidas your sorrow is not dead,
Sunk though he be beneath the wat'ry floor;
So sinks the daystar in the ocean bed,
And yet anon repairs his drooping head,
And tricks his beams, and with new-spangled ore
Flames in the forehead of the morning sky:
So Lycidas sunk low, but mounted high,
Through the dear might of Him that walk'd the waves;
Where, other groves and other streams along,
With nectar pure his oozy locks he laves,
And hears the unexpressive nuptial song,
In the blest kingdoms meek of joy and love.

There entertain him all the saints above,
In solemn troops, and sweet societies,
That sing, and singing in their glory move,
And wipe the tears for ever from his eyes.
Now, Lycidas, the shepherds weep no more;
Henceforth thou art the genius of the shore,
In thy large recompense, and shalt be good
To all that wander in that perilous flood.

   Thus sang the uncouth swain to the oaks and rills,
While the still morn went out with sandals grey;
He touch'd the tender stops of various quills,
With eager thought warbling his Doric lay:
And now the sun had stretch'd out all the hills,
And now was dropt into the western bay:
At last he rose, and twitch'd his mantle blue:
To-morrow to fresh woods, and pastures new.

SONNETS.

ON HIS BEING ARRIVED AT THE AGE OF TWENTY-THREE.

How soon hath Time, the subtle thief of youth,
  Stol'n on his wing my three-and-twentieth year!
  My hasting days fly on with full career,
  But my late spring no bud or blossom shew'th.
Perhaps my semblance might deceive the truth,
  That I to manhood am arrived so near,
  And inward ripeness doth much less appear,
  That some more timely-happy spirits indu'th.
Yet be it less or more, or soon or slow,
  It shall be still in strictest measure even
  To that same lot, however mean or high,
Tow'rd which time leads me, and the will of heaven;
  All is, if I have grace to use it so,
  As ever in my great task-master's eye.

On his Blindness.

When I consider how my light is spent,
  Ere half my days, in this dark world and wide,
  And that one talent, which is death to hide,
  Lodg'd with me useless, though my soul more bent
To serve therewith my Maker, and present
  My true account, lest he, returning, chide ;
  'Doth God exact day-labour, light denied ?'
  I fondly ask : but Patience, to prevent
That murmur, soon replies, 'God doth not need
  Either man's work, or his own gifts ; who best
  Bear his mild yoke, they serve him best : his state
Is kingly ; thousands at his bidding speed,
  And post o'er land and ocean without rest ;
  They also serve who only stand and wait.'

On the late Massacre in Piedmont.

Avenge, O Lord, thy slaughter'd saints, whose bones
  Lie scatter'd on the Alpine mountains cold ;
  Ev'n them who kept thy truth so pure of old,
  When all our fathers worshipt stocks and stones,
Forget not : in thy book record their groans
  Who were thy sheep, and in their ancient fold
  Slain by the bloody Piedmontese that roll'd
  Mother with infant down the rocks. Their moans
The vales redoubl'd to the hills, and they
  To heaven. Their martyr'd blood and ashes sow
  O'er all the Italian fields, where still doth sway
The triple tyrant ; that from these may grow
  A hundred fold, who, having learnt thy way,
  Early may fly the Babylonian woe.

To the Lord General Cromwell, May 1652,

On the proposals of certain Ministers at the Committee for Propagation of the Gospel.

Cromwell, our chief of men, who through a cloud
    Not of war only, but detractions rude,
    Guided by faith and matchless fortitude,
    To peace and truth thy glorious way hast plough'd,
And on the neck of crowned Fortune proud
    Hast rear'd God's trophies, and his work pursued,
    While Darwen stream, with blood of Scots imbrued,
    And Dunbar field, resounds thy praises loud,
And Worcester's laureate wreath : yet much remains
    To conquer still ; peace hath her victories
    No less renowned than war : new foes arise,
Threatening to bind our souls with secular chains.
    Help us to save free conscience from the paw
    Of hireling wolves, whose gospel is their maw.

From 'Paradise Lost.'

[1658–1665 ; æt. 50-57.]

BOOK I.

Of Man's first disobedience, and the fruit
Of that forbidden tree, whose mortal taste
Brought death into the world, and all our woe,
With loss of Eden, till one greater Man
Restore us, and regain the blissful seat,
Sing, heavenly muse, that on the secret top
Of Oreb, or of Sinai, didst inspire
That shepherd who first taught the chosen seed,
In the beginning how the heavens and earth
Rose out of chaos : or, if Sion hill
Delight thee more, and Siloa's brook that flow'd

Fast by the oracle of God, I thence
Invoke thy aid to my adventrous song,
That with no middle flight intends to soar
Above the Aonian mount, while it pursues
Things unattempted yet in prose or rhyme.
And chiefly thou, O Spirit, that dost prefer
Before all temples the upright heart and pure,
Instruct me, for thou know'st; thou from the first
Wast present, and, with mighty wings outspread,
Dove-like sat'st brooding on the vast abyss,
And mad'st it pregnant: what in me is dark,
Illumine; what is low, raise and support;
That to the height of this great argument
I may assert eternal Providence,
And justify the ways of God to men.
    Say first, for Heaven hides nothing from thy view,
Nor the deep tract of hell; say first, what cause
Moved our grand parents, in that happy state,
Favour'd of Heaven so highly, to fall off
From their Creator, and transgress his will
For one restraint, lords of the world besides?
Who first seduced them to that foul revolt?
The infernal Serpent; he it was, whose guile,
Stirr'd up with envy and revenge, deceived
The mother of mankind, what time his pride
Had cast him out from heaven, with all his host
Of rebel angels; by whose aid, aspiring
To set himself in glory above his peers,
He trusted to have equall'd the Most High,
If he opposed; and, with ambitious aim
Against the throne and monarchy of God,
Raised impious war in heaven, and battle proud,
With vain attempt. Him the Almighty Power
Hurl'd headlong flaming from the ethereal sky,
With hideous ruin and combustion, down
To bottomless perdition; there to dwell
In adamantine chains and penal fire,
Who durst defy the Omnipotent to arms.
Nine times the space that measures day and night

To mortal men, he with his horrid crew
Lay vanquish'd, rolling in the fiery gulf,
Confounded, though immortal : but his doom
Reserved him to more wrath ; for now the thought
Both of lost happiness and lasting pain
Torments him : round he throws his baleful eyes,
That witness'd huge affliction and dismay,
Mix'd with obdurate pride and steadfast hate :
At once, as far as angel's ken, he views
The dismal situation waste and wild ;
A dungeon horrible on all sides round,
As one great furnace flamed ; yet from those flames
No light, but rather darkness visible
Served only to discover sights of woe,
Regions of sorrow, doleful shades, where peace
And rest can never dwell, hope never comes
That comes to all ; but torture without end
Still urges, and a fiery deluge, fed
With ever-burning sulphur unconsumed :
Such place eternal justice had prepared
For those rebellious ; here their prison ordain'd
In utter darkness, and their portion set
As far removed from God and light of heaven,
As from the centre thrice to the utmost pole.
O, how unlike the place from whence they fell !
There the companions of his fall, o'erwhelm'd
With floods and whirlwinds of tempestuous fire,
He soon discerns, and weltering by his side
One next himself in power, and next in crime,
Long after known in Palestine, and named
Beëlzebub. To whom the arch-enemy,
And thence in heaven call'd Satan, with bold words
Breaking the horrid silence, thus began :
'If thou beest he ; but O, how fallen ! how changed
From him, who, in the happy realms of light,
Clothed with transcendent brightness, didst outshine
Myriads though bright ! If he whom mutual league,
United thoughts and counsels, equal hope
And hazard in the glorious enterprise,

Join'd with me once, now misery hath join'd
In equal ruin : into what pit thou seest
From what height fallen, so much the stronger proved
He with his thunder : and till then who knew
The force of those dire arms ? Yet not for those,
Nor what the potent Victor in his rage
Can else inflict, do I repent or change,
Though changed in outward lustre, that fix'd mind,
And high disdain from sense of injured merit,
That with the Mightiest raised me to contend,
And to the fierce contention brought along
Innumerable force of spirits arm'd,
That durst dislike his reign, and, me preferring,
His utmost power with adverse power opposed
In dubious battle on the plains of heaven,
And shook his throne. What though the field be lost,
All is not lost ; the unconquerable will,
And study of revenge, immortal hate,
And courage never to submit or yield,
And what is else not to be overcome ;
That glory never shall his wrath or might
Extort from me. To bow and sue for grace
With suppliant knee, and deify his power
Who from the terror of this arm so late
Doubted his empire ; that were low indeed,
That were an ignominy, and shame beneath
This downfall : since by fate the strength of gods,
And this empyreal substance cannot fail :
Since through experience of this great event
In arms not worse, in foresight much advanced,
We may with more successful hope resolve
To wage by force or guile eternal war,
Irreconcilable to our grand foe,
Who now triumphs, and in the excess of joy
Sole reigning, holds the tyranny of heaven.'

  So spake the apostate angel, though in pain,
Vaunting aloud, but rack'd with deep despair:
And him thus answered soon his bold compeer.
  ' O prince, O chief of many-throned powers,

That led the embattled seraphim to war
Under thy conduct, and in dreadful deeds
Fearless, endanger'd heaven's perpetual King,
And put to proof his high supremacy,
Whether upheld by strength, or chance, or fate ;
Too well I see, and rue the dire event,
That with sad overthrow, and foul defeat,
Hath lost us heaven, and all this mighty host
In horrible destruction laid thus low,
As far as gods and heavenly essences
Can perish: for the mind and spirit remain
Invincible, and vigour soon returns,
Though all our glory extinct, and happy state
Here swallow'd up in endless misery.
But what if he our Conqueror (whom I now
Of force believe almighty, since no less
Than such could have o'erpower'd such force as ours)
Have left us this our spirit and strength entire
Strongly to suffer and support our pains,
That we may so suffice his vengeful ire,
Or do him mightier service as his thralls
By right of war, whate'er his business be,
Here in the heart of hell to work in fire,
Or do his errands in the gloomy deep?
What can it then avail, though yet we feel
Strength undiminish'd, or eternal being
To undergo eternal punishment?'
Whereto with speedy words the arch-fiend replied :
    ' Fall'n cherub, to be weak is miserable
Doing or suffering ; but of this be sure,
To do aught good never will be our task,
But ever to do ill our sole delight,
As being the contrary to his high will
Whom we resist. If then his providence
Out of our evil seek to bring forth good,
Our labour must be to pervert that end,
And out of good still to find means of evil,
Which ofttimes may succeed, so as perhaps
Shall grieve him, if I fail not, and disturb

His inmost counsels from their destined aim.
But see, the angry Victor hath recall'd
His ministers of vengeance and pursuit
Back to the gates of heaven : the sulphurous hail,
Shot after us in storm, o'erblown, hath laid
The fiery surge, that from the precipice
Of heaven received us falling ; and the thunder,
Wing'd with red lightning and impetuous rage,
Perhaps hath spent his shafts, and ceases now
To bellow through the vast and boundless deep.
Let us not slip the occasion, whether scorn
Or satiate fury yield it from our foe.
Seest thou yon dreary plain, forlorn and wild,
The seat of desolation, void of light,
Save what the glimmering of these livid flames
Casts pale and dreadful ? Thither let us tend
From off the tossing of these fiery waves ;
There rest, if any rest can harbour there ;
And, reassembling our afflicted powers,
Consult how we may henceforth most offend
Our enemy ; our own loss how repair ;
How overcome this dire calamity ;
What reinforcement we may gain from hope ;
If not, what resolution from despair.'

Thus Satan, talking to his nearest mate,
With head uplift above the wave, and eyes
That sparkling blazed ; his other parts besides
Prone on the flood, extending long and large,
Lay floating many a rood ; in bulk as huge
As whom the fables name of monstrous size,
Titanian, or Earth-born, that warr'd on Jove ;
Briareos or Typhon, whom the den
By ancient Tarsus held ; or that sea-beast
Leviathan, which God of all his works
Created hugest that swim the ocean stream :
Him, haply, slumbering on the Norway foam,
The pilot of some small night-founder'd skiff
Deeming some island, oft, as seamen tell,
With fixed anchor in his scaly rind

Moors by his side under the lee, while night
Invests the sea, and wished morn delays :
So stretch'd out huge in length the archfiend lay
Chain'd on the burning lake : nor ever thence
Had risen, or heaved his head ; but that the will
And high permission of all-ruling heaven
Left him at large to his own dark designs ;
That with reiterated crimes he might
Heap on himself damnation, while he sought
Evil to others ; and, enraged, might see
How all his malice served but to bring forth
Infinite goodness, grace, and mercy, shewn
On man by him seduced ; but on himself
Treble confusion, wrath, and vengeance pour'd.
Forthwith upright he rears from off the pool
His mighty stature ; on each hand the flames,
Driven backward, slope their pointing spires, and, roll'd
In billows, leave in the midst a horrid vale.
Then with expanded wings he steers his flight
Aloft, incumbent on the dusky air,
That felt unusual weight ; till on dry land
He lights, if it were land that ever burn'd
With solid, as the lake with liquid fire ;
And such appear'd in hue, as when the force
Of subterranean wind transports a hill
Torn from Pelorus, or the shatter'd side
Of thundering Ætna, whose combustible
And fuell'd entrails thence conceiving fire,
Sublimed with mineral fury, aid the winds,
And leave a singed bottom all involved
With stench and smoke : such resting found the sole
Of unblest feet. Him follow'd his next mate :
Both glorying to have 'scaped the Stygian flood
As gods, and by their own recover'd strength,
Not by the sufferance of supernal power.
  'Is this the region, this the soil, the clime,'
Said then the lost archangel, 'this the seat
That we must change for heaven ; this mournful gloom
For that celestial light ? Be it so, since he

Who now is Sovereign, can dispose and bid
What shall be right ; farthest from him is best,
Whom reason hath equall'd, force hath made supreme
Above his equals.   Farewell, happy fields,
Where joy for ever dwells !   Hail horrors, hail
Infernal world, and thou profoundest hell,
Receive thy new possessor ; one who brings
A mind not to be changed by place or time :
The mind is its own place, and in itself
Can make a heaven of hell, a hell of heaven.
What matter where, if I be still the same,
And what I should be ; all but less than he
Whom thunder hath made greater ?   Here at least
We shall be free ; the Almighty hath not built
Here for his envy, will not drive us hence :
Here we may reign secure, and, in my choice,
To reign is worth ambition, though in hell :
Better to reign in hell than serve in heaven.
But wherefore let we then our faithful friends,
The associates and copartners of our loss,
Lie thus astonish'd on the oblivious pool,
And call them not to share with us their part
In this unhappy mansion, or once more,
With rallied arms, to try what may be yet
Regain'd in heaven, or what more lost in hell ?'
   So Satan spake, and him Beëlzebub
Thus answer'd.   ' Leader of those armies bright,
Which but the Omnipotent none could have foil'd,
If once they hear that voice, their liveliest pledge
Of hope in fears and dangers, heard so oft
In worse extremes, and on the perilous edge
Of battle when it raged, in all assaults
Their surest signal, they will soon resume
New courage and revive ; though now they lie
Grovelling and prostrate on yon lake of fire,
As we erewhile, astounded and amazed ;
No wonder, fall'n such a pernicious height.'
   He scarce had ceased when the superior fiend
Was moving toward the shore : his ponderous shield,

Ethereal temper, massy, large, and round,
Behind him cast ; the broad circumference
Hung on his shoulders like the moon, whose orb
Through optic glass the Tuscan artist views
At evening from the top of Fesole,
Or in Valdarno, to descry new lands,
Rivers, or mountains, in her spotty globe.
His spear, to equal which the tallest pine
Hewn on Norwegian hills, to be the mast
Of some great ammiral, were but a wand
He walk'd with, to support uneasy steps
Over the burning marle, not like those steps
On heaven's azure ; and the torrid clime
Smote on him sore besides, vaulted with fire :
Nathless he so endured, till on the beach
Of that inflamed sea he stood, and call'd
His legions, angel forms, who lay entranced
Thick as autumnal leaves that strew the brooks
In Vallombrosa, where the Etrurian shades,
High over-arch'd, embower ; or scatter'd sedge
Afloat, when with fierce winds Orion arm'd
Hath vex'd the Red-Sea coast, whose waves o'erthrew
Busiris and his Memphian chivalry,
While with perfidious hatred they pursued
The sojourners of Goshen, who beheld
From the safe shore their floating carcasses
And broken chariot wheels : so thick bestrewn,
Abject and lost, lay these, covering the flood,
Under amazement of their hideous change.
He call'd so loud, that all the hollow deep
Of hell resounded. 'Princes, potentates,
Warriors, the flower of heaven, once yours, now lost,
If such astonishment as this can seize
Eternal spirits ; or have ye chosen this place
After the toil of battle to repose
Your wearied virtue, for the ease you find
To slumber here, as in the vales of heaven ?
Or in this abject posture have ye sworn
To adore the Conqueror ? who now beholds

Cherub and seraph rolling in the flood
With scatter'd arms and ensigns, till anon
His swift pursuers from heaven-gates discern
The advantage, and descending, tread us down
Thus drooping, or with linked thunderbolts
Transfix us to the bottom of this gulf,—
Awake, arise, or be for ever fall'n.'
   They heard, and were abash'd, and up they sprung
Upon the wing; as when men wont to watch
On duty, sleeping found by whom they dread,
Rouse and bestir themselves ere well awake.
Nor did they not perceive the evil plight
In which they were, or the fierce pains not feel;
Yet to their general's voice they soon obey'd,
Innumerable. As when the potent rod
Of Amram's son, in Egypt's evil day,
Wav'd round the coast, upcall'd a pitchy cloud
Of locusts, warping on the eastern wind,
That o'er the realm of impious Pharaoh hung
Like night, and darken'd all the land of Nile:
So numberless were those bad angels seen
Hovering on wing under the cope of hell,
Twixt upper, nether, and surrounding fires;
Till at a signal given, the uplifted spear
Of their great sultan waving to direct
Their course, in even balance down they light
On the firm brimstone, and fill all the plain:
A multitude like which the populous north
Pour'd never from her frozen loins, to pass
Rhene or the Danaw, when her barbarous sons
Came like a deluge on the south, and spread
Beneath Gibraltar to the Libyan sands.
Forthwith from every squadron and each band
The heads and leaders thither haste where stood
Their great commander; godlike shapes and forms
Excelling human, princely dignities;
And powers that erst in heaven sat on thrones,
Though of their names in heavenly records now
Be no memorial; blotted out and rased

By their rebellion from the books of life.
Nor had they yet among the sons of Eve
Got them new names ; till, wandering o'er the earth,
Through God's high sufferance for the trial of man,
By falsities and lies the greatest part
Of mankind they corrupted to forsake
God their Creator, and the invisible
Glory of him that made them to transform
Oft to the image of a brute, adorn'd
With gay religions, full of pomp and gold,
And devils to adore for deities :
Then were they known to men by various names
And various idols through the heathen world.

 Say, muse, their names then known, who first, who last
Roused from the slumber on that fiery couch,
At their great emperor's call, as next in worth
Came singly where he stood on the bare strand,
While the promiscuous crowd stood yet aloof.
The chief were those, who, from the pit of hell,
Roaming to seek their prey on earth, durst fix
Their seats long after next the seat of God,
Their altars by his altar, gods adored
Among the nations round, and durst abide
Jehovah thundering out of Sion, throned
Between the cherubim ; yea, often placed
Within his sanctuary itself their shrines,
Abominations ; and with cursed things
His holy rites and solemn feasts profaned,
And with their darkness durst affront his light.
First, Moloch, horrid king, besmear'd with blood
Of human sacrifice, and parents' tears ;
Though for the noise of drums and timbrels loud
Their children's cries unheard, that pass'd through fire
To his grim idol. Him the Ammonite
Worshipp'd in Rabba and her watery plain,
In Argob and in Basan, to the stream
Of utmost Arnon. Nor content with such
Audacious neighbourhood, the wisest heart
Of Solomon he led by fraud to build

His temple right against the temple of God
On that opprobrious hill ; and made his grove
The pleasant valley of Hinnom, Tophet thence
And black Gehenna call'd, the type of hell.
Next, Chemos, the obscene dread of Moab's sons,
From Aroer to Nebo, and the wild
Of southmost Abarim ; in Hesebon
And Horonaim, Seon's realm, beyond
The flowery dale of Sibma clad with vines,
And Eleäle to the asphaltic pool.
Peor his other name, when he enticed
Israel in Sittim, on their march from Nile,
To do him wanton rites, which cost them woe.
Yet thence his lustful orgies he enlarged
Even to that hill of scandal, by the grove
Of Moloch homicide ; lust hard by hate ;
Till good Josiah drove them thence to hell.
With these came they, who, from the bordering flood
Of old Euphrates to the brook that parts
Egypt from Syrian ground, had general names
Of Baälim and Ashtaroth ; those male,
These feminine : for spirits, when they please,
Can either sex assume, or both ; so soft
And uncompounded is their essence pure ;
Not tied or manacled with joint or limb,
Nor founded on the brittle strength of bones,
Like cumbrous flesh ; but, in what shape they choose
Dilated or condensed, bright or obscure,
Can execute their airy purposes,
And works of love or enmity fulfil.
For those the race of Israel oft forsook
Their living strength, and unfrequented left
His righteous altar, bowing lowly down
To bestial gods ; for which their heads as low
Bow'd down in battle, sunk before the spear
Of despicable foes. With these in troop
Came Astoreth, whom the Phœnicians call'd
Astarte, queen of heaven, with crescent horns ;
To whose bright image nightly by the moon

Sidonian virgins paid their vows and songs;
In Sion also not unsung, where stood
Her temple on the offensive mountain, built
By that uxorious king, whose heart, though large,
Beguiled by fair idolatresses, fell
To idols foul. Thammuz came next behind,
Whose annual wound in Lebanon allured
The Syrian damsels to lament his fate
In amorous ditties all a summer's day;
While smooth Adonis from his native rock
Ran purple to the sea, supposed with blood
Of Thammuz yearly wounded: the love-talc
Infected Sion's daughters with like heat,
Whose wanton passions in the sacred porch
Ezekiel saw, when, by the vision led,
His eye survey'd the dark idolatries
Of alienated Judah. Next came one
Who mourn'd in earnest, when the captive ark
Maim'd his brute image, head and hands lopp'd off
In his own temple, on the grunsel-edge,
Where he fell flat, and shamed his worshippers
Dagon his name, sea-monster, upward man
And downward fish: yet had his temple high
Rear'd in Azotus, dreaded through the coast
Of Palestine, in Gath and Ascalon,
And Accaron and Gaza's frontier bounds.
Him follow'd Rimmon, whose delightful seat
Was fair Damascus, on the fertile banks
Of Abana and Pharphar, lucid streams.
He also 'gainst the house of God was bold
A leper once he lost, and gain'd a king;
Ahaz his sottish conqueror, whom he drew
God's altar to disparage and displace
For one of Syrian mode, whereon to burn
His odious offerings, and ad_re the gods
Whom he had vanquish'd. After these appear'd
A crew, who, under names of old renown,
Osiris, Isis, Orus, and their train,
With monstrous shapes and sorceries abused

Fanatic Egypt and her priests, to seek
Their wandering gods disguised in brutish forms
Rather than human. Nor did Israel 'scape
The infection, when their borrow'd gold composed
The calf in Oreb ; and the rebel king
Doubled that sin in Bethel and in Dan,
Likening his Maker to the grazed ox ;
Jehovah, who in one night, when he pass'd
From Egypt marching, equall'd with one stroke
Both her first-born and all her bleating gods.
Belial came last, than whom a spirit more lewd
Fell not from heaven, or more gross to love
Vice for itself : to him no temple stood,
Or altar smoked ; yet who more oft than he
In temples and at altars, when the priest
Turns atheist, as did Eli's sons, who fill'd
With lust and violence the house of God ?
In courts and palaces he also reigns
And in luxurious cities, where the noise
Of riot ascends above their loftiest towers,
And injury and outrage : and when night
Darkens the streets, then wander forth the sons
Of Belial, flown with insolence and wine.
Witness the streets of Sodom, and that night
In Gibeah, when the hospitable door
Exposed a matron, to avoid worse rape.
These were the prime in order and in might :
The rest were long to tell, though far renown'd,
The Ionian gods, of Javan's issue ; held
Gods, yet confess'd later than heaven and earth,
Their boasted parents : Titan, heaven's first-born,
With his enormous brood, and birthright seized
By younger Saturn ; he from mightier Jove,
His own and Rhea's son, like measure found ;
So Jove usurping reign'd : these first in Crete
And Ida known, thence on the snowy top
Of cold Olympus, ruled the middle air,
Their highest heaven ; or on the Delphian cliff,
Or in Dodona, and through all the bounds

Of Doric land : or who with Saturn old
Fled over Adria to the Hesperian fields,
And o'er the Celtic roam'd the utmost isles.
   All these and more came flocking ; but with looks
Downcast and damp, yet such wherein appear'd
Obscure some glimpse of joy, to have found their chief
Not in despair, to have found themselves not lost
In loss itself : which on his countenance cast
Like doubtful hue : but he, his wonted pride
Soon recollecting, with high words, that bore
Semblance of worth, not substance, gently raised
Their fainting courage, and dispell'd their fears.
Then straight commands, that at the warlike sound
Of trumpets loud and clarions be uprear'd
His mighty standard ; that proud honour claim'd
Azazel as his right, a cherub tall :
Who forthwith from the glittering staff unfurl'd
The imperial ensign ; which, full high advanced
Shone like a meteor streaming to the wind,
With gems and golden lustre rich emblazed,
Seraphic arms and trophies ; all the while
Sonorous metal blowing martial sounds ;
At which the universal host up-sent
A shout, that tore hell's concave, and beyond
Frighted the reign of Chaos and old Night.
All in a moment through the gloom were seen
Ten thousand banners rise into the air
With orient colours waving : with them rose
A forest huge of spears ; and thronging helms
Appear'd, and serried shields in thick array
Of depth immeasurable : anon they move
In perfect phalanx to the Dorian mood
Of flutes and soft recorders ; such as raised
To height of noblest temper heroes old
Arming to battle ; and instead of rage,
Deliberate valour breathed, firm and unmoved
With dread of death to flight or foul retreat :
Nor wanting power to mitigate and 'suage
With solemn touches troubled thoughts, and chase

Anguish, and doubt, and fear, and sorrow, and pain
From mortal or immortal minds. Thus they,
Breathing united force, with fixed thought,
Moved on in silence to soft pipes, that charm'd
Their painful steps o'er the burnt soil : and now
Advanced in view they stand ; a horrid front
Of dreadful length and dazzling arms, in guise
Of warriors old with order'd spear and shield !
Awaiting what command their mighty chief
Had to impose : he through the armed files
Darts his experienced eye, and soon traverse
The whole battalion views, their order due,
Their visages and stature as of gods ;
Their number last he sums. And now his heart
Distends with pride, and hardening in his strength
Glories ; for never since created man
Met such embodied force, as named with these
Could merit more than that small infantry
Warr'd on by cranes : though all the giant brood
Of Phlegra with the heroic race were join'd
That fought at Thebes and Ilium, on each side
Mix'd with auxiliar gods ; and what resounds
In fable or romance of Uther's son
Begirt with British and Armoric knights ;
And all who since, baptized or infidel,
Jousted in Aspramont, or Montalban,
Damasco, or Marocco, or Trebisond,
Or whom Biserta sent from Afric shore,
When Charlemain with all his peerage fell
By Fontarabia. Thus far these beyond
Compare of mortal prowess, yet observed
Their dread commander ; he, above the rest
In shape and gesture proudly eminent,
Stood like a tower ; his form had yet not lost
All her original brightness, nor appear'd
Less than archangel ruin'd, and the excess
Of glory obscured ; as when the sun, new risen,
Looks through the horizontal misty air
Shorn of his beams ; or from behind the moon,

In dim eclipse, disastrous twilight sheds
On half the nations, and with fear of change
Perplexes monarchs. Darken'd so, yet shone
Above them all the archangel; but his face
Deep scars of thunder had intrench'd; and care
Sat on his faded cheek; but under brows
Of dauntless courage, and considerate pride
Waiting revenge; cruel his eyes, but cast
Signs of remorse and passion, to behold
The fellows of his crime, the followers rather
(Far other once beheld in bliss), condemn'd
For ever now to have their lot in pain:
Millions of spirits for his fault amerced
Of heaven, and from eternal splendours flung
For his revolt; yet faithful how they stood,
Their glory wither'd: as when heaven's fire
Hath scathed the forest oaks, or mountain pines,
With singed top their stately growth, though bare,
Stands on the blasted heath. He now prepared
To speak; whereat their doubled ranks they bend
From wing to wing, and half enclose him round
With all his peers: attention held them mute.
Thrice he assay'd, and thrice, in spite of scorn,
Tears, such as angels weep, burst forth: at last
Words interwove with sighs found out their way.
  'O myriads of immortal spirits! O powers
Matchless, but with the Almighty; and that strife
Was not inglorious, though the event was dire,
As this place testifies, and this dire change
Hateful to utter! but what power of mind,
Foreseeing or presaging, from the depth
Of knowledge, past or present, could have fear'd,
How such united force of gods, how such
As stood like these, could ever know repulse?
For who can yet believe, though after loss,
That all these puissant legions, whose exile
Hath emptied heaven, shall fail to reascend
Self-raised, and repossess their native seat?
For me, be witness all the host of heaven,

If counsels different, or dangers shunn'd
By me, have lost our hopes. But he who reigns
Monarch in heaven, till then as one secure
Sat on his throne, upheld by old repute,
Consent or custom; and his regal state
Put forth at full, but still his strength conceal'd,
Which tempted our attempt, and wrought our fall.
Henceforth his might we know, and know our own ;
So as not either to provoke, or dread
New war, provoked ; our better part remains
To work in close design, by fraud or guile,
What force effected not : that he no less
At length from us may find, who overcomes
By force, hath overcome but half his foe.
Space may produce new worlds ; whereof so rife
There went a fame in heaven that he ere long
Intended to create, and therein plant
A generation, whom his choice regard
Should favour equal to the sons of heaven :
Thither, if but to pry, shall be perhaps
Our first eruption : thither or elsewhere ;
For this infernal pit shall never hold
Celestial spirits in bondage, nor the abyss
Long under darkness cover. But these thoughts
Full counsel must mature : peace is despair'd ;
For who can think submission ? War then, war,
Open or understood, must be resolved.'

   He spake ; and, to confirm his words, out-flew
Millions of flaming swords, drawn from the thighs
Of mighty cherubim ; the sudden blaze
Far round illumined hell : highly they raged
Against the Highest, and fierce with grasped arms
Clash'd on their sounding shields the din of war,
Hurling defiance toward the vault of heaven.

   There stood a hill not far, whose grisly top
Belch'd fire and rolling smoke ; the rest entire
Shone with a glossy scurf, undoubted sign
That in his womb was hid metallic ore,
The work of sulphur. Thither, winged with speed,

A numerous brigade hasten'd : as when bands
Of pioneers, with spade and pickaxe arm'd
Forerun the royal camp, to trench a field,
Or cast a rampart. Mammon led them on,
Mammon, the least erected spirit that fell
From heaven ; for e'en in heaven his looks and thoughts
Were always downward bent, admiring more
The riches of heaven's pavement, trodden gold,
Than aught divine or holy else enjoy'd
In vision beatific : by him first
Men also, and by his suggestion taught,
Ransack'd the centre, and with impious hands
Rifled the bowels of their mother earth
For treasures, better hid. Soon had his crew
Open'd into the hill a spacious wound,
And digg'd out ribs of gold. Let none admire
That riches grow in hell ; that soil may best
Deserve the precious bane. And here let those
Who boast in mortal things, and wondering tell
Of Babel, and the works of Memphian kings,
Learn how their greatest monuments of fame,
And strength and art, are easily outdone
By spirits reprobate, and in an hour,
What in an age they with incessant toil
And hands innumerable scarce perform.
Nigh on the plain, in many cells prepared,
That underneath had veins of liquid fire
Sluiced from the lake, a second multitude
With wondrous art founded the massy ore,
Severing each kind, and scumm'd the bullion dross :
A third as soon had form'd within the ground
A various mould, and from the boiling cells,
By strange conveyance, fill'd each hollow nook ;
As in an organ, from one blast of wind
To many a row of pipes the sound-board breathes,
Anon out of the earth a fabric huge
Rose like an exhalation, with the sound
Of dulcet symphonies and voices sweet,
Built like a temple, where pilasters round

Were set, and Doric pillars overlaid
With golden architrave ; nor did there want
Cornice or frieze, with bossy sculptures graven ;
The roof was fretted gold. Not Babylon,
Nor great Alcairo, such magnificence
Equall'd in all their glories, to enshrine
Belus or Serapis, their gods, or seat
Their kings, when Egypt with Assyria strove
In wealth and luxury. The ascending pile
Stood fix'd her stately height : and straight the doors,
Opening their brazen folds, discover wide
Within, her ample spaces o'er the smooth
And level pavement : from the arched roof
Pendent by subtle magic many a row
Of starry lamps and blazing cressets, fed
With naphtha and asphaltus, yielded light
As from a sky. The hasty multitude
Admiring enter'd ; and the work some praise,
And some the architect : his hand was known
In heaven by many a tower'd structure high,
Where sceptred angels held their residence,
And sat as princes ; whom the supreme King
Exalted to such power, and gave to rule,
Each in his hierarchy, the orders bright.
Nor was his name unheard or unadored
In ancient Greece ; and in Ausonian land
Men call'd him Mulciber ; and how he fell
From heaven, they fabled, thrown by angry Jove
Sheer o'er the crystal battlements : from morn
To noon he fell, from noon to dewy eve,
A summer's day ; and with the setting sun
Dropped from the zenith like a falling star,
On Lemnos the Ægean isle : thus they relate,
Erring ; for he with this rebellious rout
Fell long before ; nor aught availed him now
To have built in heaven high towers ; nor did he 'scape
By all his engines, but was headlong sent
With his industrious crew to build in hell.
    Meanwhile the winged heralds, by command

Of sovereign power, with awful ceremony
And trumpet's sound, throughout the host proclaim
A solemn council forthwith to be held
At Pandemonium, the high capital
Of Satan and his peers: their summons call'd
From every band and squared regiment
By place or choice the worthiest ; they anon
With hundreds and with thousands trooping came
Attended : all access was throng'd, the gates
And porches wide, but chief the spacious hall
(Though like a cover'd field, where champions bold
Wont ride in arm'd, and at the soldan's chair
Defied the best of Panim chivalry
To mortal combat, or career with lance),
Thick swarm'd, both on the ground and in the air
Brush'd with the hiss of rustling wings. As bees
In spring-time, when the sun with Taurus rides,
Pour forth their populous youth about the hive
In clusters ; they among fresh dews and flowers
Fly to and fro, or on the smoothed plank,
The suburb of their straw-built citadel,
New rubb'd with balm, expatiate and confer
Their state affairs : so thick the airy crowd
Swarm'd and were straiten'd ; till, the signal given,
Behold a wonder ! They but now who seem'd
In bigness to surpass earth's giant sons,
Now less than smallest dwarfs, in narrow room
Throng numberless, like that pygmean race
Beyond the Indian mount, or fairy elves,
Whose midnight revels, by a forest-side
Or fountain, some belated peasant sees,
Or dreams he sees, while over head the moon
Sits arbitress, and nearer to the earth
Wheels her pale course ; they, on their mirth and dance
Intent, with jocund music charm his ear ;
At once with joy and fear his heart rebounds.
Thus incorporeal spirits to smallest forms
Reduc'd their shapes immense, and were at large,
Though without number still, amidst the hall

Of that infernal court. But far within,
And in their own dimensions, like themselves,
The great seraphic lords and cherubim
In close recess and secret conclave sat,
A thousand demigods on golden seats,
Frequent and full. After short silence then
And summons read, the great consult began.

BOOK IV.

O, for that warning voice, which he, who saw
The Apocalypse, heard cry in heaven aloud,
Then when the Dragon, put to second rout,
Came furious down to be revenged on men,
'Woe to the inhabitants on earth!' that now,
While time was, our first parents had been warn'd
The coming of their secret foe, and 'scaped,
Haply so 'scaped his mortal snare : for now
Satan, now first inflamed with rage, came down,
The tempter ere the accuser of mankind,
To wreak on innocent frail man his loss
Of that first battle, and his flight to hell :
Yet, not rejoicing in his speed, though bold
Far off and fearless, not with cause to boast,
Begins his dire attempt ; which nigh the birth
Now rolling boils in his tumultuous breast,
And like a devilish engine back recoils
Upon himself ; horror and doubt distract
His troubled thoughts, and from the bottom stir
The hell within him ; for within him hell
He brings, and round about him, nor from hell
One step, no more than from himself, can fly,
By change of place : now conscience wakes despair,
That slumber'd ; wakes the bitter memory
Of what he was, what is, and what must be
Worse ; of worse deeds worse sufferings must ensue.
Sometimes towards Eden, which now in his view
Lay pleasant, his grieved look he fixed sad ;
Sometimes towards heaven, and the full-blazing sun,
Which new sat high in his meridian tower:

Then, much revolving, thus in sighs began :
  'O thou, that, with surpassing glory crown'd,
Look'st from thy sole dominion like the god
Of this new world ; at whose sight all the stars
Hide their diminish'd heads ; to thee I call,
But with no friendly voice, and add thy name,
O sun ! to tell thee how I hate thy beams,
That bring to my remembrance from what state
I fell, how glorious once above thy sphere ;
Till pride and worse ambition threw me down,
Warring in heaven against heaven's matchless King :
Ah, wherefore ? he deserved no such return
From me, whom he created what I was
In that bright eminence, and with his good
Upbraided none ; nor was his service hard.
What could be less than to afford him praise,
The easiest recompense, and pay him thanks,
How due ! yet all his good proved ill in me,
And wrought but malice ; lifted up so high
I 'sdain'd subjection, and thought one step higher
Would set me highest, and in a moment quit
The debt immense of endless gratitude,
So burdensome still paying, still to owe :
Forgetful what from him I still received,
And understood not that a grateful mind
By owing owes not, but still pays, at once
Indebted and discharged ; what burden then ?
O had his powerful destiny ordain'd
Me some inferior angel, I had stood
Then happy ; no unbounded hope had raised
Ambition. Yet why not ? some other power
As great might have aspired, and me, though mean,
Drawn to his part ; but other powers as great
Fell not, but stand unshaken, from within
Or from without, to all temptations arm'd.
Hadst thou the same free will and power to stand ?
Thou hadst : whom hast thou then or what to accuse,
But heaven's free love dealt equally to all ?
Be then his love accursed, since love or hate,

To me alike, it deals eternal woe.
Nay, cursed be thou ; since against his thy will
Chose freely what it now so justly rues,
Me miserable ! which way shall I fly
Infinite wrath, and infinite despair?
Which way I fly is hell ; myself am hell ;
And, in the lowest deep, a lower deep
Still threatening to devour me opens wide,
To which the hell I suffer seems a heaven.
O, then, at last relent : is there no place
Left for repentance, none for pardon left?
None left but by submission ; and that word
Disdain forbids me, and my dread of shame
Among the spirits beneath, whom I seduced
With other promises and other vaunts
Than to submit, boasting I could subdue
The Omnipotent. Ah me ! they little know
How dearly I abide that boast so vain ;
Under what torments inwardly I groan,
While they adore me on the throne of hell,
With diadem and sceptre high advanced,
The lower still I fall, only supreme
In misery : such joy ambition finds.
But say I could repent, and could obtain,
By act of grace, my former state ; how soon
Would height recall high thoughts, how soon unsay
What feign'd submission swore ! Ease would recant
Vows made in pain, as violent and void.
For never can true reconcilement grow
Where wounds of deadly hate have pierced so deep :
Which would but lead me to a worse relapse
And heavier fall : so should I purchase dear
Short intermission bought with double smart.
This knows my punisher ; therefore as far
From granting he, as I from begging peace :
All hope excluded thus, behold, instead
Of us out-cast, exiled, his new delight,
Mankind created, and for him this world.
So farewell hope, and with hope farewell fear,

Farewell remorse: all good to me is lost :
Evil, be thou my good : by thee at least
Divided empire with heaven's King I hold,
By thee, and more than half perhaps will reign,
As man ere long, and this new world shall know.'
    Thus while he spake, each passion dimm'd his face
Thrice changed with pale ire, envy, and despair ;
Which marr'd his borrow'd visage, and betray'd
Him counterfeit, if any eye beheld :
For heavenly minds from such distempers foul
Are ever clear. Whereof he soon aware,
Each perturbation smooth'd with outward calm,
Artificer of fraud ; and was the first
That practised falsehood under saintly show,
Deep malice to conceal, couch'd with revenge
Yet not enough had practised to deceive
Uriel once warn'd : whose eye pursued him down
The way he went, and on the Assyrian mount
Saw him disfigured, more than could befall
Spirit of happy sort : his gestures fierce
He mark'd, and mad demeanour, then alone,
As he supposed, all unobserved, unseen.
So on he fares, and to the border comes
Of Eden, where delicious Paradise,
Now nearer, crowns with her enclosure green,
As with a rural mound, the champaign head
Of a steep wilderness, whose hairy sides
With thicket overgrown, grotesque and wild,
Access denied ; and over-head up-grew
Insuperable height of loftiest shade,
Cedar, and pine, and fir, and branching palm,
A sylvan scene ; and, as the ranks ascend
Shade above shade, a woody theatre
Of stateliest view. Yet higher than their tops
The verdurous wall of Paradise up-sprung :
Which to our general sire gave prospect large
Into his nether empire neighbouring round :
And higher than that wall a circling row
Of goodliest trees, loaden with fairest fruit,

Blossoms and fruits at once of golden hue,
Appear'd, with gay enamell'd colours mix'd :
On which the sun more glad impress'd his beams
Than in fair evening cloud, or humid bow,
When God hath shower'd the earth ; so lovely seem'd
That landscape : and of pure now purer air
Meets his approach, and to the heart inspires
Vernal delight and joy, able to drive
All sadness but despair : now gentle gales,
Fanning their odoriferous wings, dispense
Native perfumes, and whisper whence they stole
Those balmy spoils. As when to them who sail
Beyond the Cape of Hope, and now are past
Mozambic, off at sea north-east winds blow
Sabean odours from the spicy shore
Of Araby the Blest ; with such delay
Well pleased they slack their course, and many a league
Cheer'd with the grateful smell old Ocean smiles :
So entertain'd those odorous sweets the fiend,
Who came their bane : though with them better pleased
Than Asmodëus with the fishy fume
That drove him, though enamour'd, from the spouse
Of Tobit's son, and with a vengeance sent
From Media post to Egypt, there fast bound.

  Now to the ascent of that steep savage hill
Satan had journey'd on, pensive and slow ;
But further way found none, so thick entwined,
As one continued brake, the undergrowth
Of shrubs and tangling bushes had perplex'd
All path of man or beast that pass'd that way.
One gate there only was, and that look'd east
On the other side : which when the arch-felon saw,
Due entrance he disdain'd ; and, in contempt,
At one slight bound high o'erleap'd all bound
Of hill or highest wall, and sheer within
Lights on his feet. As when a prowling wolf,
Whom hunger drives to seek new haunt for prey,
Watching where shepherds pen their flocks at eve
In hurdled cotes amid the field secure,

Leaps o'er the fence with ease into the fold:
Or as a thief bent to unhoard the cash
Of some rich burgher, whose substantial doors,
Cross-barr'd and bolted fast, fear no assault,
In at the window climbs, or o'er the tiles:
So clomb the first grand thief into God's fold;
So since into his church lewd hirelings climb.
Thence up he flew, and on the tree of life,
The middle tree and highest there that grew,
Sat like a cormorant; yet not true life
Thereby regain'd, but sat devising death
To them who lived; nor on the virtue thought
Of that life-giving plant, but only used
For prospect, what well used had been the pledge
Of immortality. So little knows
Any, but God alone, to value right
The good before him, but perverts best things
To worst abuse, or to their meanest use.
Beneath him with new wonder now he views,
To all delight of human sense exposed,
In narrow room, nature's whole wealth, yea more,
A heaven on earth: for blissful Paradise
Of God the garden was, by him in the east
Of Eden planted; Eden stretch'd her line
From Auran eastward to the royal towers
Of great Seleucia, built by Grecian kings,
Or where the sons of Eden long before
Dwelt in Telassar: in this pleasant soil
His far more pleasant garden God ordain'd:
Out of the fertile ground he caused to grow
All trees of noblest kind for sight, smell, taste;
And all amid them stood the tree of life,
High eminent, blooming ambrosial fruit
Of vegetable gold; and next to life,
Our death, the tree of knowledge, grew fast by,
Knowledge of good, bought dear by knowing ill.
Southward through Eden went a river large
Nor changed his course, but through the shaggy hill
Pass'd underneath ingulf'd; for God had thrown

That mountain as his garden-mound high-raised
Upon the rapid current, which through veins
Of porous earth with kindly thirst up-drawn,
Rose a fresh fountain, and with many a rill
Water'd the garden ; thence united fell
Down the steep glade, and met the nether flood,
Which from his darksome passage now appears,
And, now divided into four main streams,
Runs diverse, wandering many a famous realm
And country, whereof here needs no account ;
But rather to tell how, if art could tell,
How from that sapphire fount the crisped brooks,
Rolling on orient pearl and sands of gold,
With mazy error under pendent shades
Ran nectar, visiting each plant, and fed
Flowers worthy of Paradise, which not nice art
In beds and curious knots, but nature boon
Pour'd forth profuse on hill, and dale, and plain,
Both where the morning sun first warmly smote
The open field, and where the unpierced shade
Imbrown'd the noontide bowers : thus was this place
A happy rural seat of various view ;
Groves whose rich trees wept odorous gums and balm ;
Others whose fruit, burnish'd with golden rind,
Hung amiable, Hesperian fables true,
If true, here only, and of delicious taste :
Betwixt them lawns, or level downs, and flocks
Grazing the tender herb, were interposed,
Or palmy hillock ; or the flowery lap
Of some irriguous valley spread her store,
Flowers of all hue, and without thorn the rose :
Another side, umbrageous grots and caves
Of cool recess, o'er which the mantling vine
Lays forth her purple grape, and gently creeps
Luxuriant ; meanwhile murmuring waters fall
Down the slope hills, dispersed, or in a lake,
That to the fringed bank with myrtle crown'd
Her crystal mirror holds, unite their streams.
The birds their quire apply ; airs, vernal airs,

Breathing the smell of field and grove, attune
The trembling leaves, while universal Pan,
Knit with the Graces and the Hours in dance,
Led on the eternal Spring. Not that fair field
Of Enna, where Proserpine gathering flowers,
Herself a fairer flower, by gloomy Dis
Was gather'd, which cost Ceres all that pain
To seek her through the world ; nor that sweet grove
Of Daphne by Orontes, and the inspired
Castalian spring, might with this Paradise
Of Eden strive ; nor that Nyseian isle
Girt with the river Triton, where old Cham,
Whom Gentiles Ammon call and Libyan Jove,
Hid Amalthea, and her florid son
Young Bacchus, from his stepdame Rhea's eye ;
Nor where Abassin kings their issue guard,
Mount Amara, though this by some supposed
True Paradise, under the Ethiop line
By Nilus' head, enclosed with shining rock,
A whole day's journey high, but wide remote
From this Assyrian garden, where the fiend
Saw, undelighted, all delight, all kind
Of living creatures, new to sight and strange.
Two of far nobler shape, erect and tall,
Godlike erect, with native honour clad,
In naked majesty seem'd lords of all :
And worthy seem'd ; for in their looks divine
The image of their glorious Maker shone,
Truth, wisdom, sanctitude severe and pure
(Severe, but in true filial freedom placed),
Whence true authority in men ; though both
Not equal, as their sex not equal seem'd ;
For contemplation he and valour form'd ;
For softness she, and sweet attractive grace ;
He for God only, she for God in him :
His fair large front and eye sublime declared
Absolute rule ; and hyacinthine locks
Round from his parted forelock manly hung
Clustering, but not beneath his shoulders broad :

She, as a veil, down to the slender waist
Her unadorned golden tresses wore
Dishevell'd, but in wanton ringlets waved,
As the vine curls her tendrils, which implied
Subjection, but required with gentle sway,
And by her yielded, by him best received,
Yielded with coy submission, modest pride,
And sweet, reluctant, amorous delay.
Nor those mysterious parts were then conceal'd ;
Then was not guilty shame ; dishonest shame
Of nature's works, honour dishonourable,
Sin-bred, how have ye troubled all mankind
With shows instead, mere shows of seeming pure,
And banish'd from man's life his happiest life,
Simplicity and spotless innocence !
So pass'd they naked on, nor shunn'd the sight
Of God or angel ; for they thought no ill :
So hand in hand they pass'd, the loveliest pair
That ever since in love's embraces met ;
Adam the goodliest man of men since born
His sons, the fairest of her daughters Eve.
Under a tuft of shade that on a green
Stood whispering soft, by a fresh fountain-side
They sat them down ; and, after no more toil
Of their sweet gardening labour than sufficed
To recommend cool zephyr, and made ease
More easy, wholesome thirst and appetite
More grateful, to their supper-fruits they fell,
Nectarine fruits, which the compliant boughs
Yielded them, sidelong as they sat recline
On the soft downy bank damask'd with flowers :
The savoury pulp they chew, and in the rind,
Still as they thirsted, scoop the brimming stream ;
Nor gentle purpose, nor endearing smiles,
Wanted, nor youthful dalliance, as beseems
Fair couple, link'd in happy nuptial league,
Alone as they.   About them frisking play'd
All beasts of the earth, since wild, and of all chase
In wood or wilderness, forest or den ;

Sporting the lion ramp'd, and in his paw
Dandled the kid; bears, tigers, ounces, pards,
Gamboll'd before them; the unwieldy elephant,
To make them mirth, used all his might, and wreath'd
His lithe proboscis; close the serpent sly,
Insinuating, wove with Gordian twine
His braided train, and of his fatal guile
Gave proof unheeded; others on the grass
Couch'd, and now fill'd with pasture gazing sat,
Or bedward ruminating; for the sun,
Declined, was hasting now with prone career
To the ocean isles, and in the ascending scale
Of heaven the stars that usher evening rose;
When Satan still in gaze, as first he stood,
Scarce thus at length fail'd speech recover'd sad.

BOOK X.

Thus Adam to himself lamented loud,
Through the still night; not now, as ere man fell,
Wholesome, and cool, and mild, but with black air
Accompanied; with damps and dreadful gloom,
Which to his evil conscience represented
All things with double terror; on the ground
Outstretch'd he lay, on the cold ground, and oft
Cursed his creation; death as oft accused
Of tardy execution, since denounced
The day of his offence. 'Why comes not death,'
Said he, 'with one thrice-acceptable stroke
To end me? Shall truth fail to keep her word,
Justice divine not hasten to be just?
But death comes not at call; justice divine
Mends not her slowest pace for prayers or cries.
O woods, O fountains, hillocks, dales, and bowers!
With other echo late I taught your shades
To answer, and resound far other song.'
Whom thus afflicted when sad Eve beheld,
Desolate where she sat, approaching nigh,
Soft words to his fierce passion she assay'd;
But her with stern regard he thus repell'd:

'Out of my sight, thou serpent! That name best
Befits thee with him leagued, thyself as false
And hateful; nothing wants, but that thy shape,
Like his, and colour serpentine, may shew
Thy inward fraud; to warn all creatures from thee
Henceforth; lest that too heavenly form, pretended
To hellish falsehood, snare them! But for thee
I had persisted happy: had not thy pride
And wandering vanity, when least was safe,
Rejected my forewarning, and disdain'd
Not to be trusted; longing to be seen,
Though by the devil himself; him overweening
To over-reach; but, with the serpent meeting,
Fool'd and beguiled; by him thou, I by thee,
To trust thee from my side; imagined wise,
Constant, mature, proof against all assaults;
And understood not all was but a show,
Rather than solid virtue; all but a rib
Crooked by nature, bent, as now appears,
More to the part sinister, from me drawn;
Well if thrown out, as supernumerary
To my just number found. O! why did God,
Creator wise, that peopled highest heaven
With spirits masculine, create at last
This novelty on earth, this fair defect
Of nature, and not fill the world at once
With men, as angels, without feminine;
Or find some other way to generate
Mankind? This mischief had not then befallen,
And more that shall befall; innumerable
Disturbances on earth through female snares,
And strait conjunction with this sex: for either
He never shall find out fit mate, but such
As some misfortune brings him, or mistake;
Or whom he wishes most shall seldom gain,
Through her perverseness, but shall see her gain'd
By a far worse; or, if she love, withheld
By parents; or his happiest choice too late
Shall meet, already link'd and wedlock bound

To a fell adversary, his hate or shame:
Which infinite calamity shall cause
To human life, and household peace confound.'
   He added not, and from her turn'd: but Eve,
Not so repulsed, with tears that ceased not flowing,
And tresses all disorder'd, at his feet
Fell humble; and, embracing them, besought
His peace, and thus proceeded in her plaint:
   'Forsake me not thus, Adam! witness Heaven
What love sincere, and reverence in my heart
I bear thee, and unweeting have offended,
Unhappily deceived! Thy suppliant
I beg, and clasp thy knees; bereave me not,
Whereon I live, thy gentle looks, thy aid,
Thy counsel, in this uttermost distress,
My only strength and stay; forlorn of thee,
Whither shall I betake me, where subsist?
While yet we live, scarce one short hour perhaps,
Between us two let there be peace; both joining
As join'd in injuries, one enmity
Against a foe by doom express assign'd us,
That cruel serpent: on me exercise not
Thy hatred for this misery befallen;
On me already lost, me than thyself
More miserable! both have sinn'd; but thou
Against God only, I against God and thee;
And to the place of judgment will return.
There with my cares importune Heaven; that all
The sentence, from thy head removed, may light
On me, sole cause to thee of all this woe;
Me, me only, just object of his ire!'
   She ended weeping; and her lowly plight,
Immoveable, till peace obtain'd from fault
Acknowledged and deplored, in Adam wrought
Commiseration; soon his heart relented
Towards her, his life so late, and sole delight,
Now at his feet submissive in distress;
Creature so fair his reconcilement seeking,
His counsel, whom she had displeased, his aid:

As one disarm'd, his anger all he lost,
And thus with peaceful words upraised her soon:
'Unwary, and too desirous, as before,
So now of what thou know'st not, who desirest
The punishment all on thyself; alas!
Bear thine own first, ill able to sustain
His full wrath, whose thou feel'st as yet least part,
And my displeasure bear'st so ill. If prayers
Could alter high decrees, I to that place
Would speed before thee, and be louder heard,
That on my head all might be visited;
Thy frailty and infirmer sex forgiven,
To me committed, and by me exposed.
But rise; let us no more contend, nor blame
Each other, blamed enough elsewhere; but strive
In offices of love, how we may lighten
Each other's burden, in our share of woe;
Since this day's death denounced, if aught I see,
Will prove no sudden, but a slow-paced evil;
A long day's dying to augment our pain,
And to our seed (O hapless seed!) derived.'

  To whom thus Eve, recovering heart, replied:
'Adam, by sad experiment I know
How little weight my words with thee can find,
Found so erroneous; thence by just event
Found so unfortunate: nevertheless,
Restored by thee, vile as I am, to place
Of new acceptance, hopeful to regain
Thy love, the sole contentment of my heart
Living or dying, from thee I will not hide
What thoughts in my unquiet breast are risen,
Tending to some relief of our extremes,
Or end; though sharp and sad, yet tolerable,
As in our evils, and of easier choice.
If care of our descent perplex us most,
Which must be born to certain woe, devour'd
By death at last; and miserable it is,
To be to others cause of misery,
Our own begotten, and of our loins to bring

Into this cursed world a woeful race,
That after wretched life must be at last
Food for so foul a monster ; in thy power
It lies, yet ere conception to prevent
The race unblest, to being yet unbegot.
Childless thou art, childless remain : so Death
Shall be deceived his glut, and with us two
Be forced to satisfy his ravenous maw.
But if thou judge it hard and difficult,
Conversing, looking, loving, to abstain
From love's due rites, nuptial embraces sweet ;
And with desire to languish without hope,
Before the present object languishing
With like desire ; which would be misery
And torment less than none of what we dread ;
Then, both ourselves and seed at once to free
From what we fear for both, let us make short,
Let us seek Death ; or, he not found, supply
With our own hands his office on ourselves.
Why stand we longer shivering under fears
That shew no end but death, and have the power,
Of many ways to die the shortest choosing,
Destruction with destruction to destroy ?'
    She ended here, or vehement despair
Broke off the rest ; so much of death her thoughts
Had entertain'd, as dyed her cheeks with pale.
But Adam with such counsel nothing sway'd,
To better hopes his more attentive mind
Labouring had raised ; and thus to Eve replied :
    'Eve, thy contempt of life and pleasure seems
To argue in thee something more sublime
And excellent, than what thy mind contemns ;
But self-destruction, therefore sought, refutes
That excellence thought in thee ; and implies
Not thy contempt, but anguish and regret
For loss of life and pleasure overloved.
Or if thou covet death, as utmost end
Of misery, so thinking to evade
The penalty pronounced ; doubt not but God

Hath wiselier arm'd his vengeful ire, than so
To be forestall'd; much more I fear lest death,
So snatch'd, will not exempt us from the pain
We are by doom to pay; rather, such acts
Of contumacy will provoke the Highest
To make death in us live: then let us seek
Some safer resolution, which methinks
I have in view, calling to mind with heed
Part of our sentence, that thy seed shall bruise
The serpent's head: piteous amends! unless
Be meant, whom I conjecture, our grand foe
Satan; who in the serpent hath contrived
Against us this deceit. To crush his head
Would be revenge indeed! which will be lost
By death brought on ourselves, or childless days
Resolved, as thou proposest; so our foe
Shall 'scape his punishment ordain'd, and we
Instead shall double ours upon our heads.
No more be mention then of violence
Against ourselves; and wilful barrenness
That cuts us off from hope; and savours only
Rancour and pride, impatience and despite,
Reluctance against God and his just yoke
Laid on our necks. Remember with what mild
And gracious temper he both heard and judged,
Without wrath or reviling; we expected
Immediate dissolution, which we thought
Was meant by death that day: when, lo! to thee
Pains only in childbearing were foretold,
And bringing forth; soon recompensed with joy,
Fruit of thy womb: on me the curse aslope
Glanced on the ground; with labour I must earn
My bread; what harm? Idleness had been worse;
My labour will sustain me; and, lest cold
Or heat should injure us, his timely care
Hath, unbesought, provided; and his hands
Clothed us unworthy, pitying while he judged;
How much more, if we pray him, will his ear
Be open, and his heart to pity incline,

And teach us further by what means to shun
The inclement seasons, rain, ice, hail, and snow?
Which now the sky, with various face, begins
To shew us in this mountain; while the winds
Blow moist and keen, shattering the graceful locks
Of these fair-spreading trees; which bids us seek
Some better shroud, some better warmth to cherish
Our limbs benumb'd, ere this diurnal star
Leave cold the night, how we his gathered beams
Reflected may with matter sere foment,
Or, by collision of two bodies, grind
The air attrite to fire; as late the clouds
Justling, or push'd with winds, rude in their shock,
Tine the slant lightning, whose thwart flame driven down,
Kindles the gummy bark of fir or pine,
And sends a comfortable heat from far
Which might supply the sun: such fire to use,
And what may else be remedy or cure
To evils which our own misdeeds have wrought,
He will instruct us praying, and of grace
Beseeching him; so as we need not fear
To pass commodiously this life, sustain'd
By him with many comforts, till we end
In dust, our final rest and native home.
What better can we do, than, to the place
Repairing where he judged us, prostrate fall
Before him reverent, and there confess
Humbly our faults, and pardon beg; with tears
Watering the ground, and with our sighs the air
Frequenting, sent from hearts contrite, in sign
Of sorrow unfeigned, and humiliation meek?
Undoubtedly he will relent, and turn
From his displeasure; in whose look serene,
When angry most he seem'd and most severe,
What else but favour, grace, and mercy, shone?'
    So spake our father penitent; nor Eve
Felt less remorse: they, forthwith to the place
Repairing where he judged them, prostrate fell
Before him reverent; and both confess'd

Humbly their faults, and pardon begg'd ; with tears
Watering the ground, and with their sighs the air
Frequenting, sent from hearts contrite, in sign
Of sorrow unfeigned, and humiliation meek.

FROM 'PARADISE REGAINED.'

[1665; æt. 58.]

BOOK I.

Meanwhile the Son of God, who yet some days
Lodged in Bethabara, where John baptized,
Musing, and much revolving in his breast,
How best the mighty work he might begin
Of Saviour to mankind, and which way first
Publish his godlike office now mature,
One day forth walk'd alone, the Spirit leading
And his deep thoughts, the better to converse
With solitude, till, far from track of men,
Thought following thought, and step by step led on,
He enter'd now the bordering desert wild,
And, with dark shades and rocks environ'd round,
His holy meditations thus pursued :
  ' O, what a multitude of thoughts at once
Awaken'd in me swarm, while I consider
What from within I feel myself, and hear
What from without comes often to my ears,
Ill sorting with my present state compared !
When I was yet a child, no childish play
To me was pleasing ; all my mind was set
Serious to learn and know, and thence to do
What might be public good ; myself I thought
Born to that end, born to promote all truth,
All righteous things : therefore, above my years,
The law of God I read, and found it sweet,
Made it my whole delight, and in it grew
To such perfection, that, ere yet my age

Had measured twice six years, at our great feast
I went into the temple, there to hear
The teachers of our law, and to propose
What might improve my knowledge or their own ;
And was admired by all : yet this not all
To which my spirit aspired : victorious deeds
Flamed in my heart, heroic acts ; one while
To rescue Israel from the Roman yoke ;
Then to subdue and quell, o'er all the earth,
Brute violence and proud tyrannic power,
Till truth were freed, and equity restored :
Yet held it more humane, more heavenly, first
By winning words to conquer willing hearts,
And make persuasion do the work of fear ;
At least to try, and teach the erring soul,
Not wilfully misdoing, but unaware
Misled ; the stubborn only to subdue.
These growing thoughts my mother soon perceiving,
By words at times cast forth, inly rejoiced,
And said to me apart, " High are thy thoughts,
O son, but nourish them, and let them soar
To what height sacred virtue and true worth
Can raise them, though above example high ;
By matchless deeds express thy matchless Sire,
For know, thou art no son of mortal man ;
Though men esteem thee low of parentage,
Thy father is the eternal King who rules
All heaven and earth, angels and sons of men ;
A messenger from God foretold thy birth
Conceived in me a virgin ; he foretold
Thou shouldst be great, and sit on David's throne,
And of thy kingdom there should be no end.
At thy nativity, a glorious quire
Of angels, in the fields of Bethlehem, sung
To shepherds, watching at their folds by night,
And told them the Messiah now was born,
Where they might see him ; and to thee they came,
Directed to the manger where thou lay'st,
For in the inn was left no better room :

A star, not seen before, in heaven appearing,
Guided the wise men thither from the East,
To honour thee with incense, myrrh, and gold ;
By whose bright course led on they found the place,
Affirming it thy star, new-graven in heaven,
By which they knew the king of Israel born.
Just Simeon and prophetic Anna, warn'd
By vision, found thee in the temple, and spake,
Before the altar and the vested priest,
Like things of thee to all that present stood."
  'This having heard, straight I again revolved
The law and prophets, searching what was writ
Concerning the Messiah, to our scribes
Known partly, and soon found, of whom they spake
I am ; this chiefly, that my way must lie
Through many a hard assay, even to the death,
Ere I the promised kingdom can attain,
Or work redemption for mankind, whose sins
Full weight must be transferr'd upon my head.
Yet, neither thus dishearten'd, nor dismay'd,
The time prefix'd I waited ; when behold
The Baptist (of whose birth I oft had heard,
Not knew by sight), now come, who was to come
Before Messiah, and his way prepare !
I, as all others, to his baptism came,
Which I believed was from above ; but he
Straight knew me, and with loudest voice proclaim'd
Me him (for it was shewn him so from heaven),
Me him, whose harbinger he was ; and first
Refused on me his baptism to confer,
As much his greater, and was hardly won :
But, as I rose out of the laving stream,
Heaven open'd her eternal doors, from whence
The Spirit descended on me like a dove ;
And last, the sum of all, my Father's voice,
Audibly heard from heaven, pronounced me his,
Me his beloved Son, in whom alone
He was well pleased ; by which I knew the time
Now full, that I no more should live obscure,

But openly begin, as best becomes
The authority which I derived from heaven.
And now by some strong motion I am led
Into this wilderness, to what intent
I learn not yet ; perhaps I need not know,
For what concerns my knowledge God reveals.

So spake our Morning-star, then in his rise,
And, looking round, on every side beheld
A pathless desert, dusk with horrid shades,
The way he came not having mark'd, return
Was difficult, by human steps untrod ;
And he still on was led, but with such thoughts
Accompanied of things past and to come
Lodged in his breast, as well might recommend
Such solitude before choicest society.

BOOK III.

So spake the Son of God ; and Satan stood
A while as mute, confounded what to say,
What to reply, confuted and convinced
Of his weak arguing and fallacious drift ;
At length, collecting all his serpent wiles,
With soothing words renew'd, him thus accosts :
'I see thou know'st what is of use to know,
What best to say canst say, to do canst do ;
Thy actions to thy words accord, thy words
To thy large heart give utterance due, thy heart
Contains of good, wise, just, the perfect shape.
Should kings and nations from thy mouth consult,
Thy counsel would be as the oracle
Urim and Thummim, those oraculous gems
On Aaron's breast ; or tongue of seers old,
Infallible : or wert thou sought to deeds
That might require the array of war, thy skill
Of conduct would be such, that all the world
Could not sustain thy prowess, or subsist
In battle, though against thy few in arms.
These god-like virtues wherefore dost thou hide,
Affecting private life, or more obscure

In savage wilderness? wherefore deprive
All earth her wonder at thy acts, thyself
The fame and glory, glory the reward
That sole excites to high attempts, the flame
Of most erected spirits, most temper'd pure
Ethereal, who all pleasures else despise,
All treasures and all gain esteem as dross,
And dignities and powers all but the highest?
Thy years are ripe, and over-ripe; the son
Of Macedonian Philip had ere these
Won Asia, and the throne of Cyrus held
At his dispose; young Scipio had brought down
The Carthaginian pride; young Pompey quell'd
The Pontic king, and in triumph had rode.
Yet years, and to ripe years judgment mature,
Quench not the thirst of glory, but augment.
Great Julius, whom now all the world admires,
The more he grew in years, the more inflamed
With glory, wept that he had lived so long
Inglorious: but thou yet art not too late.'
    To whom our Saviour calmly thus replied:
'Thou neither dost persuade me to seek wealth
For empire's sake, nor empire to affect
For glory's sake, by all thy argument.
For what is glory but the blaze of fame,
The people's praise, if always praise unmix'd?
And what the people but a herd confused,
A miscellaneous rabble, who extol
Things vulgar, and, well weigh'd, scarce worth the praise?
They praise, and they admire, they know not what,
And know not whom, but as one leads the other;
And what delight to be by such extoll'd,
To live upon their tongues, and be their talk,
Of whom to be dispraised were no small praise,
His lot who dares be singularly good?
The intelligent among them and the wise
Are few, and glory scarce of few is raised.
This is true glory and renown; when God,
Looking on the earth, with approbation marks

The just man, and divulges him through heaven
To all his angels, who with true applause
Recount his praises ; thus he did to Job,
When to extend his fame through heaven and earth,
As thou to thy reproach may'st well remember,
He ask'd thee, "Hast thou seen my servant Job?"
Famous he was in heaven, on earth less known ;
Where glory is false glory, attributed
To things not glorious, men not worthy of fame.
They err, who count it glorious to subdue
By conquest far and wide, to overrun
Large countries, and in fields great battles win,
Great cities by assault : what do these worthies,
But rob and spoil, burn, slaughter, and enslave
Peaceable nations, neighbouring or remote,
Made captive, yet deserving freedom more
Than those their conquerors, who leave behind
Nothing but ruin wheresoe'er they rove,
And all the flourishing works of peace destroy ;
Then swell with pride, and must be titled gods,
Great benefactors of mankind, deliverers,
Worshipp'd with temple, priest, and sacrifice !
One is the son of Jove, of Mars the other ;
Till conqueror Death discover them scarce men,
Rolling in brutish vices and deform'd,
Violent or shameful death their due reward.
But if there be in glory aught of good,
It may by means far different be attain'd,
Without ambition, war, or violence ;
By deeds of peace, by wisdom eminent,
By patience, temperance : I mention still
Him, whom thy wrongs, with saintly patience borne,
Made famous in a land and times obscure ;
Who names not now with honour patient Job?
Poor Socrates (who next more memorable ?)
By what he taught, and suffer'd for so doing,
For truth's sake suffering death, unjust, lives now
Equal in fame to proudest conquerors.
Yet if for fame and glory aught be done,

Aught suffer'd; if young African for fame
His wasted country freed from Punic rage;
The deed becomes unpraised, the man at least,
And loses, though but verbal, his reward:
Shall I seek glory then, as vain men seek,
Oft not deserved? I seek not mine, but his
Who sent me; and thereby witness whence I am.'
　　To whom the tempter murmuring thus replied:
'Think not so slight of glory; therein least
Resembling thy great Father: he seeks glory,
And for his glory all things made, all things '
Orders and governs; nor content in heaven
By all his angels glorified, requires
Glory from men, from all men, good or bad,
Wise or unwise, no difference, no exemption;
Above all sacrifice, or hallow'd gift,
Glory he requires, and glory he receives,
Promiscuous from all nations, Jew or Greek,
Or barbarous, nor exception hath declared;
From us, his foes pronounced, glory he exacts.'
　　To whom our Saviour fervently replied:
'And reason; since his word all things produced,
Though chiefly not for glory as prime end,
But to shew forth his goodness, and impart
His good communicable to every soul
Freely; of whom what could he less expect
Than glory and benediction, that is, thanks,
The slightest, easiest, readiest recompense
From them who could return him nothing else,
And, not returning that, would likeliest render
Contempt instead, dishonour, obloquy?
Hard recompense, unsuitable return,
For so much good, so much beneficence!
But why should man seek glory, who of his own
Hath nothing, and to whom nothing belongs
But condemnation, ignominy, and shame?
Who for so many benefits received,
Turn'd recreant to God, ingrate and false,
And so of all true good himself despoil'd;

Yet, sacrilegious, to himself would take
That which to God alone of right belongs :
Yet so much bounty is in God, such grace,
That who advance his glory, not their own,
Them he himself to glory will advance.'
   So spake the Son of God ; and here again
Satan had not to answer, but stood struck
With guilt of his own sin ; for he himself,
Insatiable of glory, had lost all ;
Yet of another plea bethought him soon :
   ' Of glory, as thou wilt,' said he, 'so deem ;
Worth or not worth the seeking, let it pass.
But to a kingdom thou art born, ordain'd
To sit upon thy father David's throne,
By mother's side thy father ; though thy right
Be now in powerful hands, that will not part
Easily from possession won with arms :
Judea now and all the promised land,
Reduced a province under Roman yoke,
Obeys Tiberius ; nor is always ruled
With temperate sway ; oft have they violated
The temple, oft the law, with foul affronts,
Abominations rather, as did once
Antiochus : and think'st thou to regain
Thy right by sitting still, or thus retiring?
So did not Maccabeus : he indeed
Retired unto the desert, but with arms ;
And o'er a mighty king so oft prevail'd,
That by strong hand his family obtain'd,
Though priests, the crown, and David's throne usurp'd,
With Modin and her suburbs once content.
If kingdom move thee not, let move thee zeal
And duty ; and zeal and duty are not slow,
But on occasion's forelock watchful wait :
They themselves rather are occasion best ;
Zeal of thy Father's house, duty to free
Thy country from her heathen servitude.
So shalt thou best fulfil, best verify
The prophets old, who sung thy endless reign ;

The happier reign, the sooner it begins :
Reign then ; what canst thou better do the while ?'
    To whom our Saviour answer thus returned :
'All things are best fulfill'd in their due time :
And time there is for all things, Truth hath said,
If of my reign prophetic writ hath told,
That it shall never end, so, when begin,
The Father in his purpose hath decreed ;
He in whose hand all times and seasons roll.
What if he hath decreed that I shall first
Be tried in humble state, and things adverse,
By tribulations, injuries, insults,
Contempts, and scorns, and snares, and violence,
Suffering, abstaining, quietly expecting,
Without distrust or doubt, that he may know
What I can suffer, how obey? Who best
Can suffer, best can do ; best reign, who first
Well hath obey'd ; just trial, ere I merit
My exaltation without change or end.
But what concerns it thee, when I begin
My everlasting kingdom ? Why art thou
Solicitous ? What moves thy inquisition ?
Know'st thou not that my rising is thy fall,
And my promotion will be thy destruction ?'
    To whom the tempter, inly rack'd, replied :
'Let that come when it comes ; all hope is lost
Of my reception into grace : what worse ?
For where no hope is left, is left no fear :
If there be worse, the expectation more
Of worse torments me than the feeling can.
I would be at the worst : worst is my port,
My harbour, and my ultimate repose ;
The end I would attain, my final good.
My error was my error, and my crime
My crime ; whatever, for itself condemn'd,
And will alike be punish'd, whether thou
Reign, or reign not ; though to that gentle brow
Willingly could I fly, and hope thy reign,
From that placid aspect and meek regard,

Rather than aggravate my evil state,
Would stand between me and thy Father's ire
(Whose ire I dread more than the fire of hell),
A shelter, and a kind of shading cool
Interposition, as a summer's cloud.
If I then to the worst that can be haste,
Why move thy feet so slow to what is best,
Happiest both to thyself and all the world,
That thou, who worthiest art, shouldst be their king?
Perhaps thou linger'st, in deep thoughts detain'd
Of the enterprise so hazardous and high!
No wonder; for though in thee be united
What of perfection can in man be found,
Or human nature can receive, consider,
Thy life hath yet been private, most part spent
At home, scarce view'd the Galilean towns,
And once a year Jerusalem, few days'
Short sojourn; and what thence couldst thou observe?
The world thou hast not seen, much less her glory,
Empires, and monarchs, and their radiant courts,
Best school of best experience, quickest insight
In all things that to greatest actions lead.
The wisest, unexperienced, will be ever
Timorous and loath; with novice modesty
(As he who, seeking asses, found a kingdom),
Irresolute, unhardy, unadventurous:
But I will bring thee where thou soon shalt quit
Those rudiments, and see before thine eyes
The monarchies of the earth, their pomp and state;
Sufficient introduction to inform
Thee, of thyself so apt, in regal arts,
And regal mysteries; that thou may'st know
How best their opposition to withstand.'
   With that (such power was given him then) he took
The Son of God up to a mountain high.
It was a mountain at whose verdant feet
A spacious plain, outstretch'd in circuit wide,
Lay pleasant: from his side two rivers flow'd,
The one winding, the other straight, and left between

Fair champaign with less rivers interveined,
Then meeting join'd their tribute to the sea:
Fertile of corn the glebe, of oil, and wine;
With herds the pastures throng'd, with flocks the hills;
Huge cities and high-tower'd, that well might seem
The seats of mightiest monarchs; and so large
The prospect was, that here and there was room
For barren desert, fountainless and dry.
To this high mountain-top the tempter brought
Our Saviour, and new train of words began.

'Well have we speeded, and o'er hill and dale,
Forest and field and flood, temples and towers,
Cut shorter many a league; here thou behold'st
Assyria, and her empire's ancient bounds,
Araxes and the Caspian lake; thence on
As far as Indus east, Euphrates west,
And oft beyond: to south the Persian bay,
And, inaccessible, the Arabian drought:
Here Nineveh, of length within her wall
Several days' journey, built by Ninus old,
Of that first golden monarchy the seat,
And seat of Salmanassar, whose success
Israel in long captivity still mourns;
There Babylon, the wonder of all tongues,
As ancient, but rebuilt by him who twice
Judah and all thy father David's house
Led captive, and Jerusalem laid waste,
Till Cyrus set them free; Persepolis,
His city, there thou seest, and Bactra there;
Ecbatana her structure vast there shews,
And Hecatompylos her hundred gates;
There Susa by Choaspes, amber stream,
The drink of none but kings; of later fame,
Built by Emathian or by Parthian hands,
The great Seleucia, Nisibis, and there
Artaxata, Teredon, Ctesiphon,
Turning with easy eye, thou may'st behold.
All these the Parthian (now some ages past,
By great Arsaces led who founded first

That empire) under his dominion holds,
From the luxurious kings of Antioch won.
And just in time thou com'st to have a view
Of his great power; for now the Parthian king
In Ctesiphon, hath gather'd all his host
Against the Scythian, whose incursions wild
Have wasted Sogdiana: to her aid
He marches now in haste; see, though from far,
His thousands, in what martial equipage
They issue forth, steel bows and shafts their arms,
Of equal dread in flight or in pursuit;
All horsemen, in which fight they most excel;
See how in warlike muster they appear,
In rhombs, and wedges, and half-moons, and wings.'
   He look'd, and saw what numbers numberless
The city-gates out-pour'd, light-armed troops,
In coats of mail and military pride;
In mail their horses clad, yet fleet and strong,
Prancing their riders bore, the flower and choice
Of many provinces from bound to bound;
From Arachosia, from Candaor east,
And Margiana, to the Hyrcanian cliffs
Of Caucasus, and dark Iberian dales;
From Atropatia, and the neighbouring plains
Of Adiabene, Media, and the south
Of Susiana, to Balsara's haven.
He saw them in their forms of battle ranged,
How quick they wheel'd, and flying behind them shot
Sharp sleet of arrowy showers against the face
Of their pursuers, and overcame by flight;
The field all iron cast a gleaming brown:
Nor wanted clouds of foot, nor on each horn
Cuirassiers all in steel for standing fight,
Chariots, or elephants indorsed with towers
Of archers; nor of labouring pioneers
A multitude, with spades and axes arm'd
To lay hills plain, fell woods, or valleys fill,
Or where plain was, raise hill, or overlay
With bridges rivers proud, as with a yoke:

Mules after these, camels, and dromedaries,
And waggons, fraught with utensils of war,
Such forces met not, nor so wide a camp,
When Agrican with all his northern powers
Besieged Albracca, as romances tell,
The city of Gallaphrone, from thence to win
The fairest of her sex, Angelica
His daughter, sought by many prowest knights,
Both Paynim, and the peers of Charlemain.
Such and so numerous was their chivalry.

SAMSON AGONISTES.

[1667; æt. 59.]

Many are the sayings of the wise,
In ancient and in modern books enroll'd,
Extolling patience as the truest fortitude ;
And to the bearing well of all calamities,
All chances incident to man's frail life,
Consolatories writ
With studied argument, and much persuasion sought,
Lenient of grief and anxious thought :
But with the afflicted in his pangs their sound
Little prevails, or rather seems a tune
Harsh, and of dissonant mood from his complaint :
Unless he feel within
Some source of consolation from above,
Secret refreshings, that repair his strength,
And fainting spirits uphold.
    God of our fathers ! what is man,
That thou towards him with hand so various,
Or might I say contrarious,
Temper'st thy providence through his short course,
Not evenly, as thou rulest
The angelic orders, and inferior creatures mute,
Irrational and brute ?
Nor do I name of men the common rout,
That, wandering loose about,

Grow up and perish, as the summer-fly,
Heads without name, no more remembered ;
But such as thou hast solemnly elected,
With gifts and graces eminently adorned,
To some great work, thy glory,
And people's safety, which in part they effect :
Yet toward these thus dignified, thou oft
Amidst their height of noon,
Changest thy countenance, and thy hand, with no regard
Of highest favours past
From thee on them, or them to thee of service.
  Nor only dost degrade them, or remit
To life obscured, which were a fair dismission,
But throw'st them lower than thou didst exalt them high,
Unseemly falls in human eye,
Too grievous for the trespass or omission ;
Oft leavest them to the hostile sword
Of heathen and profane, their carcasses
To dogs and fowls a prey, or else captived ;
Or to the unjust tribunals, under change of times,
And condemnation of the ungrateful multitude.
If these they 'scape, perhaps in poverty
With sickness and disease thou bow'st them down,
Painful diseases and deform'd,
In crude old age ;
Though not disordinate, yet causeless suffering
The punishment of dissolute days : in fine,
Just or unjust, alike seem miserable,
For oft alike both come to evil end.

ANDREW MARVELL.

[BORN at Winestead near Hull, March 31, 1621; died in London, 1678. His poems were first collected by his widow, and published in a folio volume, 1681, but since that time about twenty-five new poems have been discovered. Mr. Grosart has published the complete works in the *Fuller Worthies' Library*.]

Andrew Marvell was not only a public man of mark and the first pamphleteer of his day, but a lyric and satiric poet. As a lyric poet he still ranks high. His range of subjects and styles is wide. He touches at different points Herbert, Cowley, Waller, Dryden, and the group of Lovelace and Suckling. But his most interesting connection is with Milton. Of that intellectual lustre which was produced by the union of classical culture and ancient love of liberty with Puritan enthusiasm, Milton was the central orb, Marvell a satellite, paler yet bright.

Like Milton, Marvell was at Cambridge, and there, after making himself an excellent Latinist, he graduated, as Milton had before him, in rebellious Liberalism by a quarrel with the authorities of his college. During his student days he was nearly drawn into the toils of the Jesuits; but he broke loose with an energy of reaction which has left its trace in *Fleckno*, his earliest satire. He afterwards spent four years on the Continent, living for some time at Rome, where, like Milton, he steeped his mind in Latin literature and inflamed his hatred of the Papacy. In 1650 Marvell became tutor to Mary the daughter of Fairfax, the general of the Parliament, who had laid down his command and was spending his quiet days in literature, gardening and collecting books and medals at his manor house of Nun Appleton in Yorkshire. Here Marvell was in a special home of the Protestant chivalry of which Spenser was the poet. Spenser accordingly appears in his satires as the spokesman of English patriotism. *The Hill and Grove at Billborow* and *Appleton House* are memorials of the sojourn in the shades of Nun Appleton, and they bear no small resemblance to the compositions of Lord Fairfax. In 1657 Marvell was recommended to Bradshaw as Assistant Latin Secretary of the Council of State by Milton, who describes him in his letter as a man of singular descent, acquainted with the French, Italian, Spanish and Dutch languages, well read in the Greek and Latin authors, and one whom if he had any feeling of rivalry or jealousy he might hesitate to bring in as a coadjutor. Marvell did not at that time receive the appointment ; but he was employed as tutor to young Dutton, Cromwell's intended son-in-law, at Eton, where he boarded with his pupil in the house of Oxenbridge, a zealous Puritan who had been driven into exile, with his wife, by prelatical persecution, and had preached in the Bermudas. By Cromwell as protector, Marvell was made joint Secretary with Milton. The connection has left memorials in several poems, including that on the Death of the Protector, in which we find a little picture, vivid and true, of the great man's look and bearing, by one who had often seen them.

> ' Where we (so once we used) shall now no more
> To fetch day press about his chamber door,
> From which he issued with that awful state,
> It seemed Mars broke through Janus' double gate,
> Yet always tempered with an air so mild,
> As April suns that e'er so gentle smiled.'

On the return of the Stuarts, Milton, the defender of regicide, was driven into retirement, where he had leisure to prove that a great man may throw himself thoroughly into the struggles, the feelings, even the passions of his time, and yet keep Art, serene and un-impaired, in the sanctuary of his mind. Marvell, far less com-promised and by no means regicidal, remained in public life, and as member for Hull sat, a Roman patriot incorruptible and in-flexible, in the corrupt and servile parliaments of Charles II. The poems of his later days were not epics or lyrics, but satires, levelled, like his renowned pamphlets, against tyranny and wickedness in Church and State ; and he died in the midst of a fierce literary affray with Parker, the most odious of the Restoration prelates, not without suspicion of poison. To Milton he remained bravely true, and his lines on *Paradise Lost* are about the earliest salutation of that sun as it rose amidst the clouds of the evil days.

As a poet Marvell is very unequal. He has depth of feeling, descriptive power, melody ; his study of the classics could not fail to teach him form ; sometimes we find in him an airy and tender grace which remind us of the lighter manner of Milton : but art with him was only an occasional recreation, not a regular pursuit ; he is often slovenly, sometimes intolerably diffuse, especially when he is seduced by the facility of the octosyllabic couplet. He was also eminently afflicted with the gift of 'wit' or ingenuity, much prized in his day. His conceits vie with those of Donne or Cowley He is capable of saying of the Halcyon :—

> ' The viscous air where'er she fly
> Follows and sucks her azure dye;
> The jellying stream compacts below,
> If it might fix her shadow so.'

And of Maria—

> ' Maria such and so doth hush
> The world and through the evening rush.
> No new-bo n comet such a train
> Draws through the sky nor star new-slain.
> For straight those giddy rockets fail
> Which from the putrid earth exhale,
> But by her flames in heaven tried
> Nature is wholly vitrified.'

The Garden is an English version of a poem written in Latin by Marvell himself. It may have gained by being cast originally in a classical mould, which would repel prolixity and extravagant conceits. In it Marvell has been said to approach Shelley : assuredly he shows a depth of poetic feeling wonderful in a political gladiator. The thoughts that dwell in 'a green shade' have never been more charmingly expressed.

A Drop of Dew, like *The Garden*, was composed first in Latin. It is a conceit, but a pretty conceit, gracefully as well as ingeniously worked out, and forms a good example of the contrast between the philosophic poetry of those days, a play of intellectual fancy, and its more spiritual and emotional counterpart in our own time. The concluding lines, with their stroke of 'wit' about the manna are a sad fall.

The Bermudas was no doubt suggested by the history of tne Oxenbridges. It is the 'holy and cheerful note' of a little band of exiles for conscience sake wafted by Providence in their 'small boat' to a home in a land of beauty.

Young Love is well known, and its merits speak for themselves. It is marred by the intrusion in the third and fourth stanzas of the fiercer and coarser passion.

The *Horatian Ode on Cromwell's Return from Ireland* cannot be positively proved to be the work of Marvell. Yet we can hardly doubt that he was its author. The point of view and the sentiment, combining admiration of Cromwell with respect and pity for Charles, are exactly his : the classical form would be natural to him ; and so would the philosophical conceit which disfigures the eleventh stanza. The epithet *indefatigable* applied to Cromwell recurs in a poem which is undoubtedly his ; and so does the emphatic expression of belief that the hero could have been happier in private life, and that he sacrificed himself to the State in taking the supreme command. The compression and severity of style are not characteristic of Marvell ; but they would be imposed on him in this case by his model. If the ode is really his, to take it from him would be to do him great wrong. It is one of the noblest in the English language, and worthily presents the figures and events of the great tragedy as they would impress themselves on the mind of an ideal spectator, at once feeling and dispassionate. The spirit of Revolution is described with a touch in the lines

> 'Though Justice against Fate complain
> And plead the ancient rights in vain
>   (But those do hold or break
>   As men are strong or weak).'

Better than anything else in our language this poem gives an idea of a grand Horatian measure, as well as of the diction and spirit of an Horatian ode.

Of the lines *On Milton's Paradise Lost* some are vigorous ; but they are chiefly interesting from having been written by one who had anxiously watched Milton's genius at work.

Marvell's amatory poems are cold ; probably he was passionless. His pastorals are in the false classical style, and of little value. *Clorinda and Damon* is about the best of them, and about the best of that is

> 'Near this a fountain's liquid bell
> Tinkles within the concave shell.'

The Satires in their day were much admired and feared : they are now for the most part unreadable. The subjects of satire as a rule are ephemeral ; but a great satirist like Juvenal or Dryden preserves his flies in the amber of his general sentiment. In Marvell's satires there is no amber: they are mere heaps of dead flies. Honest indignation against iniquity and lewdness in high places no doubt is there ; but so are the meanness of Restoration politics and the dirtiness of Restoration thought. The curious may look at *The Character of Holland*, the jokes in which are as good or as bad as ever, though the cannon of Monk and De Ruyter have ceased to roar ; and in *Britannia and Raleigh* the passage of which giving ironical advice to Charles II is a specimen of the banter which was deemed Marvell's peculiar gift, and in which Swift and Junius were his pupils.

Like Milton, Marvell wrote a number of Latin poems. One of them had the honour of being ascribed to Milton.

GOLDWIN SMITH.

THE GARDEN.

How vainly men themselves amaze,
To win the palm, the oak, or bays,
And their incessant labours see
Crowned from some single herb, or tree,
Whose short and narrow-verged shade
Does prudently their toils upbraid,
While all the flowers and trees do close
To weave the garlands of repose !

Fair Quiet, have I found thee here,
And Innocence, thy sister dear?
Mistaken long, I sought you then
In busy companies of men.
Your sacred plants, if here below,
Only among the plants will grow ;
Society is all but rude
To this delicious solitude.

No white nor red was ever seen
So amorous as this lovely green.
Fond lovers, cruel as their flame,
Cut in these trees their mistress' name .
Little, alas ! they know or heed,
How far these beauties her exceed !
Fair trees ! where'er your barks I wound,
No name shall but your own be found.

When we have run our passion's heat,
Love hither makes his best retreat.
The gods, who mortal beauty chase,
Still in a tree did end their race ;
Apollo hunted Daphne so,
Only that she might laurel grow ;
And Pan did after Syrinx speed,
Not as a nymph, but for a reed.

What wondrous life is this I lead !
Ripe apples drop about my head ;
The luscious clusters of a vine
Upon my mouth do crush their wine ;
The nectarine, and curious peach,
Into my hands themselves do reach ;
Stumbling on melons, as I pass,
Ensnared with flowers, I fall on grass.

Meanwhile the mind, from pleasure less,
Withdraws into its happiness ;—
The mind, that ocean where each kind
Does straight its own resemblance find ;
Yet it creates, transcending these,
Far other worlds, and other seas,
Annihilating all that 's made
To a green thought in a green shade.

Here at the fountain's sliding foot,
Or at some fruit-tree's mossy root,
Casting the body's vest aside,
My soul into the boughs does glide :
There, like a bird, it sits and sings,
Then whets and claps its silver wings,
And, till prepared for longer flight,
Waves in its plumes the various light.

Such was that happy garden-state,
While man there walked without a mate !
After a place so pure and sweet,
What other help could yet be meet !
But 'twas beyond a mortal's share
To wander solitary there :
Two paradises are in one,
To live in paradise alone.

How well the skilful gardener drew
Of flowers, and herbs, this dial new,
Where, from above, the milder sun
Does through a fragrant zodiac run,

And, as it works, the industrious bee
Computes its time as well as we !
How could such sweet and wholesome hours
Be reckoned but with herbs and flowers ?

A DROP OF DEW.

See, how the orient dew,
Shed from the bosom of the morn,
    Into the blowing roses,
(Yet careless of its mansion new,
For the clear region where 'twas born,)
    Round in itself incloses
And, in its little globe's extent,
Frames, as it can, its native element.
    How it the purple flower does slight,
        Scarce touching where it lies ;
    But gazing back upon the skies,
        Shines with a mournful light,
            Like its own tear,
Because so long divided from the sphere.
    Restless it rolls, and unsecure,
        Trembling, lest it grow impure ;
    Till the warm sun pities its pain,
And to the skies exhales it back again.
        So the soul, that drop, that ray,
Of the clear fountain of eternal day,
Could it within the human flower be seen,
    Remembering still its former height,
    Shuns the sweet leaves and blossoms green,
    And, recollecting its own light,
Does, in its pure and circling thoughts express
        The greater heaven in a heaven less.
        In how coy a figure wound,
        Every way it turns away,
        So the world excluding round,
        Yet receiving in the day,
        Dark beneath, but bright above,
        Here disdaining, there in love.

How loose and easy hence to go ;
How girt and ready to ascend ;
Moving but on a point below,
It all about does upward bend.
Such did the manna's sacred dew distil,
White and entire although congealed and chill ;
Congealed on earth ; but does, dissolving, run
Into the glories of the almighty sun.

THE BERMUDAS.

Where the remote Bermudas ride,
In the ocean's bosom unespied,
From a small boat, that rowed along,
The listening winds received this song.

'What should we do but sing his praise.
That led us through the watery maze,
Unto an isle so long unknown,
And yet far kinder than our own?
Where he the huge sea-monsters wracks,
That lift the deep upon their backs,
He lands us on a grassy stage,
Safe from the storms, and prelates' rage.
He gave us this eternal spring
Which here enamels every thing,
And sends the fowls to us in care,
On daily visits through the air ;
He hangs in shades the orange bright,
Like golden lamps in a green night,
And does in the pomegranates close
Jewels more rich than Ormus shows ;
He makes the figs our mouths to meet,
And throws the melons at our feet,
But apples plants of such a price,
No tree could ever bear them twice.
With cedars chosen by his hand
From Lebanon, he stores the land

And makes the hollow seas that roar
Proclaim the ambergrease on shore ;
He cast (of which we rather boast)
The Gospel's pearl upon our coast,
And in these rocks for us did frame
A temple where to sound his name.
Oh ! let our voice his praise exalt,
'Till it arrive at heaven's vault,
Which then (perhaps) rebounding may
Echo beyond the Mexique Bay.'

Thus sung they, in the English boat,
A holy and a cheerful note,
And all the way, to guide their chime,
With falling oars they kept the time.

YOUNG LOVE.

Come, little infant, love me now,
 While thine unsuspected years
Clear thine aged father's brow
 From cold jealousy and fears.

Pretty surely 'twere to see
 By young Love old Time beguil'd,
While our sportings are as free
 As the nurse's with the child.

Common beauties stay fifteen ;
 Such as yours should swifter move,
Whose fair blossoms are too green
 Yet for lust, but not for love.

Love as much the snowy lamb,
 Or the wanton kid, does prize
As the lusty bull or ram
 For his morning sacrifice.

Now then love me : Time may take
 Thee before thy time away ;
Of this need we 'll virtue make,
 And learn love before we may.

So we win of doubtful fate,
　And, if good to us she meant,
We that good shall antedate,
　Or, if ill, that ill prevent.

Thus do kingdoms, frustrating
　Other titles to their crown,
In the cradle crown their king,
　So all foreign claims to drown.

So to make all rivals vain,
　Now I crown thee with my love :
Crown me with thy love again.
　And we both shall monarchs prove.

A Horatian Ode upon Cromwell's Return from Ireland.

The forward youth that would appear
Must now forsake his muses dear,
　　Nor in the shadows sing
　　His numbers languishing :
'Tis time to leave the books in dust,
And oil the unused armour's rust,
　　Removing from the wall
　　The corselet of the hall.
So restless Cromwell could not cease
In the inglorious arts of peace,
　　But through adventurous war
　　Urged his active star ;
And, like the three-forked lightning, first
Breaking the clouds where it was nurst,
　　Did thorough his own side
　　His fiery way divide ;
(For 'tis all one to courage high,
The emulous, or enemy,
　　And with such to inclose,
　　Is more than to oppose ;)

Then burning through the air he went,
And palaces and temples rent;
    And Cæsar's head at last
    Did through his laurels blast.
'Tis madness to resist or blame
The force of angry heaven's flame;
    And if we would speak true,
    Much to the man is due,
Who from his private gardens, where
He lived reserved and austere,
    As if his highest plot
    To plant the bergamot,
Could by industrious valour climb
To ruin the great work of Time,
    And cast the kingdoms old,
    Into another mould.
Though Justice against Fate complain,
And plead the ancient rights in vain,
    (But those do hold or break,
    As men are strong or weak,)
Nature, that hateth emptiness,
Allows of penetration less,
    And therefore must make room
    Where greater spirits come.
What field of all the civil war,
Where his were not the deepest scar?
    And Hampton shows what part
    He had of wiser art;
Where, twining subtile fears with hope,
He wove a net of such a scope
    That Charles himself might chase
    To Carisbrook's narrow case,
That thence the royal actor borne
The tragic scaffold might adorn,
    While round the armed bands,
    Did clap their bloody hands:
He nothing common did, or mean,
Upon that memorable scene,

But with his keener eye
The axe's edge did try;
Nor called the gods with vulgar spite
To vindicate his helpless right,
But bowed his comely head
Down, as upon a bed.

This was that memorable hour,
Which first assured the forced power;
So, when they did design
The capitol's first line,
A bleeding head, where they begun,
Did fright the architects to run;
And yet in that the State
Foresaw its happy fate.

And now the Irish are ashamed
To see themselves in one year tamed.
So much one man can do,
That does both act and know.

They can affirm his praises best,
And have, though overcome, confessed
How good he is, how just,
And fit for highest trust;
Nor yet grown stiffer with command,
But still in the republic's hand,
(How fit he is to sway,
That can so well obey!)

He to the Commons' feet presents
A kingdom for his first year's rents;
And, what he may, forbears
His fame, to make it theirs;
And has his sword and spoils ungirt,
To lay them at the public's skirt:
So when the falcon high
Falls heavy from the sky,
She, having killed, no more doth search,
But on the next green bough to perch;
Where, when he first does lure,
The falconer has her sure.

What may not then our isle presume,
While victory his crest does plume?
  What may not others fear,
   If thus he crowns each year?
As Cæsar, he, ere long, to Gaul,
To Italy a Hannibal,
  And to all states not free
   Shall climacteric be.
The Pict no shelter now shall find
Within his party-coloured mind,
  But, from this valour sad,
   Shrink underneath the plaid;
Happy, if in the tufted brake
The English hunter him mistake,
  Nor lay his hounds in near
   The Caledonian deer.
But thou, the war's and fortune's son,
March indefatigably on,
  And for the last effect,
   Still keep the sword erect;
Beside the force it has to fright
The spirits of the shady night,
  The same arts that did gain
   A power, must it maintain.

ON MILTON'S PARADISE LOST.

When I beheld the poet blind yet bold
In slender book his vast design unfold,
Messiah crown'd, God's reconcil'd decree,
Rebelling angels, the forbidden tree,
Heaven, hell, earth, chaos, all; the argument
Held me awhile misdoubting his intent,
That he would ruin (for I saw him strong)
The sacred truths to fable and old song;
So Sampson groped the temple's posts in spite,
The world o'erwhelming to revenge his sight.

Yet as I read, soon growing less severe,
I liked his project, the success did fear;
Through that wide field how he his way should find,
O'er which lame faith leads understanding blind;
Lest he'd perplex the things he would explain,
And what was easy he should render vain.

Or if a work so infinite he spanned,
Jealous I was that some less skilful hand
(Such as disquiet always what is well,
And by ill imitating would excel)
Might hence presume the whole creation's day
To change in scenes, and show it in a play.

Pardon me, mighty poet, nor despise
My causeless yet not impious surmise.
But I am now convinced, and none will dare
Within thy labours to pretend a share.
Thou hast not missed one thought that could be fit,
And all that was improper dost omit;
So that no room is here for writers left,
But to detect their ignorance or theft.

That majesty which through thy work doth reign
Draws the devout, deterring the profane;
And things divine thou treat'st of in such state
As them preserves, and thee, inviolate.
At once delight and horror on us seize,
Thou sing'st with so much gravity and ease,
And above human flight dost soar aloft,
With plume so strong, so equal, and so soft:
The bird named from that paradise you sing
So never flags, but always keeps on wing.
Where couldst thou words of such a compass find?
Whence furnish such a vast expanse of mind?
Just heaven thee, like Tiresias, to requite,
Rewards with prophecy thy loss of sight.

Well might thou scorn thy readers to allure
With tinkling rhyme, of thy own sense secure,
While the Town-Bayes writes all the while and spells,
And like a pack-horse tires without his bells.
Their fancies like our bushy points appear :
The poets tag them, we for fashion wear.
I too, transported by the mode, offend,
And while I meant to praise thee, must commend ;
Thy verse created like thy theme sublime,
In number, weight, and measure, needs not rhyme.

SAMUEL BUTLER.

[SAMUEL BUTLER was born at Strensham in Worcestershire in 1612, and died in London in 1680.]

Samuel Butler, grievously miscalled 'the Hogarth of Poetry,' seems to have been mainly a self-taught man. After leaving Worcester Cathedral School he started in life as justice's clerk to a Mr. Jefferies, at Earl's Croome. He was next at Wrest in Bedfordshire, in the service of the Countess of Kent, and here he met and worked for John Selden. Finally he formed part of the household of Sir Samuel Luke, a Presbyterian Colonel, 'scout-master for Bedfordshire and governor of Newport Pagnell.' At the Restoration he was made secretary to the President of Wales and steward of Ludlow Castle, and in 1662, at full fifty years old, he published the first part of the immense lampoon whose author-ship has given him his place in English letters. The second part of *Hudibras* was issued in 1663; the third in 1678. Two years afterwards Butler died. The circumstances of his life during this final period are wholly dubious. He is said to have been rich, and he is said to have been poor; to have married a widow of means, and to have had no fortune with his wife but a parcel of bad securities; to have had a royal gift of £300 and been Buck-ingham's secretary, and to have had neither reward nor prefer-ment of any sort; to have been in a position to refuse as insufficient such places as were offered him, and to have lived and died a disappointed starveling. Aubrey, who was of his friends, describes him as a 'good fellow' but 'cholerique' and 'of a severe and sound judgement'; and adds in this connection, 'satyrical wits disoblige whom they converse with, and consequently make them-selves many enemies and few friends, and this was his case.' So that the 'mist of obscurity' in which his latter years were past may after all have been a mist of his own raising.

During his lifetime Butler published but the three parts of *Hudibras*, a couple of pamphlets, and an ode on the exploits and renown of the illustrious Claude Duval, which last, in its grave extravagance of irony, is, by anticipation, not unsuggestive of Fielding's 'Jonathan Wild.' Three volumes of 'Remains,' mostly spurious, were published in 1715; but in 1759 Thyer of Manchester put forth a couple of volumes of prose and verse selected from Butler's manuscripts, and these, with some scraps printed later on, are all that is known to exist of him. His chief work, that one on which his fame is wholly founded and of which he was himself most careful and diligent, is *Hudibras.* As a whole it is now-a-days hard reading. It is long, antiquated, exasperatingly dis-cursive. The greater part of it has fallen naturally into disuse and disregard. The most popular of its innumerable *dicta* have got degraded into mere colloquialisms, and remind us of coins effaced and smoothed by centuries of currency. But *Hudibras* is none the less as notable in these days as it was at the epoch of its birth. It has been more largely read and quoted than almost any book in the language. It contains the best and brightest of Butler, and is a perfect reflex of his mind and temper. To give an idea of it by means of extracts is almost impossible. The poet's fecundity of illustration and argument is astonishing; his volubility is bewildering; his intelligence of things is indefatigable. He treats of much, and that at such length that he takes many thousand verses to pass his heroes through some two or three adventures. To know him as he was, his work must be read as a whole, and diligently.

His literary origins in *Hudibras* are not far to seek. His matter he must have acquired during his stay with Sir Samuel Luke, when he had such opportunity of study from the life as has fallen to the lot of but few. It was in the work of Canon Le Roy and the band of brave wits responsible for the *Satyre Menippée* that he learned to make a proper use of the material he had gathered, and acquired in perfection the art of placing his butts and victims in an absolutely odious light. His genius, it is true, had little or nothing dramatic in it; and the harangues of Hudibras and the Lady and the Squire have not the personal and human ring in them that is to be discerned in those of Mayenne and the Sieur de Pierrefont. But they proceed on the same principle with these; like these, they extenuate nothing and set down everything in malice; of these they are in some sort the worthy successors. For his manner, Butler found a something of it in Cleveland. The acute, imaginative intelligence of abuse that is a distinguishing feature in that wandering satirist is a distinguishing feature in Butler also. In Cleveland, flashing his random speeches at the enemies of his party and his king, there are to be found as it were the rough beginnings of the patient, persistent, laborious author of *Hudibras*. The broken scholar, hawking at a parcel of lay-elders, ' Those state-dragoons, Made up of ears and ruffs like ducatoons'; or girding at the members of a ' Mixed Assembly' as so many ' parboiled lobsters, where there rules The fading azure and the coming gules'; or reflecting, in connection with the Scots he hated, ' Lord ! what a godly thing is want of shirts'; or crying out of Rupert that he had ' a copyhold of victory,' is not remote from the maker of disparates and burlesque apophthegms, the epigrammatist, now contumelious and now the reverse, we know in *Hudibras*. It must be added that Butler is not less polished and orderly than Cleveland is rough and careless ; that Butler is nearly always apt enough to be final, and that Cleveland hangs or misses fire a dozen times for once he hits ; that Butler in fine is an artist in raillery, and that Cleveland is at best but a clever amateur. Lastly, it was from Cervantes that Butler took the idea of his fable and of his chief personages. His object was to vilify and scourge the Roundheads and not to imitate or parody Cervantes ; otherwise the act that converted the good Alonso Quijada into an evil caricature of the Abstract Presbyterian Colonel, and Panza his squire into a monstrous and unseemly *charge* of an Independent servitor, would be not less infamous than the doings of Wycherly with Molière and Shakespeare. Butler however, did but choose the great originals of his grotesques as the two most popular figures in European literature, and his instinct in this matter—the instinct of the true parodist—did him yeoman service ; the public of the Restoration must have felt to Hudibras and Ralpho as to the oldest friends they had. Thus much secured, the rest was easy. It was not for Butler to make his figments human ; for, as Mr. Saintsbury has observed, 'to represent anything but monsters some alleviating strokes must have been introduced'; and as Butler wanted, not to finally embody the sectaries he hated, but to make as much fun out of them as possible, he did right to deal in monsters, and in monsters only. Hudibras, accordingly, is but a hunched back, a beard, and a collection of old clothes and rusty iron ; Ralpho has no outward presence at all ; while spiritually both man and master are merely compact of vileness and of folly. Butler had the court at his back, and the crowd as well ; he gave them of the stuff they liked ; and it was his function for some twenty years to pelt and belabour and defile the brace of pitiful scarecrows he had contrived, and so make sport for a winning side that could not forget it once had been in other circumstances.

It is the steady and persistent exercise of this function that has procured him much of the neglect with which he is visited. Fashions change ; the bogies of one epoch become the heroes of the next, and what yesterday was apt and humorous is balderdash and out of date to-morrow. That which we praise in Butler now is that for which two centuries ago no man regarded him. He is tedious, trivial, spiteful, ignoble, where he once was sprightly, exact, magnanimous, heroic. But he had an abundance of wit of the best and truest sort ; he was an indefatigable observer ; he knew opinions well, and books even better ; he had considered life acutely and severely : as a rhythmist he proceeded from none and has had no successor ; his vocabulary is of its kind incomparable ; his work is a very hoard of sentences and saws, of vigorous locutions and picturesque colloquialisms, of strong sound sense and robust English. And when all against him has been said that can be, there remains enough of good in his verse to prove that, great as it is, his reputation was well earned and justly bestowed.

W. E. HENLEY.

[From *Hudibras*, Part I.]

ARGUMENTATIVE THEOLOGY.

He could raise scruples dark and nice,
And after solve 'em in a trice ;
As if Divinity had catched
The itch on purpose to be scratched ;
Or, like a mountebank, did wound
And stab herself with doubts profound,
Only to show with how small pain
The sores of faith are cured again.

THE PRESBYTERIANS.

        That stubborn crew
Of errant saints whom all men grant
To be the true Church Militant.
Such as do build their faith upon
The holy text of pike and gun ;
Decide all controversies by
Infallible artillery ;
And prove their doctrine orthodox
With apostolic blows and knocks ;
Call fire and sword and desolation
A godly, thorough Reformation,
Which always must be going on,
And still be doing, never done,
As if Religion were intended
For nothing else but to be mended :
A sect whose chief devotion lies
In odd, perverse antipathies,
In falling out with that or this
And finding somewhat still amiss ;
More peevish, cross, and splenetic
Than dog distract or monkey sick :
That with more care keep holyday
The wrong, than others the right way ;

Compound for sins they are inclined to
By damning those they have no mind to.
Still so perverse and opposite
As if they worshipped God for spite,
The self-same thing they will abhor
One way and long another for ;
Freewill they one way disavow,
Another, nothing else allow ;
All piety consists therein
In them, in other men all sin.
Rather than fail they will defy
That which they love most tenderly ;
Quarrel with mince-pies, and disparage
Their best and dearest friend plum-porridge ;
Fat pig and goose itself oppose,
And blaspheme custard through the nose.

'NEW LIGHT.'

'Tis a dark lantern of the spirit,
Which none see by but those that bear it ;
A light that falls down from on high,
For spiritual trades to cozen by ;
An *ignis fatuus* that bewitches
And leads men into pools and ditches,
To make them dip themselves, and sound
For Christendom in dirty pond ;
To dive like wildfowl for salvation,
And fish to catch regeneration.

THE MUSE OF DOGGEREL.

Thou that with ale or viler liquors
Didst inspire Withers, Prynne, and Vickars,
And force them, though it was in spite
Of nature and their stars, to write ;
Who (as we find in sullen writs
And cross-grained works of modern wits)

With vanity, opinion, want,
The wonder of the ignorant,
The praises of the author, penned
By himself or wit-ensuring friend,
The itch of picture in the front
With bays and wicked rhymes upon't
(All that is left o' the Forkèd Hill
To make men scribble without skill),
Canst make a poet, spite of Fate,
And teach all people to translate
Though out of languages in which
They understand no part of speech. . . .

MARTIAL MUSIC.

Instead of trumpet and of drum
That makes the warrior's stomach come,
Whose noise whets valour sharp, like beer
By thunder turned to vinegar ;
For if a trumpet sound or drum beat
Who has not a month's mind to combat ?

HONOUR.

He that is valiant and dares fight,
Though drubbed, can lose no honour by't.
Honour's a lease for lives to come,
And cannot be extended from
The legal tenant : 'Tis a chattel
Not to be forfeited in battle.
If he that in the field is slain
Be in the bed of honour lain,
He that is beaten may be said
To lie in honour's truckle-bed.
For as we see the eclipsèd sun
By mortals is more gazed upon
Than when, adorned with all his light,
He shines in serene sky most bright,
So valour in a low estate
Is most admired and wondered at.

[From Part II.]

NIGHT.

The sun grew low and left the skies,
Put down, some write, by ladies' eyes.
The moon pulled off her veil of light
That hides her face by day from sight
(Mysterious veil, of brightness made
That 's both her lustre and her shade !),
And in the lantern of the night
With shining hours hung out her light ;
For darkness is the proper sphere
Where all false glories use to appear.
The twinkling stars began to muster
And glitter with their borrowed lustre,
While sleep the wearied world relieved,
By counterfeiting death revived.

MORNING.

The sun had long since in the lap
Of Thetis taken out his nap,
And, like a lobster boiled, the morn
From black to red began to turn.

SPIRITUAL TRIMMERS.

Some say the soul 's secure
Against distress and forfeiture ;
Is free from action, and exempt
From execution and contempt ;
And to be summoned to appear
In the other world 's illegal here ;
And therefore few make any account
Into what encumbrances they run 't.
For most men carry things so even
Between this world and hell and heaven,

Without the least offence to either
They freely deal in all together,
And equally abhor to quit
This world for both, or both for it;
And when they pawn and damn their souls
They are but prisoners on paroles.

[From Part III.]

MARRIAGE.

There are no bargains driven;
Nor marriages, clapped up in heaven,
And that's the reason, as some guess,
There is no heaven in marriages.
Two things that naturally press
Too narrowly to be at ease,
Their business there is only love,
Which marriage is not like to improve:
Love that's too generous to abide
To be against its nature tied;
For where 'tis of itself inclined
It breaks loose when it is confined,
And like the soul, its harbourer,
Debarred the freedom of the air,
Disdains against its will to stay,
And struggles out and flies away,
And therefore never can comply
To endure the matrimonial tie
That binds the female and the male,
Where the one is but the other's bail,
Like Roman jailers, when they slept
Chained to the prisoners they kept.

AMANTIUM IRAE.

Although some fits of small contest
Sometimes fall out among the best,

That is no more than every lover
Does from his hackney-lady suffer,
That makes no breach of faith and love,
But rather sometimes serves to improve.
For as in running every pace
Is but between two legs a race,
In which both do their uttermost
To get before and win the post,
Yet when they're at their races' ends
They're still as kind and constant friends,
And, to relieve their weariness,
By turns give one another ease;
So all those false alarms of strife
Between the husband and the wife,
And little quarrels, often prove
To be but new recruits of love,
When those who're always kind or coy
In time must either tire or cloy.

[From *Miscellanies.*]

An Apology for Plagiaries.

As none but kings have power to raise
A levy which the subject pays,
And though they call that tax a loan
Yet when 'tis gathered 'tis their own;
So he that's able to impose
A wit-excise on verse or prose,
And still the abler authors are
Can make them pay the greater share,
Is prince of poets of his time
And they his vassals that supply him;
Can judge more justly of what he takes
Than any of the best he makes,
And more impartially conceive
What's fit to choose and what to leave.
For men reflect more strictly upon
The wit of others than their own;

And wit that's made of wit and sleight
Is richer than the plain downright :
As salt that's made of salt's more fine
Than when it first came from the brine,
And spirit's of a nobler nature
Drawn from the dull ingredient matter.

Upon the Weakness and Misery of Man.

Our pains are real things, and all
Our pleasures but fantastical.
Diseases of their own accord,
But cures come difficult and hard.
Our noblest piles and stateliest rooms
Are but outhouses to our tombs ;
Cities though ne'er so great and brave
But mere warehouses to the grave.
Our bravery's but a vain disguise
To hide us from the world's dull eyes,
The remedy of a defect
With which our nakedness is decked,
Yet makes us smile with pride and boast
As if we had gained by being lost.

Distichs and Saws.

[From *Hudibras* and *Miscellanies*.]

(1)   Rhyme the rudder is of verses,
With which like ships they steer their courses.

(2)   In the hurry of a fray
'Tis hard to keep out of harm's way.

(3) Honour is like a widow, won
With brisk attempt and putting on,
With entering manfully and urging ;
Not slow approaches, like a virgin.

(4) Great commanders always own
What's prosperous by the soldier done.

(5) Great conquerors greater glory gain
By foes in triumph led than slain.

(6) Ay me! what perils do environ
The man that meddles with cold iron!

(7) Valour's a mousetrap, wit a gin,
That women oft are taken in.

(8) In all the trade of war no feat
Is nobler than a brave retreat,
For those that run away and fly
Take place at least of the enemy.

(9) He that runs may fight again,
Which he can never do that's slain.

(10) Fools are known by looking wise,
As men tell woodcocks by their eyes.

(11) Night is the sabbath of mankind
To rest the body and the mind.

(12) As if artillery and edge-tools
Were the only engines to save souls!

(13) Money that, like the swords of kings,
Is the last reason of all things.

(14) He that complies against his will
Is of his own opinion still.

(15) Those that write in rhyme still make
The one verse for the other's sake.

(16) He that will win his dame must do
As Love does when he bends his bow:
With one hand thrust the lady from,
And with the other pull her home.

(17) What is worth in anything
But so much money as 'twill bring?

(18) The Public Faith, which every one
Is bound to observe, is kept by none.

(19) He that imposes an oath makes it,
   Not he that for convenience takes it.

(20) Opinion governs all mankind,
   Like the blind's leading of the blind.

(21) The worst of rebels never arm
   To do their king and country harm,
   But draw their swords to do them good,
   As doctors use, by letting blood.

(22) The soberest saints are more stiff-neckèd
   Than the hottest-headed of the wicked.

(23) Wedlock without love, some say,
   Is like a lock without a key.

(24) Too much or too little wit
   Do only render the owners fit
   For nothing, but to be undone
   Much easier than if they had none.

(25) In little trades more cheats and lying
   Is used in selling than in buying;
   But in the great unjuster dealing
   Is used in buying than in selling,

(26)   Loyalty is still the same,
   Whether it win or lose the game;
   True as the dial to the sun,
   Although it be not shined upon.

(27)   The subtler all things are,
   They're but to nothing the more near.

(28) Things said false and never meant
   Do oft prove true by accident.

(29) Authority is a disease and cure
   Which men can neither want nor well endure.

ROSCOMMON.

[WENTWORTH DILLON, Earl of Roscommon, was born in Ireland in 1634. He spent the best part of his life in France and Italy, and died in London Jan. 17, 1684–85.]

Lord Roscommon was a man of taste and judgment, who had imbibed in France a liking for Academic forms of literature, and who attempted to be to English poetry what Boileau was to French. He did not come forward as a writer till late in life, when he produced two thin quartos of frigid critical poetry, *An Essay on Translated Verse*, 1681, and *Horace's Art of Poetry*, 1684. There was little originality in these polite exercises, but they were smoothly and sensibly written, with a certain gentlemanlike austerity. Pope has noted that, 'in all Charles' days, Roscommon only boasts unspotted lays.' He was the friend of Dryden, and the admirer of Milton, whose sublimity he lauded in terms that recall the later praise of Addison.

EDMUND. W. GOSSE.

FROM THE 'ESSAY ON TRANSLATED VERSE.'

On sure foundations let your fabric rise,
And with attractive majesty surprise;
Not by affected, meretricious arts,
But strict harmonious symmetry of parts,
Which through the whole insensibly must pass,
With vital heat to animate the mass;
A pure, an active, an auspicious flame,
And bright as heaven, from whence the blessing came;
But few, few spirits, pre-ordained by fate,
The race of gods, have reached that envied height,
No rebel Titan's sacrilegious crime,
By heaping hills on hills, can thither climb.
The grizly ferry-man of hell denied
Æneas entrance, till he knew his guide;
How justly then will impious mortals fall,
Whose pride would soar to heaven without a call?
Pride, of all others the most dangerous fault,
Proceeds from want of sense, or want of thought;
The men who labour and digest things most
Will be much apter to despond than boast;
For if your author be profoundly good,
'Twill cost you dear before he 's understood.
How many ages since has Virgil writ?
How few are they who understand him yet?
Approach his altars with religious fear,
No vulgar deity inhabits there;
Heav'n shakes not more at Jove's imperial nod,
Than poets should before their Mantuan god.
Hail, mighty Maro! may that sacred name
Kindle my breast with thy celestial flame;
Sublime ideas and apt words infuse,
The Muse instruct my voice. and thou inspire the Muse!

DORSET.

[CHARLES SACKVILLE, Earl of Dorset, was born January 24, 1637. Immediately after the Restoration he was elected to represent East Grinstead in parliament, and distinguished himself in the House of Commons. He went as a volunteer to the First Dutch War in 1665, and after this devoted himself to a learned leisure. He succeeded to the earldom in 1677, and again took a part in public business till 1698, when his health failed. He died at Bath, January 29, 1705-6.]

It is recorded of Lord Dorset that he refused all offers of political preferment in early life that he might give his mind more thoroughly to study. He was the friend and patron of almost all the poets from Waller to Pope ; Dryden adored him in one generation, and Prior in the next : nor was the courtesy that produced this affection mere idle complaisance, for no one was more fierce than he in denouncing mediocrity and literary pretension. Of all the poetical noblemen of the Restoration, Lord Dorset alone reached old age, yet with all these opportunities and all this bias towards the art, the actual verse he has left behind him is miserably small. A splendid piece of society verse, a few songs, some extremely foul and violent satires, these are all that have survived to justify in the eyes of posterity the boundless reputation of Lord Dorset.

The famous song was written in 1665, when the author, at the age of twenty-eight, had volunteered under the Duke of York in the first Dutch war. It was composed at sea the night before the critical engagement in which the Dutch admiral Opdam was blown up, and thirty ships destroyed or taken. It may be considered as inaugurating the epoch of vers-de-société, as it has flourished from Prior down to Austin Dobson.

EDMUND W. GOSSE.

Song written at Sea.

To all you Ladies now at land
    We men at sea indite;
But first would have you understand
    How hard it is to write;
The Muses now, and Neptune too,
We must implore to write to you.

For though the Muses should prove kind,
    And fill our empty brain,
Yet if rough Neptune rouse the wind
    To wave the azure main,
Our paper, pen, and ink, and we,
Roll up and down our ships at sea.

Then if we write not by each post,
    Think not we are unkind,
Nor yet conclude our ships are lost
    By Dutchmen, or by wind;
Our tears we 'll send a speedier way,
The tide shall waft them twice a day.

The King with wonder and surprise
    Will swear the seas grow bold,
Because the tides will higher rise,
    Than e'er they did of old;
But let him know it is our tears
Bring floods of grief to Whitehall-stairs.

Should foggy Opdam chance to know
    Our sad and dismal story,
The Dutch would scorn so weak a foe,
    And quit their fort at Goree,
For what resistance can they find
From men who 've left their hearts behind?

Let wind and weather do its worst,
    Be you to us but kind,
Let Dutchmen vapour, Spaniards curse,
    No sorrow we shall find;
'Tis then no matter how things go,
Or who's our friend, or who's our foe.

To pass our tedious hours away,
    We throw a merry main,
Or else at serious ombre play,
    But why should we in vain
Each other's ruin thus pursue?
We were undone when we left you!

But now our fears tempestuous grow
    And cast our hopes away,
Whilst you, regardless of our woe,
    Sit careless at a play,—
Perhaps permit some happier man
To kiss your hand or flirt your fan.

When any mournful tune you hear,
    That dies in every note,
As if it sighed with each man's care,
    For being so remote,
Think then how often love we've made
To you, when all those tunes were played.

In justice you can not refuse
    To think of our distress,
When we for hopes of honour lose
    Our certain happiness;
All those designs are but to prove
Ourselves more worthy of your love.

And now we've told you all our loves,
    And likewise all our fears,
In hopes this declaration moves
    Some pity from your tears:
Let's hear of no inconstancy,
We have too much of that at sea.

SONG.

Dorinda's sparkling wit and eyes
    United cast too fierce a light,
Which blazes high, but quickly dies,
    Pains not the heart, but hurts the sight.

Love is a calmer, gentler joy,
    Smooth are his looks, and soft his pace,
Her Cupid is a blackguard boy,
    That runs his link full in your face.

SONG.

Phillis, for shame, let us improve
    A thousand different ways
Those few short moments snatched by love
    From many tedious days.

If you want courage to despise
    The censure of the grave,
Though love's a tyrant in your eyes
    Your heart is but a slave.

My love is full of noble pride,
    Nor can it e'er submit
To let that fop, Discretion, ride
    In triumph over it.

False friends I have, as well as you,
    Who daily counsel me
Fame and ambition to pursue,
    And leave off loving thee.

But when the least regard I show
    To fools who thus advise,
May I be dull enough to grow
    Most miserably wise.

SIR CHARLES SEDLEY.

[SIR CHARLES SEDLEY was born at Aylesford in 1639, and died August 20, 1701. His most famous comedy, *The Mulberry Garden*, appeared in 1668; his poetical and dramatic works were collected in 1719.]

Sedley was one of the most graceful and refined of the mob of Restoration noblemen who wrote in prose and verse. For nearly forty years he was recognised as a patron of the art of poetry, and as an amateur of more than usual skill. Three times, at intervals of ten years, he produced a play in the taste of the age, and when his clever comedy of *Bellamira* was refused at the Duke's Theatre, on account of its intolerable indelicacy, he sulked for the remainder of his life, and left to his executors three more plays in manuscript. His songs are bright and lively, but inferior to those of Rochester in lyrical force. A certain sweetness of diction in his verse delighted his contemporaries, who praised his 'witchcraft' and his 'gentle prevailing art.' In his plays he seems to be successively inspired by Etheredge, Shadwell and Crowne. Two lines in his most famous song have preserved his reputation from complete decay.

EDMUND W. GOSSE.

SONG.

Love still has something of the sea,
　　From whence his Mother rose ;
No time his slaves from love can free,
　　Nor give their thoughts repose.

They are becalm'd in clearest days,
　　And in rough weather tost ;
They wither under cold delays,
　　Or are in tempests lost.

One while they seem to touch the port,
　　Then straight into the main
Some angry wind in cruel sport
　　Their vessel drives again.

At first disdain and pride they fear,
　　Which, if they chance to 'scape,
Rivals and falsehood soon appear
　　In a more dreadful shape.

By such degrees to joy they come,
　　And are so long withstood,
So slowly they receive the sum,
　　It hardly does them good.

'Tis cruel to prolong a pain,
　　And to defer a bliss,
Believe me, gentle Hermoine,
　　No less inhuman is.

An hundred thousand oaths your fears
　　Perhaps would not remove,
And if I gazed a thousand years,
　　I could no deeper love.

'Tis fitter much for you to guess
   Than for me to explain,
But grant, oh! grant that happiness,
   Which only does remain.

SONG.

[From *The Mulberry Garden.*]

Ah! Chloris, that I now could sit
   As unconcerned as when
Your infant beauty could beget
   No pleasure, nor no pain!

When I the dawn used to admire
   And praised the coming day,
I little thought the growing fire
   Must take my rest away.

Your charms in harmless childhood lay,
   Like metals in the mine,
Age from no face took more away
   Than youth concealed in thine.

But as your charms insensibly
   To their perfection prest,
Fond love as unperceived did fly,
   And in my bosom rest.

My passion with your beauty grew,
   And Cupid at my heart,
Still as his mother favoured you,
   Threw a new flaming dart.

Each gloried in their wanton part;
   To make a lover, he
Employed the utmost of his art,
   To make a beauty she.

Though now I slowly bend to love,
   Uncertain of my fate,
If your fair self my chains approve
   I shall my freedom hate.

Lovers, like dying men, may well
　　At first disordered be,
Since none alive can truly tell
　　What fortune they must see.

SONG.

Phillis is my only joy,
　　Faithless as the winds or seas,
Sometimes cunning, sometimes coy,
　　Yet she never fails to please;
　　　　If with a frown
　　　　I am cast down,
　　　　Phillis smiling
　　　　And beguiling
Makes me happier than before.

Though alas! too late I find
　　Nothing can her fancy fix,
Yet the moment she is kind
　　I forgive her with her tricks;
　　　　Which though I see,
　　　　I can't get free,—
　　　　She deceiving,
　　　　I believing,—
What need lovers wish for more.

MRS. BEHN.

[ASTHRA BEHN, whose maiden name was Johnson, was born in Canterbury in 1642, and died in London, April 16, 1689. Her most famous comedy, *The Rover*, was printed in 1677; her *Poems* appeared in 1685.]

Mrs. Behn was the first Englishwoman who made her livelihood by the profession of literature. After a youth of much vicissitude and some not inconsiderable social splendour, she seems to have lost her fortune, and to have turned at the age of twenty-nine to her pen for support. She was a woman of no learning, but of great enthusiasm for scholarship in others, and of unbounded veneration for wit and genius. Wit she herself possessed, and something, too, of genius, though not enough to lift her above the mean standard of a debased and grovelling age. But while we condemn the laxity of her manners, and exclaim, with Pope, 'how loosely does Astræa tread the stage,' we must not deny her the praise due to honest work unwearily performed through nearly twenty years of poverty and failing health. Living among men, struggling by the side of Settle and of Shadwell for the dingy honours of the stage, she forgot the dignity of her sex, and wrote like a man. In eighteen years she saw nineteen of her dramas applauded or hissed by the debauched and idle groundlings of the Duke's Theatre ; and forced to write what would please, she wrote in a style that has put a later generation very justly to the blush. But in power of sustained production she surpassed all her contemporaries except Dryden, since beside this ample list of plays, she published eight novels, some collections of poetry, and various miscellaneous volumes. The bulk of her writings, and the sustained force so considerable a body of literature displays, are more marked than the quality of her style, which is very irregular, uncertain and untutored. She possessed none of that command over her pen which a university training had secured to the best male poets of her time. But she has moments of extraordinary fire and audacity, when her verse throws off its languor, and progresses with harmony and passion. Her one long poem, *The Voyage to the Isle of Love*, which extends to more than two thousand lines, is a sentimental allegory, in a vague and tawdry style, almost wholly without value; her best pieces occur here and there in her plays and among her miscellaneous poems. It is very unfortunate that one who is certainly to be numbered, as far as intellectual capacity goes, in the first rank of English female writers, should have done her best to remove her name from the recollection of posterity by the indelicacy and indiscretion of her language.

EDMUND W. GOSSE.

SONG.

[From *Abdelazar*.]

Love in fantastic triumph sate,
　　Whilst bleeding hearts around him flowed,
For whom fresh pains he did create,
　　And strange tyrannic power he showed ;
From thy bright eyes he took his fires,
　　Which round about in sport he hurled ;
But 'twas from mine he took desires
　　Enough to undo the amorous world.

From me he took his sighs and tears,
　　From thee his pride and cruelty,
From me his languishment and fears,
　　And every killing dart from thee ;
Thus thou, and I, the god have armed,
　　And set him up a deity,
But my poor heart alone is harmed,
　　While thine the victor is, and free.

THE DREAM.

The grove was gloomy all around,
　　Murmuring the stream did pass,
Where fond Astræa laid her down
　　Upon a bed of grass ;
I slept and saw a piteous sight,
　　Cupid a-weeping lay,
Till both his little stars of light
　　Had wept themselves away.
Methought I asked him why he cried ;
　　My pity led me on,—
All sighing the sad boy replied,
　　'Alas ! I am undone !
As I beneath yon myrtles lay,
　　Down by Diana's springs,
Amyntas stole my bow away,
　　And pinioned both my wings.'

'Alas !' I cried, "'twas then thy darts
　　Wherewith he wounded me ?
Thou mighty deity of hearts,
　　He stole his power from thee ?
Revenge thee, if a god thou be,
　　Upon the amorous swain,
I 'll set thy wings at liberty,
　　And thou shalt fly again ;
And, for this service on my part,
　　All I demand of thee,
Is, wound Amyntas' cruel heart,
　　And make him die for me.'
His silken fetters I untied,
　　And those gay wings displayed,
Which gently fanned, he mounting cried,
　　' Farewell, fond easy maid !'
At this I blushed, and angry grew
　　I should a god believe,
And waking found my dream too true,
　　For I was still a slave.

On the Death of Waller.

How to thy sacred memory shall I bring,
Worthy thy fame, a grateful offering?
I, who by toils of sickness am become
Almost as near as thou art to a tomb,
While every soft and every tender strain
Is ruffled and ill-natured grown with pain?
But at thy name my languished muse revives,
And a new spark in the dull ashes strives ;
I hear thy tuneful verse, thy song divine,
And am inspired by every charming line.
But oh !
What inspiration, at the second hand,
Can an immortal elegy command?
Unless, like pious offerings, mine should be
Made sacred, being consecrate to thee.

Eternal as thy own almighty verse,
Should be those trophies that adorn thy hearse,
The thought illustrious and the fancy young,
The wit sublime, the judgment fine and strong,
Soft as thy notes to Sacharissa sung ;
Whilst mine, like transitory flowers, decay,
That come to deck thy tomb a short-lived day,
Such tributes are, like tenures, only fit
To show from whom we hold our right to wit.

Long did the untun'd world in ignorance stray,
Producing nothing that was great and gay,
Till taught by thee the true poetic way ;
Rough were the tracks before, dull and obscure,
Nor pleasure nor instruction could procure ;
Their thoughtless labours could no passion move,
Sure, in that age, the poets knew not love.
That charming god, like apparitions, then,
Was only talked on, but ne'er seen by men.
Darkness was o'er the Muses' land displayed,
And even the chosen tribe unguided strayed,
Till, by thee rescued from the Egyptian night,
They now look up and view the god of light,
That taught them how to love, and how to write.

ROCHESTER.

[JOHN WILMOT, second Earl of Rochester, was born in 1647, and died July 26, 1680. The best edition of his poems appeared posthumously in 1691.]

By a strange and melancholy paradox the finest lyrical poet of the Restoration was also its worst-natured man. Infamous in a lax age for his debaucheries, the Earl of Rochester was unfaithful as a subject, shifting and treacherous as a friend, and untrustworthy as a man of honour. His habitual drunkenness may be taken perhaps as an excuse for the physical cowardice for which he was notorious, and his early decline in bodily strength as the cause of his extreme bitterness of tongue and savage malice. So sullen was his humour, so cruel his pursuit of sensual pleasure, that his figure seems to pass through the social history of his time, like that of a veritable devil. Yet there were points at which the character of this unfortunate and abandoned person was not wholly vile. Within our own age his letters to his wife have surprised the world by their tenderness and quiet domestic humour, and, above all, the finest of his songs reveal a sweetness and purity of feeling for which the legends of his life are very far from preparing us.

The volumes which continued to be reprinted for nearly a century under the title of Rochester's Poems form a kind of ' Parnasse Satyrique' into which a modern reader can scarcely venture to dip. Of this notorious collection a large part was spurious ; the offensive matter that had to be removed from the writings of Dorset, Buckinghamshire, Butler, and other less famous profligate poets, found an asylum under the infamy of the name of Rochester. But readers who are fortunate enough to secure the volume edited by the dead poet's friends in 1691 will find no more indiscretions than are familiar in all poetry of the Restoration, and will discover, what they will not find elsewhere, the exquisite lyrics on which the fame of Rochester should rest. His satires, as trenchant and vigorous as they are foul, are not included in this edition ; he uses the English language in them as Poggio and Filelfo had used Latin. As a dramatist he is only known by his adaptation, or travesty, of Fletcher's tragedy of *Valentinian* ; of which the sole point of interest is that he omitted all Fletcher's exquisite songs, including the unequalled 'Hear ye ladies that despise,' and introduced a very good song of his own, the latter as characteristically of the Restoration as the former were Elizabethan.

With Rochester the power of writing songs died in England until the age of Blake and Burns. He was the last of the cavalier lyrists, and in some respects the best. In the qualities that a song demands, simplicity, brevity, pathos and tenderness, he arrives nearer to pure excellence than any one between Carew and Burns. His style is without adornment, and, save in this one matter of song-writing, he is weighed down by the dryness and inefficiency of his age. But by the side of Sedley or of Congreve he seems as fresh as by the side of Dryden he seems light and flowing, turning his trill of song brightly and sweetly, with the consummate artlessness of true art. Occasionally, as in the piece, not quoted here, called *The Mistress*, he is surprisingly like Donne in the quaint force and ingenuity of his images. But the fact is that the muse of Rochester resembles nothing so much as a beautiful child which has wantonly rolled itself in the mud, and which has grown so dirty that the ordinary wayfarer would rather pass it hurriedly by, than do justice to its native charms.

EDMUND W. GOSSE.

SONG.

My dear Mistress has a heart
  Soft as those kind looks she gave me;
When, with love's resistless art,
  And her eyes, she did enslave me;
But her constancy's so weak,
  She's so wild and apt to wander,
That my jealous heart would break
  Should we live one day asunder.

Melting joys about her move,
  Killing pleasures, wounding blisses,
She can dress her eyes in love,
  And her lips can arm with kisses;
Angels listen when she speaks,
  She's my delight, all mankind's wonder,
But my jealous heart would break
  Should we live one day asunder.

CONSTANCY.

I cannot change, as others do,
  Though you unjustly scorn,
Since that poor swain that sighs for you,
  For you alone was born;
No, Phillis, no, your heart to move
  A surer way I'll try,—
And to revenge my slighted love,
  Will still love on, and die.

When, killed with grief, Amintas lies,
  And you to mind shall call
The sighs that now unpitied rise,
  The tears that vainly fall,
That welcome hour that ends his smart,
  Will then begin your pain,
For such a faithful tender heart
  Can never break in vain.

THE BOWL.

Contrive me, Vulcan, such a cup
    As Nestor used of old,
Shew all thy skill to trim it up,
    Damask it round with gold.

Make it so large, that, filled with sack
    Up to the swelling brim,
Vast toasts on that delicious lake,
    Like ships at sea, may swim.

Engrave not battle on his cheek,
    With war I've nought to do,
I'm none of those that took Maestrick,
    Nor Yarmouth leaguer knew.

Let it no name of planets tell,
    Fixed stars or constellations,
For I am no Sir Sindrophel,
    Nor none of his relations.

But carve thereon a spreading vine;
    Then add two lovely boys;
Their limbs in amorous folds entwine,
    The types of future joys.

Cupid and Bacchus my saints are,
    May Drink and Love still reign,
With wine I wash away my care,
    And then to love again.

SONG.

[From *Valentinian.*]

Nymph.

Injurious charmer of my vanquished heart,
    Canst thou feel love, and yet no pity know?
Since of myself from thee I cannot part,
    Invent some gentle way to let me go;

For what with joy thou didst obtain,
　And I with more did give,
In time will make thee false and vain,
　And me unfit to live.

Shepherd.

Frail angel, that would'st leave a heart forlorn,
　With vain pretence Falsehood therein might lie,
Seek not to cast wild shadows o'er your scorn,
　You cannot sooner change than I can die;
　　To tedious life I'll never fall,
　　　Thrown from thy dear-lov'd breast;
　　He merits not to live at all,
　　　Who cares to live unblest.

SONG.

When on those lovely looks I gaze,
　To see a wretch pursuing,
In raptures of a blest amaze,
　His pleasing happy ruin,
'Tis not for pity that I move;
　His fate is too aspiring,
Whose heart, broke with a load of love,
　Dies wishing and admiring.

But if this murder you'd forego,
　Your slave from death removing,
Let me your art of charming know,
　Or you learn mine of loving;
But whether life or death betide,
　In love 'tis equal measure,
The victor lives with empty pride,
　The vanquished dies with pleasure.

SONG.

Absent from thee I languish still,
　　Then ask me not, when I return?
The straying fool 'twill plainly kill
　　To wish all day, all night to mourn.

Dear, from thine arms then let me fly,
　　That my fantastic mind may prove
The torments it deserves to try,
　　That tears my fixed heart from my love.

When, wearied with a world of woe,
　　To thy safe bosom I retire,
Where love and peace and honour flow,
　　May I contented there expire.

Lest once more wandering from that heaven,
　　I fall on some base heart unblessed,
Faithless to thee, false, unforgiven,
　　And lose my everlastlng rest.

EPITAPH ON CHARLES II.

Here lies our Sovereign Lord the King,
　　Whose word no man relies on,
Who never said a foolish thing,
　　Nor ever did a wise one.

THOMAS OTWAY.

[THOMAS OTWAY was born at Trottin, in Sussex, March 3, 1651, and died at Tower Hill, April 14, 1685, choked by a mouthful of bread ravenously eaten when he was at the brink of starvation. His most famous tragedies, *The Orphan*, and *Venice Preserved*, were printed respectively in 1680 and 1682.]

This is not the place to dwell on the splendid tragic genius of Otway, or to discuss his abject failure as a comedian. He claims our attention here on the score of two slender quartos of non-dramatic verse, *The Poet's Complaint of his Muse*, 1680, and *Windsor Castle*, 1685. The latter is a political and descriptive piece in the heroic measure ; it is modelled on Denham's *Cooper's Hill*, and betrays, notwithstanding some felicitous passages, the fatigue which was stealing over the dying author. But *The Poet's Complaint of his Muse* is a much more original and powerful poem ; it is written in the irregular measure called ‘Pindaric,’ and contains a satirical portrait of the poet and of his times, drawn without charm or colour, but in firm, bold lines, like a harsh engraving. Otway displays more observation of nature than most of his contemporaries ; but when he draws the world we live in, he is a draughtsman even sterner than Crabbe. We quote as an example of this important but rugged and unattractive poem the first strophe, which contains some picturesque and vivid lines. It should be remarked that Otway was absolutely unable to write even a fairly good song.

EDMUND W. GOSSE.

FROM 'THE POET'S COMPLAINT OF HIS MUSE.'

To a high hill where never yet stood tree,
  Where only heath, coarse fern, and furzes grow,
    Where, nipped by piercing air,
  The flocks in tattered fleeces hardly graze,
    Led by uncouth thoughts and care,
  Which did too much his pensive mind amaze,
A wandering bard, whose Muse was crazy grown,
Cloyed with the nauseous follies of the buzzing town,
  Came, looked about him, sighed, and laid him down.
  'Twas far from any path, but where the earth
  Was bare, and naked all as at her birth,
    When by the Word it first was made,
        Ere God had said :—
  Let grass and herbs and every green thing grow,
With fruitful herbs after their kinds, and it was so.
  The whistling winds blew fiercely round his head ;
    Cold was his lodging, hard his bed ;
  Aloft his eyes on the wide heavens he cast,
  Where, we are told, peace only is found at last ;
  And as he did its hopeless distance see,
  Sighed deep, and cried 'How far is peace from me!'

JOHN OLDHAM.

[BORN August 9, 1653, at Shipton, near Tedbury, in Gloucestershire; after taking his degree at Oxford, spent three years as usher at the Croydon Free School, and not long afterwards settled among the wits in London. He died December 9, 1683, on a visit to the Earl of Kingston at Holmes-Pierpont in Nottinghamshire.]

Certain features in the brief life of Oldham, as well as in the verse to which his name owes its celebrity, have very naturally engaged the attention of historical enquirers, while others have attracted the sympathy of literary students. He seems really to have valued that independence of which authors too often only prate ; he left it to the leaders of fashionable society and of fashionable literature to seek him out in his obscurity ; and when he ventured to publish his poems, he published them without a patron. But if he had a high spirit, he lacked the equally noble possession of an unfettered mind. Even a domestic chaplain in the Restoration days—such a one as Oldham has painted in one of the following extracts, and such as Macaulay, largely following Oldham, has re-painted in a well-known passage of his *History*—may have in him more of human dignity and freedom than the flatterer of popular fury and the pandar to mob-prejudice. Oldham was the laureate of the Popish Plot frenzy ; and his laurels are accordingly stained with much mire and with much blood.

To what lengths the fanaticism of excited popular feeling, together with an inborn love of strong language, can carry a bold and facile pen, the second of the following extracts will suffice to show. It illustrates the indignation which inspired Oldham's most sustained series of efforts, and the unreasoning violence and malignant exuberance of his invective, together with its frequent bad rhymes and occasional bad grammar. He has been repeatedly compared with Dryden, whose earlier and worse manner he imitated in his own earlier efforts, but whom he preceded as a satirist. It is in the latter capacity only that Oldham is memorable among our poets; for his panegyrical and other odes are laboured without being effective; his paraphrases have the flatness too common to their kind; and the rest of his verse, though occasionally pleasing, has no peculiar value. But on the roll of our later poetic satirists, which begins with Donne and ends with Gifford, Oldham occupies a far from insignificant place. Both Johnson and Pope may have owed something to him; but by Dryden he was valued and acknowledged as to him the most congenial of his fellow-authors. At the time of Oldham's death Dryden, though a supporter of the Court, was not yet a Roman Catholic; and there was accordingly no stint in the praise which, with his usual magnanimity, he offered on the early death of his younger predecessor. He had but one exception to take, and even this he was ready himself to overrule. Had Oldham lived longer, Dryden wrote, advancing age

> 'might (what Nature never gives the young)
> Have taught the numbers of thy native tongue;
> But satire needs not these, and wit will shine
> Through the harsh cadence of a rugged line.'

To us there is much besides defects of form to overlook or forgive in Oldham. His most famous satires have the reek of an essentially grosser flame than that in which the greatest masters of poetic satire, ancient or modern, forged their darts. But he was capable of productions tempered with nicer art if with less expenditure of vigour than those by which he is best known. His *Imitations* of Horace, Juvenal, and Boileau are all more or less felicitous; and in a few shorter original pieces of the same cast he shows occasional lightness as well as his habitual strength of touch. It should certainly not be forgotten that he died at thirty-one, and that the species of poetry in which he was chiefly gifted for excelling was one more especially suited to matured powers. And to have been the foremost English writer of satire at a time when Dryden was already famous, though not in this branch of poetry, was to have secured a fair title to remembrance.

A. W. WARD.

The Jesuits.

[From the *Second* of the *Satires upon the Jesuits.* 1860.]

These are the Janissaries of the cause,
The life-guard of the Roman Sultan, chose
To break the force of Huguenots and foes ;
The Church's hawkers in divinity,
Who, 'stead of lace and ribbons, doctrine cry ;
Rome's strollers, who survey each continent,
Its trinkets and commodities to vent ;
Export the Gospel, like mere ware, for sale,
And truck 't for indigo, or cochineal,
As the known factors here, the brethren, once
Swopped Christ about for bodkins, rings, and spoons.

And shall these great Apostles be contemned,
And thus by scoffing heretics defamed ?
They, by whose means both Indies now enjoy
The two choice blessing, lust and Popery ?
Which buried else in ignorance had been,
Nor known the worth of beads and Bellarmine[1] ?

It pitied holy Mother Church to see
A world so drowned in gross idolatry ;
It grieved to see such goodly nations hold
Bad errors and unpardonable gold.
Strange ! what a fervent zeal can coin infuse,
What charity pieces of eight[2] produce !
So were you chosen the fittest to reclaim
The pagan world, and give 't a Christian name.
And great was the success : whole myriads stood
At font, and were baptized in their own blood ;
Millions of souls were hurled from hence to burn
Before their time, be damned in their own turn.

Yet these were in compassion sent to Hell,
The rest reserved in spite, and, worse to feel,

---

[1] Cardinal Bellarmin, the great Jesuit controversialist, opposed by James I.
[2] The Spanish *pieza de à ocho,* a dollar, or eight silver *reals.*

Compelled instead of fiends to worship ycu,
The more inhuman devils of the two.
Rare way and method of conversion this,
To make your votaries your sacrifice !
If to destroy be Reformation thought,
A plague as well might the good work have wrought.
  Now see we why your founder, weary grown,
Would lay his former trade of killing down[1] :
He found 'twas dull ; he found a crown would be
A fitter case, and badge of cruelty.
Each snivelling hero seas of blood can spill,
When wrongs provoke, and honour bids him kill ;—
Give me your through-paced rogue, who scorns to be
Prompted by poor revenge, or injury,
But does it of true inbred cruelty ;
Your cool and sober murderer, who prays
And stabs at the same time, who one hand has
Stretched up to Heaven, the other to make the pass.
  So the late saints of blessèd memory,
Cut-throats in godly pure sincerity,
So they with lifted hands, and eyes devout,
Said grace, and carved a slaughtered monarch out.
  When the first traitor Cain (too good to be
Thought patron of this black fraternity)
His bloody tragedy of old designed,
One death alone quenched his revengeful mind,
Content with but a quarter of mankind :
Had he been Jesuit, and but put on
Their savage cruelty, the rest had gone ;
His hand had sent old Adam after too,
And forced the Godhead to create anew.

THE DOMESTIC CHAPLAIN.

[From *A Satire addressed to a Friend that is about to leave the University, and come abroad in the world.*]

Some think themselves exalted to the sky,
If they light in some noble family.

---

[1] Loyola ceased to be a soldier after the siege of Pampeluna.

Diet, a horse, and thirty pounds a year,
Besides the advantage of his lordship's ear,
The credit of the business, and the state,
Are things that in a youngster's sense sound great.
Little the inexperienced wretch does know,
What slavery he oft must undergo,
Who, though in silken scarf and cassock dressed,
Wears but a gayer livery at best.
When dinner calls, the implement must wait,
With holy words to consecrate the meat,
But hold it for a favour seldom known,
If he be deigned the honour to sit down—
Soon as the tarts appear, Sir Crape, withdraw !
Those dainties are not for a spiritual maw.
Observe your distance, and be sure to stand
Hard by the cistern with your cap in hand ;
There for diversion you may pick your teeth,
Till the kind voider[1] comes for your relief.
For mere board wages such their freedom sell,
Slaves to an hour, and vassals to a bell ;
And if the enjoyment of one day be stole,
They are but prisoners out on parole :
Always the marks of slavery remain,
And they, though loose, still drag about their chain.
  And where's the mighty prospect after all,
A chaplainship served up, and seven years' thrall ?
The menial thing, perhaps, for a reward
Is to some slender benefice preferred,
With this proviso bound : that he must wed ⎫
My lady's antiquated waiting-maid   ⎬
In dressing only skilled, and marmalade.   ⎭

[1] Basket for the scraps of dinner.

JOHN DRYDEN.

[BORN in 1631, at Aldwincle All Saints, in the valley of the Nen in
Northamptonshire, of Puritan parentage; and educated at Westminster
School and Trinity College, Cambridge. He appears to have become
a Londoner about the middle of the year 1657. At the Restoration he
changed into an ardent royalist; and towards the close of 1663 married the
daughter of a royalist nobleman, the Earl of Berkshire. In 1670 he was
appointed Historiographer-Royal and Poet-Laureate. After having hitherto
been conspicuous as a dramatist and a panegyrical poet, he in 1681, by the
publication of the *First Part* of *Absalom and Achitophel*, sprang into fame as
a writer of satirical verse. In December 1683 he was appointed Collector
of Customs in the port of London. His offices were renewed to him on the
accession of King James II, but his pension of 100*l.* was not renewed till
rather more than a year later. About the same time Dryden became a
Roman Catholic; and in April 1687, he published *The Hind and the Panther*.
Deprived of both offices and pension by the Revolution of 1688, he again
for a time wrote for the stage, but after a few years finally abandoned
dramatic composition for translation. Some of his greatest lyrics likewise
belong to his later years. He died at his house in Gerard Street, Soho,
May 1, 1700, and was buried with great pomp in Westminster Abbey.]

Dryden has been called the greatest writer of a little age; but it
may well be doubted whether he for one would have cared to
accept either limb of the antithesis. None of his moral qualities
better consorted with his magnificent genius than the real modesty
which underlay his buoyant self-assertion. His attitude towards
the great literary representative of an age earlier than that to which
his own maturity belonged was from first to last one of reverent
recognition; and though the lines written by Dryden under
Milton's portrait have more sound than point, they should not
be forgotten as testifying to the spirit which dictated them. Of
Oldham, in both the species of verse to which he owed his reputa-
tion infinitely Dryden's inferior, the elder poet wrote that their
souls were near allied, and cast in the same poetic mould. To
Congreve, his junior by full forty years, he declared that he would

gladly have resigned the laureateship, in which he had been sup-
planted by a Whig poetaster. On the other hand, whatever aspect
the Restoration age, either in politics or in literature, may wear in
our eyes, in its own it assumed any semblance rather than that of
an age of decline. And indeed, to speak of its literature only, it
must be admitted that there are not a few considerations to be
urged against the acceptance of such a designation. It is common
enough to find the literature of the Restoration age set down as
essentially a foreign literature, reproduced and imitated. Yet a
survey of Dryden's works alone, both dramatic and non-dramatic,
should suffice to shake the foundations of any such criticism. The
'heroic plays'—a species in which Dryden had rivals but no
equal—differed from the courtly romances of the Scudéry school as
full-bodied Burgundy differs from diluted claret. The so-called
Restoration comedy—of the later and more perfect growth of which
Dryden's efforts were but the precursors—is both for better and
for worse as genuinely national as it is unmistakeably real. It
would of course be extremely absurd to deny the great influence in
this period of French literature upon our own ; but it was an
influence of much greater importance for the future of our litera-
ture, both prose and verse, as to form than as to matter. Yet
though the clearness as well as the pointedness of the Restoration
style was partly due to French example, these qualities were some-
thing very different from the imported fashions of a season. Dryden
may be charged with more than his usual audacity when, in a
Prologue of 1672, he spoke of 'our wit' as far excelling 'foreign
wit,' after, in an Epilogue of 1670, he had extolled his own times as
not only wittier but 'more refined and free' in their use of the
native tongue than any preceding age. Yet inasmuch as during
two centuries English writers have on the whole followed Dryden
and his contemporaries instead of reverting to their predecessors
of the Elizabethan and earlier Stuart periods, it would savour of
rashness contemptuously to dismiss the claims to literary honours
of an age which formed for itself a style of so proved a merit.
With the aid of this style it virtually called into life a new
species of English poetry—that satirical poetry of which Dryden
is not indeed the originator, but in which he was the first as he has
in most respects remained the greatest master.

Whatever view be taken of the general features of the age of
which Dryden was the chief literary ornament—while Milton's
muse, like the blind poet himself, dwelt apart—it is certain that

this age speaks to us from the pages of its most brilliant writer. He was not formed, as a man or as a poet, to live out of his times. Yet neither was he, in character or in genius, one of those who merely give back what they have received, more or less changed in form or intensified in manner. He has been decried as a time-server in politics, as a turncoat in religion, and in literature as the flexible follower of a succession of schools. The reasons for and against these charges cannot be examined here ; and there seems something specially unsuitable in treating of Dryden in a tone of apology. At the same time both his life and works, the relations between which are peculiarly intimate, often require to be protected from some of the commentaries with which they have been visited. Many of our poets have been subjected to ungenerous criticism ; but none has, so to speak, been 'hansardised' so mercilessly as Dryden.

He was the descendant of Puritan ancestors on both the father's and the mother's side ; his own father—according to an adversary of the poet's—was a Committee-man, and one of his maternal cousins was a peer of Oliver's creation. Nothing could therefore be more natural or becoming than that on the Protector's death, Dryden, then a young man of twenty-seven, should have sung the praises of 'our Prince,' generally selecting for celebration qualities which even Cromwell's angriest enemies would not have denied him to have possessed. That the author of the *Heroic Stanzas* should with the Restoration have blossomed forth as a royalist implies no tergiversation at all. It should not be forgotten that the Restoration was not a mere party act ; and that much had happened between it and the death of Oliver Cromwell. Whatever may have been the hereditary politics of Dridens and Pickerings, John Dryden was a born royalist, and with the Restoration his political changes were at an end. Panegyrical poetry was the fashion of the age, and the exuberant inventiveness and felicitous readiness of Dryden's genius made it easy for him to excel in this kind of composition. To be sure, even the most willing and the most fluent muse must rapidly exhaust such a theme as the virtues of King Charles II ; and in his *Threnodia Augustalis*, written on the King's death, Dryden found little to add to what he had sung in the *Astræa Redux*, composed in honour of the Restoration,—except that his Majesty died hard. In shorter pieces in honour of the King, the Duchess of York, and Lord Clarendon, Dryden displayed the same talent for waving gorgeous banners of courtly praise, till in *Britannia Rediviva* he hailed the birth of a prince whom half the nation regarded as a pretender before he and his parents were exiles. No laureate has ever earned like Dryden the butt of sack which the economy of King James' new reign cut off from his salary. Of all the *tours de force* executed by him, however, the most extraordinary is that in which he under-took to flatter the nation, as well as the dynasty, to the top of their bent. The fire and spirit of the *Annus Mirabilis* are nothing short of amazing, when the difficulties which beset the author (though partly by his own choosing) are remembered. There was, first, the difficulty of his subject, which, as a perusal of the poem cannot fail to reveal to the most unsuspecting reader, was by no means made up altogether of materials for congratulation. Yet the *Annus Mirabilis* must really have 'done good' to the public; even at the present day it agreeably warms the John Bull sentiment, com-pounded of patriotism and prejudice, in the corner of an English-man's heart. Another difficulty, but in this instance a self-imposed one, was the form of verse in which the poem was written. It was chosen for the sake of its dignity, but (as Dryden well knew, and told Davenant, from whose *Gondibert* it was borrowed) it put a far greater strain upon the ingenuity and skill of the author. Thus though Dryden has written much that is more thoroughly enjoyable, he has written nothing that is more characteristic of himself than this long series of quatrains. The glorious *dash* of the performance is his own, and so is the victorious struggle against the drag of a difficult and rather dull metre.

But it was a yet different kind of poem by which the loyal adherent of the Stuart throne first became a *force* in English politics. No modern reader, whether his sympathies be with the Jebusites, or whether he think that there may be something to be said even in favour of the Solymæan rout, is likely to refuse his admiration to the greatest—greatest without even a suggestion of rivalry—of English political satires. This position in a literature rich in contributions of the same kind to political controversy *Absalom and Achitophel* (or rather the *First Part* of the satire) owes to the reason which made it so singularly effective at the season of its publication. Besides being executed with incom-parable vigour and *verve*, and as finished in detail as it is im-petuous in flow, it has the supreme merit (for a work of this kind) of being completely adapted to its special purpose. *Absalom and Achitophel* is a political satire pure and simple, not, like *Hudibras,*

a burlesque on a whole cauldron-full of political and religious controversy. The allegorical form of the satire, while so familiar in itself as to save all trouble in guessing the author's enigmas, just suffices for veiling the real theme beneath a decent disguise ; but it by no means interferes with a quality necessary for the effectiveness of the work—its directness. Accordingly, every shaft flies home ; in every character, from Achitophel and Zimri to the lesser which are as it were merely touched in passing, precisely those features are marked as to which it is desirable to strengthen and sharpen the suspicions of the popular instinct. The object of the writer being, not to furnish a satirical narrative of a complete historical episode, but to give a striking picture of the influences which had led to the situation existing at the time when Shaftesbury was to be placed on his trial for treason, the real completion of the plot of the poem would have been furnished by the event which it was designed to bring about—namely the conviction and condemnation of its treacherous hero. Thus, the *First Part* combines with its vehement invective and fervent enthusiasm a moderation proving the author's hand to be that of a shrewd as well as a keen politician. The blows are not dealt indiscriminately, as in an Aristophanic comedy to which nothing is sacred, or in the wantonness of partisan wit, such as Canning poured forth against the impotence he disliked not less than against the fanaticism he abhorred,—but with care and even with self-restraint. Absalom (Monmouth) is 'lamented' rather than 'accused'; even Achitophel himself where he deserves praise receives it from the candour of his politic assailant. When Dryden revised the poem for a second edition, he was least of all anxious to sharpen the sting of incidental passages ; for his purpose had not been to vilify all the opponents of the Court, but to ensure the downfall of the false Achitophel, who was first among them all.

Johnson has commended Dryden's *Absalom and Achitophel* as ' comprising all the excellences of which the subject is capable '; and not a jot need be abated from this at once high and judicious encomium. In what other poem of the kind will be found, together with so much versatility of wit, so incisive a directness of poetic eloquence ? Dryden is here at his best ; and being at his best, he is entirely free from that irrepressible desire to outdo himself, which in a great author as in a great actor so greatly interferes with our enjoyment of his endeavours, and to which in productions of a different kind Dryden often gave way. This self-control was the more to his credit, since he had not yet shot all the bolts in his quiver, and declared himself quite prepared to convince those who thought otherwise 'at their own cost, that he could write severely with more ease than he could write gently.' The successors and the sequel, however, to the *First Part* of *Absalom and Achitophel* have the diminished fire of polemics composed after the crisis is over. The pungent satire of *The Medal*, written after the throwing out of the bill of indictment against Shaftesbury by the London grand jury, ridicules the hypocrisy of the hero of the Puritan Londoners, and the sovereign stupidity of his worshippers, the mob —a stupidity against which 'even gods contend in vain':

> 'Almighty crowd! thou shortenest all dispute;
> Power is thy essence, wit thy attribute!
> Nor faith nor reason make thee at a stay:
> Thou leap'st o'er all eternal truths in thy Pindaric way.'

(The last line, by the way, is an admirable example of one of Dryden's favourite metrical devices—unfortunately too frequently and too indiscriminately employed by him—the incidental Alexandrine.) Among the Whig writers who took upon themselves to reply to *The Medal*, was Thomas Shadwell, 'the true-blue poet,'— who was afterwards to supersede Dryden as laureate, and who as a comic dramatist displays a measure of power which makes it necessary to take exception to the sweeping contemptuousness of Dryden's satire against him. Shadwell is the hero of *Mac Flecnoe*, to which brilliant but not very generous *jeu d'esprit* a harmless scribbler (who had even to the best of his ability extolled Dryden himself) was made to give his name. This most happily executed retort upon a by no means despicable antagonist has a double claim to immortality:—its own delightful execution, and the fact that this attempt to extinguish a single Dunce suggested to Pope the heroic idea of annihilating the whole tribe. The list of Dryden's satirical poetry closes with his contributions to the *Second Part* of *Absalom and Achitophel*, of which Nahum Tate (afterwards Poet-Laureate in his turn) was the principal author. Tate's muse might well wax faint in striving to raise her own feeble efforts to the level of 'the song of Asaph'; nor will his name be linked by posterity with Dryden's as it is with Brady's. The characters of Og (Shadwell) and Doeg (Elkanah Settle, the city poet, whose political opinions changed more than once, without landing him in a competency at the end) are in Dryden's most successful, and in his most rollicking, manner.

Thus, in what were at once the earliest and among the bitterest

days of modern English party life, the court poet had thrown him-
self heart and soul into the conflict, and had constituted himself
the chief literary champion of a side which in any case must have
engaged his goodwill and sympathy. At home and abroad, the
adversaries of the Stuarts were the natural objects of his satire ;
for how could a born partisan of centralised authority love either
Dutchmen or Dissenters? It would be hard to say which he
attacked with greater zest, whenever opportunity arose. His
attempt to inflame popular sentiment against the Dutch in the
sensation drama of *Amboyna* is a disgraceful illustration of too
common a misgrowth of patriotism. Even in the pleasant *Epistle*
which quite at the close of his life he addressed to his kinsman,
and which he himself considered as well written as anything he
had ever composed, he had originally introduced some reflexions
on Dutch valour, though a Dutchman sat on the throne. His
antipathy against the Nonconformists he was to exhibit under
circumstances creditable at all events to the ingenuousness of his
partisanship.

The history of Dryden's religious opinions has called forth very
various and much cruel comment. The latter term will seem ap-
posite if it be simply remembered how frequently instances of a
change of creed analogous to Dryden's have occurred and continue
to occur, and how deeply in most cases of the kind the insinuation
of an interested motive would be resented by those best acquainted
with their origin and progress. All that is possible on the pre-
sent occasion is to suggest, as indispensable to any enquiry into
the process and motives of Dryden's conversion to the Church of
Rome, a candid and impartial examination of his two poems, the
Religio Laici (published in November 1682) and *The Hind and the
Panther* (April 1687). In his most amusing comedy of *The Spanish
Friar* (1681) it is difficult to discover anything bearing on the
subject beyond evidence that Dryden hated priests,—a feeling to
which he steadily adhered even after he had become a member of
the Church of Rome.

There is nothing whatever to show that the *Religio Laici* was
called forth by any special occasion, or juncture of circumstances,
in the life of its author. Nor can it be looked upon as the declara-
tion of any creed in particular ; for there are surely few members
of any Protestant *Church* who would care to accept the Layman's
exposition of his standpoint as a summary of their beliefs. Un-
willing to take refuge in natural religion, unable to accept the

theory of an infallible Church, and resenting the practice of leaving the truth revealed in the Bible at the mercy of the rabble, the Layman is content to bow to authority where it deserves the name, to leave obscure points aside, and where he cannot agree with the Church, to waive his private judgment for the sake of peace :

> ' For points obscure are of small use to learn,
> But common quiet is the world's concern.'

That a Protestant whose Protestantism stood on so very weak a footing should have been led after all into the bosom of a Church claiming infallibility, seems a fact easily accounted for ; and in truth the *Religio Laici* might almost be called a halfway-house in the road along which Dryden was travelling. A reverence for authority was implanted in his nature ; he was a Tory before he was a Catholic ; moreover, he was at no time a man to strain at minor difficulties ; and it was therefore almost inevitable that the Layman's simple Creed would sooner or later cease to satisfy a mind inclined and accustomed to look at things in the grand style.

If, in point of fact, this time came very soon, there is no reason to deny that events happening and currents in operation around him, may have hastened the change. There are seasons specially favourable for a roll-call in the moral as in the political world ; and apart from the bias in his mind, Dryden was probably not one of the converts whom Rome has found it most difficult to secure. But to attribute his conversion to the renewal of a trumpery pension—whether granted immediately before or just after his declaration of his change of faith—is not less ignoble than it is idle vaguely to suggest that he was influenced by 'visions of greater worldly advantage.' If his conversion finds sufficient explanation as a process natural to a mind and disposition constituted like his, and subjected to the general influences of an age like that in which he lived, there remains no controversy to be discussed. That after becoming a Roman Catholic he should have felt a strong desire to offer to the world a defence of a position not new to the world, but new and therefore in a sense uneasy to himself, seems quite in accordance with experience. But that *The Hind and the Panther* was not published in order to conciliate the favour of King James II, is manifest from a very noteworthy circumstance. This poem, a species of *eirenicon* (as it might almost be called) to the Church of England on behalf of the Church of Rome, and an invitation to the former to unite with the latter against the

Nonconformists, appeared a fortnight after the Declaration of Indulgence, by which the king had sought to conciliate the support of 'the Bear, the Boar and every savage name' willing to listen to the voice of the charmer.

The Hind and the Panther has been censured by critics and burlesqued by wits on account of the supposed incongruity of its characters and dialogue. But there is no reason why beasts should not talk theology or politics—or anything else under the sun—in a piece constructed not as an allegory, but as a fable; and moreover, as Sir Wa'ter Scott has pointed out, Dryden might have appealed for precedents to the works of both Chaucer and Spenser. The lengthiness of parts of the poem may at the same time be undeniable; but its wit and vigour of expression, aided by a versification which Pope declared to be the most correct to be found in Dryden, render it a unique contribution to controversial literature. That the author of *The Hind and the Panther* had lost little, if any, of his power as a satirist, will be evident from some of the passages cited below as being more suitable for extraction than snatches of controversy—the description of the Nonconformist sects, the character of Father Petre (judiciously put into the Panther's lips) and that of Dr. (afterwards Bishop) Burnet, whom Dryden had already attacked in passing as Balak in *Absalom and Achitophel*, and who replied in his *History of his own Time* by signating Dryden as 'a master of immodesty and impurity of all sorts.'

This retort, or the element of truth contained in its violence, cannot be waved aside like the charges brought against Dryden of political and religious dishonesty. The licentiousness of the Restoration drama, which it would have mightily amused the Restoration dramatists to see explained as mere imaginative frolicsomeness, found in him a too willing representative, to be distinguished from the rest only because he had a genius to pervert and to profane. But it should be remembered in his honour that though he was not strong enough to resist temptation, he was true enough to his nobler self to feel and to record the degradation of his weakness. Posterity need utter no severer censure on one who has spoken of his 'second fall' with the solemn severity of self-knowledge displayed by Dryden in the incomparably beautiful *Ode to the Memory of Anne Killigrew.* His nature was too fine and too manly petulantly to defy any criticism which he thought in any measure just, although he might deprecate exaggerated rigour, and despise a preciseness of censure which to men of his mould is virtually unintelligible.

Undoubtedly, though the strength and pointedness of his style makes him recognisable in almost everything he has written—a Hercules truly to be guessed from a mere bit of himself—Dryden is one of those authors to whom complete justice can never be done by those who study him in selections only. The inexhaustible fertility and grandiose ease of his style require the vast expanse of his collected works for their full display. But what cannot be exhibited in completeness, may be indicated by contrast. Truly great as a satirical, and unusually effective as a didactic poet, Dryden as an ode-writer surpassed even Cowley in execution, and at times equalled him in felicity of conception. From the panegyrical strains of his earlier days he passed in his later to a twofold treatment of a theme not less difficult and far loftier than the praise of earthly crowns and their wearers. The two famous lyrics in honour of St. Cecilia's Day are almost equally brilliant in execution ; but the earlier and shorter is not altogether successful in avoiding the dangers incidental to any attempt of a more elaborate kind to make 'the sound appear an echo to the sense.' *Alexander's Feast*, on the other hand, may not be without a certain operatic artificiality ; but affectation alone can pretend to be insensible to the magnificent impetus of its movement, or to the harmonious charm of its *finale*. Of Dryden's art as a translator only one example could find a place here—the simple but singularly powerful version, familiar to many generations, of the *Veni, Creator Spiritus*. Yet this kind of literary work was one which neither he nor his contemporaries were inclined to undervalue. He possessed one of two qualities essential to a master in translation, and lacked the other. While gifted with an almost instinctive power of seizing upon the salient points in his original, and wonderfully facile in rendering these by ingenious turns of thought and phrase in his own tongue, he had neither the nature nor the training of a scholar. He is accordingly at once the most felicitous and the most reckless of English poetic translators. His modernisations of Chaucer, which with translations from Homer, Ovid, and Boccaccio made up his last publication, the *Fables*, show his mastery over his form at least as strikingly as any other of his works. In the days in which we live Dryden's long popular re-castings of Chaucer happily can receive no other praise than this. But something more than a mere shred of purple seemed required by way of example of these famous 'translations' by one great English poet of another and greater.

As a dramatist he cannot here be discussed; but room has been found for an example of one or two of his *Prologues* and *Epilogues*, in which the poet, following the fashion of his times, converses at his ease with his public through the medium of a favourite actor—or (since King David's happy restoration) of a favourite actress. But nowhere do the wit and the 'frankness' of the age (to use the term applied to it by one of its most popular comedians) find readier expression than in these sallies of badinage, occasionally intermixed with a grain of salt satire, or doing duty as acrid invective or patriotic bluster; and nowhere is the genial freespokenness of Dryden more thoroughly at home than in these confidences between dramatist and public. Lastly, it should not be forgotten that as a prose critic of dramatic poetry and its laws Dryden remains much more than readable at the present day; his inconsistencies any tiro can point out, but it is better worth while to appreciate the force of much that he says on whatever side of a question he may advocate. Among all our poets few have found better reasons for their theories, or for the practice they have based on the theories of others.

In Dryden it is futile to seek for poetic qualities which he neither possessed nor affected. Wordsworth remarked of him that there is not 'a single image from nature in the whole body of his works.' One may safely add to this, that he is without lyric depth, and incapable of true sublimity—a quality which he revered in Milton. If it be too much to say that the magnificent instrument through which his genius discourses its music lacks the *vox humana* of poetry speaking to the heart, the still rarer presence of the *vox angelica* is certainly wanting to it. But he is master of his poetic form—more especially of that heroic couplet to which he gave a strength unequalled by any of his successors, even by Pope, who surpassed him in finish. And if there is grandeur in the pomp of kings and the march of hosts, in the 'trumpet's loud clangour' and in tapestries and carpetings of velvet and gold, Dryden is to be ranked with the grandest of English poets. The irresistible impetus of an invective which never falls short or flat, and the savour of a satire which never seems dull or stale, give him an undisputed place among the most glorious of English wits.

A. W. WARD.

Verses to Her Royal Highness the Duchess,

On the Memorable Victory gained by the Duke against the Hollanders, June 3, 1665[1], and on her Journey afterwards into the North.

Madam,
When for our sakes your hero you resigned
To swelling seas and every faithless wind,
When you released his courage and set free
A valour fatal to the enemy,
You lodged your country's cares within your breast,
The mansion where soft love should only rest,
And, ere our foes abroad were overcome,
The noblest conquest you had gained at home.
Ah, what concerns did both your souls divide!
Your honour gave us what your love denied:
And 'twas for him much easier to subdue
Those foes he fought with than to part from you.
That glorious day, which two such navies saw
As each unmatched might to the world give law,
Neptune, yet doubtful whom he should obey,
Held to them both the trident of the sea:
The winds were hushed, the waves in ranks were cast
As awfully as when God's people past,
Those yet uncertain on whose sails to blow,
These where the wealth of nations ought to flow.
Then with the Duke your Highness ruled the day;)
While all the brave did his command obey,   }
The fair and pious under you did pray.   )
How powerful are chaste vows! the wind and tide
You bribed to combat on the English side.
Thus to your much-loved lord you did convey
An unknown succour, sent the nearest way;

[1] James Duke of York's naval victory off Lowestoft.

New vigour to his wearied arms you brought
(So Moses was upheld while Israel fought,)
While from afar we heard the cannon play,
Like distant thunder on a shiny day.
For absent friends we were ashamed to fear,
When we considered what you ventured there.
Ships, men, and arms our country might restore,
But such a leader could supply no more.
With generous thoughts of conquest he did burn,
Yet fought not more to vanquish than return.
Fortune and victory he did pursue
To bring them as his slaves to wait on you :
Thus beauty ravished the rewards of fame,
And the fair triumphed when the brave o'ercame.
Then, as you meant to spread another way
By land your conquests far as his by sea,
Leaving our southern clime, you marched along
The stubborn North, ten thousand Cupids strong.
Like Commons, the nobility resort
In crowding heaps to fill your moving court :
To welcome your approach the vulgar run,
Like some new envoy from the distant sun,
And country beauties by their lovers go,
Blessing themselves and wondering at the show.
So, when the new-born phœnix first is seen,
Her feathered subjects all adore their queen,
And while she makes her progress through the East,
From every grove her numerous train's increast ;
Each poet of the air her glory sings,
And round him the pleased audience clap their wings.

THE ATTEMPT AT BERGHEN.

[From *Annus Mirabilis, the Year of Wonders* : 1666.]

And now approached their fleet from India, fraught
   With all the riches of the rising sun,
And precious sand from southern climates brought,
   The fatal regions where the war begun.

Like hunted castors conscious of their store,
 Their way-laid wealth to Norway's coasts they bring;
There first the North's cold bosom spices bore,
 And winter brooded on the eastern spring.

By the rich scent we found our perfumed prey,
 Which, flanked with rocks, did close in covert lie;
And round about their murdering cannon lay,
 At once to threaten and invite the eye.

Fiercer than cannon and than rocks more hard,
 The English undertake the unequal war:
Seven ships alone, by which the port is barred,
 Besiege the Indies and all Denmark dare.

These fight like husbands, but like lovers those;
 These fain would keep and those more fain enjoy;
And to such height their frantic passion grows
 That what both love both hazard to destroy.

Amidst whole heaps of spices lights a ball,
 And now their odours armed against them fly:
Some preciously by shattered porcelain fall,
 And some by aromatic splinters die.

And though by tempests of the prize bereft,
 In Heaven's inclemency some ease we find;
Our foes we vanquished by our valour left,
 And only yielded to the seas and wind.

Nor wholly lost we so deserved a prey,
 For storms repenting part of it restored,
Which as a tribute from the Baltic sea
 The British ocean sent her mighty lord.

Go, mortals, now and vex yourselves in vain
 For wealth, which so uncertainly must come;
When what was brought so far and with such pain
 Was only kept to lose it nearer home.

The son who, twice three months on the ocean tost,
 Prepared to tell what he had passed before,
Now sees in English ships the Holland coast,
 And parents' arms in vain stretched from the shore

This careful husband had been long away,
　Whom his chaste wife and little children mourn,
Who on their fingers learned to tell the day
　On which their father promised to return.

Such are the proud designs of human kind,
　And so we suffer shipwrack everywhere !
Alas, what port can such a pilot find
　Who in the night of Fate must blindly steer !

The Fire of London.

[From *Annus Mirabilis.*]

Such was the rise of this prodigious fire,
　Which, in mean buildings first obscurely bred,
From thence did soon to open streets aspire,
　And straight to palaces and temples spread.

The diligence of trades, and noiseful gain,
　And luxury, more late, asleep were laid ;
All was the Night's, and in her silent reign
　No sound the rest of Nature did invade.

In this deep quiet, from what source unknown,
　Those seeds of fire their fatal birth disclose ;
And first few scattering sparks about were blown,
　Big with the flames that to our ruin rose.

Then in some close-pent room it crept along,
　And, smouldering as it went, in silence fed ;
Till the infant monster, with devouring strong,
　Walked boldly upright with exalted head.

Now, like some rich or mighty murderer,
　Too great for prison which he breaks with gold,
Who fresher for new mischiefs does appear,
　And dares the world to tax him with the old,

So scapes the insulting fire his narrow jail,
　And makes small outlets into open air ;
There the fierce winds his tender force assail,
　And beat him downward to his first repair.

The winds, like crafty courtesans, withheld
   His flames from burning but to blow them more:
And, every fresh attempt, he is repelled
   With faint denials, weaker than before.

And now, no longer letted of his prey,
   He leaps up at it with enraged desire,
O'erlooks the neighbours with a wide survey,
   And nods at every house his threatening fire.

The ghosts of traitors from the Bridge descend,
   With bold fanatic spectres to rejoice;
About the fire into a dance they bend,
   And sing their sabbath notes with feeble voice[1].

Our guardian angel saw them where they sate,
   Above the palace of our slumbering King;
He sighed, abandoning his charge to Fate,
   And drooping oft looked back upon the wing.

At length the crackling noise and dreadful blaze
   Called up some waking lover to the sight;
And long it was ere he the rest could raise,
   Whose heavy eyelids yet were full of night.

The next to danger, hot pursued by fate,
   Half-clothed, half-naked, hastily retire;
And frighted mothers strike their breasts too late
   For helpless infants left amidst the fire.

Their cries soon waken all the dwellers near;
   Now murmuring noises rise in every street;
The more remote run stumbling with their fear,
   And in the dark men justle as they meet.

So weary bees in little cells repose;
   But if night-robbers lift the well-stored hive,
An humming through their waxen city grows,
   And out upon each other's wings they drive.

---

[1] The heads of persons executed for treason were displayed on London Bridge.

Now streets grow thronged and busy as by day ;
   Some run for buckets to the hallowed quire ;
Some cut the pipes, and some the engines play,
   And some more bold mount ladders to the fire.

In vain ; for from the east a Belgian wind
   His hostile breath through the dry rafters sent ;
The flames impelled soon left their foes behind,
   And forward with a wanton fury went.

A key[1] of fire ran all along the shore,
   And lightened all the river with a blaze ;
The wakened tides began again to roar,
   And wondering fish in shining waters gaze.

Old Father Thames raised up his reverend head,
   But feared the fate of Simois[2] would return ;
Deep in his ooze he sought his sedgy bed,
   And shrank his waters back into his urn.

The fire meantime walks in a broader gross[3] ;
   To either hand his wings he opens wide ;
He wades the streets, and straight he reaches cross,
   And plays his longing flames on the other side.

At first they warm, then scorch, and then they take ;
   Now with long necks from side to side they feed ;
At length, grown strong, their mother-fire forsake,
   And a new colony of flames succeed.

To every nobler portion of the town
   The curling billows roll their restless tide ;
In parties now they straggle up and down,
   As armies unopposed for prey divide.

One mighty squadron, with a sidewind sped,
   Through narrow lanes his cumbered fire does haste,
By powerful charms of gold and silver led
   The Lombard bankers and the Change to waste.

[1] *Key* = quay.   [2] See *Iliad,* bk. xxi (of the Xanthos).   [3] *gross,* bulk.

Another backward to the Tower would go,
   And slowly eats his way against the wind;
But the main body of the marching foe
   Against the imperial palace is designed.

Now day appears; and with the day the King,
   Whose early care had robbed him of his rest;
Far off the cracks of falling houses ring,
   And shrieks of subjects pierce his tender breast.

Near as he draws, thick harbingers of smoke
   With gloomy pillars cover all the place;
Whose little intervals of night are broke
   By sparks that drive against his sacred face.

More than his guards his sorrows made him known,
   And pious tears which down his cheeks did shower;
The wretched in his grief forgot their own;
   So much the pity of a king has power.

He wept the flames of what he loved so well,
   And what so well had merited his love;
For never prince in grace did more excel,
   Or royal city more in duty strove.

ACHITOPHEL.

[From *Absalom and Achitophel,* Part I; 1681.]

Of these the false Achitophel[1] was first,
A name to all succeeding ages curst:
For close designs and crooked counsels fit,
Sagacious, bold, and turbulent of wit,
Restless, unfixed in principles and place,
In power unpleased, impatient of disgrace;
A fiery soul which, working out its way,
Fretted the pigmy body to decay
And o'er-informed the tenement of clay.

     [1] *Achitophel* = Shaftesbury.

A daring pilot in extremity,
Pleased with the danger, when the waves went high,
He sought the storms ; but, for a calm unfit,
Would steer too nigh the sands to boast his wit.
Great wits are sure to madness near allied,
And thin partitions do their bounds divide ;
Else, why should he, with wealth and honour blest,
Refuse his age the needful hours of rest ?
Punish a body which he could not please,
Bankrupt of life, yet prodigal of ease ?
And all to leave what with his toil he won
To that unfeathered two-legged thing, a son,
Got, while his soul did huddled notions try,
And born a shapeless lump, like anarchy.
In friendship false, implacable in hate,
Resolved to ruin or to rule the state ;
To compass this the triple bond he broke [1],
The pillars of the public safety shook,
And fitted Israel for a foreign yoke ;
Then, seized with fear, yet still affecting fame,
Usurped a patriot's all-atoning name.
So easy still it proves in factious times [2]
With public zeal to cancel private crimes.
How safe is treason and how sacred ill,
Where none can sin against the people's will,
Where crowds can wink and no offence be known,
Since in another's guilt they find their own !
Yet fame deserved no enemy can grudge ;
The statesman we abhor, but praise the judge.
In Israel's courts ne'er sat an Abbethdin
With more discerning eyes or hands more clean,
Unbribed, unsought, the wretched to redress,
Swift of despatch and easy of access.

[1] *The triple bond* is the Triple Alliance of 1667, undone by the alliance concluded with France in 1670, when Shaftesbury was a member of the Cabal.

[2] This and the following lines, referring to Shaftesbury's conduct as Lord Chancellor, were inserted in the second edition. The *Abbethdin* was the Jewish Chief Justice.

Oh ! had he been content to serve the crown
With virtues only proper to the gown,
Or had the rankness of the soil been freed
From cockle that oppressed the noble seed,
David for him his tuneful harp had strung
And Heaven had wanted one immortal song.
But wild ambition loves to slide, not stand,
And Fortune's ice prefers to Virtue's land.
Achitophel, grown weary to possess
A lawful fame and lazy happiness,
Disdained the golden fruit to gather free,
And lent the crowd his arm to shake the tree.
Now, manifest of crimes contrived long since,
He stood at bold defiance with his Prince,
Held up the buckler of the people's cause
Against the crown, and skulked behind the laws.
The wished occasion of the Plot he takes [1];
Some circumstances finds, but more he makes ;
By buzzing emissaries fills the ears
Of listening crowds with jealousies and fears
Of arbitrary counsels brought to light,
And proves the King himself a Jebusite.[2]
Weak arguments ! which yet he knew full well
Were strong with people easy to rebel.
For, governed by the moon, the giddy Jews
Tread the same track when she the prime renews :
And once in twenty years their scribes record,
By natural instínct they change their lord.

THE MALCONTENTS. ZIMRI.

[From *Absalom and Achitophel*, Part I.]

To further this, Achitophel unites
The malcontents of all the Israelites,
Whose differing parties he could wisely join
For several ends to serve the same design ;

---

[1] *The Plot* is the Popish Plot.　　[2] *Jebusites* = Roman Catholics.

The best, (and of the princes some were such,)
Who thought the power of monarchy too much ;
Mistaken men and patriots in their hearts,
Not wicked, but seduced by impious arts ;
By these the springs of property were bent
And wound so high they cracked the government.
The next for interest sought to embroil the state
To sell their duty at a dearer rate,
And make their Jewish markets of the throne,
Pretending public good to serve their own.
Others thought kings an useless heavy load,
Who cost too much and did too little good.
These were for laying honest David by
On principles of pure good husbandry.
With them joined all the haranguers of the throng
That thought to get preferment by the tongue.
Who follow next a double danger bring,
Not only hating David, but the King ;
The Solymaean rout [1], well versed of old
In godly faction and in treason bold,
Cowering and quaking at a conqueror's sword,
But lofty to a lawful prince restored,
Saw with disdain an Ethnic plot begun
And scorned by Jebusites to be outdone.
Hot Levites [2] headed these ; who, pulled before
From the ark which in the Judges' days they bore,
Resumed their cant, and with a zealous cry
Pursued their old beloved theocracy,
Where Sanhedrin and priest enslaved the nation,
And justified their spoils by inspiration ;
For who so fit for reign as Aaron's race,
If once dominion they could found in grace?
These led the pack ; though not of surest scent,
Yet deepest mouthed against the government.

---

[1] *The Solymaean rout* is the rabble of the City. (Hierosolyma, or
Jerusalem = London.)

[2] *Levites* = Presbyterian ministers.

A numerous host of dreaming saints succeed
Of the true old enthusiastic breed:
'Gainst form and order they their power employ,
Nothing to build and all things to destroy.
But far more numerous was the herd of such
Who think too little and who talk too much.
These out of mere instínct, they knew not why,
Adored their fathers' God and property,
And by the same blind benefit of Fate
The Devil and the Jebusite did hate:
Born to be saved even in their own despite,
Because they could not help believing right.
Such were the tools; but a whole Hydra more
Remains of sprouting heads too long to score.
Some of their chiefs were princes of the land;
In the first rank of these did Zimri[1] stand,
A man so various that he seemed to be
Not one, but all mankind's epitome:
Stiff in opinions, always in the wrong,
Was everything by starts and nothing long;
But in the course of one revolving moon
Was chymist, fiddler, statesman, and buffoon;
Then all for women, painting, rhyming, drinking,
Besides ten thousand freaks that died in thinking.
Blest madman, who could every hour employ
With something new to wish or to enjoy!
Railing and praising were his usual themes,
And both, to show his judgment, in extremes:
So over violent or over civil
That every man with him was God or Devil.
In squandering wealth was his peculiar art;
Nothing went unrewarded but desert.
Beggared by fools whom still he found too late,
He had his jest, and they had his estate.
He laughed himself from Court; then sought relief
By forming parties, but could ne'er be chief:

---

[1] *Zimri* is George Villiers, second Duke of Buckingham, a member of the Cabal, but after his dismissal a member of the Opposition. He had ridiculed Dryden as Bayes in *The Rehearsal.*

For spite of him, the weight of business fell
On Absalom and wise Achitophel;
Thus wicked but in will, of means bereft,
He left not faction, but of that was left.

SHADWELL.

[From *Mac Flecknoe*; October, 1682.]

All human things are subject to decay,
And, when Fate summons, monarchs must obey.
This Flecknoe[1] found, who, like Augustus, young
Was called to empire and had governed long,
In prose and verse was owned without dispute
Through all the realms of Nonsense absolute.
This aged prince, now flourishing in peace
And blest with issue of a large increase,
Worn out with business, did at length debate
To settle the succession of the state;
And pondering which of all his sons was fit
To reign and wage immortal war with wit,
Cried, "'Tis resolved, for Nature pleads that he
Should only rule who most resembles me.
Shadwell alone my perfect image bears,
Mature in dulness from his tender years;
Shadwell alone of all my sons is he
Who stands confirmed in full stupidity.
The rest to some faint meaning make pretence,
But Shadwell never deviates into sense.
Some beams of wit on other souls may fall,
Strike through and make a lucid interval;
But Shadwell's genuine night admits no ray,
His rising fogs prevail upon the day.
Besides, his goodly fabric fills the eye
And seems designed for thoughtless majesty,

[1] Richard Flecknoe had died in 1678. He was an Irishman by birth.

Thoughtless as monarch oaks that shade the plain,
And, spread in solemn state, supinely reign.
Heywood and Shirley[1] were but types of thee,
Thou last great prophet of tautology.
Even I, a dunce of more renown than they,
Was sent before but to prepare thy way,
And coarsely clad in Norwich drugget[2] came
To teach the nations in thy greater name.

DOEG AND OG.

[From *Absalom and Achitophel*, Part II; November, 1682.]

Doeg[3], though without knowing how or why,
Made still a blundering kind of melody;
Spurred boldly on, and dashed through thick and thin,
Through sense and nonsense, never out nor in;
Free from all meaning, whether good or bad,
And, in one word, heroically mad,
He was too warm on picking-work to dwell,
But faggoted his notions as they fell,
And, if they rhymed and rattled, all was well.
Spiteful he is not, though he wrote a satire,
For still there goes some thinking to ill-nature;
He needs no more than birds and beasts to think,
All his occasions are to eat and drink.
If he call rogue and rascal from a garret,
He means you no more mischief than a parrot;
The words for friend and foe alike were made,
To fetter them in verse is all his trade.
Let him be gallows-free by my consent,
And nothing suffer, since he nothing meant;
Hanging supposes human soul and reason,
This animal's below committing treason:

[1] Thomas Heywood and James Shirley were both extremely prolific dramatists.
[2] Shadwell was a Norfolk man.
[3] *Doeg* = Elkanah Settle.

Shall he be hanged who never could rebel?
That's a preferment for Achitophel.
Railing in other men may be a crime,
But ought to pass for mere instinct in him;
Instinct he follows and no farther knows,
For to write verse with him is to transprose[1];
'Twere pity treason at his door to lay
Who makes heaven's gate a lock to its own key;
Let him rail on, let his invective Muse
Have four and twenty letters to abuse,
Which if he jumbles to one line of sense,
Indict him of a capital offence.
In fire-works[2] give him leave to vent his spite,
Those are the only serpents he can write;
The height of his ambition is, we know,
But to be master of a puppet-show[3];
On that one stage his works may yet appear,
And a month's harvest keeps him all the year

Now stop your noses, readers, all and some,
For here's a tun of midnight work to come,
Og[4] from a treason-tavern rolling home.
Round as a globe, and liquored every chink,
Goodly and great he sails behind his link.
With all this bulk there's nothing lost in Og,
For every inch that is not fool is rogue:
A monstrous mass of foul corrupted matter,
As all the devils had spewed to make the batter.
When wine has given him courage to blaspheme,
He curses God, but God before cursed him;

---

[1] Settle had written a reply to the *First Part* of *Absalom and Achitophel*, entitled *Absalom Senior, or Achitophel Transprosed*. The next line but one is cited from this poem.

[2] The allusion is to the burning of the Pope in a pageant at Temple Bar, superintended by the City Poet.

[3] This taunt was verified when Settle acted the Dragon in an adaption of his operatic spectacle, *The Siege of Troy*, for Mrs. Mynn's booth at Bartholomew Fair.

[4] *Og* = Shadwell.

And if man could have reason, none has more,
That made his paunch so rich and him so poor.
With wealth he was not trusted, for Heaven knew
What 'twas of old to pamper up a Jew ;
To what would he on quail and pheasant swell
That even on tripe and carrion could rebel?
But though Heaven made him poor, with reverence speaking,
He never was a poet of God's making ;
The midwife laid her hand on his thick skull,
With this prophetic blessing—Be thou dull ;
Drink, swear, and roar, forbear no lewd delight
Fit for thy bulk, do anything but write.
Thou art of lasting make, like thoughtless men,
A strong nativity—but for the pen ;
Eat opium, mingle arsenic in thy drink,
Still thou mayest live, avoiding pen and ink.
I see, I see, 'tis counsel given in vain,
For treason, botched in rhyme, will be thy bane ;
Rhyme is the rock on which thou art to wreck,
'Tis fatal to thy fame and to thy neck.
Why should thy metre good king David blast?
A psalm of his will surely be thy last.
Darest thou presume in verse to meet thy foes,
Thou whom the penny pamphlet foiled in prose?
Doeg, whom God for mankind's mirth has made,
O'ertops thy talent in thy very trade ;
Doeg to thee, thy paintings are so coarse,
A poet is, though he's the poet's horse.
A double noose thou on thy neck dost pull
For writing treason and for writing dull ;
To die for faction is a common evil,
But to be hanged for nonsense is the devil.
Hadst thou the glories of thy King exprest,
Thy praises had been satires at the best ;
But thou in clumsy verse, unlicked, unpointed,
Hast shamefully defied the Lord's anointed :
I will not rake the dunghill of thy crimes,
For who would read thy life that reads thy rhymes

But of king David's foes be this the doom,
May all be like the young man Absalom;
And for my foes may this their blessing be,
To talk like Doeg and to write like thee.

TRADITION.

[From *Religio Laici;* November, 1682.]

Must all tradition then be set aside?
This to affirm were ignorance or pride.
Are there not many points, some needful sure
To saving faith, that Scripture leaves obscure,
Which every sect will wrest a several way?
For what one sect interprets, all sects may.
We hold, and say we prove from Scripture plain,
That Christ is GOD; the bold Socinian
From the same Scripture urges he's but MAN.
Now what appeal can end the important suit?
Both parts talk loudly, but the rule is mute.
Shall I speak plain, and in a nation free
Assume an honest layman's liberty?
I think, according to my little skill,
To my own mother Church submitting still,
That many have been saved, and many may,
Who never heard this question brought in play.
The unlettered Christian, who believes in gross,
Plods on to Heaven and ne'er is at a loss;
For the strait gate would be made straiter yet,
Were none admitted there but men of wit.
The few by Nature formed, with learning fraught,
Born to instruct, as others to be taught,
Must study well the sacred page; and see
Which doctrine, this or that, does best agree
With the whole tenour of the work divine,
And plainliest points to Heaven's revealed design;
Which exposition flows from genuine sense,
And which is forced by wit and eloquence.

Not that tradition's parts are useless here,
When general, old, disinteressed, and clear:
That ancient Fathers thus expound the page
Gives truth the reverend majesty of age,
Confirms its force by biding every test,
For best authorities, next rules, are best;
And still the nearer to the spring we go,
More limpid, more unsoiled, the waters flow.
Thus, first traditions were a proof alone,
Could we be certain such they were, so known:
But since some flaws in long descent may be,
They make not truth but probability.
Even Arius and Pelagius durst provoke
To what the centuries preceding spoke.
Such difference is there in an oft-told tale,
But truth by its own sinews will prevail.
Tradition written, therefore, more commends
Authority than what from voice descends:
And this, as perfect as its kind can be,
Rolls down to us the sacred history:
Which, from the Universal Church received,
Is tried, and after for its self believed.

The Sects. Private Judgment.

[From *The Hind and the Panther*, Part I; April, 1687.]

Panting and pensive now she ranged alone,
And wandered in the kingdoms once her own.
The common hunt, though from their rage restrained
By sovereign power, her company disdained,
Grinned as they passed, and with a glaring eye
Gave gloomy signs of secret enmity.
'Tis true she bounded by and tripped so light,
They had not time to take a steady sight;
For truth has such a face and such a mien
As to be loved needs only to be seen.
The bloody Bear, an independent beast,
Unlicked to form, in groans her hate expressed.

Among the timorous kind the quaking Hare
Professed neutrality, but would not swear.
Next her the buffoon Ape, as atheists use,
Mimicked all sects and had his own to choose;
Still, when the Lion looked, his knees he bent,
And paid at church a courtier's compliment.
The bristled baptist Boar, impure as he,
But whitened with the foam of sanctity,
With fat pollutions filled the sacred place
And mountains levelled in his furious race;
So first rebellion founded was in grace.
But, since the mighty ravage which he made
In German forests[1] had his guilt betrayed,
With broken tusks and with a borrowed name,
He shunned the vengeance and concealed the shame,
So lurked in sects unseen. With greater guile
False Reynard fed on consecrated spoil;
The graceless beast by Athanasius first
Was chased from Nice, then by Socinus nursed,
His impious race their blasphemy renewed,
And Nature's King through Nature's optics viewed;
Reversed they viewed him lessened to their eye,
Nor in an infant could a God descry.
New swarming sects to this obliquely tend,
Hence they began, and here they all will end.

What weight of ancient witness can prevail,
If private reason hold the public scale?
But, gracious God, how well dost Thou provide
For erring judgments an unerring guide!
Thy throne is darkness in the abyss of light,
A blaze of glory that forbids the sight.
O teach me to believe Thee thus concealed,
And search no farther than Thyself revealed;
But her alone for my director take,
Whom Thou hast promised never to forsake!
My thoughtless youth was winged with vain desires;
My manhood, long misled by wandering fires,

---

[1] The allusion is more especially to the Anabaptist doings at Münster.

Followed false lights ; and when their glimpse was gone,
My pride struck out new sparkles of her own.
Such was I, such by nature still I am ;
Be Thine the glory and be mine the shame !

THE UNITY OF THE CATHOLIC CHURCH.

[From *The Hind and the Panther,* Part II.]

'One in herself, not rent by schism, but sound,
Entire, one solid shining diamond,
Not sparkles shattered into sects like you :
One is the Church, and must be to be true,
One central principle of unity ;
As undivided, so from errors free ;
As one in faith, so one in sanctity.
Thus she, and none but she, the insulting rage
Of heretics opposed from age to age ;
Still when the giant-brood invades her throne,
She stoops from heaven and meets them half way down,
And with paternal thunder vindicates her crown.
But like Egyptian sorcerers you stand,
And vainly lift aloft your magic wand
To sweep away the swarms of vermin from the land.
You could like them, with like infernal force,
Produce the plague, but not arrest the course.
But when the boils and botches with disgrace
And public scandal sat upon the face,
Themselves attacked, the Magi strove no more,
They saw God's finger, and their fate deplore ;
Themselves they could not cure of the dishonest sore.
'Thus one, thus pure, behold her largely spread,
Like the fair ocean from her mother-bed ;
From east to west triumphantly she rides,
All shores are watered by her wealthy tides.
The gospel-sound, diffused from pole to pole,
Where winds can carry and where waves can roll,
The self-same doctrine of the sacred page
Conveyed to every clime, in every age.

THE BUZZARD[1].

[From *The Hind and the Panther*, Part III.]

'A portly prince, and goodly to the sight,
He seemed a son of Anak for his height :
Like those whom stature did to crowns prefer ;
Black-browed and bluff, like Homer's Jupiter ;
Broad-backed and brawny built for love's delight,
A prophet formed to make a female proselyte.
A theologue more by need than genial bent ;
By breeding sharp, by nature confident,
Interest in all his actions was discerned ;
More learned than honest, more a wit than learned ;
Or forced by fear or by his profit led,
Or both conjoined, his native clime[2] he fled :
But brought the virtues of his heaven along ;
A fair behaviour, and a fluent tongue.
And yet with all his arts he could not thrive,
The most unlucky parasite alive.
Loud praises to prepare his paths he sent,
And then himself pursued his compliment ;
But by reverse of fortune chased away,
His gifts no longer than their author stay ;
He shakes the dust against the ungrateful race,
And leaves the stench of ordures in the place.
Oft has he flattered and blasphemed the same,
For in his rage he spares no sovereign's name :
The hero and the tyrant change their style
By the same measure that they frown or smile.
When well received by hospitable foes,
The kindness he returns is to expose ;
For courtesies, though undeserved and great,
No gratitude in felon-minds beget ;
As tribute to his wit, the churl receives the treat.
His praise of foes is venomously nice ;

---

[1] Burnet, afterwards Bishop of Salisbury.   [2] Scotland.

So touched, it turns a virtue to a vice:
A Greek, and bountiful, forewarns us twice[1].
Seven sacraments he wisely does disown,
Because he knows Confession stands for one;
Where sins to sacred silence are conveyed,
And not for fear or love to be betrayed [2]:
But he, uncalled, his patron to control,
Divulged the secret whispers of his soul;
Stood forth the accusing Satan of his crimes,
And offered to the Moloch of the times.
Prompt to assail, and careless of defence,
Invulnerable in his impudence,
He dares the world and, eager of a name,
He thrusts about and justles into fame.
Frontless and satire-proof, he scours the streets,
And runs an Indian muck at all he meets.
So fond of loud report, that not to miss
Of being known (his last and utmost bliss,)
He rather would be known for what he is.

'Such was and is the Captain of the Test,
Though half his virtues are not here exprest;
The modesty of fame conceals the rest.
The spleenful Pigeons never could create
A prince more proper to revenge their hate;
Indeed, more proper to revenge than save;
A king whom in His wrath the Almighty gave:
For all the grace the landlord had allowed
But made the Buzzard and the Pigeons proud,
Gave time to fix their friends and to seduce the crowd.
They long their fellow-subjects to enthral,
Their patron's promise into question call,
And vainly think he meant to make them lords of all.

---

[1] '*Timeo Danaos et dona ferentes.*' Verg. Æn. ii. 49.

[2] The allusion is to the evidence given by Burnet against the Earl of Lauderdale before the House of Commons in 1675.

[3] The allusion seems to be to Burnet's defence of the obnoxious Test against Parker, Bishop of Oxford.

Prologue to Aureng-Zebe, or The Great Mogul; 1675[1].

Our author by experience finds it true,
'Tis much more hard to please himself than you;
And, out of no feigned modesty, this day
Damns his laborious trifle of a play;
Not that it's worse than what before he writ,
But he has now another taste of wit;
And, to confess a truth, though out of time,
Grows weary of his long-loved mistress, Rhyme.
Passion's too fierce to be in fetters bound,
And Nature flies him like enchanted ground:
What verse can do he has performed in this,
Which he presumes the most correct of his;
But spite of all his pride, a secret shame
Invades his breast at Shakespeare's sacred name:
Awed when he hears his godlike Romans rage,
He in a just despair would quit the stage;
And to an age less polished, more unskilled,
Does with disdain the foremost honours yield.
As with the greater dead he dares not strive,
He would not match his verse with those who live:
Let him retire, betwixt two ages cast,
The first of this and hindmost of the last.
A losing gamester, let him sneak away;
He bears no ready money from the play.
The fate which governs poets thought it fit
He should not raise his fortunes by his wit.
The clergy thrive, and the litigious bar;
Dull heroes fatten with the spoils of war:
All southern vices, Heaven be praised, are here;
But wit's a luxury you think too dear.

---

[1] *Aureng-Zebe*, the last of Dryden's tragedies in rhyme, was produced at the Theatre Royal. 'Our neighbours' in line 37 refers to the rival house in Dorset Garden.

When you to cultivate the plant are loth,
'Tis a shrewd sign 'twas never of your growth:
And wit in northern climates will not blow,
Except, like orange trees, 'tis housed from snow.
There needs no care to put a playhouse down,
'Tis the most desert place of all the town :
We and our neighbours, to speak proudly, are,
Like monarchs, ruined with expensive war ;
While, like wise English, unconcerned you sit,
And see us play the tragedy of Wit.

To the Pious Memory of the accomplished young lady
Mrs. Anne Killigrew[1], excellent in the two sister
arts of poesy and painting. An Ode. 1686.

Thou youngest virgin-daughter of the skies,
  Made in the last promotion of the blest ;
Whose palms, new plucked from Paradise,
In spreading branches more sublimely rise,
  Rich with immortal green above the rest :
Whether, adopted to some neighbouring star,
Thou roll'st above us in thy wandering race,
  Or in procession fixed and regular
Moved with the heaven's majestic pace,
  Or called to more superior bliss,
Thou tread'st with seraphims the vast abyss :
Whatever happy region be thy place,
Cease thy celestial song a little space ;
Thou wilt have time enough for hymns divine,
Since Heaven's eternal year is thine.
Hear then a mortal Muse thy praise rehearse,
      In no ignoble verse,

---

[1] Anne Killigrew, maid of honour to the Duchess of York, died of the
small-pox in 1685, in the twenty-fifth year of her age. She was of a
literary family, and herself a poetess as well as a painter. Dryden's Ode
was prefixed to a posthumous edition of her poems.

But such as thy own voice did practise here,
When thy first fruits of poesy were given,
To make thyself a welcome inmate there;
　　While yet a young probationer,
　　And candidate of Heaven.

If by traduction[1] came thy mind,
　　Our wonder is the less to find
A soul so charming from a stock so good;
Thy father was transfused into thy blood:
So wert thou born into the tuneful strain,
(An early, rich, and inexhausted vein.)
　　But if thy pre-existing soul
Was formed at first with myriads more,
　　It did through all the mighty poets roll
Who Greek or Latin laurels wore,
And was that Sappho last, which once it was before.
If so, then cease thy flight, O heaven-born mind!
Thou hast no dross to purge from thy rich ore:
　　Nor can thy soul a fairer mansion find
　　Than was the beautious frame she left behind:
Return, to fill or mend the quire of thy celestial kind.

　　May we presume to say that, at thy birth,
New joy was sprung in heaven as well as here on earth?
For sure the milder planets did combine
On thy auspicious horoscope to shine,
And even the most malicious were in trine[2].
Thy brother-angels at thy birth
　　Strung each his lyre, and tuned it high,
　　　That all the people of the sky
Might know a poetess was born on earth;
　　　And then, if ever, mortal ears
　　　Had heard the music of the spheres.

[1] *traduction* = derivation from one of the same kind (Johnson).
[2] *trine*, the conjunction of three planets in the three angles of a triangle.

And if no clustering swarm of bees
On thy sweet mouth distilled their golden dew,
    'Twas that such vulgar miraclēs
    Heaven had not leisure to renew:
For all the blest fraternity of love
Solemnized there thy birth, and kept thy holiday above.

O gracious God! how far have we
Profaned thy heavenly gift of Poesy!
Made prostitute and profligate the Muse,
Debased to each obscene and impious use,
Whose harmony was first ordained above,
For tongues of angels and for hymns of love!
Oh wretched we! why were we hurried down
    This lubric and adulterate age,
    (Nay, added fat pollutions of our own,)
    To increase the steaming ordures of the stage?
What can we say to excuse our second fall?
Let this thy Vestal, Heaven, atone for all:
    Her Arethusian stream remains unsoiled,
    Unmixed with foreign filth and undefiled;
Her wit was more than man, her innocence a child.

Art she had none, yet wanted none,
    For Nature did that want supply:
So rich in treasures of her own,
    She might our boasted stores defy:
Such noble vigour did her verse adorn
That it seemed borrowed, where 'twas only born.
Her morals too were in her bosom bred,
    By great examples daily fed,
What in the best of books, her father's life, she read.
    And to be read herself she need not fear;
    Each test and every light her Muse will bear,
    Though Epictetus with his lamp were there.
    Even love (for love sometimes her Muse exprest),
Was but a lambent flame which played about her breast;
    Light as the vapours of a morning dream,
    So cold herself, whilst she such warmth exprest,
    'Twas Cupid bathing in Diana's stream.

Born to the spacious empire of the Nine,
One would have thought she should have been content
To manage well that mighty government ;
But what can young ambitious souls confine ?
   To the next realm she stretched her sway,
   For Painture[1] near adjoining lay,
A plenteous province and alluring prey.
A Chamber of Dependences was framed,
(As conquerors will never want pretence,
   When armed, to justify the offence),
And the whole fief in right of Poetry she claimed.
   The country open lay without defence ;
For poets frequent inroads there had made,
   And perfectly could represent
   The shape, the face, with every lineament,
And all the large domains which the dumb Sister swayed ;
   All bowed beneath her government,
   Received in triumph whereso'er she went.
Her pencil drew whate'er her soul designed,
And oft the happy draught surpassed the image in her mind.
   The sylvan scenes of herds and flocks
   And fruitful plains and barren rocks ;
   Of shallow brooks that flowed so clear,
   The bottom did the top appear ;
   Of deeper too and ampler floods
   Which, as in mirrors, showed the woods ;
   Of lofty trees, with sacred shades
   And perspectives of pleasant glades,
   Where nymphs of brightest form appear,
   And shaggy satyrs standing near,
   Which them at once admire and fear.
   The ruins too of some majestic piece,
   Boasting the power of ancient Rome or Greece,
   Whose statues, friezes, columns, broken lie,
   And, though defaced, the wonder of the eye ;

---

[1] *Painture* (peinture) and *picture* are both used in the sense of 'painting' by Dryden.

What nature, art, bold fiction, e'er durst frame,
Her forming hand gave feature to the name.
So strange a concourse ne'er was seen before,
But when the peopled ark the whole creation bore.

The scene then changed; with bold erected look
Our martial King the sight with reverence strook:
For, not content to express his outward part,
Her hand called out the image of his heart:
His warlike mind, his soul devoid of fear,
His high-designing thoughts were figured there,
As when by magic ghosts are made appear.
Our phœnix queen was portrayed too so bright,
Beauty alone could beauty take so right:
Her dress, her shape, her matchless grace,
Were all observed, as well as heavenly face.
With such a peerless majesty she stands,
As in that day she took the crown from sacred hands;
Before a train of heroines was seen,
In beauty foremost, as in rank the queen.
Thus nothing to her genius was denied,
But like a ball of fire, the farther thrown,
Still with a greater blaze she shone,
And her bright soul broke out on every side.
What next she had designed, Heaven only knows:
To such immoderate growth her conquest rose
That Fate alone its progress could oppose.

Now all those charms, that blooming grace,
The well-proportioned shape and beauteous face,
Shall never more be seen by mortal eyes;
In earth the much-lamented virgin lies.
Not wit nor piety could Fate prevent;
Nor was the cruel Destiny content
To finish all the murder at a blow,
To sweep at once her life and beauty too;
But, like a hardened felon, took a pride
To work more mischievously slow,
And plundered first, and then destroyed.
O double sacrilege on things divine,

To rob the relic, and deface the shrine!
  But thus Orinda[1] died:
Heaven by the same disease did both translate;
As equal were their souls, so equal was their fate.
Meantime, her warlike brother on the seas
His waving streamers to the winds displays,
And vows for his return with vain devotion pays.
  Ah, generous youth! that wish forbear,
  The winds too soon will waft thee here!
  Slack all thy sails, and fear to come;
Alas! thou knowst not, thou art wrecked at home.
No more shalt thou behold thy sister's face,
Thou hast already had her last embrace.
But look aloft, and if thou kenst from far,
Among the Pleiads, a new-kindled star,
If any sparkles than the rest more bright,
'Tis she that shines in that propitious light.

When in mid-air the golden trump shall sound,
  To raise the nations under ground;
  When in the Valley of Jehosophat
The judging God shall close the book of Fate,
  And there the last assizes keep
  For those who wake and those who sleep;
  When rattling bones together fly
  From the four corners of the sky;
When sinews o'er the skeletons are spread,
Those clothed with flesh, and life inspires the dead;
The sacred poets first shall hear the sound,
And foremost from the tomb shall bound,
For they are covered with the lightest ground;
And straight, with inborn vigour, on the wing,
Like mounting larks, to the new morning sing.
There thou, sweet saint, before the quire shalt go,
As harbinger of Heaven, the way to show,
The way which thou so well hast learned below.

[1] *Orinda*, the poetess Katharine Philips, who died of small-pox in 1664 in her thirty-third year. Anne Killigrew wrote some verses in her honour.

A Song for St. Cecilia's Day, November 22, 1687.

From harmony, from heavenly harmony
    This universal frame began ;
  When Nature underneath a heap
    Of jarring atoms lay,
  And could not heave her head,
The tuneful voice was heard from high,
    Arise, ye more than dead.

Then cold and hot and moist and dry
  In order to their stations leap,
    And Music's power obey.
From harmony, from heavenly harmony,
    This universal frame began :
    From harmony to harmony
Through all the compass of the notes it ran,
The diapason closing full in Man.

What passion cannot Music raise and quell?
    When Jubal struck the chorded shell,
  His listening brethren stood around,
    And, wondering, on their faces fell
  To worship that celestial sound :
Less than a god they thought there could not dwell
  Within the hollow of that shell,
  That spoke so sweetly, and so well.
What passion cannot Music raise and quell?

    The trumpet's loud clangor
      Excites us to arms
    With shrill notes of anger
      And mortal alarms.
    The double double double beat
      Of the thundering drum
      Cries, hark ! the foes come ;
Charge, charge, 'tis too late to retreat.

The soft complaining flute
In dying notes discovers
The woes of hopeless lovers,
Whose dirge is whispered by the warbling lute.

Sharp violins proclaim
Their jealous pangs and desperation,
Fury, frantic indignation,
Depth of pains and height of passion,
For the fair, disdainful dame.

But oh! what art can teach,
What human voice can reach
The sacred organ's praise?
Notes inspiring holy love,
Notes that wing their heavenly ways
To mend the choirs above.

Orpheus could lead the savage race,
And trees unrooted left their place,
Sequacious of the lyre;
But bright Cecilia raised the wonder higher:
When to her organ vocal breath was given,
An angel heard, and straight appeared,
Mistaking earth for heaven.

Grand Chorus.

As from the power of sacred lays
The spheres began to move,
And sung the great Creator's praise
To all the blessed above;
So when the last and dreadful hour
This crumbling pageant shall devour,
The trumpet shall be heard on high,
The dead shall live, the living die,
And Music shall untune the sky.

ALEXANDER'S FEAST; OR, THE POWER OF MUSIC.

A song in honour of St. Cecilia's Day, 1697.

'Twas at the royal feast for Persia won
    By Philip's warlike son:
    Aloft in awful state
    The godlike hero sate
    On his imperial throne;
His valiant peers were placed around;
Their brows with roses and with myrtles bound:
    (So should desert in arms be crowned.)
The lovely Thais, by his side,
Sate like a blooming Eastern bride,
In flower of youth and beauty's pride.
    Happy, happy, happy pair!
      None but the brave,
      None but the brave,
None but the brave deserves the fair.

Chorus.

    Happy, happy, happy pair!
      None but the brave,
      None but the brave,
None but the brave deserves the fair.

    Timotheus, placed on high
    Amid the tuneful quire,
With flying fingers touched the lyre:
    The trembling notes ascend the sky,
    And heavenly joys inspire.
The song began from Jove,
Who left his blissful seats above,
(Such is the power of mighty love.)

A dragon's fiery form belied the god :
Sublime on radiant spires he rode,
When he to fair Olympia pressed ;
And while he sought her snowy breast,
Then round her slender waist he curled,
And stamped an image of himself, a sovereign of the world.
The listening crowd admire the lofty sound,
A present deity, they shout around ;
A present deity, the vaulted roofs rebound :
    With ravished ears
    The monarch hears,
    Assumes the god,
    Affects to nod,
And seems to shake the spheres.

Chorus.

    With ravished ears
    The monarch hears,
    Assumes the god,
    Affects to nod,
And seems to shake the spheres.

The praise of Bacchus then the sweet musician sung,
Of Bacchus ever fair, and ever young.
The jolly god in triumph comes ;
Sound the trumpets, beat the drums ;
    Flushed with a purple grace
    He shows his honest face :
Now give the hautboys breath ; he comes, he comes.
Bacchus, ever fair and young,
    Drinking joys did first ordain ;
Bacchus' blessings are a treasure,
Drinking is the soldier's pleasure ;
    Rich the treasure,
    Sweet the pleasure,
Sweet is pleasure after pain.

Chorus.

Bacchus' blessings are a treasure,
Drinking is the soldier's pleasure ;
Rich the treasure,
Sweet the pleasure,
Sweet is pleasure after pain.

Soothed with the sound the king grew vain ;
Fought all his battles o'er again ;
And thrice he routed all his foes, and thrice he slew the slain
The master saw the madness rise,
His glowing cheeks, his ardent eyes ;
And while he heaven and earth defied,
Changed his hand, and checked his pride.
He chose a mournful Muse,
Soft pity to infuse ;
He sung Darius great and good,
By too severe a fate,
Fallen, fallen, fallen, fallen,
Fallen from his high estate,
And weltering in his blood ;
Deserted at his utmost need
By those his former bounty fed ;
On the bare earth exposed he lies,
With not a friend to close his eyes.
With downcast looks the joyless victor sate,
Revolving in his altered soul
The various turns of chance below ;
And, now and then, a sigh he stole,
And tears began to flow.

Chorus.

Revolving in his altered soul
The various turns of chance below ;
And, now and then, a sigh he stole,
And tears began to flow.

The mighty master smiled to see
That love was in the next degree;
'Twas but a kindred-sound to move,
For pity melts the mind to love.
　　Softly sweet, in Lydian measures,
　　Soon he soothed his soul to pleasures.
War, he sung, is toil and trouble;
Honour but an empty bubble;
　　Never ending, still beginning,
　　Fighting still, and still destroying:
　　If the world be worth thy winning,
Think, O think it worth enjoying:
　　Lovely Thais sits beside thee,
　　Take the good the gods provide thee.
The many rend the skies with loud applause;
So Love was crowned, but Music won the cause.
　　The prince, unable to conceal his pain,
　　　　Gazed on the fair
　　　　Who caused his care,
　　And sighed and looked, sighed and looked,
　　Sighed and looked, and sighed again;
At length, with love and wine at once oppressed,
The vanquished victor sunk upon her breast.

Chorus.

　　The prince, unable to conceal his pain,
　　　　Gazed on the fair
　　　　Who caused his care,
　　And sighed and looked, sighed and looked,
　　Sighed and looked, and sighed again;
At length, with love and wine at once oppressed,
The vanquished victor sunk upon her breast.

Now strike the golden lyre again;
A louder yet, and yet a louder strain.
Break his bands of sleep asunder,
And rouse him, like a rattling peal of thunder.

Hark, hark, the horrid sound
　　Has raised up his head ;
　　As awaked from the dead,
　And, amazed, he stares around.
'Revenge, revenge!' Timotheus cries ;
　　' See the Furies arise ;
　　See the snakes that they rear,
　　How they hiss in their hair,
　And the sparkles that flash from their eyes !
　　Behold a ghastly band,
　　Each a torch in his hand !
Those are Grecian ghosts, that in battle were slain,
　　　　And unburied remain
　　　　Inglorious on the plain :
　　　　Give the vengeance due
　　　　To the valiant crew.
Behold how they toss their torches on high,
　How they point to the Persian abodes,
And glittering temples of their hostile gods.'
The princes applaud with a furious joy;
And the king seized a flambeau with zeal to destroy ;
　　　Thais led the way,
　　　To light him to his prey,
And, like another Helen, fired another Troy.

Chorus.

And the king seized a flambeau with zeal to destroy ;
　　　Thais led the way,
　　　To light him to his prey,
And, like another Helen, fired another Troy.

　　　Thus long ago,
　Ere heaving bellows learned to blow,
　　While organs yet were mute,
　　Timotheus, to his breathing flute
　　　And sounding lyre,
Could swell the soul to rage, or kindle soft desire.
　At last divine Cecilia came,
　Inventress of the vocal frame ;

The sweet enthusiast, from her sacred store,
   Enlarged the former narrow bounds,
   And added length to solemn sounds,
With Nature's mother-wit, and arts unknown before.
   Let old Timotheus yield the prize,
     Or both divide the crown :
   He raised a mortal to the skies ;
     She drew an angel down.

Grand Chorus.

   At last divine Cecilia came,
   Inventress of the vocal frame ;
The sweet enthusiast, from her sacred store,
   Enlarged the former narrow bounds,
   And added length to solemn sounds,
With Nature's mother-wit, and arts unknown before.
   Let old Timotheus yield the prize,
     Or both divide the crown :
   He raised a mortal to the skies ;
     She drew an angel down.

LINES PRINTED UNDER THE ENGRAVED PORTRAIT OF MILTON,

In Tonson's Folio Edition of the ' Paradise Lost,' 1688 [1].

Three poets, in three distant ages born,
Greece, Italy, and England did adorn.
The first in loftiness of thought surpassed,
The next in majesty, in both the last.
The force of Nature could no farther go ;
To make a third she joined the former two.

---

[1] Malone has suggested that these lines are an amplification of a distich
addressed to Milton when at Rome by Salvaggi (otherwise unknown to fame) :
   ' Græcia Mæonidem. jactet sibi Roma Maronem,
     Anglia Miltonum jactat utrique parem.'

To my Friend, Mr. Congreve,

On his Comedy called The Double Dealer, 1693.

Well then, the promised hour is come at last,
The present age of wit obscures the past :
Strong were our sires, and as they fought they writ,
Conquering with force of arms and dint of wit :
Theirs was the giant race before the flood ;
And thus, when Charles returned, our empire stood.
Like Janus[1] he the stubborn soil manured,
With rules of husbandry the rankness cured ;
Tamed us to manners, when the stage was rude,
And boisterous English wit with art endued.
Our age was cultivated thus at length,
But what we gained in skill we lost in strength.
Our builders were with want of genius curst ;
The second temple was not like the first ;
Till you, the best Vitruvius, come at length,
Our beauties equal, but excel our strength.
Firm Doric pillars found your solid base,
The fair Corinthian crowns the higher space ;
Thus all below is strength, and all above is grace.
In easy dialogue is Fletcher's praise ;
He moved the mind, but had not power to raise.
Great Jonson did by strength of judgment please,
Yet, doubling Fletcher's force, he wants his ease.
In differing talents both adorned their age,
One for the study, t'other for the stage.
But both to Congreve justly shall submit,
One matched in judgment, both o'ermatched in wit,
In him all beauties of this age we see,
Etherege his courtship, Southern's purity,
The satire, wit, and strength of manly Wycherly.
All this in blooming youth you have achieved ;

---

[1] *Janus*, the primitive and deified king of Latium.

Nor are your foiled contemporaries grieved.
So much the sweetness of your manners move,
We cannot envy you, because we love.
Fabius might joy in Scipio, when he saw
A beardless Consul made against the law,
And join his suffrage to the votes of Rome,
Though he with Hannibal was overcome.
Thus old Romano bowed to Raphael's fame,
And scholar to the youth he taught became.

O that your brows my laurel had sustained !
Well had I been deposed, if you had reigned :
The father had descended for the son,
For only you are lineal to the throne.
Thus, when the State one Edward did depose,
A greater Edward in his room arose :
But now, not I, but poetry is curst ;
For Tom the second reigns like Tom the first.[1]
But let them not mistake my patron's part
Nor call his charity their own desert.
Yet this I prophesy,—Thou shalt be seen,
Though with some short parenthesis between,
High on the throne of wit, and, seated there,
Not mine—that's little—but thy laurel wear.
Thy first attempt an early promise made ;
That early promise this has more than paid.
So bold, yet so judiciously you dare,
That your least praise is to be regular.
Time, place, and action may with pains be wrought,
But genius must be born, and never can be taught.
This is your portion, this your native store:
Heaven, that but once was prodigal before,
To Shakespeare gave as much; she could not give him more.
Maintain your post : that's all the fame you need ;
For 'tis impossible you should proceed.

---

[1] Thomas Shadwell was succeeded as Historiographer Royal by Thomas Rymer, who was the right man for the post, though he was a poet of no mark and a critic of no merit. In the poet-laureateship Shadwell was succeeded by Tate.

Already I am worn with cares and age,
And just abandoning the ungrateful stage:
Unprofitably kept at Heaven's expense,
I live a rent-charge on His providence:
But you, whom every Muse and grace adorn,
Whom I foresee to better fortune born,
Be kind to my remains; and oh, defend,
Against your judgment, your departed friend!
Let not the insulting foe my fame pursue,
But shade those laurels which descend to you:
And take for tribute what these lines express;
You merit more, nor could my love do less.

PALAMON AND ARCITE [1].

[Book III. vv. 524-635; 1698 or 1699.]

The herald ends: the vaulted firmament
With loud acclaims and vast applause is rent:
' Heaven guard a Prince so gracious and so good,
So just, and yet so provident of blood!'
This was the general cry. The trumpets sound,
And warlike symphony is heard around.
The marching troops through Athens take their way,
The great Earl-marshal orders their array.
The fair from high the passing pomp behold;
A rain of flowers is from the windows rolled.
The casements are with golden tissues spread,
And horses' hoofs, for earth, on silken tapestry tread.
The King goes midmost, and the rivals ride
In equal rank, and close his either side.
Next after these there rode the royal wife,
With Emily, the cause and the reward of strife.
The following cavalcade, by three and three,
Proceed by titles marshalled in degree.

---

[1] A version of part of *The Knightes Tale* in the *Canterbury Tales*, vv. 2563-1638.

Thus through the southern gate they take their way,
And at the list arrived ere prime of day.
There, parting from the King, the chiefs divide,
And wheeling east and west, before their many ride.
The Athenian monarch mounts his throne on high,
And after him the Queen and Emily:
Next these, the kindred of the crown are graced
With nearer seats, and lords by ladies placed.
Scarce were they seated, when with clamours loud
In rushed at once a rude promiscuous crowd,
The guards, and then each other overbare,
And in a moment throng the spacious theatre.
Now changed the jarring noise to whispers low,
As winds forsaking seas more softly blow,
When at the western gate, on which the car
Is placed aloft that bears the God of War,
Proud Arcite entering armed before his train
Stops at the barrier, and divides the plain.
Red was his banner, and displayed abroad
The bloody colours of his patron god.
    At that self moment enters Palamon
The gate of Venus, and the rising Sun ;
Waved by the wanton winds, his banner flies,
All maiden white, and shares the people's eyes.
From east to west, look all the world around,
Two troops so matched were never to be found ;
Such bodies built for strength, of equal age,
In stature sized ; so proud an equipage :
The nicest eye could no distinction make,
Where lay the advantage, or what side to take.
    Thus ranged, the herald for the last proclaims
A silence, while they answered to their names :
For so the king decreed, to shun with care
The fraud of musters false, the common bane of war.
The tale was just, and then the gates were closed ;
And chief to chief, and troop to troop opposed.
The heralds last retired, and loudly cried,
'The fortune of the field be fairly tried !'

At this the challenger, with fierce defy,
His trumpet sounds ; the challenged makes reply:
With clangour rings the field, resounds the vaulted sky.
Their vizors closed, their lances in the rest,
Or at the helmet pointed or the crest,
They vanish from the barrier, speed the race,
And spurring see decrease the middle space.
A cloud of smoke envelopes either host,
And all at once the combatants are lost :
Darkling they join adverse, and shock unseen,
Coursers with coursers justling, men with men :
As labouring in eclipse, a while they stay,
Till the next blast of wind restores the day.
They look anew : the beauteous form of fight
Is changed, and war appears a grisly sight.
Two troops in fair array one moment showed,
The next, a field with fallen bodies strowed :
Not half the number in their seats are found,
But men and steeds lie grovelling on the ground.
The points of spears are stuck within the shield,
The steeds without their riders scour the field.
The knights unhorsed, on foot renew the fight ;
The glittering fauchions cast a gleaming light ;
Hauberks and helms are hewed with many a wound,
Out spins the streaming blood, and dyes the ground.
The mighty maces with such haste descend,
They break the bones, and make the solid armour bend
This thrusts amid the throng with furious force ;
Down goes, at once, the horseman and the horse :
That courser stumbles on the fallen steed,
And, floundering, throws the rider o'er his head.
One rolls along, a football to his foes ;
One with a broken truncheon deals his blows.
This halting, this disabled with his wound,
In triumph led, is to the pillar bound,
Where by the king's award he must abide ;
There goes a captive led on t' other side.
By fits they cease, and leaning on the lance,
Take breath a while, and to new fight advance.

Full oft the rivals met, and neither spared
His utmost force, and each forgot to ward :
The head of this was to the saddle bent,
The other backward to the crupper sent :
Both were by turns unhorsed ; the jealous blows
Fall thick and heavy, when on foot they close.
So deep their fauchions bite, that every stroke
Pierced to the quick ; and equal wounds they gave and took.
Borne far asunder by the tides of men,
Like adamant and steel they met again.

So when a tiger sucks the bullock's blood,)
A famished lion issuing from the wood }
Roars lordly fierce, and challenges the food.)
Each claims possession, neither will obey,
But both their paws are fastened on the prey ;
They bite, they tear ; and while in vain they strive,
The swains come armed between, and both to distance drive.

TO MY HONOURED KINSMAN, JOHN DRYDEN,[1]

Of Chesterton, in the county of Huntingdon, Esq.; 1699.

How blessed is he who leads a country life,
Unvexed with anxious cares and void of strife !
Who, studying peace and shunning civil rage,
Enjoyed his youth and now enjoys his age :
All who deserve his love he makes his own ;
And, to be loved himself, needs only to be known.

Just, good, and wise, contending neighbours come)
From your award to wait their final doom, }
And, foes before, return in friendship home.)
Without their cost you terminate the cause
And save the expense of long litigious laws,
Where suits are traversed, and so little won
That he who conquers is but last undone.

---

[1] John Dryden, first cousin of the poet, was Member for Huntingdonshire, and seems to have belonged to the Opposition, which called itself the Country party.

Such are not your decrees ; but so designed,
The sanction leaves a lasting peace behind,
Like your own soul serene, a pattern of your mind. }

Promoting concord and composing strife,
Lord of yourself, uncumbered with a wife ;
Where, for a year, a month, perhaps a night,
Long penitence succeeds a short delight :
Minds are so hardly matched, that even the first,
Though paired by Heaven, in Paradise were cursed.
For man and woman, though in one they grow,
Yet, first or last, return again to two ;
He to God's image, she to his was made ;
So farther from the fount the stream at random strayed.

How could he stand, when, put to double pain,
He must a weaker than himself sustain?
Each might have stood perhaps, but each alone ;
Two wrestlers help to pull each other down.

Not that my verse would blemish all the fair ;
But yet, if some be bad, 'tis wisdom to beware, }
And better shun the bait than struggle in the snare.
Thus have you shunned and shun the married state,
Trusting as little as you can to Fate.

No porter guards the passage of your door,
To admit the wealthy and exclude the poor ;
For God, who gave the riches, gave the heart
To sanctify the whole by giving part.
Heaven, who foresaw the will, the means has wrought,
And to the second son a blessing brought !
The first-begotten had his father's share,
But you, like Jacob, are Rebecca's heir.[1]

So may your stores and fruitful fields increase,
And ever be you blessed, who live to bless.
As Ceres sowed where'er her chariot flew,
As Heaven in deserts rained the bread of dew,
So free to many, to relations most,
You feed with manna your own Israel host.

---

[1] John Dryden inherited from his mother.

With crowds attended of your ancient race,
You seek the champian[1] sports or sylvan chace ;
With well-breathed beagles you surround the wood,
Even then industrious of the common good ;
And often have you brought the wily fox
To suffer for the firstlings of the flocks,
Chased even amid the folds, and made to bleed,
Like felons, where they did the murderous deed.
This fiery game your active youth maintained,
Not yet by years extinguished, though restrained ;
You season still with sports your serious hours,
For age but tastes of pleasures, youth devours.
The hare in pastures or in plains is found,
Emblem of human life ; who runs the round,
And, after all his wandering ways are done, ⎫
His circle fills, and ends where he begun, ⎬
Just as the setting meets the rising sun. ⎭
Thus princes ease their cares ; but happier he,
Who seeks not pleasure through necessity,
Than such as once on slippery thrones were placed,
And, chasing, sigh to think themselves are chased.

So lived our sires, ere doctors learned to kill,
And multiplied with theirs the weekly bill.
The first physicians by debauch were made ;
Excess began, and sloth sustains the trade.
Pity the generous kind their cares bestow
To search forbidden truths (a sin to know),
To which if human science could attain,
The doom of death, pronounced by God, were vain.
In vain the leech would interpose delay ;
Fate fastens first, and vindicates the prey.
What help from art's endeavours can we have? ⎫
Guibbons[2] but guesses, nor is sure to save ; ⎬
But Maurus[3] sweeps whole parishes, and peoples every grave. ⎭

[1] *Champian sports*, country sports.

[2] A celebrated physician of the day, who attended Dryden himself.

[3] Sir Richard Blackmore, ' Knight Physician ' and ' City Bard,' who had attacked Dryden in the preface to his moral epic, *Prince Arthur*, and in a *Satire upon Wit*. Luke Milbourn was a clergyman who had written a pamphlet in hostile criticism of Dryden's *Virgil*.

And no more mercy to mankind will use
Than when he robbed and murdered Maro's muse.
Wouldst thou be soon dispatched, and perish whole,
Trust Maurus with thy life, and Milbourn with thy soul
By chase our long-lived fathers earned their food ;
Toil strung the nerves and purified the blood :
But we their sons, a pampered race of men,
Are dwindled down to threescore years and ten.
Better to hunt in fields for health unbought
Than fee the doctor for a nauseous draught.
The wise for cure on exercise depend ;
God never made his work for man to mend.

The tree of knowledge, once in Eden placed,
Was easy found, but was forbid the taste ;
O, had our grandsire walked without his wife,
He first had sought the better plant of life !
Now both are lost : yet wandering in the dark,
Physicians for the tree have found the bark ;
They, labouring for relief of human kind,
With sharpened sight some remedies may find ;
The apothecary-train is wholly b'ind.
From files a rand)m recipe they take,
And many deaths of one prescription make.
Garth [1], generous as his Muse, prescribes and gives ;
The shopman sells, and by destruction lives :
Ungrateful tribe ! who, like the viper's brood,
From Medicine issuing, suck their mother's blood !
Let these obey, and let the learned prescribe,
That men may die without a double bribe ;
Let them, but under their superiors, kill,
When doctors first have signed the bloody bill :
He scapes the best, who, nature to repair,
Draws physic from the fields in draughts of vital air.

You hoard not health for your own private use,
But on the public spend the rich produce.
When, often urged, unwilling to be great,
Your country calls you from your loved retreat,

---

[1] Sir Samuel Garth, an eminent physician, and author (whatever the overwise might say) of the poem *The Dispensary.*

And sends to senates, charged with common care,
Which none more shuns, and none can better bear:
Where could they find another formed so fit
To poise with solid sense a sprightly wit?
Were these both wanting, (as they both abound,)
Where could so firm integrity be found?

Well-born and wealthy, wanting no support,
You steer betwixt the country and the court;
Nor gratify whate'er the great desire,
Nor grudging give what public needs require.
Part must be left, a fund when foes invade;
And part employed to roll the watery trade;
Even Canaan's happy land, when worn with toil,
Required a sabbath-year to mend the meagre soil.

Good senators (and such are you) so give,
That kings may be supplied, the people thrive;
And he, when want requires, is truly wise,
Who slights not foreign aids nor over-buys,
But on our native strength in time of need relies.
Munster was bought, we boast not the success[1];
Who fights for gain for greater makes his peace.

Our foes, compelled by need, have peace embraced[2];
The peace both parties want is like to last;
Which if secure, securely we may trade,
Or not secure, should never have been made.
Safe in our selves, while on our selves we stand,
The sea is ours, and that defends the land.
Be then the naval stores the nation's care,
New ships to build, and battered to repair.

Observe the war in every annual course;
What has been done was done with British force.
Namur subdued is England's palm alone;
The rest besieged, but we constrained the town:

---

[1] The Bishop of Münster, the notorious Bernhard von Galen, received English pay when taking part in the war against the Dutch; but on the intervention of France he laid down his arms in 1666.

[2] The Peace of Ryswick (1697), concluded two years after William the Third's capture of Namur, referred to a few lines further on.

We saw the event that followed our success ;
France, though pretending arms, pursued the peace,
Obliged by one sole treaty to restore
What twenty years of war had won before.
Enough for Europe has our Albion fought :
Let us enjoy the peace our blood has bought.
When once the Persian king was put to flight,
The weary Macedons refused to fight :
Themselves their own mortality confessed,
And left the son of Jove to quarrel for the rest.

Even victors are by victories undone :
Thus Hannibal, with foreign laurels won,
To Carthage was recalled, too late to keep his own.
While sore of battle, while our wounds are green,
Why should we tempt the doubtful die again ?
In wars renewed uncertain of success,
Sure of a share, as umpires of the peace.

A patriot both the king and country serves,
Prerogative and privilege preserves.
Of each our laws the certain limit show ;
One must not ebb, nor t' other overflow.
Betwixt the Prince and Parliament we stand ;
The barriers of the State on either hand :
May neither overflow, for then they drown the land.
When both are full, they feed our blessed abode,
Like those that watered once the Paradise of God.

Some overpoise of sway by turns they share ;
In peace the people, and the prince in war :
Consuls of moderate powers in calms were made ;
When the Gauls came, one sole dictator swayed.

Patriots in peace assert the people's right,
With noble stubbornness resisting might :
No lawless mandates from the court receive,
Nor lend by force, but in a body give.
Such was your generous grandsire, free to grant[1]
In parliaments that weighed their Prince's want :

---

[1] *Your generous grandsire;* Sir Erasmus Dryden, who was likewise the poet's grandfather. He was imprisoned under Charles I for refusing to contribute to the general loan in 1626.

But so tenacious of the common cause
As not to lend the king against his laws ;
And, in a loathsome dungeon doomed to lie, ⎫
In bonds retained his birth-right liberty,   ⎬
And shamed oppression, till it set him free. ⎭
　O true descendant of a patriot line,
Who, while thou sharest their lustre, lend'st them thine,
Vouchsafe this picture of thy soul to see ;
'Tis so far good as it resembles thee.
The beauties to the original I owe,
Which when I miss, my own defects I show.
Nor think the kindred Muses thy disgrace ;
A poet is not born in every race.
Two of a house few ages can afford,
One to perform, another to record.
Praiseworthy actions are by thee embraced ;
And 'tis my praise to make thy praises last.
For even when death dissolves our human frame, ⎫
The soul returns to Heaven from whence it came, ⎬
Earth keeps the body, verse preserves the fame. ⎭

VENI CREATOR SPIRITUS [1].

Creator Spirit, by whose aid
The world's foundations first were laid,
Come, visit every pious mind ;
Come, pour thy joys on humankind ;
From sin and sorrow set us free,
And make thy temples worthy thee.
　O source of uncreated light,
The Father's promised Paraclete !
Thrice holy fount, thrice holy fire,
Our hearts with heavenly love inspire ;

---

[1] This paraphrase of the Latin hymn popularly attributed to Charlemagne was first printed in Tonson's folio edition of Dryden's *Poems,* 1701.

Come, and thy sacred unction bring
To sanctify us, while we sing.

Plenteous of grace, descend from high,
Rich in thy sevenfold energy!
Thou strength of his Almighty hand,
Whose power does heaven and earth command.
Proceeding Spirit, our defence,
Who dost the gift of tongues dispense,
And crown'st thy gift with eloquence.

Refine and purge our earthy parts;
But, oh, inflame and fire our hearts!
Our frailties help, our vice control,
Submit the senses to the soul;
And when rebellious they are grown,
Then lay thy hand, and hold them down.

Chase from our minds the infernal foe,
And peace, the fruit of Love, bestow;
And lest our feet should step astray,
Protect and guide us in the way.

Make us eternal truths receive,
And practise all that we believe:
Give us thy self, that we may see
The Father and the Son by thee.

Immortal honour, endless fame,
Attend the Almighty Father's name:
The Saviour Son be glorified,
Who for lost man's redemption died:
And equal adoration be,
Eternal Paraclete, to thee!